Remaking American Theater

An account of contemporary theater practice in its most collaborative and dynamic form, this is the first book-length study of two of the most important American theater artists at the start of the twenty-first century. For twenty-five years, Mee and Bogart have pursued independent but sympathetic visions of theater rooted in the avant-garde of the 1960s, guided by a view of art and culture as a perpetual process of "remaking." Since 1992, the SITI Company has pioneered the unique combination of three training practices (Viewpoints, Suzuki, and Composition) as the basis for collective creations that layer language, gesture, and image in a complex and often stunning fashion. This study provides both a general introduction to Mee's unorthodox playwriting, Bogart's innovative directing, the ensemble work of the SITI Company, and an in-depth case study of their work together on *bobrauschenbergamerica*, a piece inspired by the art of Robert Rauschenberg.

SCOTT T. CUMMINGS teaches courses in dramatic literature and playwriting and directs plays in the Theater Department of Boston College. His productions there include Charles L. Mee's *A Summer Evening in Des Moines*, Shakespeare's *The Comedy of Errors* and Beckett's *Endgame*. As a theater critic and arts journalist he has written for *American Theatre*, the *Boston Globe* and the *Boston Phoenix*. His scholarly essays and reviews have appeared in *Theatre Journal*, *Modern Drama* and *Journal of Dramatic Theory and Criticism*, among others.

Remaking American Theater

Charles Mee, Anne Bogart and the SITI Company

SCOTT T. CUMMINGS

CAMBRIDGE
UNIVERSITY PRESS

CAMBRIDGE UNIVERSITY PRESS
Cambridge, New York, Melbourne, Madrid, Cape Town, Singapore, São Paulo

CAMBRIDGE UNIVERSITY PRESS
The Edinburgh Building, Cambridge CB2 2RU, UK
Published in the United States of America by Cambridge University Press, New York

www.cambridge.org
Information on this title: www.cambridge.org/9780521818209

First published 2006

Printed in the United Kingdom at the University Press, Cambridge

A catalogue record for this book is available from the British Library

Library of Congress cataloging in publication data
Cummings, Scott T., 1953–
Remaking American theater: Charles Mee, Anne Bogart and the SITI Company / Scott
T. Cummings.
p.   cm. – (Cambridge Studies in American Theatre and Drama)
Includes bibliographical references and index.
ISBN 0 521 81820 6 (hardback)
1.   SITI Company. 2.   Theater – New York (State) – New York – History – 20th century.
3.   Mee, Charles, 1938 – 4.   Bogart, Anne, 1951– I.   Title. II.   Series.
PN2277.N5C86 2006
792.09747′109045–dc22
2005032570

ISBN-13 978-0-521-81820-9 hardback
ISBN-10 0-521-81820-6 hardback

for Janet
with abiding love

She would not say of any one in the world now that they were this or were that. She felt very young; at the same time unspeakably aged. She sliced like a knife through everything; at the same time was outside, looking on. She had a perpetual sense, as she watched the taxi cabs, of being out, out, far out to sea and alone; she always had the feeling that it was very, very dangerous to live even one day. Not that she thought herself clever, or much out of the ordinary.

Virginia Woolf, Mrs. Dalloway (1925)

Carlo watched this silly madness with slitted eyes. Finally he slapped his knee and said, "I have an announcement to make."

"Yes? Yes?"

"What is the meaning of this voyage to New York? What kind of sordid business are you on now? I mean, man, whither goest thou? Whither goest thou, America, in thy shiny car in the night?"

"Whither goest thou?" echoed Dean with his mouth open. We sat and didn't know what to say; there was nothing to talk about any more. The only thing to do was go.

Jack Kerouac, On the Road (1957)

My art is just about paying attention – about the extremely dangerous possibility that *you* might be art.

Robert Rauschenberg (Interview by Barbara Rose, 1987)

Contents

Illustrations

Acknowledgments

I first met Charles Mee in January 2000 when I interviewed him for an article I was writing for the Boston *Phoenix*. He mentioned that he was in the early stages of a new play that he would create with Anne Bogart and the SITI Company inspired by the art of Robert Rauschenberg. I knew little of Mee's work at that time, but I had been following Bogart and the SITI Company with interest since their *Going, Going, Gone* in 1996. I had a hunch that this might prove to be a unique and fruitful collaboration, and so, not knowing at first what might come of it, I asked for permission to observe the process leading to the premiere of what was already titled *bobrauschenbergamerica*.

I got lucky – on at least two counts. First, permission was granted. To observe an artist at work is a privilege. Even the most scrupulous bug on the wall cannot claim to be a neutral presence. At any moment in my research I could not have blamed those involved for shutting the door on me. That never happened, which is a courtesy and a gift for which I am forever grateful. Second, the play turned out to have a life. Since its premiere in Louisville in 2001, *bobrauschenbergamerica* has traveled on different occasions to Stamford, Champaign-Urbana, Chicago, Brooklyn, and Minneapolis, as well as to Bonn and Paris. This itinerary-after-the-fact lends some validation to my impulse to center my research on the collaboration of Mee, Bogart, and SITI on a single project.

The book that has resulted would not have been possible without the aid and participation of a great many people. At Boston College, where I teach, material and moral support have come from all corners, including Joseph F. Quinn, Dean of the College of Arts and Sciences; Michael A. Smyer, Associate Vice President for Research; and my colleagues in the Theater Department, especially Stuart J. Hecht and John Houchin. At Media Technology Services, Michael Swanson and April Rondeau advised on the cover design and Stephen Vedder went above and beyond in preparing the photographs for publication with care. The cast and crew of my 2002 production of *A Summer Evening in Des Moines* helped me to understand Mee's dramaturgy from the inside out. Over the years, my dedicated undergraduate research assistants – Claire Darby, Dan Brunet, Marin Kirby, Megan Rulison, and Sarah Lunnie – provided much valuable help, from fact-checking to hand-holding to proof-reading and other services. They were great.

This book is based primarily on field research, which means that I have communicated through in-depth interviews and casual conversations, in emails and phone calls and face-to-face meetings, with many people who have worked or studied with Mee, Bogart, and SITI over the years. These people include (in alphabetical order) Elissa Adams, Christopher Akerlind, Michi Barall, Wendell Beavers, Melina Bielefelt, Claudia Brown, Rebecca Brown, Kyle Chepulis, Jane Comfort, Tom Damrauer, John Dillon, Michael Dixon, Alec Duffy, Leslie Ferreira, Christian Frederickson, Tali Gai, Jackie Goldhammer, Rachel Grimes, Anne Hamburger, Eric Hill, Naomi Iizuka, Tina Landau, Troy Lavallee, Gideon Lester, Jon Jory, Brian Jucha, Marc Masterson, Erin Mee, Carol Mullins, Jason Noble, Tanya Palmer, Aileen Passloff, Sandy Robbins, Susan Ryan, Zan Sawyer-Dailey, David Schweizer, Kathleen Turco-Lyon, Les Waters, Kenn Watt, Amy Wegener, Julia Whitworth, Matthew Wilder, Laurie Williams, and Robert Woodruff. Very few of these people are quoted directly in the book, which nonetheless rests in part on their collective experience. I thank them (and others not mentioned here) for the gift of their time and their insight.

Artists would not survive without institutions to nurture and promote them. I pay tribute here to the many theaters, presenting organizations, and universities who have supported the artists discussed in this book, and I thank the many individuals at these institutions who helped me to gain access to information about their work. In particular, I would single out the staffs of the Actors Theatre of Louisville and the American Repertory Theatre for their friendly and generous accommodation of my repeated presence on their premises and my requests for all manners of help.

At Cambridge University Press, Commissioning Editor Victoria Cooper, Assistant Editor Rebecca Jones, Production Editors Alison Powell and Elizabeth Davey, and Copy-editor Maureen Leach have all demonstrated uncommon patience with me and my fussiness over innumerable details regarding the manuscript. Series Editor Don B. Wilmeth provided unwavering support and a calming influence throughout the entire (prolonged) process. I owe him a great debt.

In an effort to save me from embarrassment, Leslie Ferreira, Greg Gunter, Adrianne Krstansky, Ed Walters, Peter Ferran, and, especially, Janet Morrison have favored me by reading portions of the manuscript and offering feedback. Any infelicities that remain are all mine. Also, at different times, I have benefited from extended dialogues with Julia Whitworth and Jennifer Schlueter, younger scholars with research interests in Mee, Bogart, and SITI Company.

Another category of gratitude altogether must be reserved for the individuals whose work is the subject of this book. Whatever the strength and commitment of its individual members, a theatrical ensemble is always a precious and delicate thing. The SITI Company's survival for more than thirteen years is perhaps their greatest accomplishment, and they are right to be protective of it. Their willingness to grant me behind-the-scenes access to their work was tested each time I showed up with a tape recorder or a notebook in hand, and despite their misgivings or wishes at moments that I would just go away, they were always welcoming, accommodating, and professional. To Ellen Lauren, Kelly Maurer, Will Bond, Tom Nelis, Barney O'Hanlon, Leon Ingulsrud, Akiko Aizawa, Stephen Webber, J. Ed Araiza, and Susan Hightower, to Darron West and Brian Scott, to James Schuette and Neil Patel, to Megan Wanlass-Szalla and Elizabeth Moreau, to Danyon Davis, Gian-Murray Gianino, and Jennifer Taher, I wish to express my sincere and personal thanks for making this book possible.

Finally, for their trust, their cooperation, their candor, and their patience, I thank Chuck Mee and Anne Bogart. Their reputation for a great generosity of spirit is legendary and, I can attest, well earned.

A note to the reader

In an effort to avoid confusion, the following notes explain some of the practices and conventions that governed the writing of this book:

1. Which Mee? The man known to friends and colleagues as Chuck Mee has been known professionally over the years as Charles L. Mee, Jr., Charles L. Mee, and sometimes Charles Mee. My usage in this book varies according to context and Mee's practice at the time of a particular reference to him. (Thankfully, Anne Bogart has always been Anne Bogart.)

2. Bibliography. In order to save space and because so much of this study is based on firsthand research, this book contains no bibliography. Full citations regarding all sources, primary and secondary, are contained in the notes. I apologize for any inconvenience this may cause the reader.

3. Quotations from Mee plays. Charles Mee is well-known for posting his plays on his website (www.charlesmee.org), and I have taken advantage of that practice by excusing myself from detailed citation of quotations from his texts. Unless otherwise specified, all quotations from Mee plays are taken from the texts on the website and can be easily found there. With longer quotes I have maintained Mee's practice of registering sentences on the page in a free-verse form that has a few words (or sometimes only one) in a line of text. With shorter quotes contained in the body of a sentence, I have indicated a Mee line-break with a back slash, as in the following quote from Phil's Girl in *bobrauschenbergamerica*: "What I think about is / I'd like to have sex with you in the parking lot / behind the Exxon station / near that diner on the Malibu highway / you know the one?"

4. Punctuation. On the American model, my practice is to use double quotation marks for all direct quotations from interviews, printed sources, and so on. This is to reserve the use of single quotation marks for setting off a word or a phrase in an effort to coin a term or to indicate an implied

quotation (as if to say, 'so to speak'). I also have a fondness – I hope not an affectation – of using a long dash to set off a parenthetical thought or observation that is of more than parenthetical importance.

5. National nomenclature. Lacking a satisfactory alternative, I use the words "America" and "American" to refer to the United States of America and characteristics of that nation. The words themselves – their resonances, their contested meanings, their cultural freight – are too central to the book's concerns to be swapped out for politically correct substitutes.

Introduction: of hiccups and fireflies

O<small>N A SUNDAY MORNING IN THE FALL OF 1953,</small> ROBERT
Rauschenberg laid down a long, narrow strip of paper on the pavement
of Fulton Street near his studio in downtown Manhattan. Then, his buddy
John Cage drove his Model A Ford along the strip of paper with slow care,
as Rauschenberg applied black house paint to one of the rear tires. The
result was *Automobile Tire Print* – 22 feet (6.5 meters) long and 16.5 inches
(42 centimeters) wide – a crude monoprint that forecast Rauschenberg's
career-long pre-occupation with making large-scale work, with collaboration, with the mechanics of making and transferring images, with everyday
objects as material and subject, with space becoming time, and with
American iconography.

That same fall, with Abstract Expressionism and the New York School
all the rage, the twenty-eight-year-old Rauschenberg asked Willem de
Kooning, "the master of the new movement in American painting,"[1] for
one of his drawings so that he might erase it and present it as a work of his
own. De Kooning obliged, providing a pencil-and-crayon drawing that he
knew would resist obliteration. After a month, Rauschenberg came back
with *Erased de Kooning Drawing*, matted, labeled, and mounted in a gold-
leaf frame, with faint smudges of de Kooning's original still visible. Here
again Rauschenberg's fascination with the surface of things and the process
of making (or unmaking) is evident, as is a puckish imagination and a young
artist's willful effort to distance himself from the Abstract Expressionism
out of which he emerged. More significant though is the provocation to
viewers to confront their assumptions about what constitutes a work of art.[2]
If the sentiment behind *Erased de Kooning Drawing* was not clear,
Rauschenberg made it plain when, in the spirit of his friend and inspiration
Marcel Duchamp, he responded to the request of a French gallery owner for

a portrait of her by sending a cable that read: "This is a portrait of Iris Clert if I say so – Robert Rauschenberg."[3]

The gesture was cheeky, even radical, in its day. If, in the first decade of the twenty-first century, it seems like a cliché, that is one measure of Rauschenberg's permanent influence on our culture. Along with his friends and collaborators, composer John Cage and dancer/choreographer Merce Cunningham, Rauschenberg was at the forefront of a post-Second World War avant-garde that changed the idea of art forever. The tire track laid down in Fulton Street led to a vast new territory, a realm of possibility in the visual and the performing arts that to this day has not yet been fully explored. While countless abominations have been created in the name of "this is a work of art because I say it is," the true legacy of this triumvirate stems from their recognition of the beauty of the ordinary and their willful incorporation of chance into the artistic process. Their transformation of the understanding of art, from an object in a museum or on a stage or in a concert hall to a mode of perception and a quality of life, has enriched the lives of millions who will never even know their names.

When director Anne Bogart first conceived a theatrical meditation on the subject of Andy Warhol and American consumerism, she approached her friend, the playwright Charles Mee, to see if he would provide a text for the piece. They had collaborated twice before in the early 1990s: on a site-specific piece for En Garde Arts called *Another Person is a Foreign Country* and on Mee's radical revision of Euripides's *Orestes*, one of two inaugural productions of what became known as the SITI Company (pronounced "city"). They were eager to work together again. So, Mee immersed himself in Warhol, only to find himself uninspired. He withdrew from the project, which went forward without him. *Culture of Desire* premiered in Pittsburgh in the fall of 1997, just as the Guggenheim Museum in New York was opening a massive retrospective of one of Warhol's chief contemporaries: Robert Rauschenberg. Already a Rauschenberg fan, Mee saw the Guggenheim exhibit and later proposed to Bogart that they collaborate on a piece inspired by it. Bogart would say later that she suspected all along that Mee, in countering Warhol with Rauschenberg, was trying to teach her and her company a friendly lesson about "what a real artist is."[4]

bobrauschenbergamerica – written by Mee, directed by Bogart, and created and performed by the SITI Company – received its world premiere as part of the Actors Theatre of Louisville's Humana Festival of New American Plays in March 2001. In keeping with the spirit of its namesake, it takes the form of a collage play. It has no plot or narrative through-line, and its eight characters are cardboard archetypes. Over the course of forty-three short, discontinuous scenes, the play presents a seemingly random series of American events. From moment to moment, there is a line dance, a back-yard picnic, a game of checkers, a square dance, an assassination, a pizza delivery, a beating, a yard sale, and lots of chicken jokes. The piece exudes a Midwestern charm and boyish insouciance, one which celebrates the feeling of freedom and adventure that begins with exploring the woods at the edge of your neighborhood and stretches as far as a man walking on the moon. While its dominant mood is happy-go-lucky, there is also a recognition of what the play calls "the dark side," the inclination towards violence, destruction, and murder that is such an integral part of American culture.

Unlike *Culture of Desire*, which has the figure of Andy Warhol at its center, Rauschenberg is nowhere to be found in *bobrauschenbergamerica*, although a character named Bob's Mom is. Despite her presence, the piece makes no attempt to convey Rauschenberg's biography or to represent Rauschenberg's art in any literal sense. Instead, it borrows images, techniques, and themes from his profuse body of work and combines them with Mee's own writing, lots of appropriated texts, and the inventions of Bogart and the SITI Company in order to create an impressionistic and personal vision of the American experience in the era of Rauschenberg, the second half of the twentieth century. Rather than a biographical portrait, Mee and company sought to create a play that generated much the same response as Rauschenberg's art itself. Mee described it this way:

> What I think is so great about Rauschenberg is that he is a great American artist. He makes work that creates a world that we all wish America would be, which is to say, without being a Pollyanna, without turning a blind eye to the violence and tragedy and nastiness, his work is very open and very small-d democratic. He brings into his work not just what has been ignored or unseen or neglected or not previously visible, but stuff that has been positively rejected, garbage that has been thrown away. He brings it in off the street and says this, too, is worthy of attention. Before there was a word inclusiveness, he was inclusive. Before anybody did sampling, he was sampling. Before the French literary theorists knew what appropriation was, Rauschenberg was doing it. When he brings stuff together the way he does – a stuffed goat with an automobile tire around its stomach standing on a platform with wheels on it – if that is a sculpture, then anything is possible. I think that is the feeling that he creates: that anything is possible. And what more do you want out of life than anything being possible?[5]

In less capable hands, this 'anything-is-possible' approach might have resulted in a work that is incoherent, pretentious, and narcissistic. Mee, Bogart, and the SITI Company managed to avoid such pitfalls and create a work that was glorious in its randomness and exhilarating in its sense of freedom. The play's disconnected, self-contained events presented themselves as individual works in a museum exhibit or independent acts in a variety show or separate attractions at an old-time amusement park. If the viewer did not care for what was happening at the moment, something different was just around the corner. Some of the bits were gratuitously weird or suspiciously ironic or just plain corny, but on balance they were imbued with a sense of wonder or simple fun that gave the action an infectious, helter-skelter momentum. The lack of continuity from one segment to the next, the radical shifts in tone or mood, and the constant theatrical non sequiturs, all seemed to be designed to test the limits of the audience's willingness to go with the flow and give their undivided attention to the present moment, whatever that happened to be. With this strategy, *bobrauschenbergamerica* went beyond being playful and carefree to generate a complex experience of freedom, which it then used to characterize both the process of artistic creation and the culture of the United States of America.

How did they do that? How do playwright, director, designer, and actor each prepare and shape their material in a way that anticipates or, better still, elicits the contributions of their collaborators? And how do all of them leave room for the audience, whose extraordinary act of paying attention constitutes the ultimate act of theatrical composition and the perceptual ground on which the whole theatrical enterprise rests? These are the questions at the heart of this study, which will introduce the work of Mee and Bogart independent of one another and then examine in detail their collaboration on *bobrauschenbergamerica*.

In life and art, Charles Mee and Anne Bogart are kindred spirits. Both are known for a tremendous personal generosity, and their professional visions as playwright and director are complementary. Both sacrifice some of the authority of their positions in order to pursue a theater that is as open, inclusive, and collaborative as it can be. Both have aesthetics that are rooted in the American avant-garde of the 1960s, particularly the off-Off-Broadway dance and theater movements centered in Greenwich Village and SoHo, and influenced by international vanguard directors from the 1970s on. Both have embraced collage as a basis for structuring new work and what each calls "stealing" as a method for filling out that structure. Both have demonstrated an abiding fascination with twentieth-century American culture and history and, more generally, with the mechanics of change, be it in styles and conventions of theatre or in national historical process. And, as the new century dawned and they set to work on *bobrauschenbergamerica*, both found themselves in the prime of their careers, major figures in the reshaping of American theater and drama.

In form and content alike, the plays of Charles Mee demonstrate his view of culture as a process in which a society sifts through the past and its artifacts, salvages what is of interest and value, and redefines itself by combining recycled materials in new ways, from a new perspective, and with new ideas and materials. This aesthetic of "remaking," as he calls it, accounts for two primary features of his playwriting. Many of his plays are radical revisions of extant texts, from Greek tragedies such as *Orestes* and *The Suppliant Women* to modern classics such as *The Lower Depths* and *The Caucasian Chalk Circle*. Mee describes his method as a matter of using a classic text as a scaffolding or armature on which to shape his own construction, which he then smashes into fragments and presents held together by a more intuitive structure. From play to play, the ur-text may remain visible and recognizable, leading some to refer to his plays as adaptations, or it may recede into the conceptual background, leaving only trace evidence and haunting the play like a ghostly spirit. Some of Mee's plays, including *bobrauschenbergamerica*, have no single, discernible antecedent, but there is always some aspect of the work that is building on the past.

Mee supplements his own writing by taking texts from his wide-ranging reading and inserting them verbatim into the play. This postmodern, quotational technique is subversive, pluralistic, and celebratory. It challenges the strict, legalistic notion of intellectual property that has evolved over the history of capitalism and has been complicated more recently by the seemingly unbounded access to information made possible by the internet. It incorporates a cacophony of voices and sensibilities into his plays, in a manner that does not smooth over their dissonance or resolve their differences; in this way, Mee adds a subtle democratic dimension to the work. And, by the sheer vehemence, lyricism, sincerity, or offensiveness of the borrowed passages, Mee celebrates First Amendment freedoms as he depicts writing, theater, art, and culture as a violent collision of images, ideas, and values that propels societies, like Walter Benjamin's angel of history, into the future facing backwards. Mee's work combines a critical perspective on the past with a cautious faith in democratic process and historical progress to create works that are complex, provocative, and imbued with the joy of life.

Anne Bogart's theater is driven by the joy of discovery. She makes plays as theatrical essays in which she investigates subjects of interest and confronts nagging questions about the world around her. She came out of high school wanting to be a director, and in the past thirty-five years, she has rarely gone a year without directing a play. Her insatiable thirst for inquiry, marked by the twin questions "What is it?" and "What is it really?," have led to a sustained and experimental investigation of traditional American drama, various forms of American popular culture, key figures in twentieth-century American culture, and the nature of artistic creation itself, particularly theatrical creation. In the process, she has demonstrated a particular fascination with the question of the audience, most obvious in her early site-specific creations on the streets of New York and in the Audience Project she conducted at the Actors Theatre of Louisville in the late 1990s. She directs plays with the mind of a choreographer, scoring the motion of bodies in time and space with a keen eye towards rhythm, visual composition, and other formal principles. At the same time, she is known for the freedom that she extends to her actors, for her commitment as a teacher to the development of young, independent theater artists, and for her long-standing pursuit of ensemble work and the ideal of company.

All she ever wanted was a company of players with whom to make theater. After pick-up work in the East Village theater community and an aborted stint as artistic director of Trinity Repertory Company, she got what she wanted – properly speaking, began to get – in 1992 when she partnered with renowned Japanese director Tadashi Suzuki to create the Saratoga International Theatre Institute, known today as the SITI Company. Over time, the SITI Company refined a unique approach to theater training that combines the rigorous physical practices pioneered in Japan by Suzuki, an improvisational orientation to theatrical space and time known as the Viewpoints, and a collective strategy for generating raw material called Composition. These techniques became the bedrock on which the SITI Company's performances rest. In addition to staging classic plays by Shakespeare, Marivaux, and Noël Coward, Bogart and the SITI Company have created a series of original works based on such influential cultural figures as Marshal McLuhan, Andy Warhol, Orson Welles, Robert Wilson, Virginia Woolf, Leonard Bernstein, and, of course, Robert Rauschenberg.

These productions have been characterized by the particular manner in which they layer three quasi-independent texts on top of each other: a spoken or verbal text, often comprised of quotations taken from outside sources; a physical or gestural text, marked by non-behavioral movement executed with crystalline precision; and a design text, a combination of scenic elements, expressionistic lighting, and near continuous sound or music. Whatever its particular subject, a SITI Company creation is always about two things: the idea of theater, how it works, the audience–actor equation; and the idea of company, collaborative creation, the rare power of people working together.

bobrauschenbergamerica came at a conspicuous moment in the respective careers of Mee, Bogart, and the SITI Company. In the six years between September 1997, when the Rauschenberg retrospective opened at the Guggenheim, and October 2003, when their homage played the Brooklyn Academy of Music's Next Wave Festival, playwright, director, and company moved from the vanguard into the mainstream, creating high-profile work at a prodigious rate and reaching expanding audiences in New York, at regional theaters and performing arts centers around the USA, and in Europe.

Mee had no fewer than eight plays receive their world premieres in this six-year period, nine if you count a modest college production of *A Summer Evening in Des Moines*.[6] Many of these received immediate second and third productions. For example, *True Love*, his riff on the Phaedra-Hippolytus myth, received its world premiere at the Holland Festival in Amsterdam (2001), inaugurated the new off-Broadway Zipper Theater (2001), and then was produced at the Deutsches Theater in Berlin (2002). At the same time, Mee's early, edgy plays, such as *Orestes* and *Trojan Women: A Love Story*, continued to be remounted by fledgling directors and start-up theaters seeking to plant their flag and establish an identity. His first success, his 1986 collaboration with director Martha Clarke on *Vienna: Lusthaus*, was "revisited" in 2002 by New York Theatre Workshop, a reunion which led Clarke and Mee to start work on a piece about Toulouse Lautrec. And in 2002, at the age of sixty-three, he won the PEN/Laura Pels Foundation Award for "an American playwright in mid-career."

In this same six-year period, Bogart and the SITI Company also premiered nine original creations and staged three operas, two Noël Coward plays, and Marivaux's *La Dispute* as well. Bogart's move into opera, not uncommon for mid-career theater directors, included two high-profile world premieres composed by Deborah Drattell: *Lilith* at New York City Opera (with Lauren Flanigan) and *Nicholas and Alexandra* at Los Angeles Opera (with Placido Domingo). Bogart directed all fifteen of these productions and found time to work outside the SITI Company as well, collaborating with Laurie Anderson on her *Songs and Stories from Moby Dick* and with Lola Pasholinski and Linda Chapman on their *Gertrude and Alice: A Likeness to Loving*. In this time, Bogart also received a Guggenheim Fellowship, published her first book, *A Director Prepares*, to generally positive reviews, and was awarded tenure at Columbia University, where she heads the graduate directing program. The SITI design team – Neil Patel (sets), James Schuette (costumes), Mimi Jordan Sherin (lighting), and Darron West (sound) – received a major design award from *Entertainment Design* magazine. The SITI Company's actor training workshops grew more and more popular as the influence of the Suzuki method, Viewpoints, and Composition work spread. And, many SITI members, actors and designers alike, did significant work outside of the company to various degrees of acclaim.

This prolonged moment of fruition is defined by what I would call the Actors Theatre of Louisville–Brooklyn Academy of Music (ATL–BAM) axis. Both Mee and Bogart had new pieces premiere at the 2000 Humana Festival in Louisville that went on to the Next Wave Festival in Brooklyn. After touring to the Edinburgh Festival, the SITI Company's *War of the Worlds*, written by Naomi Iizuka, played BAM in October 2000. Mee's *Big Love*, directed by Les Waters, ended up at BAM in December 2001, after stops at Long Wharf Theatre in New Haven, Berkeley Repertory Theatre, and Chicago's Goodman Theatre. *bobrauschenbergamerica* premiered at Humana in March 2001, and two and a half years later, it opened the Next Wave Festival in October 2003. If the Humana Festival is the resident regional theater's premiere showcase for new American plays and the Next Wave Festival is New York's premiere American showcase for vanguard work from home and around the world, then there can be little argument that Mee, Bogart, and SITI were at the forefront of the American theater at the start of the twenty-first century. The coincidence of this zenith with their collaboration on *bobrauschenbergamerica* makes it all the more appropriate as an object of study and a lens through which to look at their body of work.

This, then, is a book about a playwright, a director, a theater company, a play, and a production of that play. To the extent that it aims to analyze the nexus of these five subjects, it cannot hope to be comprehensive about all of them. Things have been left out. For example, the SITI Company's important trilogy of solo pieces – *Bob*, *Room*, and *Score* – receives scant attention here. I have sacrificed a measure of breadth for the sake of depth, but in chronicling the step-by-step development of *bobrauschenbergamerica*, I do not mean to suggest that this is always how Charles Mee writes or Anne Bogart directs or the SITI Company creates a play. Each process of creation is unique, and if artists do not grow in their work, it gets repetitive and dull. Nevertheless, the practices and principles incorporated in this one collaboration do reflect aspects of their work in general and my hope is that a close examination of it will shed some light on them as artists. If I focus on minutiae at moments, it is because theatrical truth dwells in the details – the choice of a word, the turn of a foot, the timing of a fade – and because any given moment onstage can be seen to represent the convergence of all time and all space. Perhaps this view is romantic. After all, *bobrauschenbergamerica* lasts only 110 minutes in performance, little more than a hiccup in the life of those who came to see it, most of whom spat it out with their toothpaste that night before they went to bed. What difference could a play make really?

Nevertheless, my ongoing fascination with the phenomenology of theater compels me to regard that insignificant hiccup, from the catch in the throat when the lights go down to the gasp of air at the curtain call, as the tipping point on which for a moment all life is balanced. In the here-and-now of performance, the past and the future, the actual and the possible, the many and the one are all held in brief, glorious suspension. If I had to choose a single moment from *bobrauschenbergamerica* as an emblem of that suspension and a paradigm of the whole, it would be one that comes almost an hour into the show. An actor, Japanese by birth and done up like Annette Funicello in a 1960s beach movie, kicks off her platform sandals, tosses aside her purse, and dives into a puddle of gin. For reasons that this book aims to make clear, this moment of hilarity for the audience is also a symbol of the joyful, ludic spirit at the heart of the play, a prime example of the unusual manner in which Mee wrote it, a crucial pivot in Bogart's orchestration of its many jumbled elements, and a demonstration of how the SITI Company's techniques give its actors a commanding presence. It is also an in-joke, but we will get to that later. Not every moment of the play is worth explicating in detail and to do so would be tedious, but the principle of close analysis remains at the heart of my enterprise.

The plan of the book is simple. It has two parts. Part I provides a general introduction to the lives and independent careers of Mee and Bogart, up through their first collaboration in 1991. It goes on to outline the early history of the SITI Company and to describe the training methods on which their work is based. It discusses in brief a number of Mee, Bogart, or SITI creations, many of which merit the same more extensive analysis given to Mee's *Full Circle* and Bogart/SITI's *Cabin Pressure* in an interlude chapter that leads to the second part. Part II is a case study of *bobrauschenbergamerica*, from its roots in the work of Robert Rauschenberg and the 1997 Guggenheim retrospective through its rehearsal and the Actors Theatre of Louisville premiere in 2001 to its revival at the Brooklyn Academy of Music in 2003. The focus here is on process, on how these theatre artists came to create something out of nothing, and on the million and one decisions that go into making a single play. In tracing the play's evolution, no doubt, I have missed things. My research has been thorough, but I could not attend every rehearsal or meeting, interview every artist involved, or examine every decision that went into the production. And trying to capture the fleeting moment of performance and put it down in words is akin to chasing fireflies. Even if you catch a jarful, the glow is not going to last for long. My hope, dear reader, is to have just enough fireflies to illuminate, if only in fits and starts, the work of some of the most interesting and important American theater artists at the beginning of the twenty-first century.

Part I

A playwright, a director, and a company

I

Mee: from accidental historian to citizen playwright

CHARLES MEE WAS A PROFESSIONAL HISTORIAN BEFORE HE WAS
a professional playwright. He started out writing about the Renaissance –
about the Medicis and Italy, the birth of the Reformation in the
confrontation between Martin Luther and Pope Leo X, and Erasmus –
in books that at first were geared for young readers and then for a general
adult audience. His political activism in opposition to the Vietnam War
and the Nixon Presidency promoted his interest in the history of the
Cold War and its origins in the First and Second World Wars. One of
his early successes was *Meeting at Potsdam* (1975), an account of the
Potsdam Conference in July 1945, when Truman, Churchill, and Stalin
met in a suburb of Berlin to carve up the post-war world. A Book-of-the-
Month Club selection, it was made into a Hallmark Hall of Fame television movie by David Susskind, starring José Ferrer as Stalin, John House-
man as Churchill, and Ed Flanders as Truman. Mee had a knack for
making history dramatic, for turning scholarly sources and primary docu-
ments such as diaries, correspondence, and official reports into vivid
confrontations between world historical figures. *Meeting at Potsdam* led
to other books on summit diplomacy and power sharing after major
military conflicts, including *The End of Order: Versailles 1919* (1980), *The
Marshall Plan: The Launching of the Pax Americana* (1984), and *The Genius
of the People* (1987), about the Constitutional Convention of 1787. All told,
Mee wrote a dozen works of history, some of which were translated into
Spanish, French, Polish, German, Persian, Chinese, Slovenian, and Japanese.

Over time though, the historian's mask of objectivity grew more and
more uncomfortable. For him, there was something mendacious about the
whole enterprise:

I never meant to be a historian. I came out of college with the intention of writing for the theater and got all caught up in the anti-Vietnam War activities, which led to political arguments which led to writing about politics and political history. Before I knew it I was drawn into this public conversation about the history of the United States and its Constitution and the values that are put in jeopardy when one has an active internationalist foreign policy. I felt like a fraud all those years. First of all because I felt not adequately schooled as an historian, and second of all because it was not for me a satisfactory way of talking about the world. The basic assumption of history is that you are going to be able to formulate dispassionate statements about events that really make you want to scream and cry out and weep. I really think the theater is more the place where I can write about the world and not pretend that my view is dispassionate.[1]

And so, over the course of the 1980s and into the 1990s, Mee turned more and more to writing for the stage. Eventually he stopped writing history altogether. Nevertheless, his identity as a historian must be seen as the chrysalis out of which the playwright emerged. His knowledge of twentieth-century Euro-American political history provides the intellectual underpinning for four early works he called the American Century plays. And even those plays that are not based on historical events are colored by his perspective as a historian.

Rejecting the American tradition of psychological realism, Mee conceives his characters as the products of politics, economics, sociology, and gender, "people through whom the culture speaks, often without the speakers' knowing it."[2] That is one reason why he has them speak words drawn, as it were, from the historical record, that is, from a myriad of popular sources, such as supermarket tabloids, internet chat rooms, and celebrity memoirs, as well as more literary works, ranging from Thucydides to Elaine Scarry to the *Pillow Book* of Sei Shonagon. Contradictory, confrontational, and open to interpretation, his plays are Rorschach tests for society at large, offering "evidence of who and how we are and what we do." His ultimate concern is to take the temperature of the body politic by filtering the culture of the past and the present through his own unabashed subjectivity. Again and again, his plays include sentences along the lines of 'that's what it is to be human.' and that is ultimately what they are about. Humanity is his subject and, in another sense, his objective, too.

Charles Louis Mee, Jr. was born September 15, 1938 in Evanston, Illinois. With two older sisters, he grew up outside of Chicago in the towns of

Palatine, Streator, and Barrington. His father, Charles Louis Mee, a devout Catholic, spent thirty-five years moving up the corporate ladder at the Commonwealth Edison Company. His mother, née Sarah Elizabeth Lowe, was a devoted housewife and homemaker and, as Mee writes, "not even quite Protestant, really, but only, vaguely, 'Christian.'"[3] Mee attended parochial schools. He had an Irish setter named Pat. He was a Boy Scout. He led a typical middle-class, Midwestern boyhood, "with buckteeth, a crew cut, a love of swimming, football, and comic books." He dreamed of playing quarterback at Notre Dame – until the summer of 1953, after his freshman year of high school, when he contracted polio and his life stopped dead in its tracks. He was fourteen.

Poliomyelitis is an acute, infectious virus that attacks the motor neurons of the central nervous system and often results in extensive, permanent muscle loss. Also known as infantile paralysis, the disease reached epidemic proportions in the USA in the late 1940s and early 1950s. It nearly killed Mee. He spent fifteen days on his back in the isolation ward of a hospital, in tremendous pain and a delirious fever, unable to move anything but his eyelids and three fingers of his left hand. His weight dropped from 160 pounds to 90. He was close enough to death that his father summoned a priest to administer last rites. ("In that instant," he later wrote, "I became an ex-Catholic."[4]) The fever eventually broke, and sensation gradually returned to parts of his body. An aggressive rehabilitation program, caring nurses, and his own fierce determination helped him to loosen and then build up strength in muscles that had turned as stiff as wood. After more than four months in the hospital, he was released, crippled for life but able to walk with the aid of a leg brace and double aluminum canes with arm cuffs. In the spring, without the leg brace, he returned to high school to resume "a nearly normal life," the title of his memoir about his battle with polio. He acted in school plays and became vice-president and president of the student council. He wrote about sports for the local paper. He got his driver's license and got into trouble with his buddies for pulling adolescent pranks. He sang square dance calls for the high school exhibition square dance team. He went to the junior prom with a cheerleader named Suzy Harvey. He graduated from high school on schedule and headed for college at Harvard. By that time, an effective polio vaccine was in development and the disease was well on its way to being under control in the USA.

A Nearly Normal Life makes clear how "such a life transforming event" shaped Mee's outlook on life and influenced his eventual choice of careers as editor, historian, and playwright. Contracting polio was for him a random occurrence without reasonable cause, one that taught him an early, unforgettable lesson about the fragility of all life. Surviving polio was a type of rebirth, a second chance at life that gave him a *carpe-diem* attitude and even a taste for delinquency. Different from the first, this second life was defined by a profound alienation from his crippled teenage body and by "the growing sensation of being an outsider," an up-and-comer relegated to the role of spectator on "the sidelines" of life.[5] Mee responded by changing the game and embracing a life of the mind. In the hospital, barely able to hold a book in his weak hands, he gave himself a short course in western philosophy, devouring Plato and the Greeks and other great books instead of *Superman* or *Archie* or *Classics Illustrated* comic books. The love of learning that took hold at this time remained with him in the decades to come. He became an omnivorous reader, a "bookish man" by his own account,[6] an editor, an author, and a bit of a gadfly among the intelligentsia. "There is love of another person, and there is love of books," he wrote in *A Nearly Normal Life*. "These are the two great loves of life. Anyone who has ever felt like an outsider knows this."[7]

At Harvard in the late 1950s, Mee's intellectual interests turned from philosophy and theology to literature and art history. He gravitated to the theater, studying with Archibald MacLeish, among others, directing and acting in shows with campus groups, and writing his own plays. In his junior year, for the fiftieth anniversary of the Harvard Dramatic Club, he directed Brecht's *The Good Woman of Setzuan* and fell in love with the woman brought in to play Shen Te, Claire Lu Thomas. They got married the next summer in Stratford, Connecticut, where she was an apprentice at the Stratford Shakespeare Festival. This early marriage lasted only a couple of years, the first in a series of relationships and marriages, mainly with actresses, that would mark Mee's personal life. He graduated from Harvard in 1960 and moved to Greenwich Village, a young buck determined to pursue a career as a playwright. Through Eric Bentley, who he had the chutzpah to contact for advice when he was directing Brecht as an undergraduate, Mee met Robert Brustein, Richard Gilman, Gordon Rogoff, and Robert Corrigan, all in early stages of their critical careers. He wrote a piece about the Living Theater for the *Tulane Drama Review*, and when Richard Schechner became its editor, Mee and Rogoff were appointed its New York editors. In 1962, three of his fledgling one-acts – *Constantinople Smith, Anyone! Anyone!*, and *The Players' Repertoire* – were produced off-Off-Broadway by the new Writers Stage Company, with Roscoe Lee Browne and James Earl Jones in the cast.[8] Not yet twenty-five, he was making his presence felt in the midst of the theatrical explosion known as off-Off Broadway, which saw rough-and-tumble, devil-may-care theater erupt in churches, cafés, basements, and lofts all over Greenwich Village.

But life – and the 1960s – led him away from theater and into politics, history, and a first career as an editor. He got married for the second time in 1962, and he and his wife, Suzi Baker, had a daughter, Erin, in 1963 and a son, Charles L. Mee III, in 1969. One of his first day jobs in New York was as a fact-checker at *Horizon*, a glossy hardbound magazine of the arts that he had admired (and subscribed to) as an undergraduate. Off and on, he worked there and for its publisher, American Heritage, for years, rising through the ranks to become managing editor and then editor of *Horizon*. By this time, he was involved in the anti-war movement, co-founding a group that supported election campaigns in swing districts of Congressional candidates opposed to the US presence in Vietnam. With his friend, Edward L. Greenfield, he wrote a wry political satire titled *Dear Prince: The Unexpurgated Counsels of N. Machiavelli to Richard Milhous Nixon* (1969). In the 1970s, following revelations about the secret bombing of Cambodia and Laos and the Watergate break-in, Mee became the co-founder and chairman of the National Committee on the Presidency, a nationwide, grass-roots organization dedicated to the impeachment of the man he referred to as "the Dark Liar." His political activism and his effort to understand the workings of current American imperialism led him from the Vietnam War back through the Cold War to the Second World War, the First World War, and the various diplomatic summits that resolved each military conflict in a way that seemed to guarantee the next. In the process, he became, almost by accident, a historian.

In the 1970s and 1980s, Mee wrote works of political history for a general readership.[9] Critics and editors kept saying that his history books read like novels, so in the late-1970s, he took a year and wrote one, living on credit cards and royalties from *Meeting at Potsdam*. In the midst of this effort, an ominous notice from the government arrived at his door one day threatening to auction off his furniture in a week's time for failure to pay back taxes. This crisis prompted a wholesale reassessment of Mee's situation in life. He set out to put his financial house in order. He ended his current relationship. (His second marriage had ended in divorce in 1975.) And he tossed his unfinished, "stillborn" novel in a curbside trash can. This was years before he owned a computer, and by the time he realized he wanted the manuscript back, the sanitation department had come and gone. There was no carbon or xerox copy. So he sat down at his typewriter

to recover what he could and found that the rush of writing that resulted
took the form of three one-act plays. This led to a revelation:

> Oh, I see, when I want to write something for myself and only for
> myself, to put down what matters most to me so it is clear and true and
> vivid and memorable, the form it takes is the form of a play. So
> I realized I ought to return to writing plays.[10]

The first play Mee undertook – the three rough one-acts were perma-
nently consigned to his bottom drawer – was *The Investigation of the
Murder in El Salvador*, which found its way into the hands of three of
the most important producing directors of the 1980s, Gordon Davidson,
Robert Brustein, and Joseph Papp. Mee knew Davidson from hanging
around the Stratford Shakespeare Festival in the summer of 1959, when
Davidson was an assistant stage manager there. Twenty-five years later, in
1984, as artistic director of the Mark Taper Forum, Davidson organized a
workshop production of *The Investigation of the Murder in El Salvador*,
which was directed by Peter Brosius. The play's political content must
have had some appeal for Robert Brustein, who Mee knew a bit from his
early days in New York, but the idea for a production at the American
Repertory Theatre, possibly directed by JoAnne Akalaitis, never got off
the drawing board. Around this time, Mee became acquainted with playwright Wallace Shawn, who worked in a copy shop that Mee patronized.
Shawn read the play and passed it on to Joe Papp, who liked it and decided
to produce it at the Public Theatre. Among the prospective directors were
Akalaitis and Martha Clarke, the choreographer-director whose hybrid
mix of movement, music, and image was attracting wider and wider
attention at the time. When Mee met Clarke, she was in the early stages
of creating a new work, an impressionistic portrait of fin-de-siècle Vienna.
Mee convinced her and her producer, Lyn Austin of Music-Theatre
Group/Lenox Arts Center, to tap his historical skills and have him provide
a text for the piece. *Vienna: Lusthaus* became a huge sensation in New York
in the spring and summer of 1986, winning the Obie for best play, drawing
critical comparisons to such visualists as Robert Wilson, Ping Chong, and
Meredith Monk, and moving from the theater at St. Clement's Episcopal
Church to a sold-out run at Papp's Public Theater.[11]

Vienna: Lusthaus

Vienna: Lusthaus takes its title from the Lusthaus, or Pleasure Pavilion, an
octagonal building at the far end of the famous Viennese park called the

Prater. It was a favored gathering place during the city's most celebrated period, the late nineteenth and early twentieth century, the glorious, glamorous, final years of the Austro-Hungarian Empire. This was the Vienna of Schiele and Schnitzler and Schonberg, of Klimt, Kokoschka, and Kraus, of Freud and Wittgenstein, none of whom appear in the piece but all of whom inform it. Instead of a historical portrait, Martha Clarke and her collaborators – composer Richard Peaslee, set and costume designer Robert Israel, lighting designer Paul Gallo, and Mee, credited in the playbill with providing "text" – created an abstract and ethereal evocation of the Viennese zeitgeist and the broader cultural forces of Eros and Thanatos that, as Freud argued in 1930, were at the heart of civilization and its discontents.

Featuring eleven performers and six musicians, the sixty-five-minute piece takes the form of a series of vignettes, each composed with precision, saturated with mood, and vivid with imagery. The piece is presented in an empty, unadorned white room, with slightly skewed walls that do not meet at the corners. The audience sees this room through a scrim that fills the proscenium's fourth wall, adding a dreamy, hazy, soft focus to many of the images. A proud soldier in a blue and red uniform circles the stage with a posture and gait that suggests the canter of a stallion. Two women on a bench share a tender, lingering kiss, and then one of them tells a story about how her mother accidentally walked out of an open window and fell to her death. A pair of young lovers, lying one on top of the other, roll across the floor in a lover's embrace, while an older woman looks on; when they stand up and release each other, the older woman steps between them and, after a moment, the man wheels and kisses her with passion. These and other related images are arresting in their beauty. Some of them – such as a sequence in which a man sets a loose-limbed woman on his lap and manipulates her like a puppet – are humorous and troubling all at once. The ethereal tones of the music, mostly harp, strings, and woodwinds; the gradual cross-fades of the chiaroscuro lighting; the slow, practiced grace of the performers' movement, neither dance nor realistic behavior; all combine to give the piece a gentle, undulating rhythm as it moves from segment to segment, generating an undeniable, if complicated, sensuality that includes and eventually yields to images of violence, death, and decay. There are reminders that the Vienna of Freud and Klimt was also the capital of European anti-Semitism and the home of an aspiring painter named Adolf Hitler. In one of the piece's few dialogues, the casual question "Is he a Jew?" has an odd, conspicuous ring. More and more, erotic impressions yield to images of death, until, in the last sequence, the figure of a dead soldier asks "What does rigor mortis actually mean?" and "What colors does a body pass through after death?" As the lights fade dimmer and dimmer, he receives matter-of-fact clinical answers: "Light pink, red, light blue, dark blue, purple-red." *Vienna: Lusthaus* ends on this mordant, matter-of-fact note.

While Mee's contribution to *Vienna: Lusthaus* was significant, the piece and its success belonged to Martha Clarke, who conceived it before Mee was on board and determined its final shape, as a choreographer would, on the basis of movement, rhythm, gesture, shape, and other compositional principles. Mee's "text" for *Vienna: Lusthaus* was comprised of brief, isolated monologues, many of them anecdotal descriptions of an odd or mysterious experience, often of a sexual nature. In one, a man describes the elaborate beauty regimen of his Aunt Cissi. In another, which begins "I was in India several thousand years ago fondling a horse," a woman describes how a blond-haired boy "came down from the horse and kissed my quim." Another, spoken by an older gentleman, simply lists a series of names – "Klara, a seamstress. Once. Elke, a shopkeeper's daughter. Twice" and so on – which becomes evident as a catalogue of his sexual conquests. While Mee based some of the texts on his own dreams, many of them were culled from his historical research into period sources, such as Wittgenstein's notebooks, Freud's love letters to his wife, and the diaries of the Hapsburgs. A number of the segments had no text at all. In this regard, Mee's role might have seemed to be more that of a dramaturg than a playwright, all the more because he had no established identity as a playwright at the time. Hindsight, however, makes clear just how much *Vienna: Lusthaus* forecast his approach to playwriting in the years to come. Appropriation and quotation out of context from a variety of sources, the absence or suppression of cause-and-effect narrative in favor of affective and associative structures, the use of collage technique to arrange theatrical fragments into 'pictures at an exhibition,' a non-hegemonic text that invites independent elaboration from an auteur director, kinky sex as a frequent topic of conversation, and an ominous aura of apocalypse are all traits of *Vienna: Lusthaus* that would come to define his larger body of work.

Vienna: Lusthaus, Mee's first produced script since his salad days off-Off Broadway in the 1960s, was the true beginning of his career as a playwright. Joe Papp's plans to produce *The Investigation of the Murder in El Salvador* never materialized, but in the spring of 1988, the downtown impresario saw Mee's *The Imperialists at the Club Cave Canem* at the

Home for Contemporary Theatre and Art on Walker Street in TriBeCa and moved it to the Public Theater for a brief run that summer. The production was a family affair. Mee's twenty-four-year-old daughter Erin, an aspiring director and, like her father, a Harvard graduate, staged the piece. The role of Karen was played by his third wife, Kathleen Tolan, an actor and playwright in her own right, who he had married in 1981.[12] Mee and Tolan had two daughters, Sarah, born in 1985, and Alice, born in 1989. That same year, *The Investigation of the Murder in El Salvador* finally received its premiere in a production directed by David Schweizer at New York Theater Workshop. By this time, Mee was attracting more and more attention in downtown circles as a historian-playwright, an exotic hybrid in a Reagan-era theater community that paid too little attention to politics and the world at large. He was invited to be one of the keynote speakers – South African playwright Athol Fugard was another – at the 1990 biennial conference of the Theatre Communications Group (TCG), the national service organization of regional resident theaters. The incoming TCG president that year happened to be Anne Bogart.

The TCG meeting came at an inauspicious moment for the nation's theaters. The crusade against the National Endowment for the Arts (NEA), triggered by the Mapplethorpe and Serrano controversies and led in Congress by Jesse Helms and Dana Rohrbacher, was in full swing.[13] NEA grantees were now required to sign a decency pledge or forfeit funding. Congressional allocations were dwindling. The future of the agency was in doubt. And soon, "the NEA Four" – performance artists Karen Finley, Holly Hughes, Tim Miller, and John Fleck – would have their awards withheld by NEA chair John Frohnmayer, triggering a legal battle that went all the way to the Supreme Court. Speaking as a political activist turned historian turned playwright and as the author of books about Lorenzo de' Medici, Rembrandt, and the connections between art, patronage, and politics, Mee raised the specter of "official art" in the USA and issued a call to arms:

> If artists are not taking the heat, if their reviews are always good, if their patrons are entirely happy, if the politicians are quiet, then the artists have failed their fellow citizens, not just the poor and the outcast, but all their fellow citizens. So, it is not up to those of us who make and produce and finance art to seek less trouble from politicians; it is up to us to seek more trouble . . . Shall we go down in history as the most easily intimidated artists and producers and boards of directors the world has ever known? I can't believe it. Let us rather learn to jump into a nasty political fight and bite back. Let us learn to demand our rights without shame and without

apology. Let's choose a few politicians, let's talk ceaselessly to our friends in the media, let's talk to the wealthy friends we have who can contribute to political campaigns, let us end a few political careers forever, and let's get on with our work.[14]

For Mee, henceforward, that work would be writing plays. The accidental historian had become a citizen playwright.

In an interview in the *New York Times* at the time of *Vienna: Lusthaus*, Mee made an explicit link between fin-de-siècle Vienna and Reagan-era America. "I see civilization sleepwalking to the edge of doom, then and now," he said. "I see it then in a way that's frightening, in that it feels so contemporary. Those people were unconscious of where they were headed in the same way that we seem to be unconscious of where we're headed, and both they and we are enormously resourceful at finding ways of avoiding reality – of insulating and isolating ourselves from ugliness, and anesthetizing ourselves to the harshness of the world."[15] Mee's return to playwriting in the 1980s signaled his new strategy for representing this sense of a world teetering on the verge of apocalypse and for getting others to pay attention to it. At this time, still active as an historian, he wrote four thematically related plays, conceived as a tetralogy of sorts and referred to as the American Century plays, that depict privileged, self-absorbed characters blind to the catastrophe gathering around them. The first three plays examine the legacy and origins of what some historians call the Pax Americana (the "American Peace," alluding to the imperialist Pax Romana), moving backwards in time, like a Greek trilogy in reverse, from contemporary US entanglements in Central America to the period of the two World Wars to European colonialism to, at least in title, the origins of the USA.[16] Though slow to be premiered and rarely, if ever, staged since then, they merit consideration here as plays that represent Mee's metamorphosis from historian into playwright and present the prospectus for what kind of playwright that might be.

The Investigation of the Murder in El Salvador

On March 24, 1980, Archbishop Oscar Arnulfo Romero, an outspoken critic of the US-backed military junta ruling El Salvador, was shot and killed by a professional assassin while celebrating mass in the Chapel of the Hospital de la Divina Providencia. Later that year, three US nuns and a Catholic lay worker in El Salvador were raped and murdered by a paramilitary death squad. These vicious incidents helped to increase awareness of widespread political repression and human rights abuses in El Salvador and other Central American countries. The depth of US involvement in these military regimes, through foreign aid and the US Army's notorious School of the Americas, was not widely known until the Iran-Contra scandal of the mid-1980s. But followers of US foreign policy, including Mee, were already familiar with the network of dubious relationships between Central American regimes, international business interests, and the US military that stretched all the way back to the days of the United Fruit Company in the nineteenth century. This is the historical context that gave rise to *The Investigation of the Murder in El Salvador*.

In its outward realism, this first play would prove to be unusual for Mee. It takes place in a single location, an elegant, sun-drenched veranda in a tropical clime, and in a single, unbroken scene, making it perhaps the longest single scene in Mee's entire oeuvre. Charles Gallejas, "half English and half Spanish or West Indian," is entertaining five guests for a leisurely luncheon that includes "copious amounts of fresh fruits, cheeses, delicacies," pyramids of finger sandwiches served on silver trays, and colorful drinks in hurricane glasses. His guests are international jetsetters and power brokers: among others, an investment banker who looks at a skyscraper and sees the beauty of the financial plan that made it possible; a silent, wheelchair-bound man who revels in his association with the likes of Averell Harriman, Albert Schweitzer, and Clare Boothe Luce; and his wife, who jabbers away, her Lhaso Apso in her lap, about shopping at Saks, inaugural parades, and cosmetic surgery. Speaking in refined, civilized tones all the while, their conversation touches on unsavory subjects. One shares a gruesome anecdote about the consequences of burying Franklin D. Roosevelt in a metal coffin. The host describes watching rats in India drinking his urine and then spells out how to filet and prepare rat as a delicacy in a light cream sauce. Over time, their responses become more defensive and guilty as they seek to justify themselves in the face of no direct accusation. "After all, I'm not killing people," says the investment banker, his eyes filling with tears.

The play hinges on the irony of its title. When Gallejas hears an offstage scream in the play's first moments, he asks the butler to make inquiries. It turns out that a bloody corpse has turned up in the dumbwaiter. A few cursory questions are asked, a minor discomfort ripples through the group, but the gossip-filled luncheon resumes. The murder remains uninvestigated. The identity of both victim and perpetrator are a matter of indifference. Dessert is served. Ambiguous references to "the situation" and "the natives," as well as telltale offstage sounds such as a helicopter hovering overhead, point to an eruption of political violence that is coming closer and closer. But host and guests alike remain nonchalant. Pressure builds and builds beneath the tranquil surface of events until it erupts with finality in the play's violent climax. The splash of waves and the songs of tropical birds are soon drowned out by screams, breaking glass, sirens, gunshots, and the shouts of a riot. Scenery falls. Strobe lights flicker. Images of "beautiful things broken" are projected. An explosion "rocks the theater." And at the very last moment, three gunshots ring out and the head of one guest explodes, splattering blood against the rear wall as the lights fade slowly.

A drawing-room murder mystery in which the intrepid detective never shows up, *The Investigation of the Murder in El Salvador* is a wry joke that masks a smoldering fury. Its extended theatrical metaphor associates the vicious violence of political repression with the smug, hedonistic "lifestyles of the rich and famous." The play has the feel of a political cartoon come to life, one that suggests – or merely indulges a wish – that this decadent elite is on the verge of annihilation. The absence of the eponymous investigation is the leading edge of an irony that offers an oblique and mordant attack on the ruling class and their blithe indifference to the crimes which make their wealth and comfort possible. If property is theft, the play suggests, capitalism is murder.

The War to End War

In 1980, Mee published *The End of Order: Versailles 1919*, his historical account of the six-month Paris Peace Conference, which sought to establish a new world order after a war that marked the end of four empires: the German, Austro-Hungarian, Ottoman, and Russian. Dedicated to "William Mee, my grandfather, who lost all 10 of his brothers in World War I," the book argues that the diplomats and statesmen who gathered in Paris "far from restoring order to the world, took the chaos of the Great War, and, through vengefulness and inadvertence, impotence and design, they sealed it as the permanent condition of our century."[17] A few years later, Mee wrote *The War to End War*, a theatrical fantasia that looks at the events of *The End of Order* through a dada kaleidoscope. Side by side, the book and the play provide the most direct and palpable measure of Mee's switch from historian to playwright. As Mee put it, "I never got it right in the book because that nineteenth-century New-tonian cause-effect construction of narrative is a lie about how history happens. In a theater piece, you can go anywhere you want; you can shift perspectives."[18]

The War to End War is written in three sections or movements, two of which are situated around the historical moment of 1919. The first, "The Treaty of Versailles," draws much of its material straight from *The End of Order*. It depicts a theatrical convergence of the four principal players in the diplomatic drama at Versailles: the British diplomat Harold Nicolson, surrogate for Lloyd George; the seventy-eight-year-old French minister of war Georges "Le Tigre" Clemençeau; President Woodrow Wilson, whose famous Fourteen Points called for the establishment of a League of Nations; and the German foreign minister Count Ulrich von Brockdorff-Rantzau. Mee calls for this section to be performed in front of a gigantic shattered mirror in several ornate, gilt frames, both an allusion to Versailles's famous Hall of Mirrors, where the much-contested treaty was finally signed, and a literalization of Mee's favorite image (shards, fragments, broken pieces) for his own dramaturgy.

"Dada," the play's second part, takes place in front of a large rusted steel wall that descends from the flies to block the shattered mirror. It presents Mee's recipe for a chaotic extravaganza in the manner of dada performance as it was practiced during and after the war in Zurich, Berlin, Hanover, Cologne, and Paris. One of its characters is Kurt Schwitters, the pioneer collage artist and writer who created his own dada form called Merz after being rejected by the Berlin dadaists in 1918. Another is philosopher Ludwig Wittgenstein, who at one point drops his pants and moons the audience with ceremonial dignity. At another point, "Mona Lisa enters, naked, with a mustache" (an allusion to Duchamp), puts her arms out, and spins in a circle around and around. At the end of this part, "a Rube Goldberg contraption of enormous complexity and stupidity slowly descends, deus ex machina fashion," whirling and rocking and then producing a light for Wittgenstein's cigar, before self-destructing in a ball of fire.

"Los Alamos," the third part, is positively serene in comparison. It shifts from the end of the First World War to the end of the Second World War and from the palace of Versailles to the desert of New Mexico. Another historical foursome, J. Robert Oppenheimer, Ernst Teller, Enrico Fermi, and John Von Neumann, major physicists involved in the development of the atom and hydrogen bombs, gather on the night before the first bomb test at Trinity Site to play poker and chat about probability and game theory. They place bets without checking their cards because "What's the fun in life if you don't estimate." While they make no mention of Los Alamos or their purpose in being there, Oppenheimer does observe that "we've transformed our home into the most perilous place in the universe." All the while, a voice-over recites "a revised Ten

Commandments, since the old ten haven't worked so well." In the end, green fog fills the stage, as it did in the beginning, and the men of science descend through trap doors while "sounds and images that call up an unreasoning love of the earth" are heard and seen.

The War to End War is a history play with a difference. It makes no attempt to represent actual events at Versailles or Zurich or Los Alamos, preferring instead to create a mosaic of broken shards of history, dislodged from the tidy logic of cause-and-effect and presented instead as a tremendous explosion, rendered with an apocalyptic whimsy inspired by dada. A stage direction at the start of the "Dada" movement reads "It can be said that THE PLAY begins here . . . What has come up to now can be considered the prologue; what follows this section can be considered the epilogue." This is a prime indication of Mee's vision of history as a chaotic dada performance, without rational beginning, middle, and end, a collision of social, political, and economic forces marked by a disorienting perpetual simultaneity. Like the Rube Goldberg invention in its midst, the play makes fun of the mechanism of cause and effect, negating traditional notions of historical progress in favor of conflating past and present in a moment of continuing and endless eruption. Hiroshima, Cabaret Voltaire, Verdun become, in effect, simultaneous events more truly understood by the blunt force of their impact: the eerie stillness that comes before, the blinding flash of light and deafening ringing in the ears that comes during, and the splatter of blood on the canvas of civilization that comes after. History, for Mee, is a bomb.

The Constitutional Convention: A Sequel

In 1987, Mee marked the bicentennial of the Constitutional Convention of 1787 by publishing *The Genius of the People*, his book about the contentious gathering in Philadelphia – another summit meeting, in effect – that yielded the foundational document of American democracy. Around that time, he wrote a jumble of a play called *The Constitutional Convention: A Sequel*, a cryptic title given the fact that the play has no American characters and no discernible link to the events of 1787. Written in nine fragmentary sections, it is perhaps the most amorphous and raw of Mee's plays, more the scenario for a performance event than a clear and complete script of a play. Productions have been few and far between.[19]

The Constitutional Convention: A Sequel centers on three characters – Arthur, Susan, and David – who come and go on three Louis XVI chairs which rise from beneath the stage. They share a series of dialogues and monologues which are juxtaposed by projections on a scrim, voiceovers, deafening musical sequences, and several unscripted "performance pieces" left to the producer's imagination.[20] The play offers no indication whatsoever of setting, situation, or relationship between the three characters. References to Swahili, the Muthaiga Club in Nairobi, and the impossibility of getting mincemeat suggest that they might be long-suffering British colonialists in East Africa or some other outpost of empire. At one point, the characters watch a movie, "a recreation of the landing of the Mayflower, or an old Katharine Hepburn film." A voiceover lists the do's and don'ts for a healthy bondage-and-domination relationship. Arthur insists that at "the first Thanksgiving" the settlers were so starved for food that they dug up their dead and ate them. There are several mentions of cannibalism after this, including Susan's suggestion that world hunger might be relieved if fat people had some of their intestines removed and sent to foreign countries with food shortages. Later, David describes how the laundry service where they take their clothes rents them out to the locals before cleaning them. National Enquirer-like headlines – "MERMAID BABY BORN TO TEEN" – are projected. Towards the end, Arthur runs in place for a very long time, with microphones strapped all over his body so that every movement – pounding his chest, slapping his arms, kicking and stomping – is amplified. The piece ends with the recording of a choir singing "a heart-rending piece" of gospel music.

In a manner similar to *The Investigation of the Murder in El Salvador*, Mee posits characters who epitomize the received notion of Civilization and then lathers them with imagery that suggests the barbarism in which their sense of privilege and superiority is rooted. "The play is about conventions and rules of all kinds," Mee explained in 1988. "Rules of what is done and what isn't done, what is acceptable behavior and what is rude behavior – all become techniques of political control."[21] While the play squeezes some comedy out of exposing the silliness of manners and other behavioral codes, no simple moral equation emerges. Through the figure of Susan in particular, its sole female character, the play ruminates on the difficulty of maintaining a sense of identity amidst the maelstrom of forces, geo-political, socio-cultural, and psycho-sexual, that bear down on the individual in the imperial era of late-capitalism. "What is a woman, finally?" asks David. "A woman is a sort of package of gesture, clothing, voice, and ice." As one of the idle rich, Susan practices photography just "so I feel I have something to do," but she professes a feeling of revulsion at turning "the people in the street" into objectified "specimens" with her camera. A slide projection that illustrates the right and wrong cut of pants for a woman to wear to work and an opaque theoretical monologue about feminism fortify the impression of Susan as a figure questioning her place as a woman in the world and looking for absolutes to anchor her in it. At one moment, she claims to feel "as though I'm coming into my own, that's the main thing, that I have this marvelous sense of myself," but at another she sees herself as "incorrectly positioned" and, as a result, never able to do the right thing or even to do anything right. Early in the play, Susan describes once meeting a transvestite who told her that he had been a woman for ten years. "That's nothing," she told him in turn, "I've been a woman for thirty-six years."

The Imperialists at the Club Cave Canem

The last of the American Century plays stands as a satyr play to the trilogy that precedes it. Unlike the others, it lacks a thick historical subtext or a direct tie to one of Mee's history books. As Mee explained to the *New York Times*, the title – "cave canem" means "beware the dog" in Latin – refers to "one of the signs that still remains engraved in stone from the late days of the Roman empire. Club Cave Canem is also the name of a restaurant in the East Village that has been a real hot spot for the chic-est of the yuppies."[22] A theatrical trifle, it wallows in its own shallowness, satirizing the 'sleepwalkers' who stumble through a world in decline with eyes wide shut.

The Imperialists at the Club Cave Canem begins with a fractured fairy tale, the story of Cinderella rendered as a humorous tongue-twister: "Rindecella was a gritty little pearl/who lived in a wottage in the coods/ with her two sugly isters and her sticked wetmother." This dyslexic prologue and an overture for solo violin serve as preamble to three different dialogues between "a couple in bed," each of which is followed by some kind of performance piece. The three dialogue-scenes borrow the daisy-chain structure of Schnitzler's *La Ronde*: first, Molly is in bed with Peter; then Peter is in bed with Karen; and finally Karen is in bed with David. Beyond their status as bedmates, their identities and relationships remain unknown. They are defined only by their vacuous conversations, which range in topic from "this guy who killed himself with his pants" to reincarnation to a deadly plane crash to television documentaries about African tribes to meeting David Bowie at the Mudd Club to the sexual habits of politicians to making love in a bathtub full of spaghetti. They talk about these and other subjects with a mix of superficial astonishment and blithe nonchalance, as if all of human experience was mere fodder for supermarket tabloids, gossip columns, and their idle chat before or after or instead of sex. They are so numbed-out and self-involved that their subjectivity has dissolved into the wider culture of narcissism that seems to have engendered them. As Karen says, "Often I hear something and I remember it and I think it happened to me."

These dialogues-in-bed alternate with three performance pieces, for which the script provides no description or direction whatsoever. As he did in *The Constitutional Convention: A Sequel,* Mee simply calls for "a performance piece" at three different moments, a virtual demand that the director or producer share in the authorship of the event and complete the work that he has started. As it turned out, this job fell to Mee's daughter, Erin, who directed the play twice, first in 1988 and then again in 2001, when the play was revived as part of the inaugural production of the short-lived Market Theatre in Cambridge, Massachusetts. At the Public Theatre in 1988, the performance artists who joined the show rotated every two weeks: "Tori Chickering tap-danced while playing the tuba, the Alien Comic did a prop-filled monologue, the Second Hand Dance Company kicked themselves in the butts rhythmically with wooden clackers, and Liz Prince, dressed in a 1920s flapper outfit with cigarette butts for fringe, sang a torch song."[23] At the Market in 2001, an art-rock band called Neptune provided pounding, deafening music from electric guitars welded out of scrap metal and percussion instruments fashioned out of saw blades, washboards, and oil drums, and a noise artist named Jessica Rylan Can't used radio static, a distortion box, a microphone, and her own voice to generate pure cacophony while gyrating and writhing in place.

These performance pieces might seem to be little more than arty interludes between the bedroom scenes, but the third dialogue in *The Imperialists at the Club Cave Canem* tempts the audience to forge more meaningful connections between the play's two continuities. It concludes with Karen's personal anecdote about going to see a piece of performance art in which a working-class Irishman got up and read from his autobiography, only to be interrupted by people in the audience here and there talking to each other, in whispers at first and then in full voice. These mounting distractions eventually prompted Karen to lose her patience and tell the noisemakers to shut the fuck up. Only after the show, when she learned that it was titled "PATTERNS OF INTERFERENCE," did she realize that this was all part of the act, which was planned as a series of disruptions that made her profane outburst the ultimate, actual content of the performance. In the end, again, it was all about her. Lying next to her in bed, David does not "get what it means."

I mean, I know, since it is a product of human intelligence or culture it must mean something even if the Irishman didn't know what it meant or what it means is unintentional or that it means something about the collective consciousness even though the Irishman doesn't get it but is just the unknowing medium through whom the culture speaks, you know, but I don't get it.

After a long pause, Karen admits that she does not get it either, leaving the audience to ponder whether *Imperialists at the Club Cave Canem* is a clever, half-serious riff on the riddle of hermeneutics or a theatrical shaggy-dog story that mocks the spectatorial reflex to find meaning.

This question depends on what relation, if any, is implied between the dialogues in bed and the performance pieces, a decision which Mee, in effect, defers to the director. While the play has no plot, it demonstrates an undeniable interest in narrative, as indicated by references to amazing stories, true stories, dreams, "stories you shouldn't believe," funny stories, "a story with a moral," stories you've heard before, fairy tales such as Cinderella, "my story," and the writing of James Joyce and Grace Paley. Is the play a light-hearted metaphysical riff on the need for stories (including histories perhaps) to hold experience together, without which all dissolves into frivolous theatrics? If the two halves of the play are seen as metaphors for each other, then the play becomes a tongue-in-cheek satire on the emptiness of Gen X intimacy or the pretensions of contemporary performance art (or both).[24] If the two halves are seen as old and new forms of theater in a head-to-head contest, then the novelty acts become the heroic avatar of Performance itself, sent to liberate theater from the death grip of domestic realism. Lasting only forty-five minutes in performance, *The Imperialists at the Club Cave Canem* raises these issues and then begs not to bear too much interpretive weight. The play stops just short of asking the sophomoric question "Does a play whose meaning is that it has no meaning have meaning?" In the end, it is a provocative lark. In this regard, a spectator would do well to bear in mind the spoonerisms of the fairy-tale prologue, which make clear that all it takes is the magic of a "gairy fodmother" to turn "the wurty dags into a drancy fess, and the hice into morses, and the cumpkins into a poach."

Taken as a whole, the American Century plays do not offer a grand mythic and national narrative on the order of *The Oresteia* or Shakespeare's *Henriad* or even Tony Kushner's *Angels in America*. They do not depict a specific historical action that ends on the brink of a new world order or present a systematic critique of American imperialism at the end of the

Cold War. These are history plays of a different stripe, plays that set a bomb beneath the idea of history itself and then detonate it in front of an audience of less-than-innocent bystanders. In this regard, the American Century plays point to Mee as the first American playwright of the Age of Terrorism, not because terrorism is their subject (it is not) and certainly not because they condone terrorism (they do not) but because they erupt on the stage with the fierce force of a devastating surprise attack. They are not predicated on established rules of aesthetic engagement. They present an overwhelming effect with no discernible, proportionate cause. In structure, they recall moments of catastrophic violence, such as the 1983 bombing of the US Marine Corps barracks in Beirut, more than the diplomatic summits that Mee chronicled in his books. In their chaotic, explosive exuberance, these early plays, as inscrutable and incomplete as they are, call for "a more robust and complex view of the world," one that is governed by the same principle of uncertainty that led Mee away from writing history.

Mee's final work of history is *Playing God: Seven Fateful Moments When Great Men Met to Change the World* (1993). As the title suggests, it focuses on seven different occasions when "two leaders meet, with the presumed power, by uttering a word, altering a position, relinquishing a claim, offering trust, telling a lie, taking a gamble, remaining firm, to transform the course of events."[25] The book's seven showdowns range from the meeting in the year 452 in northern Italy between Pope Leo I and Attila the Hun, whose barbarian army was poised to attack Rome, to the 1815 Congress of Vienna, which re-apportioned much of Europe in the wake of Napoleon's final defeat, to the G-7 summit in London in 1991 between the world's wealthiest nations and Mikhail Gorbachev, who came, hat in hand, hoping the economic giants would prop up a crumbling Soviet Union. Each is presented not only as brief case study in international politics but as a prime instance of how those who would shape history through the peaceful arts of rhetoric and negotiation, rather than by force of arms, can make a basic mistake and fall short of their designed goal. Mee defines seven "conceptual pitfalls"[26] that thwart those who practice the fine art of high-stakes diplomacy: the Problem of Knowing, the Illusion of Power, the Inevitability of Surprise, the Principle of Contingency, the False Lessons of History, the Rule of Unintended Consequences, and the Fantasy of Realism.

Given its retroactive status as Mee's farewell to history, *Playing God* also asks to be read as a meta-history, that is, as a chronicle of the occupational hazards of the professional historian. The Problem of Knowing refers to the need to take action on the basis of incomplete and possibly faulty information. The Principle of Contingency stipulates that "everything depends on everything else" without knowing exactly how, just as the Rule of Unintended Consequences demonstrates that any course of action will have unplanned (as well as planned) results. The False Lessons of History lead to the erroneous assumption that the past is a sound basis for anticipating the future, which is informed by the Inevitability of Surprise, in the form of random chance, freak acts of nature, dumb luck, and other unpredictable factors. With all these variables in play, identifying the exact cause of an event or predicting the precise effect of a certain course of action becomes folly, for statesman and historian alike. As Mee writes in *Playing God*,

> Even if we were to identify all the classes of cause of historical events, we could not construct a complete causal explanation of any given moment. Because each cause has a previous cause, if we were to attempt to explain the complete causes of events, we should soon become trapped in an infinite regression of explanation . . . It is for this reason that there can be no laws of history, that each individual moment is singular, a constellation of causes and effects that never recurs in exactly the same way.[27]

This conviction is at the heart of all his plays: they obey no laws of history. In detailing the pitfalls of the profession that he was leaving behind, *Playing God* suggests through a kind of *via negativa* the principles that would govern his work in the profession that lay ahead. In his plays, Mee escapes the "vexing difficulty of seeing the facts of the matter clearly" by making little or no effort to make the facts of the matter clear. He looks at the world around him or the history of civilization or his own life knowing that facts are missing, that appearances are deceiving, that accidents happen, that contingency rules, and so on, and then, with unapologetic subjectivity, he presents what appeals to him, what feels true or good, what resonates with his empirical sense of things, as rooted in his own experiences and refined through decades of intellectual inquiry and surveying the cultural landscape. Cause and effect, the backbone of Aristotelian drama and the bane of the historian's existence, have no place in his unconventional dramaturgy. Instead of a plot, a chain of causally related events working their way towards their 'inevitable,' teleological end, a Mee play progresses (to use a misnomer) from one singular "individual moment" to the next, like an assortment of colorful beads cut loose from the string of theatrical time, each one a twinkling instant surrounded by a "network of limitless interrelations," each one free, if not independent, of what came before and what comes after.

In his memoir, Mee makes an explicit connection between his adolescent battle with polio and his impulses as a writer:

> Intact people should write intact books with sound narratives built of sound paragraphs that unfold with a sense of dependable cause and effect, solid structures you can rely on. That is not my experience of the world. I like a book that feels like a crystal goblet that has been thrown to the floor and shattered, so that its pieces, when they are picked up and arranged on a table, still describe a whole glass, but the glass itself lies in shards. To me, sentences should veer and smash up, careen out of control; get under way and find themselves unable to stop, switch directions suddenly and irrevocably, break off, come to a sighing inconclusiveness. If a writer's writings constitute a "body of work," then my body of work, to feel true to me, must feel fragmented. And then, too, if you find it hard to walk down the sidewalk, you like, in the freedom of your mind, to make a sentence that leaps and dances now and then before it comes to a sudden stop.[28]

This image of shards, fragments, or fractured pieces of a once robust whole comes up again and again in Mee's work and in his discussions of it, as if to demonstrate a biographical imperative for his rejection of conventional forms. Such a psychological understanding would be critically simplistic, of course, but on a human level it adds a certain resonance to such elements of his plays as the preponderance of dance and movement sequences, his cracking open of others' texts to extract pieces for his own use, and his rejection of shapely narrative structures.

What story there is in Mee's plays is often borrowed from myth, from Greek tragedy or romantic comedy, taken for granted, and then used as a binding agent or armature for what amounts to a miscellany of ideas, images, actions, and speeches. Even in his more narrative plays, Mee's true form is collage. He takes bits and pieces of theatrical material, written artifacts from other sources, skeletal plots from Sophocles or Shakespeare or Brecht, archetypal characters, moments of spectacle stolen from other productions, the dreams of his lovers, and his own veiled confessions of faith in humanity, and combines them in ways that generate their own "patterns of interference." Whatever unity they have stems from the sensibility that selects and arranges them. That is why the last line of *bobrauschenbergamerica* is "OK, that feels good to me." When Mee took up playwriting again in his mid forties, old enough to see no future in it, he wrote only to please himself, to register his impression of how things are, putting things together on a whim, as evidence of the world or his own inner roilings, and then chancing that this mélange of material might appeal to the sensibilities of others. If it did not, he would still end up with a document that reflected his true sense of being in the world, something which writing history did not do. As it turned out, it led to perhaps the toughest thing for a playwright in the USA to achieve: a career.

2

Bogart: engendering space, or building a nest

In 1977, ANNE BOGART WROTE HER MASTER'S THESIS AT New York University about five important theater directors: Method acting guru Lee Strasberg and four contemporary avant-gardists, Robert Wilson, Richard Foreman, Andrei Serban, and, her thesis advisor, Richard Schechner. Twenty-five years later, in what must have been a gratifying experience, an exhibition at the Exit Art Gallery in SoHo celebrated Bogart's work and career side by side with two of her early inspirations, Foreman and Wilson, as well as that of Reza Abdoh, Meredith Monk, and Peter Schumann. Curated by Norman Frisch and mounted in the summer of 2002, "SHOW PEOPLE: Downtown Directors and the Play of Time" profiled six pioneers of downtown experimental theater and offered their careers as a source of inspiration for a generation of younger artists. Abdoh, who died of AIDS in 1995 at the age of thirty-two, was represented by a video library of his work for theater and film. The other five directors, all in their fifties and sixties and still very active, dipped into their archives to create retrospective installations out of production photographs, manuscript pages, design sketches, costumes and props, sound loops, and video projections. Robert Wilson included a few of his famous chairs, and Peter Schumann filled a gallery with large-scale Bread and Puppet figures gathered under a muslin tent. Meredith Monk traced the history of her work by lining up side by side a long row of shoes that she had worn in various performances over the years. Richard Foreman created a chaotic, cerebral environment, much like the mindscapes he designs for his plays, which included a graffiti manifesto titled "10 Things I Hate About Theater."

Bogart's installation offered a thorough introduction to her work, in substance and symbol alike. Simple yet subtle in design, it had two adjacent parts, one open and full, the other closed and empty, each equal in size and mirroring the other with a veiled symmetry. The first part featured more than fifty production photographs, most black-and-white, some in color, mounted in two rows on the wall or attached to rigid wires stretching from floor to ceiling. In the middle of this area, beckoning visitors from across the room, stood a memorable prop from *bobrauschenbergamerica*, a stuffed deer with a pink tutu around its midsection mounted on a tuft of artificial turf. The production photographs presented a thorough retrospective of Bogart's career, from a "deconstruction" of *Macbeth* in 1975 up through a production of *Hay Fever* at the Actors Theatre of Louisville in 2002. Each was accompanied by a brief caption from Bogart, casual in tone, full of enthusiasm, and friendly. For *The Women* at Hartford Stage, she explained, "In casting the 16 women, the criterion was that each actress could also play Medea. I wanted strength and humor fueled by outrage. It worked!" For the Elmer Rice classic, she wrote, "*The Adding Machine* is a big expressionist masterpiece, part of the rich tradition of American non-realism that we seem to have forgotten about. Touch these plays and they leap to life." The photograph from *bobrauschenbergamerica*, which showed actor Barney O'Hanlon frolicking in a pile of white laundry, had this caption: "It was with this production that Chuck Mee taught the SITI Company to follow what feels joyful."

The second half of the Bogart installation, titled "ROOM," was in a separate, enclosed gallery, shuttered from the photographic display by a partition. Before entering, a visitor faced the following list of instructions stenciled on the wall:

> Leave belongings on the hooks provided.
> Enter with an awareness of what is already under way. Listen and be
>   attentive with your whole body.
> Do not speak.
> Relax and soften the eyes so that you are not directly looking at any one
>   person or thing in the room.
> Sustain a distinct closeness or distance from other people and
>   architectural elements.
> Be patient.
> What happens?

Upon entering, the room revealed itself as a proverbial empty space, roughly 30 feet (9 meters) across by 20 feet (6 meters) deep. Speakers overhead generated a mechanical drone, white noise to match the white walls and floor. On opposite sides of the room, facing each other, were two plain plywood benches, lighted from beneath by fluorescent tubes.

At first, the whole thing feels like a joke – the room is empty! there's nothing there! – and those who derogate Bogart's theater as the theatrical equivalent of the Emperor's new clothes would find supporting evidence here. But the low industrial hum, the four white walls, the deep blue of the ceiling, and the benches opposite each other combined to insist that there was something there: the viewer who is taking it all in, the one who has entered to look and listen. The day that I visited, no one else was there, so the room became a simple, resonant space that invited a moment's idle meditation. On busier days, the coming and going of viewers must have added a social dimension to the experience, as people negotiated the sharing of the space and the degree of their complicity with the instructions for being there. Do you play by the rules and maintain silence? If so, what other sounds are revealed? Do you avoid looking at others? What happens if you stand close to someone? How long do you stay? Does patience have its rewards? Does something happen?

This "Room" – not to be confused with the SITI Company's one-person play about Virginia Woolf with the same title – needs to be seen as a simple paradigm for Bogart's art. Hers is an ontological theater, a place of being in which the rhythm of shared presence substitutes for a conventional dramatic action. Whatever the subject of a particular work, she never loses sight of the basic transaction between spectator and performer – and the possibilities, mutual obligations, and repercussions that derive therefrom. Her sense of event is predicated on the assumption that beyond what is happening on the surface there is another level of action, often inscrutable, which asks for a broader, deeper understanding. When she rehearses a play, she does not work to predetermine the event or force the action so much as she tries to establish the conditions which will make it possible for something to happen and then, as much as possible, to follow wherever that leads. This means that she relies on her collaborators – actors, designers, and audience – to be active, independent, creative, and attentive so that their energies can coalesce and move in a direction determined by no one of them. Bogart facilitates this process by narrowing the field of inquiry to a topic (or an established dramatic text) and a few basic questions, laying down certain guidelines and principles that will bound that inquiry, and then leaving 'room' for the creative expression of others. She constitutes a space in which something might occur, sets things in motion within that space, and then pulls back to see what happens. This means that it can be difficult to gauge Bogart's presence or absence in the work. She is everywhere and nowhere in it, just as she was everywhere and nowhere in the empty white room that represented her in the Exit Art installation.

Instead of a strict chronological presentation, Bogart chose to organize the production photographs in her Exit Art exhibit into six categories, worth recounting here for the accurate overview they provide of her work:

"Classic Explosions," mostly of modernist masters (Büchner, Gorky, Strindberg, no Ibsen or Shaw) and twentieth-century American classics (Rice, Kaufman and Hart, Williams, Inge, no O'Neill or Miller), with a fondness for Noël Coward thrown in for good measure;

"Site Specific," early experiments in New York City and in Europe in leading an audience on unusual journeys that took them to "rooftops, construction sites, basements, a Romanian meeting hall, discos, clubs, a detective agency, an abandoned schoolhouse and many other places ripe for invasion;"[1]

"Dance/Theatre," mostly works from the 1980s reflecting a desire to create work driven by movement more than text and by an obsession with the enigma of male/female relationships (regarding which, one caption reads, "How does that work? How fascinating! How strange!");

"Living Playwrights," including collaborations with Mac Wellman, Eduardo Machado, Charles Mee, Naomi Iizuka, and the world premieres of two Paula Vogel plays, *Hot'n Throbbing* and *The Baltimore Waltz*;

"Music Theatre," everything from classic Broadway musicals turned on their heads (*South Pacific, On the Town*) to chamber pieces for Lyn Austin's Music Theater Group (*The Making of Americans, Between Wind, Cinderella/Cendrillon*) to new opera on a grand scale (*Lilith* at New York City Opera, *Nicholas and Alexander* at Los Angeles, both composed by Deborah Drattell);

"Devised Works," original collage pieces, many woven out of texts taken from a single author (Strindberg, Brecht, Inge) or around a single figure (Marshall McLuhan, Andy Warhol, Robert Wilson), mostly created in close collaboration with the SITI Company.

As meaningful as Bogart's own taxonomy is, it can be further reduced to two basic procedures for making theater: she puts original pieces together ("Devised Works") or she takes established plays apart ("Classic Explosions"). That is, she either collects pieces of text drawn from various sources and, through her collaboration with actors, designers, and some-times dramaturgs or playwrights, builds them up into an assemblage which has shape, rhythm, and the sense of a whole. Or, she takes an established text and disrupts or supplements its surface integrity in order to make it more immediate and more urgent, often by reconfiguring its core action through the use of a metatheatrical frame or comparable device. Bogart has never called herself a playwright, although the etymological sense of "-wright" as a maker, an artificer, a forger of forms certainly makes her one. Her devised works are, in effect, new plays, theatrical compositions structured more on the principles of dance and music than the conventional dramaturgy of plot, character, and dialogue. Similar to a Mee play, the texts for these pieces consist of an anthology of quotations or excerpts taken from a variety of published sources, interviews, novels and stories, theoretical writings, autobiographies, and even other plays. Collage is her natural form, too.

Bogart traces this practice back to her senior thesis production at Bard College. She set out to select an Ionesco play to direct, but the more she read, the more she found she was interested in sections from this play or that but never the entire script. So, she changed course, compiled her favorite bits and pieces into an Ionesco miscellany, and then staged the whole thing under the title *Knocks, A Collection*. Since then, Bogart has pursued much the same strategy in creating original work, a predilection that she attributes to what she calls her "scavenger mentality."

> I am a scavenger. I am not an original thinker and I am not a true creative artist. So the notion of scavenging appeals to me. That is what I do. Like a bird that goes and pulls different things and makes a nest. I think it is more a nesting impulse, of taking this and that and weaving it together to make some sort of marriage of ideas. I read a lot and I take little bits of what I read and I put them together into thoughts and ideas. I juxtapose ideas. I like the satisfaction of putting things together like that. That is my talent, if I have any talent, to be able to hold up a number of things in the air at the same time.[2]

Bogart's association of her scavenger mentality with a nesting impulse is meaningful as a metaphor for the way that she engenders space through her work. She creates an environment, for actors in rehearsal and for spectators in performance, that is bounded and protective and nurturing enough that certain challenges, difficulties, and everyday terrors can be confronted within it.

Bogart's "classic explosions" might be seen as devised in a broader sense, insofar as she often invents a new reality for the action, a new present tense, either through changing periods or adding a frame situation to the play as given. For example, in 1983, she approached Gorky's *The Lower Depths*, presented under its more literal title of *At the Bottom*, by wondering, "What would happen if a bunch of East Village skinhead punks found the play and decided to perform it once a week in a deserted basketball court?"[3] Exploring this question became the collective task of her cast, students in the Experimental Theater Wing at New York University. During the 1980s, she worked variations on this frame strategy in other productions there. Büchner's *Danton's Death* was undertaken as if by a group of downtown "celebutantes" who had decided to act the play for the French Revolution "theme night" at their favorite East Village club. Supplemented by the music of Lieber and Stoller, Wedekind's *Spring Awakening* was presented "by an imagined spaceship crew who had discovered the play as a document of how humans used to live"[4] on planet Earth. Most famously, Bogart triggered the ire of the Rodgers and Hammerstein estates when she staged *South Pacific* at New York University as if it was being performed by US military veterans of Grenada and Beirut with post-traumatic stress disorder who were graduating from a hospital treatment program.

This hypothetical 'what if' technique, which might be traced back to the central conceit of Peter Weiss's *Marat/Sade*, is well suited for working with students. It treats the classic drama as an artifact, a found object, perhaps even a talisman, which must be examined without presumption and researched in detail in order to release its powerful secrets. It then dislodges the presentation of that drama from its original, historical context and transposes it into the more familiar key of contemporary youth. It stipulates a recognizable, tight-knit community (street punks, Gen X-ers, war veterans) out of which the production emerges. It challenges the cast as a whole to develop a strong sense of ensemble, through improvisation, theater games, and other rehearsal techniques. It calls upon the individual student actor to take responsibility for his or her performance by inventing a fictional persona within that community. The actor plays, in effect, a version of himself who then plays a theatrical role. This approach satisfies, at least in principle, the paradoxical need of a post-Artaudian, post-Brechtian generation to make theater that is immediate and visceral, more *real* than realism, without succumbing to the noxious illusion that acting is anything more than role-playing.

In 1990, near the end of her brief tenure as artistic director of the Trinity Repertory Company, Bogart staged *On the Town* (1944), the Leonard Bernstein musical with book by Adolph Green and Betty Comden, as if it was being performed on the deck of an aircraft carrier in the Pacific Ocean at the height of the Second World War. The play's given setting, a glittery, romanticized Manhattan where three sailors on shore leave share a twenty-four-hour adventure, became a remote fantasy of

home for a crew of shipboard performers whose show might be interrupted at any moment by a Japanese air raid. After this production,
Bogart's use of such an explicit metatheatrical frame dwindled, but her
dislocation of a play's setting or the suggestion of an implicit or withheld
frame continued to define her staging of established texts. Sometimes this
is achieved by the use of supernumeraries. In Bogart's 2002 production of
Noël Coward's *Hay Fever* at the Actors Theatre of Louisville, the Bliss
family home in Cookham, England was transformed by Neil Patel's design
into an ultra-modern glass mansion in Bucks County, Pennsylvania, which
might have been designed by Mies van der Rohe or Richard Meier. Bogart
added six extras to the cast – "maintenance workers" such as a window
washer, a landscaper, a housemaid, and an exterminator – who contributed
to the household mayhem at moments but more often served as working-
class witnesses to the bourgeois antics of the main characters. A year
later at the American Repertory Theatre, Bogart directed Marivaux's *La
Dispute*, an Enlightenment, romantic comedy that explores the origins of
infidelity. She amplified the play's changing-partners theme by adding a
long movement prologue, choreographed by Barney O'Hanlon as a sultry
promenade for nine men and nine women, many of whom then watched
the main action of the play from a catwalk high above the stage. In one
form or another, a Bogart production will often include an onstage
audience, figures whose presence serves to draw attention to the action
as something that is performed, something to be watched. In *bobrauschenbergamerica*, that figure is a cheerleader on roller skates, a stand-in for
Bogart herself, who watches much of the play as if peering over a backyard
fence at a family gathering going on next door.

This incorporation of onstage observers into her productions reflects
Bogart's positioning of herself as the first audience for a piece that is in the
process of being created. Once the groundwork has been laid, she relies on
her collaborators to take the raw materials she has gathered and make
something of them. In the rehearsal room, often perched on a stool with
the script in front of her on a music stand, she pays close attention to her
actors. Her focus is relaxed but sharp. Once a scene gets under way, even in
the early stages, she may not speak for long intervals, preferring to look
and listen without particular expectation, open to possibility, trying to
follow the tide of events more than lead them. She traces this strategy to a
job she had in the late-1970s leading a theater workshop at a halfway house
in Manhattan for schizophrenics. When interest in her planned activities
waned and participation in the workshop dropped, she asked the group
what they wanted to do, and they said they just wanted to do musical

comedies. So, she acceded to their wish, explaining that she did not know much about musical comedy and that they would have to show her. And they did. In the weeks that followed, the group erupted with excitement and activity, attendance spiked, and people were bouncing off the walls with energy. "It was like riding a hurricane," Bogart explained. "I didn't know where it was going to go. That is how I learned that is what I do. You enable people to create. That is where I learned it, from these people, who are deeply creative but cannot control their lives. I don't try to control things. I ride what is happening."[5]

If you ask Anne Bogart where she grew up, she says in an instant, "The Navy." In her Trinity Rep production of *On the Town*, she named the aircraft carrier on the set the USS Essex as a tribute to her father, Gerard S. Bogart, a career naval officer who commanded the Essex for a year in the early 1960s. He also served as an aviator, a naval attaché, an intelligence officer, a division chief for the Military Advisory Assistance Group in Japan, the commanding officer of a Navy oiler, and an administrator at the Naval War College in Rhode Island. Her mother, Margaret Spruance Bogart, was the daughter of a very important admiral in US military history. Admiral Raymond Spruance is widely credited for the stunning US victory in the Battle of Midway (June 3–6, 1942), the turning point in the Pacific campaign of the Second World War. A brilliant strategist who shied away from publicity, he went on to become Commander of the Fifth Fleet, President of the Naval War College (1946–48), and US Ambassador to the Philippines (1952–55). As Bogart will tell you, "In the movie *Midway*, which I never saw, he is played by Glenn Ford."[6]

Born September 25, 1951 in Newport, Rhode Island, Anne Bogart led the peripatetic childhood of a "Navy brat." Her father's career took the family from Newport to Coronado, California (near San Diego); Tokyo (for two and a half years, around the time she was six); the Philippines; Washington DC; Quonset, Rhode Island; Virginia Beach, Virginia; Norfolk, Virginia; and then again back to Rhode Island. With an older and a younger brother in a family steeped in military tradition, Bogart found that not much was expected of her as the female child, a benign disregard that contributed to her becoming self-reliant, ambitious, and independent. As a girl, she loved horses and riding, although the family's frequent moves made it impractical for her to have her own horse. She became good at meeting people fast, making temporary friends, and then letting go, a rhythm of life that she later associated with her eventual involvement with theater: "You have this intense experience; you get very close over a short period of time, and then it's over. That's something I accept."[7]

In 1967, Bogart saw her first professional theater production, thanks to Project Discovery, an enrichment program sponsored by the newly formed National Endowment for the Arts and the US Department of Education. This Great Society initiative made it possible for every high school student in Rhode Island to see free of charge a play at what was then the Trinity Square Repertory Company. Bogart saw an environmental production of *Macbeth* directed by Adrian Hall and designed by Eugene Lee; though mystified and a bit overwhelmed by the experience, it left an indelible impression on her. She was already involved in theater at Middletown High School, working backstage, hunting down props, taking notes for the director, and the like. In tenth grade, she was helping her French teacher Jill Warren direct a high school production of *The Bald Soprano*; when the director got the flu ten days before opening, Bogart had to take over and finish the job. The production was a success, and Bogart, a fifteen-year-old high school sophomore, was hooked for life on directing. In the forty years since then, she has directed more than one hundred productions, rarely going more than a few months without being in rehearsal.

Bogart's college years were just as peripatetic as her childhood. She applied to prestigious women's colleges such as Sarah Lawrence, Vassar, and Sweet Briar and was admitted to none of them. So, she spent a year at a junior college called Briarcliff (now defunct), then a year in Greece studying in the "College Year in Athens" program at the American Hellenic Center, and a semester at Emerson College in Boston, before ending up at Bard College, where she spent two years and graduated with her BA in 1974. It was around this time that Bogart became a lesbian. As she describes it, "I essentially decided to be gay in the summer between my junior and senior years in college. I had the worst series of guy relationships and I had just had it with men. So, I literally went to a bookstore and took out a book on how to be gay, read the book, found somebody to have sex with for the first time, and it was great. I cut my hair short, wore corduroy pants and brown leather jackets, drank Jack Daniels, and smoked nonfiltered Lucky Strikes. For a while, I just played right into that role and had a great time."[8]

At Bard, Bogart joined Via Theater, a fledgling theater company started by fellow student David Ossian Cameron in order to explore the "poor theater" techniques of Jerzy Grotowski. For almost two years, a small, dedicated ensemble met daily to train in the rigorous physical disciplines of Grotowski and to develop a piece about love, sex, and violence called *Tower of Babel – First Story.* In the spring of 1974, they performed the piece at Bard and at St. Mark's Church in the East Village (where Mee's fledgling play *The Gate* had been done a decade earlier). This led to an invitation from a theater company in India to come to Delhi to perform and work there. In December, in Tel Aviv, en route to India, things fell apart and Via Theater disbanded rather suddenly. With her unused travel money as a grubstake, Bogart returned to New York City to pursue a career as a director. She rented a spacious loft on Grand Street in SoHo for $325 a month, began a series of odd jobs, and started studying tai chi. She saw as much downtown theater and dance as she could, including multiple visits to Richard Schechner's Performance Group production of *Mother Courage and Her Children.* She started making her own theater on a shoestring, including early pieces based on *Macbeth* and Virginia Woolf's *The Waves.* She enrolled as a graduate student in New York University's Department of Drama (soon to become the Department of Performance Studies), received her MA in 1977, and, two years later, began to teach and direct in the newly formed Experimental Theatre Wing of New York University's Tisch School of the Arts. In 1980, her early work was profiled in a "Women and Performance" issue of *The Drama Review.*[9] Not yet thirty, Bogart was making her presence felt in the hothouse world of downtown theater, just as a young Chuck Mee had fifteen years earlier.

For the next ten years, Bogart cut her teeth as an experimental director with an interest in site-specific performance, movement-based theater work, and metatheatrical treatments of classic plays. In the late 1970s, she moved to Montreal for a year, where she fell in love with an architect named Sarah Bonnemaison and began a relationship that lasted ten years. That year in Montreal, Bogart happened to see the film version of Peter Stein's Schaübhne production of Gorky's *Summerfolk.* Its passionate acting, intellectual rigor, and sheer beauty had a profound, "galvanizing" effect on her and prompted an obsessive interest in contemporary German theater. She studied German at the Goethe Institute, hosted German newcomers to New York with theater interests, and poured over the glossy pages of *Theater Heute*, looking for inspiration and even memorizing the names and credits of people in Peter Stein's company, seeing what she might glean about the methods of the richest theater in Germany and apply to her poor theater in the streets of New York. This led, oddly enough, to an article about her in *Theater Heute* and then to periods of time traveling, living, and directing in Europe, including productions at theater conservatories in Berlin and Bern. Bogart's effort to turn herself into a 'German' director on the model of Peter Stein or Klaus Michael Grüber led to what she has called "a big personal revelation that saved me." As Bogart tells it, while staying in a *pensione* in the Dolomites of northern Italy,

> I realized with profound conclusiveness that I was an American; I had an American sense of humour, an American sense of structure, rhythm and logic. I thought like an American. I moved like an American. And, all at once, it was clear to me that the rich American tradition of history and people exists to tap into and own. Suddenly I was free.[10]

She returned home and proceeded to invent herself as an American artist. She directed American plays, investigated American history, and embraced American performance traditions. In Northampton, Massachusetts in 1982, under the conspicuously German title *Sehnsucht*, she directed a version of Tennessee Williams's *A Streetcar Named Desire*, which included eight Stanley Kowalskis and a dozen Blanche Duboises, one of them a man. In 1983, for the Danspace Project at St. Mark's Church, she created an original dance-theater piece called *History, An American Dream*, which combined public speeches spoken from a railed balcony by such figures as Thomas Paine, Emma Goldman, Joseph McCarthy, Vince Lombardi, and Angela Davis with movement sequences below featuring a chorus of men and women, variously presented as lovers, soldiers, and families. She directed a piece based on the plays of William Inge at the East Village of New York theatre venue PS 122 in 1984 and the Al Carmines-Leon Katz adaptation of Gertrude Stein's *The Making of Americans* for Lyn Austin's Music-Theater Group in 1985. The next year, with playwright Mac Wellman, she created *1951*, a chaotic, expressionistic investigation of McCarthyism and its chilling effect on artists who challenged the status quo. "Through a brutally effective mechanism," Bogart later wrote, "artists were directed to disengage from issues facing the real world," in the process bringing public art to a virtual end, sealing off certain populist and socialist aspects of the first half of the century, and promoting narrower, more inward-looking and private modes of expression, such as Method acting and abstract expressionism.[11] Bogart wanted to find ways to re-open some of the avenues closed down by the Red Scare, make contact with traditions and playwrights from the first half of the twentieth century (especially popular entertainment forms and 1920s expressionism), and deal with history and politics without being limited to a strict documentary approach.

During this time, a widening community of interest gathered around Bogart, fueled in part by former students from New York University who wanted to continue working with her. And her interest in having a company, a continuing fellowship of artists with whom she could build a vocabulary and a set of relationships that would be used to create plays as a group, developed into a compelling need. In an oft-repeated anecdote, she tells of the epiphany that followed a brief encounter in Berlin with Ariane Mnouchkine in which the French director asked her the rhetorical question, "What are you going to do without a company?" There was plenty of local evidence to support this contention, from the Living Theater to the Open Theater, from the Performance Group to the Wooster Group, not to mention any number of lesser known, shorter-lived collectives that sprung up like wild mushrooms during the 1960s and 1970s. In 1987, Via Theater was revived as the name of a new organization dedicated to producing Bogart's work, among others, starting with a dance theater piece called *Assimil*. A year later, in conjunction with the Talking Band and Otrabanda, Bogart and Via created *No Plays No Poetry but Philosophical Reflections Practical Instructions Provocative Prescriptions Opinions and Pointers From A Noted Critic and Playwright*.

The noted critic and playwright in question was Bertolt Brecht, and the piece took bits and pieces from "The Messingkauf Dialogues" and the invaluable John Willett volume *Brecht on Brecht* and converted, subverted, and perverted them into a carnival of theory.[12] The audience was greeted by a sideshow barker, puffing a cigar and sporting a leather jacket à la Brecht, who harangued against the history of theater to date. Then, they were guided into a large, open, warehouse-like space that, like a fairground midway, featured various exhibits or scenes demonstrating, sometimes tongue-in-cheek, Brecht's concepts. In one area, an actress "portrays Brecht playing Charlie Chaplin playing Hitler giving instructions on how an actor should play a Nazi."[13] In another, an actress dons a fake mustache and a garter belt to illustrate in crude fashion a Brechtian alienation effect. There were spontaneous outbursts of music, echoing Weill and Eisler, and eventually, the audience was gathered in one spot for a satirical panel discussion on the nature of theater, which imploded under the weight of its own ideas. Later, sipping champagne and all aswoon, a man and a woman played a seductive love scene out of the sentimental, "culinary" theater that Brecht hated, except their dialogue was composed of Brecht epigrams instead of, say, Noël Coward witticisms. With reverent disrespect, *No Plays No Poetry* praised Brecht with faint damning and in the process skewered a few of the postmodern affectations of the 1980s avant-garde. In the spring of 1988, the piece earned Bogart her first Obie.

That August, a month before her thirty-seventh birthday, Bogart was on her way out to Omaha, Nebraska to direct an opera when she stopped overnight at a hotel in Dubuque, Iowa and found a lump on her breast. Diagnosed with breast cancer, she had a breast and lymph node removed within a month, recovering fully and quickly enough that within a year she could joke to a reporter, "See, flat as a boy."[14] Still, Bogart's intimation of her own mortality had an understandable *carpe-diem* effect, one which intensified her interest in being a candidate to succeed the departing Adrian Hall as head of the Trinity Repertory Company. On December 13, 1988, her appointment as artistic director (effective the following September) was announced, signaling her return to her native state of Rhode Island and to the theater that twenty years earlier had sparked her interest with a memorable rendition of *Macbeth*.[15] For many, it was a surprising choice. Bogart had no administrative experience as the head of an arts organization, not to mention a large institution such as Trinity, with its not-for-profit corporate structure and multi-million dollar budget. She was a creature of downtown theater and a product of the 1970s avant-garde, well-known below 14th Street but unknown outside New York. For others, her 'avant-garde' pedigree made her the perfect choice to succeed a regional pioneer like Hall, who along with designer Eugene Lee put Trinity on the map with their muscular brand of epic theater. It was to be the passing of the torch to a new generation.[16]

On May 21, 1990, only nine months into her new job, Bogart resigned as Trinity's artistic director when the board of directors slashed the initial $4 million budget for her second season by 25 percent.[17] Publicly, the split was cordial, but the board's action was understood by many, including Bogart, as not only an economic necessity but also a calculated move to force her departure. She had come on strong at Trinity, replacing the director of its in-house conservatory training program, releasing members of the large resident acting company, and bringing in her own team of downtown collaborators, including Jeff Halpern, Tina Landau, Brian Jucha, and Victoria Hunter. By her own admission, she did nothing to help herself in programming her first season like a "kid in a candy store."[18] She remounted *No Plays No Poetry* as an inaugural celebration. She started the regular subscription season with Gorky's *Summerfolk*, which was followed by three controversial and dark productions of obscure plays that left many Trinity regulars scratching their heads or averting the eyes. Maria Irene Fornes directed her sprawling, four-part *And What of the Night?* Molly Smith directed Darrah Cloud's adaptation of the Jose Donoso novel *The Obscene Bird of Night*. And Robert Woodruff directed a "ferocious and orgiastic" production of Brecht's *Baal*.[19] By the time Bogart's production of the Leonard Bernstein musical *On the Town* opened in the spring, damage control was in full swing, with *mea culpae* in the newspaper, a special town meeting for disgruntled patrons, and the announcement of a more subscriber-friendly second season, anchored by Kaufman and Hart, Shakespeare, Ibsen, O'Casey, and Fugard. But it was already too late. At a two-day planning retreat, Bogart threatened to resign if the board of directors insisted on their intention to cut $1 million from the budget, thereby compelling her to make drastic changes. The board insisted, and, unwilling to jeopardize her vision for the theater and renege on her commitments to a number of artists, Bogart found herself walking away, almost before she knew it.

Bogart's "one glorious, terrible year" at Trinity was devastating to her, all the more for its sudden, shocking conclusion. She had come to town with hopes of putting down roots in her native Rhode Island, of building her own company there, and of advancing her teaching interests through the Trinity Conservatory. But the effort to graft a fledgling, ragtag East Village theater group onto a venerable, hidebound regional theater institution did not take. She did not return to the city of Providence for more than a decade. At some personal cost, Bogart learned that "you cannot take over someone else's company. You have to start from scratch."[20] She had started from scratch with Via Theater, but the Trinity job intervened. Before long, she would try again, with a major boost from a man on the other side of the world.

The rebound off of Trinity put Bogart in a different league. She served a two-year term (1991–93) as president of Theatre Communications Group. She went on to direct elsewhere two plays originally slated for her second Trinity season, Kaufman and Hart's *Once in a Lifetime* at the American Repertory Theatre in 1990 and the world premiere of Paula Vogel's *The Baltimore Waltz* at the Circle Repertory Company, which earned her a second Obie in 1992. Jon Jory brought her to the Actors Theatre of Louisville to direct Eduardo Machado's *In the Eye of the Hurricane* at the 1991 Humana Festival, the first of a dozen productions she would show at ATL in the coming years.[21] That fall, in a collaboration with Mabou Mines, she directed Brecht's *In the Jungle of Cities*, the first production in JoAnne Akalaitis's brief tenure as Joe Papp's hand-picked successor at the Public Theater in New York. She proceeded with plans for a trilogy of plays based on popular culture forms, creating *American Vaudeville* in 1992 at the Alley Theatre in Houston with Tina Landau, her partner in life and art at that time. She directed Clare Boothe Luce's *The Women* at San Diego Rep in 1992 and again at Hartford Stage in 1993. Mixed in among all these engagements at notable resident theaters in New York and around the country came *Another Person is a Foreign Country*, an unusual production at an unusual theater that brought Anne Bogart and Charles Mee together for the first time.

In the winter of 1990, while Bogart had her hands full in Providence, Mee happened to see the En Garde Arts production of Mac Wellman's *Crowbar* in the crumbling, abandoned Victory Theater on 42nd Street near Times Square. Built by Oscar Hammerstein (grandfather of the famous lyricist) in 1900 as one of the first legitimate playhouses on 42nd Street, the theater was operated for many years by David Belasco and was later home to a long-running production of *Abie's Irish Rose*. But since its glory days as a glittering Broadway show palace, it had devolved from a burlesque house to a movie theater, and, eventually, a porno house, which was showing *Hot Saddle Tramp* and *Fantasex Girls* when it closed for good in the late 1980s.[22] At that point, the property was caught up in a real-estate tug-of-war over the future of West 42nd Street. With litigation pending and the theater in limbo, producer Anne Hamburger proposed to borrow the Victory as the site – and the subject – for an En Garde Arts production. For the past five years, this had been Hamburger's modus operandi: finding and borrowing neglected places around New York and using them as the settings for unexpected theater performances. She had already produced Maria Irene Fornes's *Hunger* and Quincy Long's *Dirty Work* on different floors of a stripped-down Greenwich Street warehouse and separate performance pieces by Stephan Balint, Penny Arcade, and David Van Tieghem in three apartments on the third floor of the Chelsea Hotel on 23rd Street. And, at the time of *Crowbar*, plans were well under way to use the cobblestone streets of the meatpacking district at Ninth Avenue and Little West 12th Street as the setting for Reza Abdoh's "festival of depravity," *Father Was a Peculiar Man*.[23]

During its thirteen-year existence, En Garde Arts represented the most significant and sustained experiment in site-specific theater in American theater history. Hamburger's project, part threnody and part breath of life for a dying city, was to identify overlooked, abandoned, ruined corners of Manhattan and match them with writers, directors, composers, and performers who would create theatrical events in response to those spaces. To accomplish this, with each project, Hamburger had to forge intricate, behind-the-scenes alliances between civic authorities, arts funders, real-estate moguls, neighborhood groups, local merchants, zoning commissions, private corporations, labor unions, police and fire departments, performers, politicians, and people on the street. This Herculean effort made En Garde Arts, in its own modest way, the most public of public theaters. While it lasted, it constituted a provocative and insistent meditation on the relationship between theater, architecture, memory, and the idea of a city. Elinor Fuchs characterized Hamburger as "one of the landscape visionaries of the American theater."[24] In an admiring essay in *Performing Arts Journal*, James Schlatter articulated the aesthetic that united En Garde's body of work:

> Like the sites themselves, the history they conjure seems both dead and gone and very much still alive. And through this act of collective imagining or conjuring, the audience essentially engages in a dialogue with itself as a gathered public body, provoking, hopefully, larger questions about the notion of progress, about the loss of a shared history, and consequently, about the shared future of the assembled spectators . . . an audience witnesses a kind of Einsteinian prospect of history continually spiraling back on itself and confronting – and potentially renewing – itself through repeated encounters with its own past.

> While it is impossible to sum up adequately En Garde Arts's theatrical "style," one might characterize many of their pieces as contemporary urban-American anti-masques. On one level, they present the whole of the society at a moment of significant historical crisis in a postmodern pageant of high and low cultural icons, political effigies, and performance forms. This form of eclectic staging enables a performance to collapse time and history into space and to compact a sprawling, fractured, and self-divided society into a (relatively) contained arena. This aggressively presentational, collage form of theatre creates a sense that entire culture, not just a few of its select representatives, is present on-stage at a critical juncture in that culture's history.[25]

A theater of this nature could not help but appeal to Mee, whose vision of a neo-Athenian public theater is summed up, in effect, in the paragraphs above. For him, En Garde was a dream come true.

Not long after seeing *Crowbar*, Mee called up Anne Hamburger and said "I want to do one of those."[26] Amenable to the prospect, she and Mee piled into her beat-up Nissan Sentra and started driving around Manhattan looking for derelict sites that might inspire a piece of theater, her practiced strategy for getting a project started. One of the places that they visited was a building at the southern end of Roosevelt Island, one that millions of New Yorkers have eyed from FDR Drive, a hospital, designed by architect James Renwick and opened in 1856 to quarantine immigrants arriving at Ellis Island with infectious diseases. By the time Mee and Hamburger got there, it was another urban ruin, exposed to the weather enough that trees were growing inside the building. Mee was inspired. He immediately conceived a piece about social outcasts staged in this abandoned hospital on what he saw as "this island of the damned." Hamburger asked Mee if he had a director in mind for the project, and he suggested Anne Bogart, knowing that, by that time, she was just then coming off from her debacle at Trinity Rep and might be available. Bogart and Mee had met professionally in the 1980s at the Music Theatre Group's summer home in the Berkshires, but they were not well acquainted. Their collaboration on *Another Person is a Foreign Country* would change all that.

Anne Bogart's role as a pioneer of site-specific theater has not been widely recognized. In 1978, she met a small audience on a street corner in lower Manhattan and took them home to her brownstone apartment in Brooklyn to see a three-character play called *Inhabitat*. While she has always claimed that her use of borrowed or abandoned spaces was less innovation than simple necessity – "Since nobody would give me a theater, the only option was to do it in the street or on rooftops or wherever"[27] – she was among the first in the USA to stage plays on a regular basis in what has come to be known as "a found environment" or "found space": "any given area, interior or exterior, that is used in its existing state for performance."[28] The historical roots of site-specific theater can be found in several alternative performance forms – the "environmental theater" of Richard Schechner, the dance and music experiments of Meredith Monk and Trisha Brown, the spectacles staged at the Festival of Shiraz in Iran by Peter Brook and Robert Wilson, the political street pageants of the Living Theatre and the Bread and Puppet Theatre, the Happenings of Allen Kaprow, Robert Whitman, and others – many of which took place outdoors, in vast natural settings or in urban plazas and parks. Bogart was among those who brought the site-specific impulse indoors, commandeering curious and available interiors and converting them into momentary performance spaces. Her initiative was a natural extension of the off-Off-Broadway ethos and the resourcefulness of producers like Joe Cino, Ellen Stewart, and Al Carmines, who turned Greenwich Village cafés, churches, lofts, even a meatpacking plant, into vestpocket theaters.

More than a matter of expediency or budgetary convenience, Bogart's experiments advanced her interest in the relationship of audience and event. In appropriating a building or a room as a temporary theater, a site-specific piece draws attention to its original architectural, historical, and aesthetic dimensions. In turn, this tends to elevate an audience's awareness of its own spectatorial role, particularly when the piece requires the audience to move from one place to another during the performance, adding a kinetic or processional dimension to the viewing experience, or when it spills out into the street, enhancing its nature as public event and availing itself of an accidental or found audience. This shift of overt emphasis onto the viewer's conscious experience of the play, the place of performance, and the act of spectating remained a trait of Bogart's directing long after she gave up her more explicitly site-specific experiments.

From the late-1970s well into the 1980s, Bogart staged a number of site-specific productions, many of which included a guide or host, either Bogart herself or an associate, who ushered a small audience to a series of borrowed or appropriated performance sites. For *Out of Sync* (1980), a loose adaptation of Chekhov's *The Seagull*, the audience gathered at the Odessa Restaurant in the East Village. At 8:00 p.m., Bogart appeared and led them down the block to a second-floor loft for the first two acts; then through a playground, down some stairs, and across a courtyard to a basement location a few streets away for another two acts; and finally to a spot on Second Avenue for the final scene, which the audience watched from all the way across the street, with traffic whizzing by in between. Throughout *Out of Sync*, Bogart changed the audience's vantage point as a way of triggering their awareness of space and their presence in it as watchers. The Treplev character in the piece was a young filmmaker, and the first act included an aborted screening of his work-in-progress, comparable to Treplev's symbolist drama of the future. This film was shot in the same locations that the audience would come to visit for the third and fourth acts of the play. It began with Karina, the Nina character, in a basement being watched through a window on the courtyard by a character named Peter; two acts later, the audience took on the same role of voyeurs and watched the third act through the same courtyard windows. There are other scenes in the piece in which a character is eavesdropping or looking on unnoticed – "seeing, unseen" as *Hamlet*'s Claudius would say – all part of Bogart's effort to implicate the spectator in the act of spectating.[29]

In those early days, Bogart kept looking for ways to test how far an audience would go. She conceived *The Emissions Project* (1980) as a theatrical soap opera, with a new episode – in a new location – each Sunday for some weeks running. As she later explained:

The audience would call my home – it was in the early days of answering machines – and they would get a message that told them where to
meet that week, like "Meet at the Basilica Restaurant and bring a
flashlight," or "Meet in Port Authority Terminal under the clock."
And when they got there, I would be the guide and I would say, "Follow
me," and we would go somewhere. We would come to a space and there
would be a scene and then we would go somewhere else. It was like a
promenade piece. Every week was a different journey, and the audience
never knew where they were going to end up.[30]

One of the eleven actors involved in *The Emissions Project* was Anne
Hamburger, a former art major at the University of Massachusetts-
Amherst with an interest in environmental sculpture, performance art,
and earth works. As a student, she spearheaded a project to draw a 1:1 scale
replica of the campus's twenty-eight-story W. E. B. Du Bois Library on
the lawn in front of the library in order to see how it might alter pedestrian
behavior. Once in New York, she was the kind of person who gravitated
into Anne Bogart's orbit. Not long after joining *The Emissions Project*, she
took over responsibility for locating interesting and available sites for the
next week's installment. Over the next couple years, Hamburger helped to
produce other Bogart projects, until in 1983, she enrolled in the graduate
program in theater management at the Yale School of Drama. Three years
later, her MFA thesis project, inspired in part by her work with Bogart,
was a proposal – from mission statement to business plan to trial-balloon
project – for a site-specific theater company in New York to be called En
Garde Arts.

If, nowadays, you go to the corner of 106th Street and Central Park West,
where the Upper West Side meets Morningside Heights, you will find a
twenty-five-story high-rise of luxury condominiums. It features on-site
valet parking, a spa and fitness center, "ambassador concierge service," and
a veiled history. On the Central Park end of the complex, there are the
remnants of a much older building, most conspicuously a series of round
towers, constructed of heavy masonry, with gothic window casements and
conical roofs, surrounding what was once a courtyard. This original
building, designed by architect Charles Coolidge Haight and financed
by real-estate baron John Jacob Astor III, opened in 1890 as Astor Pavilion, the first American hospital devoted exclusively to the care of cancer
patients. In keeping with the latest medical theories, the towers were
round to allow for lots of windows (and therefore steady light and air
circulation) and to eliminate corners (where dirt, stagnant air, and perhaps

infectious germs might accumulate). When the hospital expanded and moved in the 1950s to become what is now Memorial Sloan Kettering, the building was converted into a 374-bed nursing home, one in a large syndicate of nursing homes operated by a man named Bernard Bergman. Years later, a criminal investigation, statehouse hearings, and a subsequent trial revealed widespread abuses of the nursing home's patients, including overcrowding, inadequate food, unheated rooms, and lack of medical treatment. In 1974, Bergman was convicted of Medicaid fraud and the Towers Nursing Home was shut down and abandoned.

Sixteen years later, when Charles Mee, Anne Bogart, and Anne Hamburger snuck onto the property to look around, the Towers was a ruin. The courtyard was strewn with rubble. The windows were shattered or broken. Electricity, heat, and water had long since been shut off. In other words, it was a perfect place to do *Another Person is a Foreign Country*. Hamburger had been unable to obtain permission to use the Renwick Ruin on Roosevelt Island, so the real-estate search had continued for some time, more narrowly focused on finding a location well suited to Mee's idea for a piece of 'outsider theater.' The search stopped as soon as permission was secured to use the Towers Nursing Home, which provided one of the more memorable backdrops for one of En Garde's more unusual productions.

Another Person is a Foreign Country

Another Person is a Foreign Country was a multi-cultural freak show. Mee set out to create a piece about difference, about Other-ness, and specifically about how physical disability, and beyond that, mental disorder, sexual orientation, race, age, and other social markers, stigmatize people who are no less human – and otherwise no different – than the able-bodied, white, heterosexual majority that defines what is considered to be normal. He was more concerned with the perception of difference by the presumptive norm than the personal experience of it by 'the afflicted,' and to force that issue, his script called for performers with all manner of disabilities. This triggered one of the most prolonged and challenging casting processes that either Bogart or Hamburger had ever encountered. Mee had been recently charmed by a recording of a choir of European singers with Down syndrome, so producer, director, and playwright drove to a Down syndrome treatment center in upstate New York to see if their chorus might participate in the production. That effort was unsuccessful, as was an attempt to find conjoined twins to be in the show. Nevertheless, the search for exceptional performers generated a buzz in the casting community at a moment when the push for "color blind" and "non-traditional" casting was gaining momentum.[31]

In the end, the cast of *Another Person is a Foreign Country* was conspicuous enough in its diversity for one critic to describe it as "*A Chorus Line* for people who can't get an audition."[32] These people included:

four blind or visually impaired members of the Lighthouse Agency Choir who sang each night, dressed in red robes, their guide dogs at their side;

an ad hoc rock-and-roll band made up of seven musicians from the Talented Handicapped Artists Workshop (THAW) at a halfway house on Long Island for recovering psychiatric in-patients;

the professional actor David J. Steinberg, a dwarf who had played roles in JoAnne Akalaitis's productions of *The Screens* and *Henry IV* Parts One and Two and in the Ron Howard film *Willow*;

a "Tiny Woman" from New Jersey named Maria J. Clark, born with a growth-stunting condition called Osteogenesis Imperfecta (aka "brittle bones"), which limited her height to 2 feet 10 inches;

a tall, blond transvestite in a gold evening gown named Terence Mintern, who played a hermaphrodite named Ethyl;

a deaf actor/playwright named Bruce Hlibok, who ran his own deaf theater group and who had appeared on Broadway in Lyle Kessler's *Runaways*;

the seventy-two-year-old resident of a retirement home down the block from the Towers, who wandered into rehearsal one day to see what was happening and volunteered to be in the show; and

a six-year-old kid named Rashid Brown.

These performers were joined by a handful of other actors, including Tom Nelis, who a year later would become a founding member of the SITI Company, and a band of "Angels," mainly recent New York University graduates, who served as ushers, extras, and a kind of manic chorus.

None of these performers played characters in any conventional sense. They were, all at once, themselves as individuals, mouthpieces for Mee's array of borrowed and original texts, representations of difference, and guests at an ostensible dinner party that was the play's main event (see figure 1). A grandstand was set up for the audience in the interior courtyard of the Towers, facing a long narrow banquet table covered by a white tablecloth and resting in a bed of sand. As Mee describes it:

The audience comes and sits in bleachers and there is a great big dining table and all these people come out of the house and sit at the table and

Figure 1. Multicultural freak show: *Another Person is a Foreign Country* (1991). (a) The cast at banquet, including Tom Nelis as the Poet (far right). (b) The chorus of Angels in the courtyard of the Towers Nursing Home. (Photographs by William Rivelli.)

perform the most basic social ritual of all: breaking bread. And the audience witnesses and, in effect, participates in a dinner party. That was it. They came out, they sat down, they had food, they had dinner table conversation, they told stories, and they left. And the experience for the audience was you are sitting there and all these freaks come out of the building and you are thinking, "Whoa, this is weird! These are really freaky people!" As it goes on, some of the stories are odd, so they draw you in. Some of them are funny, some are sad, so you begin to feel warmth towards these people and finally comfort with them, with being with them, until you finally felt you were part of the same human community, and that was the end of the evening. That was the structure of the piece. That was the event.[33]

The dinner conversation challenged conventional notions of civility and manners in a manner similar to *The Investigation of the Murder in El Salvador*. The guests chatted about such subjects as body piercings or a preference for rough sex as though they were discussing the latest beauty treatment or fitness craze. The topic soon turned to natural history and more and more to zoological anomalies, bizarre animals, and other freaks of nature. "We're all specimens," observed Mike the dwarf, standing on top of the table. He then proceeded to give a graphic and embarrassing description of the male and female genitals of Ethyl, the hermaphrodite, which concluded: "There are those who say that most people go through life in fear that they will have a traumatic experience, that they will be violated somehow in their bodies or in their innermost selves. And that those who were born with their traumas have already passed the test in life. They are the aristocrats."[34]

The play turned on this simple inversion: reconfiguring the abnormal and grotesque in terms of "the exquisite" or "the uniqueness of things," presenting outsiders as aristocrats, conflating culture and nature, civilization and barbarism. The piece climaxed with a helter-skelter after-dinner entertainment that filled the courtyard, the scaffolding against the side of the building, and several upper-story windows with a wild, pantomimic orgy. While the band rocked out, the entire cast, along with the chorus of Angels, humped and bumped, grinded and gyrated, kissed and copulated with violent abandon, eventually giving birth to a series of surreal aberrations out of Hieronymous Bosch, such as a giant ear or "a birdhead with legs coming out of its mouth." The fury of this orgy spent, the guests settled down again around the table for the play's final round of speeches, including one that catalogued the abuses perpetuated by the Towers Nursing Home decades earlier.

In what was by all accounts the play's most memorable and poignant testimony, Bruce Hlibok, playing a role called Ajax, described how his parents forced him to take music lessons "in an effort to make me average," even though he was deaf. He told how a sadistic piano teacher asked again and again, "Do you hear the lovely music?" The actor, refusing all the while to have his impaired speech translated by a fellow cast member, finally concluded, "If she had asked me if I *felt* the music, I would have said yes, because it was true. And, in fact, I came to love the piano for its shape, and its beauty, and its silence." In the play's final moments, as plaintive music played, a carefully rigged pipe across the top of the courtyard wall released a gentle cascade of water, as if to suggest that the building itself, which had witnessed a century of pain, was moved to tears.

Critical response to *Another Person is a Foreign Country* was favorable but mixed, with some critics taking issue with the contradictory impulse at the heart of its conception. "The production, with its loving reliance on the contributions of the exceptional artists, keeps teaching us to recognize the humanity we share with them; the text, at the same time, proudly insists on their difference, on the arbitrary meaninglessness of nature in making us all different from one another," wrote Michael Feingold in the *Village Voice*.[35] In a similar vein, Jan Stuart found the piece "forever at odds with itself, adrift in some murky zone between stressing the otherness of its subjects and rendering that otherness a palpable part of our own experience."[36] The critic in the *New York Post* wrote, "the surface effects of this show are spectacular. But isn't the point to look beneath the surface?"[37] In fact, the point seemed to be to look *at* the surfaces of things, from the physiology of the performers to the façade of the Towers Nursing Home to the jarring images in the play's borrowed pieces of text. All of these might be seen as just the sort of shards and broken fragments of a 'normal' whole out of which Mee prefers to construct his work. In *Another Person is a Foreign Country*, he and Bogart took a 'broken' site and a 'fragmented' cast and illuminated their rough surfaces with a spectacle of music, movement, light, and language.

Like most En Garde offerings, this first collaboration between Mee and Bogart was an unrepeatable, one-of-a-kind event. A year later, they would team up for a second time on *Orestes*, the inaugural production of the SITI Company. Both continued to work independently with Anne Hamburger on site-specific En Garde productions. In 1994, Bogart directed *Marathon Dancing*, the second installment in her trio of pieces about American popular culture in the first half of the twentieth century. It presented a kaleidoscopic portrait of the Depression-era dance marathon craze, set within "the ironic frame"[38] of an opulent grand ballroom on the third floor of the Masonic Hall on West 23rd Street in Chelsea. Two of Mee's riffs on the Greeks were directed for En Garde Arts by Tina Landau. In 1993, she staged *Orestes* on an abandoned pier on the Hudson River, with the glittering lights of New Jersey in the distance. In 1996, she did *Trojan Women: A Love Story* in the graffiti-strewn ruins of the East River Amphitheatre, a WPA building which, one summer forty years earlier, had been the first outdoor home of Joseph Papp's fledgling New York Shakespeare Festival.[39]

In 1999, a changing civic, economic, and real-estate climate in New York and sheer exhaustion prompted Hamburger to shut down operations in favor of becoming artistic director of the La Jolla Playhouse in San Diego. A year later, she jumped ship to become an executive vice-president at Disney, in charge of night-time spectacles, day-time parades, and splashy short-form musicals seen at Disney theme parks around the world. In effect, she would now do site-specific theater on a multi-million dollar, multi-national, corporate scale. In the meantime, En Garde Arts, a theater of ghosts, became a ghost itself, but its place in the careers of Bogart and Mee and in the history of theater in New York should not be forgotten.

3

Mee: putting on the Greeks

Eᴀʀʟʏ ɪɴ 1991, ᴀʀᴏᴜɴᴅ ᴛʜᴇ ᴛɪᴍᴇ ᴏғ ᴛʜᴇ ɢᴜʟғ ᴡᴀʀ, ɢᴏʀᴅᴏɴ Davidson, artistic director of the Mark Taper Forum, contacted director Robert Woodruff to see if he had a project in mind for a workshop aimed at developing new takes on classic plays. Woodruff, in turn, got hold of his friend Chuck Mee to see what he had in the works, and when Mee reported having nothing suitable in hand, Woodruff proposed that they work on an adaptation of Euripides's *Orestes* as a post-war tragedy of madness. Woodruff went off to Los Angeles to start work with a group of ten actors, while Mee, who remained in New York, faxed new material to the West Coast to be interpolated into the ancient text at designated moments. After two weeks of workshopping material, Woodruff returned to New York and presented Mee with the results, which the playwright later described as "this pile of crap: the play, my stuff, everybody's stuff, his notes." In sifting through it and distilling it down to some kind of script, Mee discovered a way of working that he would favor for years to come: "I took the Greek play *Orestes*, stuck a bunch of stuff on it, threw the scaffolding away, and what was left retained the form of what was now absent, only it was different."[1]

The resulting play proved to be a breakthrough in both Mee's evolving dramaturgy and his developing career. In earlier plays, he had already adopted the practice of appropriating passages from his readings and research and including them more or less verbatim in his scripts. Now, in a manner that brings to mind the postmodern methods of Heiner Müller, he was taking the plot and characters of a classic drama and writing his own play on top of that, generating a confrontation with history and a theatrical palimpsest that demonstrated no particular concern about where the original author's work left off and his own began.[2] Mee's version of *Orestes* became the first in a series of free interpretations of Greek tragedies. Each one is different in its fidelity and proximity to the original, inviting critical debate about whether the plays should be regarded as original works or adaptations and demonstrating in practical terms Mee's evolving ideas about culture – and even the writing of a single play – as a process of remaking.

Alluding to the labeling practices of software manufacturers, he titled his 1993 take on Euripides's last play *The Bacchae 2.1*, as if to suggest that the core play was still in place but that enhancements had been added to make it as up-to-the-minute and functional as possible. This titular gesture is more than hip; the perpetual rewriting and upgrading of software programs can be seen as a metaphor for the symbiotic manner in which a text (a programming code or an entire culture) and the conventions surrounding its use are revised and restructured over time to suit changing needs, interests, and technical possibilities. In turning to Greek tragedy, with its coincidence with the birth of democracy, Mee was declaring both his sincere desire for a public theater in the spirit of fifth-century Athens and his unapologetic intention to use Greek models as the basis for his own civic-minded dramas. On a more practical level, the Greeks offered big, broad plays rooted in sensational myths and populated by complicated characters who are driven by heroic passions and moral confusion to commit outrageous acts of violence. That is good, juicy stuff for any playwright who wants to work outside the psychological box of domestic realism.

Orestes 2.0, as the play came to be known,[3] was a breakthrough for Mee in part because of the interest in his work that it elicited from a community of directors and in particular from the trio of Robert Woodruff, Anne Bogart, and Tina Landau. In the context of this book, *Orestes 2.0* is significant as the second collaboration of Mee and Bogart and the inaugural production of the Saratoga International Theater Institute (SITI), but Bogart was the third director to get her hands on the play. After the initial 1991 workshop at the Taper, Woodruff directed the play a year later at University of California, San Diego. Landau did the play with students in the American Repertory Theatre's Institute for Advanced Theatre Training in January 1992 and then followed it in June 1993 with a celebrated En Garde Arts production staged on an abandoned pier on the Hudson River.[4] Bogart's SITI production, the play's professional premiere, came in the summer of 1992 (see figure 2). David Schweizer directed *Orestes 2.0* in March 1994 as part of the inaugural offering of the Actors Gang in Los Angeles, and other independent productions followed the next year in San Francisco and Seattle. The play clearly

Figure 2. Apocalypse now: two versions of Mee's *Orestes 2.0.* (a) Anne Bogart's production in Saratoga Springs (1992), with Eric Hill (center) as Menelaus standing over Richard Thompson as Orestes. (Photograph by Clemems Kalischer.) (b) Tina Landau's production on the Hudson River (1993), with (from left to right) Theresa McCarthy as Electra, Jayne Amelia Larson as Helen, and Elvin Velez as Phrygian Slave. (Photograph by William Rivelli.)

appealed to adventurous directors who sought to create their own unique theatrical event around and on top of the playwright's text, just as Mee had with the Greek original.

Subsequent Mee plays had much the same appeal to a widening circle of directors, including Brian Kulick in New York, Matt Wilder in San Diego, and Kenn Watt in San Francisco. The openness of Mee's scripts, their insistence that they contain a spectrum of possible productions and no single, authoritative one, makes it difficult to evaluate them independent of the directors who interpret them. Pure textual criticism of Mee plays has its limits. Nevertheless, a brief examination of four plays from the 1990s based on Greek tragedies – *Orestes 2.0*, *Trojan Women: A Love Story*, *True Love*, and *Big Love* – demonstrates his new strategy of building a new play on the skeleton of a classic and suggests how the tone and focus of Mee's work shifted as the conditions of his life and art changed over the course of the decade.

Orestes 2.0

First presented in Athens in 408 BC, Euripides's *Orestes* takes place outside the palace of Argos, six days after Orestes's murder of his mother Clytemnestra. In the grip of a terrible delirium brought on by the Furies, Orestes is cared for by his loving sister Electra while they wait to find out what form his capital punishment will take. His only hope of survival rests with Menelaus, just back from the Trojan War, but pleas for his uncle's intercession are met by empty promises and mincing words of advice. A messenger provides a detailed account of the trial. Menelaus did not even appear to testify. Both Orestes and Electra were condemned to death; the assembly's only concession was to allow them to carry out the sentences themselves by suicide. At this point, Pylades, Orestes's friend and accomplice, intervenes, insisting that they fight back and take revenge against Menelaus by killing his much-reviled wife Helen, cause of the long war. Electra proposes that they take Helen's daughter Hermione hostage and threaten to kill her if they are not allowed to escape. With Orestes's will to live revived, everything goes according to plan until he is about to deal the death blow to Helen. In this instant, reports a Phrygian slave, Helen disappeared into thin air. When Menelaus runs out to see what has happened, Orestes (with a knife at Hermione's throat), Electra (torches in hand), and Pylades appear on the roof, threatening to kill the girl and set the palace ablaze. At the height of this furor, with catastrophe certain, Apollo appears from above as deus ex machina, with Helen at his side, and proclaims an abrupt and amicable resolution to the whole mess. Orestes will spend a year in exile and then stand trial in Athens, where he will be acquitted and return to rule Argos and marry Hermione. Pylades will marry Electra. Menelaus will rule Sparta as compensation for the loss of his wife, who is to be enshrined as an immortal star in the heavens to light the way for mariners at night. With amity restored, Apollo ascends with Helen, and all's well that seems to end well.

This implausible and peremptory happy ending has sparked considerable critical debate, postive and negative, about Euripides's command of his art in *Orestes*. Imagine, for instance, the effect on stage when Hermione is told she will marry the man with a knife at her throat. Whether this deus ex machina makes a mockery of the tragic situation or projects a dark, penetrating irony back over it, its absurdity can be seen as a measure of the runaway madness that defines Orestes's spirit throughout the play. The issue for Euripides here is less the path to civic justice than the suffering of extreme emotion, by Orestes first and foremost, and then by his comrades in arms, Electra and Pylades. In its manic subjectivity, *Orestes* can be seen as an instance of Attic expressionism, one announced by Electra's first lines in the play:

> There is no form of anguish with a name –
> No suffering, no fate, no fall
> Inflicted by heaven, however terrible –
> Whose tortures human nature could not bear
> Or might not have to bear.

All that follows from there – the melodramatic vacillations of the plot; the violent swings of emotion from hatred, guilt, madness, and despair to love, loyalty, and the sudden will to survive; the rooftop climax out of a Hollywood, action-adventure movie – add up to a case study in human affliction.

That, at least, would seem to be the basis for Mee's interest in the tragedy, which he makes strikingly contemporary while preserving more of the original than an unknowing spectator might suspect. Mee stays close to Euripides's plot, retains much of his dialogue, and even includes a number of specific and evocative character gestures from Euripides, such as Electra wiping away a foamy excretion from Orestes's lips when he wakes up from tormented sleep. As might be expected, Mee's most obvious interventions concern the play's setting and the treatment of the chorus. The palace at Argos becomes "a palatial white Newport-style or Palm Beach-style beach house," and the Greek aristocrats become American jetsetters, outfitted in designer fashions by Armani, Chanel, and Jean Paul Gautier. Mee stipulates that "the setting is both inside and out," with its broad, pockmarked lawn doubling as something like the psychiatric ward in a military hospital. There is a row of white hospital beds for a small chorus of "damaged war victims," who are kept under control by a trio of nurses as they play mah jong, break into ironic renditions of contemporary pop songs, talk about sex, and listen to the radio "as though it were the only thing still working in a backyard in which all life has been recently annihilated." This sense of general ruin and the aftermath of widespread catastrophe, absent in Euripides, pervades the entire play. Mee magnifies Orestes's madness to suggest a civilization in apocalypse, a favorite theme of his early plays.[5]

In *Orestes 2.0*, ground zero for this apocalypse is the human body itself. The hospital setting suggests as much, as does the first speech of the play: an autopsy report that describes in clinical detail the physical condition of a female murder victim whose throat was cut while in the bathtub.[6] This, of course, is Clytemnestra. The variety of texts that Mee "sticks on" the play – taken from sources ranging from *Vogue* and *Soap Opera Digest* to Brazilian political theorist Roberto Mangabeira Unger to serial killer John Wayne Gacy – make the corporal focus conspicuous. The narcissistic Helen describes a beauty regimen – "I cleanse, tone, moisturize, and exfoliate" – that makes plain her preoccupation with healthy skin. Two of the deranged veterans exchange lines that name different torture techniques often used on political prisoners, prisoners of war, and spies. One of the nurses describes in comic and graphic detail how she became "a slave to my orgasms," masturbating up to six hours a day. In aggregate, the many descriptions of sex and violence draw attention to ways in which the human body is treated as a material object which receives an action that results either in pleasure or, much more often in the world of this play, pain. In two instances, Mee makes this objectification literal and a joke. When Electra tells Helen to send her daughter Hermione to Clytemnestra's grave with an offering, a nurse wheels on a large doll on a tricycle wearing "a white, floral Betsy Johnson sun dress with matching leggings." At the end of the play, when Apollo appears as deus ex machina with Helen at his side, she takes the form at that moment of "a giant blow-up fuck-me doll."

More than simple sensationalism, Mee's focus on the body-as-object gives theatrical expression to ideas found in Elaine Scarry's *The Body in Pain* (1987), a seminal work in cultural studies that examines the phenomenology of pain: its inexpressibility; its capacity through torture and war to deconstruct the world of its sufferers; and its inverse relationship to the imagination as a creative and constructive operation. One of Mee's invented characters in *Orestes 2.0* is known as Tapemouth Man, a hospital inmate "tied up in a wheelchair with tape over his mouth," who manages to wriggle free three times over the course of the play long enough to speak extended passages from Scarry's book before being bound, gagged, and silenced again. The first passage, a Homeric roll call of fallen warriors, makes the point that the action of war and the pain it inflicts result in more than injury or the loss of individual life; they amount to the "unmaking" of the civilization that has sent men into battle to defend or advance it, insofar as each death diminishes that civilization's human stock of certain valued attributes. Soldiers who die for their country take a part of their country with them, and those who survive with injury find their identities unmade as well.[7] At the end of *Orestes 2.0*, while changing a bandage, one of the nurses asks a wounded veteran, "Do you have any pain?," to which his response is "Oh, yes. I'd say that's the least of it. I'd say: I'm not myself any more."

The Tapemouth Man's second monologue advances these ideas by describing "the way the nation inscribes itself in the body," whether by defining citizenship as physical residence within certain geo-political boundaries or by establishing tort laws that determine liability of certain products that enter or come into contact with the body, such as food, cosmetics, automobiles, and so on. The history and culture of the nation, Tapemouth Man (and Scarry) argue, is written on the body of its citizens, in wartime in the cuneiform of a soldier's wounds and in peacetime in the social gestures and physical customs of people at work and play. From this perspective, Orestes's lunatic pain needs to be seen not as the psychotic delusions of a guilty matricide but as the register of the state, be it Euripides's Athens or Mee's USA, on its number-one native son. Orestes is not himself anymore either. He has lost not only identity but also genuine agency. The 'reduction' of his sentence to death-by-suicide and his doomed attempt at a rooftop escape are both the state's way of getting him to finish the task of unmaking that it has already begun. In Euripides, Apollo arrives as deus ex machina just in time to abort Orestes's order to burn down the palace, but Mee allows the destruction to go forth, despite his Apollo's ludicrous hope that "things have not gone so far that not even a god can put things to right." The city goes on burning for the rest of the play until all that remains is "a smoking ruin, a smoldering fire" and a silence penetrated only by the sound of a radio – "like the music," Mee writes, "that continues on the radio after a car wreck." Civilization, such as it is, has been laid waste by what amounts to a self-inflicted wound.

This dystopic view is typical of Mee's early work, but Tapemouth Man's third monologue follows Scarry in articulating the antithesis and, in some

sense, the antidote for the operation of pain: the imagination and its
capacity for making and remaking worlds that have been undone through
torture, war, and other, less obvious and less violent performances of
power. If pain unmakes the world, Scarry argues, the imagination remakes
it. Given the importance to Mee of the idea of "remaking," Tapemouth
Man's speech, which the playwright says is to be delivered "cheerfully, like
a smiling Buddha," is worth quoting in full:

> The imagination
> is less a separate faculty
> than a quality of all our mental faculties:
> the quality of seeing more things
> and making more connections among ideas about things
> than any list of theories and discourses
> can countenance.
> The imagination works
> by a principle of sympathy
> with the suppressed and subversive elements in experience.
> It sees the residues,
> the memories, and the reports of past or faraway social worlds
> and of neglected or obscure perceptions
> as the main stuff with which we remake our contexts.
> It explains the operation of a social order
> by representing what the remaking of this order would require.
> It generalizes our ideas
> by tracing a penumbra of remembered or intimated possibility
> around present or past settlements.
> By all these means
> it undermines
> the identification of the actual
> with the possible.

This passage comes as close as any in Mee's body of work to articulating
his theoretical orientation as an artist, that is, as one who makes the practice
of the imagination his profession. To be sure, in the onward rush of performance, Tapemouth Man's speeches might come across more like the ravings
of a madman than a brief dissertation on aesthetics. Their dense thematic
implications must be difficult for a listener to grasp on the fly, especially
given the immediate response the third monologue provokes: Tapemouth
Man's fellow inmates pounce on him, gag him, drag him upstage, throw him
to the floor, kick him in the head or, the script offers, just shoot him dead.
This stifling of speech provides an active demonstration of how the state,

here through the ironic agency of its own war victims, resists the subversive work of the imagination and inscribes itself on the body.

At the time of creating *Orestes 2.0*, Mee was still in the process of winding down his career as a historian (with its professional demeanor of dispassionate objectivity) in favor of embracing what Scarry calls the imagination's "principle of sympathy with the suppressed and subversive elements in experience." The quotational plays to come would be composed out of "the residues, the memories, and the reports of past or faraway social worlds" or selected fragments from the mediatized world of present-day popular culture. In tracing the penumbra of ancient Greek tragedies, his radical revisions would undermine "the identification of the actual with the possible," and, as much by the forcefulness of their expression as their overt political content, offer resistance to the mechanism by which the dominant social and economic order writes itself on the body politic.

Trojan Women: A Love Story

A familiar state of cataclysm defines the first act of *Trojan Women: A Love Story*, Mee's fourth venture into remaking the Greeks, following treatments of *The Bacchae* (1993) and *Agamemnon* (1994). In this piece, Mee altered his initial practice of using a single Greek model as a point of departure and created what amounts to a theatrical diptych. The first act, which Mee divides into sections called "The Prologue" and "The Play," mirrors the action of Euripides's *The Trojan Women* and its depiction of the fate of the women of Troy in the immediate aftermath of the Greeks' victory. The second act, dubbed "The Musical," draws on *Les Troyens* (1858), the grand Romantic opera by Hector Berlioz (itself a two-part work), as well as Virgil's *Aeneid*, to present a contemporary version of Aeneas's famous sojourn in Carthage while en route to Italy to found the city of Rome and a new empire. Filled with enough pop songs to prompt Michael Feingold to call it a ballad opera, it contrasts the unmitigated pathos of Euripides with a pastoral idyll that takes place in a sexual utopia.[8] In the process, it introduces a theme that will bend Mee's work towards comedy in the years to come: the difference between women and men.

A city in shock, the Troy of the first half is "a smoking, still-burning ruin" with black ash raining down from the sky (see figure 3). The action takes place at the same liminal moment between war and peace that inspired so much of Mee's historical writing, although in this case "playing God" means seizing the spoils of war by the throat rather than negotiating their distribution through the art of diplomacy. Mee calls for a chorus of

Figure 3. Theatrical diptych - *The Trojan Women: A Love Story* at the old East River Park Amphitheatre (1996). (a) Troy as ruin, with Nancy Hume as Andromache (center) and Stephen Webber as Ray Bob. (b) Carthage as spa with Jason Danieley (down center, saluting) as Aeneas and his men posing for Harriett D. Foy (right, in pool) as Dido. (Photographs by William Rivelli.)

"a hundred dark-skinned 'Third World' women making computer components at little work tables." Their litany of woe is drawn verbatim from
testimonials by survivors of Hiroshima, the Holocaust, and other modern
catastrophes. Talthybius, the Greek herald, comes to announce (just as he
does in Euripides) which Greek generals will take which Trojan women as
slave, concubine, and trophy. Astyanax, infant son of Hector (and, like
Hermione in *Orestes 2.0*, represented by a doll), is killed. Helen manipulates her husband Menelaus into taking her back. Polyxena is sacrificed at
Achilles's grave. And Hecuba, wife of Priam, queen of Troy, and mother of
all suffering, makes every effort to absorb the tragedy of war unto herself
and end the cycle of barbarism. She says:

> There is nothing predestined in all this:
> if rage and violence is in our bones
> then let us rise beyond it –
> this is what it is to be civilized.

But Mee departs from Euripides when he has Hecuba succumb in the end
to the thirst for revenge – "This pain must be answered with more pain, / this
brutality with brutality in kind," she says – and sends for Aeneas, who comes
out of hiding to receive his marching orders. He is to travel to a new country,
"make a nation that can endure," and return one day to destroy Greece.

The Carthage of the second half, Mee stipulates, is a "dreamland, a
world of drift, heaven," which takes the form of a fancy health spa, with
exercise machines, massage tables, piles of fluffy towels, bowls of luscious
fruit, and a hot tub (see figure 3). Until the wayward Trojans arrive, the
spa's inhabitants are all female, prompting one of Aeneas's men to ask "Is
this a club for women only?" When Dido, queen of Carthage, sees Aeneas,
she is transfixed by love, observing:

> You know,
> a cave that has been dark for a million years
> will become bright
> the moment a candle is lit inside it.
> Things can happen so suddenly.

Dido and Aeneas proceed to talk about what each of them finds attractive
in the opposite sex and about love at first sight – "I think it's the only kind
there is," she says – and then they relax in each other's arms, in a state of
blissful undress, while the other men and women describe the pleasures of
sexual positions outlined in the Kama Sutra: the Honey Bee, the Swan
Sport, the Lovely Lady in Control, the Coitus of the Gods, Inviting the

Nectar, Sucking a Mango, and so on. A ripple of anxiety disturbs the tranquility of this erotic paradise when Dido reads Aeneas's Tarot, and before long, the lovers come to quarrel. The restless Aeneas insists that he has "certain obligations" to uphold and a need "to achieve something." In Virgil and in Berlioz, this masculine compulsion leads Aeneas to set sail for Italy, and Dido, in distressed response, to immolate herself on a pyre of his possessions. But Mee, as he did in the first half of the play, reverses final events and has Dido grab Aeneas by the hair and try to drown him in the hot tub, while the chorus ends the play by singing a few stanzas of "When Somebody Loves You."

In performance, these lineaments of a plot are less pronounced than the summary here might suggest. As in his other takes on the Greeks, Mee withholds much of the conventional exposition; those ignorant of the myth will not learn it from watching the play. The suffering of the Trojan women and the passion of Dido and Aeneas function more as bulletin boards on which he pins a myriad of texts and songs that plumb the differences between men and women and examine the mysterious desire that attracts such seeming opposites to each other. In the Troy act, a Special Forces soldier says, "The natural state of a man, / the ecstatic state, will find itself in the visions of things that appear suddenly: cadavers, for example, / nudity, explosions, spilled blood, sunbursts, abscesses, thunder." In contrast, a member of the female chorus describes feminist utopias as places "where egalitarian, consensual, and cooperative relationships flourish and where both sexes are able to engage in meaningful work," places that "celebrate what we usually think of as traditionally female tasks and traits: nurturance, expressiveness, support or personal growth and development, a link with the land or earth."[9] Theoretical banter such as this sits side by side with more colloquial dialogue about gender roles. Andromache, "wearing torn Lagerfeld clothes," talks about "having been a good wife" and the proper way for a married woman to sign a letter. Polyxena regrets facing death at age thirteen partly because there is a lot she doesn't know yet, like "why do guys insist on driving?" and "why is a guy who sleeps around a stud / but a girl who does is a slut?" The humor here turns mordant when, a moment later, Polyxena is gagged and dragged off to be murdered.

In the Carthage act, in which, Mee says, "the dramaturgical rules have shifted," frequent romantic ballads and torch songs give the action more the feel of a musical revue. The Edenic fantasy here focuses on the power of love between a woman and a man and, in particular, on why a man, having experienced that rapture, would turn his back and walk away. Carthage is "a woman's world," Aeneas says, and he needs to live in a man's world, a world of his own making, "a world / without / false hope / or sentiment." Dido wonders what he is afraid of – loss of control? her superstitious belief in things like astrology and the I Ching? the threat that love will pass? the threat that it might prove eternal and never pass? or her sheer otherness as a woman? – but all he can say to justify his departure is, in effect, 'a man's gotta do what a man's gotta do.' "There may even be some deep biological thing to this," Aeneas admits, copping to a genetic determinism that in the moment seems weak and unconvincing. His rationale echoes an idea voiced in the first act: "Men act. / We know this. / Attach no value to it, / particularly. / To act is to be. / No more no less." In the end, though, it is Dido who takes action, but in a way that concludes the play on an explicit note of uncertainty. When the two lovers hug each other good-bye, Dido grabs Aeneas's head and thrusts it under the water in the hot tub again and again, until his body goes limp and she collapses exhausted on the floor. Mee leaves it to the director to decide whether he dies or he drags himself, nearly dead, out of the tub to collapse at Dido's side. There is no meaning per se in either choice because how things turn out in the end is not Mee's real concern.

What matters and what shapes the audience's experience is the impression of two utterly different worldspaces, an idea made literal and performative by Tina Landau when she staged the play in 1996 at two different sites on the grounds of the old East River Amphitheater.[10] Both Troy and Carthage are defined by choruses of women, and in Hecuba and Dido, each is represented by a strong female leader, but the cities themselves are gendered as male and female respectively. This distinction tops a list of oppositions – war and peace, pain and pleasure, violence and sex, Thanatos and Eros, sun and moon, hell and heaven, tragedy and pastoral – that characterizes the two panels of the play's diptych. What is a man? What is a woman? What is that love that draws them together in breathless desire but does not sustain them once they catch their breaths? On a superficial level, the play's answers to these questions seem simplistically Manichean, but the contrast of Troy and Carthage is better understood as a bifocal lens through which to contemplate the masculine and the feminine as complicated terms in a dialectic that has no synthesis. There is no third gender.

True Love

Mee wrote *True Love*, his take on the myth of Phaedra and Hippolytus, for Laurie Williams, an actress who he first met when she was in *The War to End War* at the Sledgehammer Theater in San Diego in 1993. In 1995, they met again, fell in love, and lived together, without marrying, until the spring of 2001, not long after the Actors Theatre of Louisville premiere of *bobrauschenbergamerica*. After a staged reading in August 1998, *True Love* did not receive its first full production until June 2001, when Ivo van Hove, the first European director to take an interest in Mee's work, staged it for the Holland Festival in Amsterdam. The play's American premiere came in November of that year, when Jeanne Donovan Fisher, a long-time friend and supporter of Mee, produced it independently at the new Zipper Theatre near Times Square, with Laurie Williams in the Phaedra role.[11] By that time, however, Williams and Mee were no longer a couple, a change of relationship that added some awkwardness to the production process and some fuel for a harrowing emotional confrontation between the Phaedra and Theseus characters in the play's final moments.

As the myth goes, while Theseus, hero-king of Athens, is away on one of his many adventures, his legitimate wife, Phaedra, finds herself unable to control a forbidden passion for her stepson Hippolytus, Theseus's son by one of his earlier conquests, Antiope, queen of the amazons. Phaedra's desperate admission of her love, along with Theseus's untimely return, lead to a series of tragic events, which have been famously dramatized by Euripides, Seneca, and Racine. Euripides centered his *Hippolytus* on the hubris of the eponymous prince in rejecting worldly love in favor of pristine chastity, a choice that angers Aphrodite, goddess of love, who gets her revenge by instigating Phaedra's desire and the tragic events that stem therefrom. Both Seneca and Racine eliminated the gods as active characters and shifted the primary focus from Hippolytus to Phaedra, making her more pathetic and more sympathetic than in Euripides. There are other variations as well – in the orchestration of the plot; in the characterization of Theseus and Phaedra's confidante, the Nurse; in Racine's introduction of a love interest for Hippolytus; in the nuances of Phaedra's psychology – but all three classical versions are still driven by the heroine's all-consuming, uncontrollable, and illicit sexual desire for her young, chaste, honorable stepson. Neither a helpless victim of the gods nor a reviled moral villain, Phaedra is a noble woman caught in the grip of an undeniable primordial emotion. Its symptoms are debilitating: it clouds vision, stifles speech, disorients thought, ravages body and soul with fever and pain, and leads to a state of psychic ruin as devastating as the trauma of war.

Mee transplants the Phaedra story from a palace in ancient Greece to a rundown gas station in the American boondocks. It might be anywhere really, but a reference to Utica suggests upstate New York, an area that includes other place-names (Syracuse, Ithaca) borrowed from the ancient Mediterranean world of Euripides and Seneca. "Surrounded wall to wall by red clay stained with oil and gas," this place smacks of ruin as well, less from the aftermath of war than the dereliction of time, a crossroads that was abandoned and rusted out when the interstate went in somewhere else. Mee calls for a "surreally supremely beautiful" gas pump, an inflatable plastic kiddie swimming pool, a doghouse with no dog, and a nearby no-tell motel with a decrepit sign ("Mo el Aph it") that alludes to the Goddess of Love. And there is an old Lincoln Town Car, wheels off, hood up, splattered with mud after being left right where it broke down who knows how long ago (see figure 4). The car belongs to Polly, thirty-four, the Phaedra figure, wearing "Armani, with some rips and stains," and Richard, her husband, in his fifties, who, Theseus-like, has been gone for six months or more, leaving his rollerblading son, Edward, age thirteen or fourteen, in her custody.

From the play's first moments, when Polly gazes long and hard at Edward in motionless silence, her penetrating desire for him is apparent, but she does not experience the same maniacal sense of sin, shame, and taboo that wracks the conscience of the other Phaedras. Her passion is more "cold and numb." She feels on some level that it is wrong, but she makes no effort to conceal or deny it, saying at one point, "And then, if you fall in love, / what can you do?" After a series of erotically charged encounters with Edward, Polly eventually takes him by the hand and leads him into the back seat of the Lincoln for what is by that time an inevitable consummation of desire. When they get out of the car and slow dance naked to Screamin Jay Hawkins's "I Put a Spell on You," Richard makes his equally inevitable return. He has a confrontation with Edward over what kind of father he was to him, followed by a confrontation with Polly over their relationship, the latter so prolonged and so full of vitriol and hateful recrimination that it suggests how profoundly they must have loved each other at one time. Then, he takes a gun and shoots her three times, before putting the pistol in his mouth and blowing his brains out. With that, the play is over.

Mee's particular variations on the plots, characters, and settings of Euripides, Seneca, and Racine are less important than, once again, his use of his source material as the organizing surface for a collage of thematically related texts.[12] In this instance, the theme is Eros in its most overtly sexual form, a choice that makes *True Love* an odd, contemporary rendition of Plato's *Symposium*, which Mee first encountered when he was hospitalized with polio.[13] Instead of Agathon, Aristophanes, Socrates, and

Figure 4. Sex and death: *True Love* and *Big Love.* (a) Laurie Williams as Polly at the Zipper (2001). (Photograph by Carol Rosegg.) (b) Karenjune Sanchez (fore-ground), former SITI actor, as Thyona, with other reluctant brides at the Actors Theatre of Louisville (2000). (Photograph by Richard Trigg.)

company, Mee surrounds Polly and Edward with a motley crew of worka-
day philosophers: Phil, a car mechanic; Bonnie, "a nasty, slatternly girl;"
Shirley, a local librarian; Jim, a guy who likes to have people smash pies in
his face; and Red Dicks, a transvestite beautician who plays the accordion.
Together, they constitute a kind of ersatz chorus for the play, by virtue
of their individual confessions about their sex lives and their collective
identity as a garage band that plays several loud rock-and-roll numbers
over the course of the action. They start off the play milling about the
gas station listening to a down-home radio talk show about love. Bobby,
the program's guest sex expert, strikes an ironic note of erudition when
he lists the various types of love outlined by the ancient Greeks: love
as friendship (philia), benevolence towards guests (senike), mutual attraction of friends (hetairike), "and then sensual love of course, or erotike."
Shirley calls in to the radio show to share her view that love is "the most
factual thing about how you are," and she goes on to elaborate at comic
length on some of the things about a man that make her "weak and shaky
with desire," such as bushy eyebrows, a comforting voice, a hairy chest, or
a certain vulnerability that allows her to hurt him and then care for him
"like a wounded animal."

In this disarmingly amusing way, frank talk about sex is established as
one of the play's main activities. Phil describes a form of "electronic
masturbation" using a low-voltage power source (like an amp), a Casio or
Yamaha synthesizer, and a small electrode inserted into the urethra. "You
can play the 'A above middle C' on the left channel," he says, "and you'll get
some very interesting tingling and throbbing sensations." Moments later,
Polly talks about how much she misses her husband Richard and the way
he holds her in bed at night, and how "touching is just as important for
human beings as eating." This leads to a theoretical disquisition on
the incest taboo and on eros as the feeling that turns a woman into "the
unwilling subject of the uncontrollable, indiscriminate excitement of pure
animal sex." And then, speaking into a microphone, she goes into a hot
sexual fantasy about calling her husband at the office and how "just the
sound of my voice / would make your cock start to swell."

As the play moves forward, the graphic discussion of sexual practices
gets more and more unorthodox, either in a comic vein or a manner that is
more stark and confrontational. One minute the characters will talk about
quirky, funny turn-ons, like sucking somebody's toes or strip-searching a
guy or cutting a hole in a paper plate, putting it over a man's genitals, and
then eating lukewarm spaghetti and meatballs off the plate, and the next
minute, Bonnie will describe how she and her husband "just don't do any

of that vanilla sex any more" because she needed "to be alternately fondled and beaten . . . cuffed and forced to masturbate / until I'm completely humiliated by my own nastiness and / insatiability." Later in the play, Jim talks about committing incest with his daughter from when she was three to age ten, and Phil talks about how when he was a boy his father forced him "to massage his penis with my mouth." Before that, Phil asks Jim if he remembers when "this teacher stuck the fork in your hiney," which leads them to recall how she made her first-graders put peanut butter and jelly on her mouth and eyes and vagina and then lick it off. Jim says, "It was fun. I thought it was funny." And Phil replies, "Of course, you get into an area like this / it's hard to judge."

And that is exactly what the play does: it gets into areas of sexual conduct that are hard to judge. The play invokes a spectrum of sexual behavior that ranges from conventional to playful to adventurous to kinky to abusive to sick to criminal – depending on who you are and where you draw the line. It provokes individual spectators to judge for themselves where the natural, normal expression of eros leaves off and where deviance, perversion, and taboo take over. In Euripides and Seneca, Hippolytus's aura of honorable chastity accentuates the moral fact that Phaedra's love, however human, is illicit, aberrant, and taboo. In contrast, Mee situates Polly's love for Edward in the middle of such a wide range of erotic practice that, despite her pangs of guilt, it does not register as automatically wrong, all the more because Edward, by his own admission no longer a virgin, gets into the backseat of the Lincoln of his own free will. Among the characters onstage and, more important, in the minds of the audience, the play instigates a theatrical symposium on what is true love and what is not. Antiquity's moral absolute is exposed as a relative construct that an individual or a society creates in order to define what it is to be civilized.

This switch from absolute to relative value is what turns *True Love*, despite the violence that ends the play, from tragedy towards comedy in the classical sense of genre. In comedy, a social polity (a family, a coterie or social class, a city-state) is jeopardized by some immoderate character or behavioral force that exceeds the bounds of what is normal, appropriate, and good for that group. From one comedy to another, the threat and the corrective action it triggers may register as transgressive, anarchic, and carnivalesque or as normative, authoritarian, and conservative, but in either case, the social group's prevailing conventions, codes, manners, and values are exercised (that is, given a workout, played around with, tested and reinforced, or granted a momentary holiday). This is what *True Love* does, not through the action of its borrowed tragic plot but through the running commentary of the characters. It exercises ideas about the nature of love and what is normal sexual behavior – without providing the closure of classic comedic form (lovers reconciled and united, weddings afoot, and social pariahs chastened or expelled). The murder-suicide at the play's climax ends up being characterized as a garden-variety crime of passion, sensationalist fodder for radio talk shows and Court TV specials. It is a perfunctory resolution for a borrowed plot that Mee uses to create a theater of public discourse that inquires into how men and women define what it is to be human.

Big Love

Near the end of *True Love*, just before Richard takes out a gun and shoots Polly, he says,

> I remember
> when we went to see the Greek play
> The Danaids
> in the abandoned marble quarry
> and I thought:
> we are connected to this human life
> and to one another
> for all eternity.

In the summer of 1996, Romanian director Silviu Purcarete's reconstruction of Aeschylus's *Les Danaïdes* was performed in an abandoned marble quarry at the Avignon Festival. Mee saw the spectacle, with its dual choruses of fifty women in deep blue and fifty saffron-clad men, and a few years later, when the Actors Theatre of Louisville commissioned him to write a play for the 2000 Humana Festival, he undertook his own version of the Danaids story. *The Suppliant Women*, the only surviving play in the Aeschylus trilogy, was thought for many years to be oldest extant play in the western world,[14] and Mee wanted to mark the new millennium by harkening back to the origins of drama itself. The result was *Big Love*, a comedy about rape.

Aeschylus's *The Suppliant Women* tells the story of the daughters of Danaos, fifty in number and descendants of Io, the long-suffering Argive priestess who, enamored by Zeus, was transformed into a cow by the jealous Hera and then chased by a vicious gadfly across the Near East all the way to Egypt. The play begins with the arrival of the Danaids in a sacred grove outside of Argos. They have fled Egypt and forced marriage to their cousins, the fifty sons of Aegyptus, and returned to their Greek homeland seeking sanctuary from Pelasgos, the Argive king. While Pelasgos consults with the Argive assembly, an Egyptian fleet arrives to reclaim the women, by force if necessary. The play ends with a tense showdown between the Egyptian Herald, who threatens war if the women are not released, and Pelasgos, who rebuffs him and welcomes the Danaids into the city. While the second and third plays of the trilogy – *The Egyptians* and *The Danaids* – have not survived, scholars have delineated a rough, presumptive outline. War breaks out. The Egyptian army defeats the Argive defenses, lays siege to the city, recaptures the unwilling brides, and proceeds with the delayed ceremonies. The Danaid women have no choice but to submit, but under their father's leadership, each one swears an oath to murder her new husband in her wedding bed on the night of the nuptials. The next morning, forty-nine men lay dead, but one of the would-be assassins, Hypermestra, explains that she spared her husband for love. An immediate trial ensues.

The difficulty of executing justice in this matter seems to have provoked the divine intervention of Aphrodite as deus ex machina. One of two substantial fragments from *The Danaids* to survive contains part of a speech explaining a verdict which seems to favor Hypermestra. Aphrodite says:

> Holy heaven longs to pierce the land,
> and longing for marriage seizes the earth. Rain,
> falling from the liquid sky, impregnates earth,
> and she, to benefit mankind, gives birth
> to grass for the herds and to grain, Demeter's gift
> of life. From the showers of this wedding flow
> the seasons when trees bear their flowers and fruits.
> Of all these things I am also the cause.[15]

Thus does the Goddess of Love, mother of Eros according to some myths, seem to enforce the union of earth and sky, female and male, wife and husband, as essential to the continuation of life itself. And thus do classical scholars regard *The Danaids* as Aeschylus's symbolic enactment of the transformation of endogamy from institutionalized rape into a civil (and perhaps spiritual) union mandated by love. Just as the *Oresteia* dramatized the mythic origins of a system of justice based on the code of law and trial by jury, the Danaid trilogy might have depicted the mythic origins of an institution of marriage based on the code of love and perpetual fidelity. In each case, the cessation of tribal violence and the transition from war to peace and, on a broader level, from barbarism to civilization is at stake. This is precisely the liminal moment that has always fascinated Mee, first as a historian and then as a playwright.

Big Love transposes the setting from a sacred grove in Greece to the marbled terrace of a ritzy Mediterranean villa on the coast of present-day Italy. The action begins with the arrival of Lydia, Olympia, and Thyona, three Greek sisters in tattered white satin wedding gowns, wearing sunglasses and lugging suitcases and steamer trunks.[16] Along with their other sisters, fifty of them all told, they have fled the altar and forced marriages to their fifty Greek-American cousins. In the kooky equivalent of the parados in Aeschylus, they proclaim their defiance by stepping center stage and singing Leslie Gore's 1964 hit, "You Don't Own Me." In the moment, the proto-feminist lyrics of this old top-40 record mask the play's serious concern with gender and power with a tongue-in-cheek irony. When the sisters meet Piero, the wealthy and influential owner of the villa, they claim international refugee status, seeking protection from kidnapping and rape and insisting on his moral obligation to embrace their plight. Piero goes off to consider the matter and to attend to his weekend houseguests, and while they await his decision, the deafening sounds of a helicopter overhead announce the arrival of the jilted grooms, Nikos, Oed, and Constantine, who enter wearing high-tech flying helmets and jump suits over their wedding tuxedos.

The brothers have come to enforce their ancient contract and reclaim their brides, against their will, if necessary. In an effort to negotiate a peaceful compromise, Piero invites the men in for a cigar, a glass of something, and a man-to-man talk. Before they go in, Constantine, Thyona's would-be groom, advises her to embrace a more realistic view about the workings of power:

> You say, you don't want to be taken against your will.
> People are taken against their will every day.
> Do you want tomorrow to come?
> Do you want to live in the future?
> Never mind. You can't stop the clock.
> Tomorrow will take today by force
> whether you like it or not.
> Time itself is an act of rape.
> Life is rape.

This is just one of numerous passages in the play that examine the concept of rape in the broader sense of being taken against one's will and subject to the will of a superior force. In a manner similar to *True Love*'s airing of ideas about sexual desire, *Big Love* generates its own quirky, troubling symposium that pushes beyond the reflexive presumption that rape is evil and wrong and prompts consideration of what rape is (and is not) and how it operates on a cultural level.

Giuliano, Piero's debonair and effeminate son, talks to the women at one point about his extensive collection of Barbie and Ken dolls and introduces the paradoxical notion that for some people rape is a choice:

> Some people like to be taken forcibly.
> If that's what they like, then that's okay.
> And if not, then not.
> I myself happen to like it.
> To have somebody grab me.
> Hold me down.
> To know they have to have me
> no matter what.
> It's not everyone's cup of tea.
> Everyone should be free to choose for themselves.

Olympia, who likes to be pampered and to "wear skirts that blow up in the wind," extends this idea when she admits:

> And I myself enjoy the freedom that submission gives me.
> I like to be tickled and tortured
> and I like to scream and scream
> and feel helpless
> and be totally controlled
> and see how good that makes someone else feel.
> It is for me the most natural high.
> It is so much better than taking drugs.
> You can just relax and enjoy yourself
> and feel alive and free inside.

Thyona, leader of the sisters and a vigilant man-hater, is hard-pressed to persuade them that their situation is not a matter of romantic enchantment or consensual submission to another. As she says, "This is about guys hauling you off to their cave."

The most radical and provocative consideration of sexual force comes at the conclusion of a wild sequence in which the three brothers rend their clothes and hurl themselves to the floor again and again as they vent their rage and frustration about how boys are socialized to take on specific gender roles and then punished for it when they play out those roles as men. Their fury spent, they collapse in exhaustion, and then, in a quiet, simple way, Constantine explains that men want to be "good" and "civilized" just as women do, but "when push comes to shove," when an enemy invades your country, raping women and killing children, then everyone wants "a man who can defend his home," "a man who can fuck someone up." This requires nurturing the capacity for violence, which then, in times of peace, a man is expected to put away somewhere "as though he didn't have such impulses" or risk being judged abusive, "despicable," or criminal if he is unable to do so. He goes on to introduce a challenging notion:

and so it may be that when a man turns this violence on a woman
in her bedroom
or in the midst of war
slamming her down, hitting her,
he should be esteemed for this
for informing her
about what it is that civilization really contains
the impulse to hurt side by side with the gentleness
the use of force as well as tenderness
the presence of coercion and necessity
because it has just been a luxury for her really
not to have to act on this impulse or even feel it
to let a man do it for her
so that she can stand aside and deplore it
whereas in reality
it is an inextricable part of the civilization in which she lives
on which she depends

Constantine's long, frighteningly rational monologue concludes with the startling idea that rape "is a gift that a man can give a woman," a gift that enables her "to know the truth of how it is to live on earth" not as a man or a woman but as a human being.

As the action of the play proceeds, this turns out to be "a gift" that the women choose to give in return. When Piero is unable to negotiate a compromise with the men, plans for a compulsory wedding ceremony gather momentum. The sisters debate whether to submit or resist, until Thyona finally persuades the other two that, without a nation to defend them, they must make their own law and kill their husbands. What begins as a traditional cut-the-cake wedding scene erupts in an orgy of violence when the brides pull knives from their garters and attack the grooms (see figure 4, page 75 above). When the bloody mayhem subsides, Lydia is discovered in the arms of her new husband, Nikos, who she has spared out of love. She is immediately placed on trial for betrayal of her promise and her sisters, with Bella, Piero's Old World mother, presiding as judge. In the end, Bella acquits Lydia of all charges, and echoing the Aphrodite fragment from Aeschylus, explains her verdict:

This is why: love trumps all.
Love is the highest law.
It can be bound by no other.
Love of another human being –
man or woman –
it cannot be wrong.

The play ends promptly with Mendelssohn's wedding march, confetti, flashbulbs, and the tossing of the bridal bouquet. This forced note of canonical harmony swells with irony in contrast with all that has come before and the dead bodies strewn about the stage. Love trumps all, but at a cost, and the happy ending is as imposed as that of any deus ex machina in fifth-century Athens. As the honeymoon begins, the uncomfortable question remains how men and women are to live together in a world where civilization is defined as much by war, rape, violence, and the use of blunt force as by the power of love.

In such early, seldom-performed works as *The Constitutional Convention: A Sequel* and *The Imperialists at the Club Cave Canem*, Mee sketched out a theatrical strategy that alternated scenes of spoken dialogue with unscripted performance pieces to be created for the production at hand. Mee's move into remaking Greek tragedy can be seen as a natural next step, since the Greeks originated the structural pattern of alternating rhetorical confrontations between speaking actors with odes that are sung and danced by a chorus. No matter how buried the plot or how chaotic the surface of events in a Mee play, the dialectical rhythm of Greek tragedy remains. Each play has its own choral group – the nurses and patients in *Orestes 2.0*; the women of Troy in part one and Aeneas's men and Dido's women in part two of *The Trojan Women: A Love Story*; Shirley, Bonnie, Jim, Phil, and Red Dicks in *True Love*; and the sister-brides and brother-grooms in *Big Love* – who perform music-and-movement sequences or discursive or lyrical monologues that are the rough equivalent of choral odes. In each case, Mee is explicit in his stage directions in emphasizing that, more than mere interludes, these karaoke numbers, variety acts, dance breaks, fight sequences, pop tunes, performance events, and physical outbursts are equal in importance to the text-based scenes with which they are intermingled. Even though the acts of violence that end these plays function more as musical resolves than resolutions of a narrative conflict, Mee had found his dramaturgical model in the Dionysian spirit and Apollonian form of Greek tragedy.

But, over the course of the 1990s, as Mee went back to the Greeks
again and again, aspects of comedy became more and more pronounced.
Orestes 2.0 is all apocalyptic tragedy at heart, an Expressionist Geschrei
and a dark portrait of civilization run amok. *The Trojan Women: A Love
Story* joins at the hip Euripides's post-war tragedy with a pastoral romance.
The vagaries of love and the differences between men and women,
staples of comedic discourse, surface in the play's borrowed texts and
in the thematic opposition of Troy and Carthage. *True Love* retains
the vestiges of tragedy in its use of the Phaedra myth and its catastrophic
conclusion, but its implicit arbitration of social norms and sexual
behavior belongs more to the world of comedy. And *Big Love* goes one
step further with its outright battle-of-the-sexes plot and compulsory
happy ending, however ironic it may be. While the shift in tone from
dark towards light and in theme from Thanatos towards Eros is far
from absolute over the decade, it does anticipate the binge of unapologetically romantic comedies that Mee would write in the years right
before and after *bobrauschenbergamerica*. For those who had come to
appreciate Mee early on as a kind of theatrical bomb-thrower, an apocalyptic playwright instigating chaotic, dystopic stage events, the eventual
change of stripes was disconcerting.

In the mid 1990s, when Mee was still a relative unknown and commercial web browsers had not yet triggered the explosion of the world wide
web, he began a practice that became a leading edge of his profile as a
playwright. At the time, still dependent on a regular job to support himself
and his family, he was editor-in-chief at Rebus, Inc. (now University
Health Publishing), a publisher of health newsletters and medical reference books for consumers. With the aid and encouragement of his colleague Tom Damrauer, Mee posted three of his plays on the nascent internet,
specifically on a site known as the English Server.[17] By 1996, Damrauer had
helped Mee to launch his own website, which posted the complete texts of
his plays along with the following invitation:

> These pieces for the theatre were taken from the public domain, and
> they are returned to the public domain here. Browsers are encouraged to
> take them, print them, perform them, cut them, add to them, re-make
> them in any way – do freely whatever they want with them.[18]

The website, dubbed "the (re)making project," represented Mee's
Golden Rule: do unto my writing as I have done unto the writing of
others, that is, appropriate material of interest from the culture at large
and make something new and personal and pleasing with it.

This was at first less a call to plagiarism than a populist gesture towards utopian visions of a free and democratic internet. "I'm attracted to the idea of things being owned in common," he said in 1996. "I'm not trying to prescribe. But to me it feels true: the culture is where stuff comes from. I believe in giving it back."[19] Mee's giveaway upload came at a time when peer-to-peer file sharing services (such as the infamous Napster), the increased use of sampling in the popular music industry, and the open source movement were raising new, thorny issues regarding intellectual property rights. In an August 17, 2000 profile on National Public Radio's *All Things Considered*, Mee was credited with "touching a raw cultural nerve" by making his plays available online for free, although he was quick to point out that for a playwright the financial stakes were puny compared to a rap musician or a software programmer.[20] Ironically, as Mee's work gained wider appeal and became trendy to produce, some people took the invitation to steal from his work as license to rewrite or, possibly, censor a play and still present it as his, a practice that led him to reiterate his initial offer in more precise terms:

> Please feel free to take the plays from this website and use them freely as a resource for your own work: that is to say, don't just make some cuts or rewrite a few passages or re-arrange them or put in a few texts that you like better, but pillage the plays as I have pillaged the structures and contents of the plays of Euripides and Brecht and stuff out of Soap Opera Digest and the evening news and the internet, and build your own, entirely new, piece – and then, please, put your own name to the work that results.

By the time it was ten years old, Mee's website was receiving more than 100,000 hits a year. While visitors interested in producing the plays as written are encouraged to contact his agent at International Creative Management, Inc. to secure performance rights, Mee's concern is less proprietary than it is personal. After a decade of experimenting with sticking pieces of found and borrowed text on the scaffold of a classical play, he came to see authorship more and more as a matter of arranging and juxtaposing his chosen materials, often on an affective or intuitive basis. Whatever the mix of old and new, his placement and sequencing of it amounted to his original creation, and for another to rearrange a piece and still call him the author was a misrepresentation. This orientation, while hardly new to Mee at the time of *bobrauschenbergamerica*, became a guiding principle of that piece's creation.

4

SITI: from Toga to "New Toga" and beyond

T HE SITI COMPANY IS THE OFFSPRING OF A THEATRICAL BLIND date. In the summer of 1988, Anne Bogart was part of a small American delegation that traveled to Japan to meet with renowned director Tadashi Suzuki, to speak about their work in the USA, and to experience his summer theater festival in the remote village of Toga-mura. The trip was organized by Peter Zeisler, executive director of the Theatre Communications Group and an early champion of Suzuki's work in the USA. Bogart had just won an Obie, her first, for *No Plays No Poetry*, and she was getting ready in the fall to assume a tenured position on the theater faculty of the University of California–San Diego. The trip to Toga was a professional junket for her, a chance to get back to Japan for the first time since she was a child and to see firsthand what all the fuss was about at Suzuki's utopian mountain hideaway. She had no idea at the time of her invitation that in a few years Suzuki would be looking for an American partner to join in the creation of a satellite operation in the USA, nor, for that matter, just how tempestuous her life would be in the four years before she became that partner.

In what proved to be a small irony of history, Anne Bogart was a little girl living with her family in Tokyo when Tadashi Suzuki was about to start his undergraduate studies across town at Waseda University. Born in 1939, Suzuki grew up in a Japan whose defeat in the Second World War was credited in part to Bogart's grandfather. Her father was part of a lingering US military presence in Japan that alienated much of Suzuki's generation. At Waseda, Suzuki studied political science and economics and was active in campus theater groups. In 1966, he and his student cohorts, including playwright Minoru Betsuyaku (dubbed by some as the Samuel Beckett of Japan), formed the Waseda Little Theatre, one of several upstart groups

86

that comprised Japan's "little theater movement." Similar to concurrent developments in the USA and Europe, Suzuki and his peers wanted to push beyond realism and logocentrism in order to explore avant-garde and actor-centered impulses. He soon began a historic collaboration with actress Kayoko Shiraishi, his leading lady until 1990, whose celebrated performance as a madwoman in *On the Dramatic Passions I* (1969) and *On the Dramatic Passions II* (1970) brought a rush of attention to Suzuki's work at home and abroad. An invitation from Jean-Louis Barrault to participate in the Théâtre des Nations Festival in Paris in 1972 helped to affirm Suzuki's vision of a theater that fused new forms with old traditions, both Japanese and western. In the coming years, he became recognized around the world as a pioneer of interculturalism and one of the world's foremost directors, ranked alongside such international masters as Peter Brook, Ariane Mnouchkine, and Eugenio Barba. In the USA though, his more enduring legacy stems from the rigorous method of actor training that bears his name and from his role in the creation of the SITI Company.

While Suzuki remained a powerful force in Japan well into the twenty-first century, his reputation abroad derives mainly from his pioneering work of the 1970s and 1980s, much of which was performed at the theatrical compound he developed over the years in Toga-mura.[1] Tucked away in the mountains of Toyama Prefecture, Toga's isolation from urban, industrial Japan appealed to Suzuki for numerous reasons. Its bucolic setting – "in the middle of nature, where man can feel free," as he put it – made it necessary to travel some distance to get there, as a tourist or a pilgrim, and then remain for a while before returning home. And there was ample, affordable space on which to develop an extended theater complex. In short, the site suited Suzuki's dream of building a holy theater that served its public as a kind of spiritual retreat, which might produce a new and necessary sense of refreshment. In 1976, the Waseda Little Theatre shifted its base of operations from Tokyo to Toga-mura, eventually reconstituting itself as the Suzuki Company of Toga (SCOT). In partnership with architect Isozaki Arata, Suzuki converted an old farmhouse into a small indoor theater, similar to a *noh* stage; years later, they built an outdoor amphitheater, similar to an Attic stage, that backed onto a small lake with a stunning mountain vista beyond. Noted for its idyllic tranquility, the Toga-mura compound, complete with rehearsal studios, dormitories, and dining facilities, grew to become a destination theater that eventually attracted 10,000 visitors a year. To make full use of this theatrical paradise, Suzuki inaugurated an annual international festival in 1982, which each summer hosted vanguard companies from around the world.

As a young rebel intent on theatrical reform, Suzuki had set out to create a visceral theater that cut across cultural and historical boundaries by borrowing elements from the modern *shingeki*, the traditional *noh* and *kabuki*, and Japanese martial arts and using them to stage pared-down versions of Greek and Shakespearean tragedy and also Chekhov. In a manner that anticipated Mee's method of remaking Greek tragedy, a trilogy of Suzuki adaptations – *The Trojan Women* (1974), *The Bacchae* (1978), and *Clytemnestra* (1983) – interpolated contemporary pop songs and borrowed texts into stripped-down, scrambled versions of the Greek original. These and subsequent productions were shaped by Suzuki's abiding conviction that human existence is a kind of illness and that consciousness of this condition makes the human race akin to a madman trapped in an asylum.[2] Again and again, this metaphor led Suzuki to frame a classic text as the memory, dream, or hallucination of a solitary patient confined in some kind of hospital setting. Inspired by the *noh* concept of *yugen*, he pursued an art of stillness, but a stillness activated by a powerful, underlying "animal energy." To contact this forgotten primal force, he led his actors in experiments with rigorous lower-body movements and exercises that emphasized forceful contact with the ground, on the assumption that "an actor's basic sense of his physicality comes from his feet"[3] (see figure 8, page 119 below). Leon Ingulsrud, a former member of SCOT and subsequent member of SITI, explains Suzuki's orientation as follows:

> The expressiveness of the human body, therefore the expressiveness of the actor, is based on an animal energy, which is something very hot and deep and powerful in an actor. The ability to express with that energy has grown dormant within us. So, the process of training is a process of waking that up. There is a technical core in the training that has to do with control of the center of gravity, control of breath, control of concentration, but all of that is in service of getting that animal energy to happen.[4]

Influenced by forms of walking in *noh* and *kabuki*, Suzuki began to develop what he called "the grammar of the feet." Some of the movements created by Suzuki and his company to wake up their animal energy became the basis for choral movements in their productions, which, in turn, came to provide the basis for rudimentary instruction in what became known as the Suzuki Method of Actor Training (described in detail in chapter 5 and referred to throughout as Suzuki Training, for short, or, where context permits, just Suzuki). Suzuki's landmark production of *The Trojan Women*, featuring Kayoko Shiraishi and two sizeable choruses (one of peasants, the other of Greek soldiers), played a crucial role in this chicken-and-egg evolution. First seen in 1974, *The Trojan Women* was such a tremendous success that it remained in the SCOT repertoire and toured the world off and on until 1990, which meant that each time the play was revived replacements had to be taught the choral sequences. For Suzuki's company in the 1970s, as in the ancient *noh* tradition, this meant that training and performance became co-extensive.

Pockets of the American theater community first became aware of the evolving Suzuki training in the late 1970s. James R. Brandon, the eminent scholar of Asian theater, spent five weeks in Japan in the winter of 1976, researching actor training and participating in Suzuki's evening training sessions with the Waseda Little Theatre. His detailed description of the exercises, plus excerpts from an interview with Suzuki, were published in *The Drama Review*.[5] Suzuki's direct, personal introduction to the USA was facilitated by two Milwaukee institutions, Milwaukee Repertory Theatre, headed by John Dillon and Sara O'Connor, and the University of Wisconsin–Milwaukee (UWM), where Sanford Robbins and Jewel Walker were creating a new professional actor training program. On a trip to Japan to investigate traditional theater training, Robbins met Suzuki, became interested in his methods, and invited his company to come to Milwaukee to perform *The Trojan Women* and to work with UWM acting students. This 1979 visit led to a joint production of *The Bacchae* a year or so later, directed by Suzuki with members of his company and actors in the UWM program. Soon, a small but growing number of American actors were traveling to Japan in the summers to train with SCOT at Toga-mura.[6] Some were cast in Suzuki productions. For example, when Suzuki created his composite tragedy *Clytemnestra* at Toga in 1983, he cast Tom Hewitt in the role of Orestes, making him the only non-Japanese actor in the production.[7] Five years later, in 1988, Hewitt played the title role in *The Tale of Lear*, a revision of his earlier *King Lear* with an all-male, all-American cast, mounted as a joint venture by Milwaukee Repertory Theatre, Arena Stage, Berkeley Repertory Theatre, and StageWest in Springfield, Massachusetts.[8]

Over the course of the 1980s, Suzuki and his company returned to the USA on numerous occasions to lead workshops, teach master classes, and show his productions. *The Trojan Women* was seen in New York in 1982, in Los Angeles at the Olympic Arts Festival in 1984, and in Washington DC in 1985. Theatre Communications Group published a number of his occasional writings under the title *The Way of Acting* in 1986. As his first American disciples became proficient, his training methods were incorporated into a handful of leading Master of Fine Arts acting programs, notably UWM, Juilliard, and University of California–San Diego (UCSD).[9] In 1989, one of Suzuki's protégés, Eric Hill, succeeded Gregory Boyd as artistic director of StageWest in Springfield, Massachusetts, which was already something of a Suzuki outpost in the USA. Hill used Suzuki-trained actors and Suzuki's aesthetics in a number of productions, including a 1991 *Hamlet*, which he staged as "a dream within a dream, taking place in the mind of Horatio, who has withdrawn to a monastery to ponder the meaning of the events he has witnessed and Hamlet's charge to tell posterity his story."[10] The cast of Hill's *Hamlet* included no fewer than five future members of the SITI Company: founding members Kelly Maurer (Hamlet), Ellen Lauren (Gertrude), and Will Bond (Horatio), as well as Stephen Webber (Ghost/Rosencrantz/Gravedigger) and Susan Hightower (Ophelia).[11]

As Suzuki's influence and interest in the resident regional theater grew, he began to think about establishing a base of operations in the USA, partly to provide a place for his American disciples to create work and partly to gain leverage in cultural politics back home in Japan. Various scenarios and possibilities were considered. In the end, with the encouragement of Peter Zeisler, Suzuki turned to Bogart, with whom he had hit it off when she first came to Toga in 1988 and who had returned to Japan in 1990 to visit Suzuki's new theater operation at Art Tower Mito, an elaborate performing and visual arts complex an hour northeast of Tokyo. Suzuki proposed that they combine forces to launch what was promoted as "a new kind of cultural organization." On the rough model of the Toga Festival, it would be part theater company, part training center, part creative think tank, and part international forum, and it would pursue "the growth of individual artists and the development of a new approach to world theater."[12] The arrangement was formalized at a June 1991 meeting between Suzuki and Bogart in New York, during the run of *Dionysus* at the New York International Festival of the Arts. Suzuki left it to Bogart to propose where this new "Institute" might be situated, and she suggested the congenial town of Saratoga Springs, New York, three hours upstate from Manhattan, on the outskirts of the Adirondacks. The town was home to the Saratoga Performing Arts Center, Skidmore College, Yaddo (the artists' colony), the famous Saratoga Race Course, and natural mineral springs that helped to make it a fashionable spa and resort back in America's Gilded Age. After seeing the town and meeting with local officials, Suzuki agreed that it was the right spot, later joking that raising start-up money at home would be easier because Saratoga means "new toga" in Japanese, a name that would have appeal to backers already accustomed to supporting the Suzuki Company of Toga.

And so, in the summer of 1992, Suzuki summoned a number of his devoted followers, Bogart gathered some of her cohorts and the Saratoga International Theater Institute was launched with dual productions based on tragedies by Euripides (see figure 5). Continuing his lifelong meditation on *The Bacchae*, Suzuki revised and restaged a bilingual version of his *Dionysus*, first created with the Acting Company of Mito in 1990.[13] Suzuki's cast included Ellen Lauren (Agave) and Kelly Maurer (in a role called the Reverend Mother), both members at one time of the Mito cast; five other Americans (Jeffrey Bihr, Tom Hewitt, Eric Hill, Tom Nelis, and Scott Rabinowitz); and a dozen Japanese SCOT members. Bogart chose to stage Mee's version of *Orestes*, a distinctly American take on the Greeks that counterbalanced Suzuki's Japanese vision. In addition to the seven American actors in *Dionysus*, her cast also included Will Bond, Joseph Haj, Susan Hightower, Tina Shepard, and Regina Byrd Smith. Both productions rehearsed in Japan and were performed at the Toga Festival that summer, before coming to Saratoga Springs in September to inaugurate the Saratoga International Theater Institute. The occasion was marked by a symposium titled "A Theater Towards the 21st Century," weekend workshops in Composition taught by Bogart, and a three-week course led by Suzuki. Nobody knew how long it would last or what exact form it would take, but the Saratoga International Theater Institute – SITI, for short – was up and running.[14]

Much of the inaugural year's activities were financed through Suzuki's auspices. His role as senior partner in the founding of the Saratoga International Theater Institute was crucial, but his direct involvement in the organization tapered off over the next few years. In the summer of 1993, a smaller group of five actors joined Bogart in Toga-mura to create the fledgling company's first original work, *The Medium*. On the model of the first year, it was presented first in Toga-mura and then in Saratoga Springs in September, along with Suzuki's production of *The Tale of Lear* and a single showing of his *Waiting for Romeo*, an anthology piece about a woman who imagines she is Juliet, created for Lauren out of texts drawn from Shakespeare, Chekhov, and Beckett. In its third summer, Bogart and an ensemble of five created and performed *Small Lives/Big Dreams* at the Toga Festival in Japan, but no Suzuki production came with it to upstate New York in the fall. And in its fourth summer, the Saratoga International Theater Institute stayed at home and developed *Going, Going, Gone* at

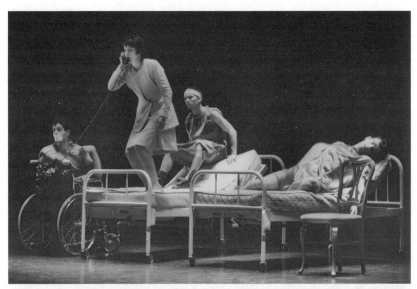

Figure 5. Euripides times two: the first SITI summer (1992). (a) Bogart's production of *Orestes 2.0*, with Ellen Lauren as Electra, Will Bond (behind her) as William, Joseph Haj as Tapemouth Man (left), and Richard Thompson as Orestes (right). (b) Suzuki's production of *Dionysus*, with Ellen Lauren as Agave and Eric Hill as Cadmus. (Photographs by Clemens Kalischer.)

Skidmore, before taking it to Toga in 1996. The nascent company's artistic home had shifted from East to West, from Toga to "New Toga."

Of the dozen American actors who performed in *Orestes* and *Dionysus* in the first summer of the Saratoga International Theater Institute, four – Will Bond, Ellen Lauren, Kelly Maurer, and Tom Nelis – stuck together and stuck with Bogart to form the nucleus of the SITI Company. Only Nelis had been recruited by Bogart. She directed him in 1989 in her *Strindberg Sonata* at UCSD, where he was an MFA acting student (and where the professional training included Suzuki work), and in 1991 in the En Garde Arts production of *Another Person is a Foreign Country*. The other three core actors had trained with Suzuki and worked together – and with artistic director Eric Hill – at StageWest for years. Lauren and Hill were company members at the Milwaukee Repertory Theatre and Maurer was a graduate student at UWM when Suzuki first came to Milwaukee. They were among the first to make regular sojourns to Toga-mura to train with SCOT. When Maurer left Milwaukee to teach at the University of Pittsburgh and act with the City Theatre there, she met Bond and introduced him to the work; before long, he was spending summers in Toga as well.

Other members who came to the SITI Company via the Suzuki path include Leon Ingulsrud, Akiko Aizawa, and Stephen Webber. Born and raised in Japan, the son of Lutheran missionaries from the USA, Ingulsrud first met Suzuki in 1987 in Minneapolis and joined the SCOT company within a year, initially as Suzuki's assistant on his American version of *King Lear*. He was very much involved in the discussions that led to establishing the Saratoga International Theater Institute; in 1993, he left SCOT to study with Bogart at Columbia and eventually to join SITI as a teacher, an assistant director, and an occasional director and actor. Aizawa, a native of Japan, was also a member of SCOT before moving to the USA in 1996 to join the SITI Company. After an acting internship at the Milwaukee Repertory Theatre, Webber trained and worked at StageWest with Maurer, Bond, and Lauren, and on their recommendation, Bogart invited him to join the group, starting, in effect, with his taking over a role in *The Medium* in early 1995.

Other actors recruited by Bogart became important members of the company. Karenjune Sanchez and Jefferson Mays, both of whom Bogart first met at UCSD and subsequently cast in other productions, joined the company in the summer of 1994 to create *Small Lives/Big Dreams*. Vital members of the group in its formative years, each of them moved on in the late 1990s for personal and professional reasons. Barney

O'Hanlon studied as an undergraduate with Bogart at New York University where he appeared in her 1986 production of *Danton's Death*; he spent the tempestuous year at Trinity Repertory Company with her, performed in *American Vaudeville* at the Alley in 1992, and then, in his first SITI Company appearance, took over a role in *Small Lives/Big Dreams* in early 1995. His special interest in movement and dance led him to become SITI's resident choreographer. J. Ed Araiza first worked with Bogart on her *Picnic* at the Actors Theatre of Louisville and joined the SITI actors when he took over a role in *The Medium* when it ran in June 1994 at the New York Theatre Workshop (NYTW), marking the company's New York City debut.

SITI began as a summertime enterprise with an uncertain future and an amorphous identity, but as strong relationships developed between Bogart and her actors and outside support for their work grew, the effort to form more of a year-round company gathered steam. Following the NYTW run of *The Medium*, SITI augmented the annual Summer Intensive in Saratoga Springs with fall and spring training sessions in New York, which continued and expanded over the next decade. From its base in Manhattan, the fledgling company was able to form connections around the country with both presenting organizations, such as the Wexner Center for the Arts at Ohio State University, and producing theaters, chief among them the Actors Theatre of Louisville (ATL). ATL was for years a mainstay for Bogart, who directed Eduardo Machado's *In the Eye of the Hurricane* for the Humana Festival there in 1991 and William Inge's *Picnic* in late 1992. In January 1995, Bogart was the celebrated focus of ATL's first-and-only Modern Masters Festival, which included showings of *The Medium* and *Small Lives/Big Dreams*, Bogart's new production of *The Adding Machine*, plenary speakers, a colloquium, an exhibit, a workshop with members of the SITI Company, a lecture-demonstration on the Viewpoints, and a book about Bogart with contributions from a number of her collaborators. For the next seven years, Bogart returned to ATL on an annual basis either to premiere an original SITI creation at the Humana Festival (*Going, Going, Gone* in 1996; *Cabin Pressure* in 1999; *War of the Worlds* in 2000; *bobrauschenbergamerica* in 2001; *Score* in 2002) or to present a fresh twist on a venerable classic (*Miss Julie* in 1997; *Private Lives* in 1998; *Hay Fever* in 2002).

In addition to providing an "artistic home" away from home for Bogart and the company, ATL also was the source of several key long-term SITI personnel. After stage managing Bogart's ATL production of *The Adding Machine*, Megan Wanlass-Szalla became SITI's company stage manager for the next five years and then its managing director, lending much-needed stability to the administrative side of the organization. Darron West was ATL's resident sound designer when Bogart started directing there. With *Picnic* in 1992 and *The Medium* in 1993, they initiated an unusual director–designer collaboration that had West in rehearsal on a daily basis, helping to shape the production and building up the sound design on an organic, gradual, trial-and-error basis rather than coming in during technical rehearsals and laying down cues on top of what the actors had rehearsed. While Bogart tends to work with the SITI Company's set, costume, and lighting designers in a more or less conventional manner, West's unique rehearsal-room partnership with her and the SITI performers – functioning in part as fellow actor, co-director, dramaturg, as well as designer of intricate "soundscapes" – is one thing that makes the company's work distinct and remarkable.

While the 1992 production of Mee's *Orestes* marked the official beginning of the Saratoga International Theater Institute, what would soon be named the SITI Company was forged in the crucible of their first three original creations: *The Medium, Small Lives/Big Dreams*, and *Going, Going, Gone*. With these works, Bogart was able to refine a method of creating new work that she had been experimenting with for years. That method can be traced all the way back to the Ionesco miscellany that she staged in her senior year at Bard, the first in a series of pieces composed of excerpts gathered from a variety of textual sources and held together by a web of music, movement, and design. She made works based on individual playwrights (Inge, Strindberg) or eras of American culture (*1951, American Vaudeville*). In the two pieces she made with Via Theater, she turned to theory for source material, basing *No Plays No Poetry* on Brecht's ruminations about theater and *Behavior in Public Places* on the sociological writing of Erving Goffman. With *The Medium*, based on the philosophy of media espoused by Marshal McLuhan, Bogart continued this focus on theory and initiated the SITI Company's investigation of important twentieth-century cultural figures, many of them American.

For a while, Bogart referred to this work as "Essay Theater."[15] She identified a field of inquiry, conceived a new piece around "a theory or theories about a certain aspect of life," conducted research and collected data, established certain parameters or ground rules for manipulating the assembled raw material, and then worked with her collaborators to shape theatrical metaphors that somehow expressed the ideas at the heart of the piece. As this method evolved, each new essay was defined by three givens:

(1) a question or set of questions, which articulated the nature of the inquiry, its focus and its curiosity; (2) an anchor, usually an important real-life cultural figure who was seen to embody the question; and (3) a structure, a familiar type of event that was used as a means to organize and arrange performance materials pertinent to the question and the anchor. These three nodal elements established a contained field for the project, within which the actors operated with tremendous creative latitude.

The Medium

Bogart's first SITI theater essay, *The Medium*, focused on the impact of television, the personal computer, and other electronic media on contemporary life: "How is the new technology changing us psychologically? How is it changing our relationships? How is it changing our art? Can we describe the future?"[16] With these starting questions in mind, Bogart found an appropriate anchor in the figure of Marshal McLuhan (1911–80), the Canadian thinker who stirred controversy in the 1960s with his sweeping pronouncements on the effects of media and technology on society. McLuhan prophesied the end of a dominant, centuries-old print-oriented culture (what he called "the Gutenberg Galaxy") and the beginning of "the global village," a new electronic age which returned to a more tribal culture, but on a planetary scale. A popular public speaker in his heyday, he suffered a series of strokes late in life and lost his capacity for speech. Taking this as her conceptual point of departure and as a metaphor for the abrupt changes in communication wrought by electronic media, Bogart expanded the traumatic moment of a stroke into a ninety-minute excursion through the suddenly shuttered mind of McLuhan, configured as a vast television wasteland through which he channel-surfs with the aid of a remote control. The piece was composed of a series of segments, each of which was based on a familiar genre of television program (newscast, talk show, sitcom, game show, western, cooking show, televangelist, variety show, and so on), except that, instead of the well-worn clichés of television dialogue, the actors spoke portentous epigrams from the writings of McLuhan or samplings from more recent high-tech magazines like *Wired* (see figure 6).

In the original production, Tom Nelis represented the figure of McLuhan as a vaudevillian pitchman, who kept repeating telltale lines such as "What's that buzzing?" and "You don't like those ideas? I've got others!" as he careened from one television frequency to another.[17] Sound designer Darron West created his first "soundscape" for a SITI production,

Figure 6. Channel-surfing: *The Medium*. Will Bond as McLuhan with Ellen Lauren at the Actors Theatre of Louisville's Modern Masters Festival (1995). (Photograph by Richard Trigg.)

making memorable use of an array of television jingles and sound effects, as well as Dionne Warwick's recording of the theme song from *Valley of the Dolls*. In creating the manic, warped television segments, the cast of five actors used a highly physical, hyperkinetic movement style variously described by reviewers as "a jerky, robotic ballet" (Brantley), "automaton-like" (Jacobson), and "as if they are stuck on a high-speed carousel, incapable of stopping" (Milvy).[18] "Like a piece of minimalist music" Fintan O'Toole wrote, *The Medium* "loops around itself, depending on rhythm and hypnotic repetition rather than on action or dialogue. Nothing moves forward, because, in the enervated, neurotic world it describes, there is no such direction."[19]

The Medium introduced what would become signature traits of the SITI Company's work: the triadic conceptual strategy of question-anchor-structure; the layering in performance of three quasi-independent texts (verbal/textual, physical/gestural, and visual/aural); a non-linear approach to theatrical time and space; and, most important, a rigorous, precise, and choreographic approach to movement on stage. Bogart staged her high-tech meditation in an intentionally low-tech fashion, eschewing the use of video, projections, and other mediated effects (except for sound) in favor of concentrating the action in the physicality of the performers. By anecdotal accounts, *The Medium* was so exhausting in its non-stop aerobic activity that on certain nights steam could be seen rising off the actors' bodies under the hot stage lights. On a thematic level, this Grotowskian physicality asserted raw corporal being against what McLuhan called "the discarnate body" of the electronic future. From a broader perspective, it heralded the abiding and pre-eminent value of the SITI Company's work: the shared, unmediated, aesthetic transaction between highly trained actors and an audience willing to go with the flow and see where it takes them. *The Medium* reached a climax with McLuhan's tortured, stroke-impeded effort to utter the epigram that was, in effect, its moral: "There is no inevitability as long as there is a willingness to contemplate what is happening." This sentence might be taken as the watchword for all of Bogart's theater essays and for the work of the SITI Company as a whole. In its rigor and its zeal, it demands the willingness to contemplate what is happening onstage. McLuhan's most famous and fundamental idea – "the medium is the message" – argued that human societies are shaped more by the *forms* of communication than by their explicit content. The SITI Company's first original creation announced that, whatever the express topic of each new theater essay, it was always also an inquiry into the medium of theater itself.

Small Lives/Big Dreams

Bogart conceived *Small Lives/Big Dreams* as a companion piece to *The Medium*. If *The Medium* contemplated the future, this next piece focused on the past and the question of memory: "Why should we remember the past? Is it true that if we are unable to remember our past, we have no future? If we lose our memory, will we lose our humanity?"[20] The anchor for these questions was Anton Chekhov, not the playwright himself but his five full-length plays. In a manner that echoed Bogart's earlier 'playwright collages,' *Small Lives/Big Dreams* was constructed wholly from material taken from *Ivanov*, *The Seagull*, *Uncle Vanya*, *Three Sisters*, and *The Cherry Orchard*. These texts were distributed in a particular fashion: each of the five actors in the piece personified one of the five major plays, as if the play itself was a character, and spoke only lines sampled from that play.[21] The structure for this anchor, logically enough, was the symphonic four-act structure of a Chekhov play, with its internal rhythms of arrival and departure spanned by other social rituals in between.

In Chekhov, such events take place in the realistic context of a provincial Russian estate, some of whose idealistic inhabitants suffer the melancholy of their own obsolescence and yearn for millennial change. In a decidedly abstract manner, the five characters of *Small Lives/Big Dreams* came together as motley wayfarers on an undefined road to nowhere, traveling in a loose procession, survivors of an unknown apocalypse that keeps happening over and over, sending them into violent convulsions with each aftershock (see figure 7). They have little or no memory of who they are and only a smattering of objects – artifacts of identity such as a clock, a pair of shoes, a silver teapot, a framed picture of a dog, or a picnic basket – to give them clues about where they came from.[22] At first, they barely acknowledged each other, speaking past one another in a manner that was unnatural, disjunctive, aphasic. They seemed to orbit in parallel universes, beyond each other's reach, but as the play moved through its four movements, they achieved a superficial contact and a momentary society, taking tea, putting on a play, posing for a group photograph, as if they might start civilization over again from scratch. At moments, they even seemed to regain the capacity for memory, but any sense of progress was superseded by a cycle of perpetual repetition as the action, as in *The Medium*, looped back around on itself again and again, like an old record player whose needle is stuck in one groove. In the end, as in Chekhov, there was a prolonged leave-taking and the echo of emptiness.

The three interwoven texts of *Small Lives/Big Dreams* – sound, speech, and movement, each one out of kilter – used the musical form of a fugue to capture the dissociative psychic condition of a fugue state. The fugue uses multiple voices in complex counterpoint, that is the interaction of the five Chekhov plays, to articulate and reiterate a basic theme, in this case the selective amnesia and wandering from home, often in response to trauma or extreme stress, that characterizes a fugue state. The result was a dense, evocative tone poem, suggestive of Beckett, an elegy for a lost world, which in its formalism was impenetrable to some, "reductionist" to others, and, for Alisa Solomon of the *Village Voice*, "the most emotional Bogart production I've ever seen, pulsating with mourning, yearning, the refusal of futility."[23] As the SITI Company's second original creation, *Small Lives/ Big Dreams* affirmed its willingness to make dense, abstruse work shaped by elaborate, veiled metaphors and complex musical structures. Its focus on memory, lost and found, extended to Bogart's work with the SITI Company her ongoing project of reconstructing the past, be it a theatrical tradition, a historical event, or an important figure from a different era.

Figure 7. Lost in space: *Small Lives/Big Dreams* (1995) and *Going, Going, Gone* (1997) at the Actors Theatre of Louisville. (a) Kelly Maurer, Will Bond, and J. Ed Araiza as three plays of Chekhov (from left to right). (b) Tom Nelis and Ellen Lauren as cosmic hosts (left) and Karenjune Sanchez and Stephen Webber as their guests (right). (Photographs by Richard Trigg.)

Going, Going, Gone

If *The Medium* and *Small Lives/Big Dreams* were about time and the problem of the future or the past, *Going, Going, Gone* was about space, on both an intimate and a cosmic scale. Inspired by a *New York Times Sunday Magazine* article that "suggested that an understanding of quantum physics is an important part of living in our modern world," Bogart situated the play on an almost bare stage that was "a living room that is also the entire universe." It contained a white sofa and a shiny cocktail cart on wheels with an ice bucket and decanters of brightly colored liquors. The outline of a white square on the shiny black floor demarcated the playing area, and two tall poles strung on guy wires indicated a doorway. This simple space suggested both a domestic interior and a closed system. Characters identified only as Man and Woman entered this field, accompanied by sound effects that made it seem as if they had penetrated a sonic barrier or entered another dimension. Man fixed drinks, and the couple interacted in a naturalistic manner, except for one strange thing: their casual dialogue was composed of dense theoretical statements concerning quantum mechanics, microphysics, cosmogony, and the nature of the universe. A few minutes later, two Guests, male and female, arrived, and as the four adults settled into a cozy, late-night cocktail party, the sexual energy between them started to build. Woman, an obvious lush, flirted with the male guest, if only to get a rise out of Man. The female guest giggled and stumbled about like a co-ed at a fraternity party. As the couples got inebriated, the conversation grew more animated, sexier, and eventually confrontational, even though it was comprised all the while of exchanges like "There can be no energy without mass," "Nature abhors a vacuum," and "To observe is to disturb."

Eventually, for many in the audience, the parallels with Edward Albee's *Who's Afraid of Virginia Woolf?* became too conspicuous to ignore. And, indeed, the actors were going through the motions of Albee's classic while speaking their anthology of scientific quotations. The tension between the surface talk about wormholes, quarks, neutrinos, and entropy and the ferocious byplay of the Albee text expanded and contracted in a manner that sounded silly one moment and astonishingly apt the next, generating a wave pattern that ultimately triggered its own theatrical Big Bang. Even for those who did not make the connection, Albee's three-act progression from "Fun and Games" to "Walpurgisnacht" to "The Exorcism" lent a coherence and an intensity to the action that the literal words did not convey. The guests and hosts interacted more and more like charged particles in a sealed environment, until the 'George' figure finally got rough with 'Martha,' who responded by launching into a long opaque story using verses from Genesis. Unable to withstand her "blasphemous" verbal assault, he stepped out of the white square, violating the fourth wall as if he was rupturing some invisible membrane. At that point, the onstage universe imploded – sofa, drinks cart, door, even the white outline on the floor all disappeared; 'Honey' and 'Nick' left – leaving Man and Woman dancing in the dark to the twinkle of a thousand stars, as Mel Torme crooned the Cole Porter lyric, "When an irresistible force such as you / Meets an old immovable object like me / You can bet as sure as you live / Something's gotta give, something's gotta give, / Something's gotta give."

As staged by Bogart and performed by Tom Nelis, Ellen Lauren, Stephen Webber, and Karenjune Sanchez, the fusion of Albee with theoretical physics released a strange and stunning energy (see figure 7, page 100 above). Anyone who saw *Going, Going, Gone* – or, for that matter, *edium* or *Small Lives/Big Dreams* – and sought its rationale in the exchange of conversational dialogue or a clear, linear narrative was disappointed, confused, and, in some cases, irritated. All three of these pieces were predicated on what I would call the Bogart Inversion, which takes the surface action of a conventional drama – be it a single play like *Who's Afraid of Virginia Woolf?*, the archetypal action of a Chekhov play, or the formulaic structure of stereotypical television shows – and makes it the subtext or scaffolding for an original creation whose seemingly random surface text pertains to quantum physics or memory loss or information theory. Bogart herself has compared the experience of seeing her plays to watching a foreign film with no subtitles, suggesting that things will make little sense until the viewer stops trying to figure out the logic of what the characters are saying and pays attention to what they are doing. If you watch *Going, Going, Gone* with your fingers in your ears, the story is fairly apparent. If you take them out and let the language sink in, without being in a rush to "get it," the convergence of text, image, and movement generate strong impressions and visceral responses, positive and negative alike. In this way, Bogart regards a play on stage as something akin to the observer-created reality of quantum mechanics and expects members of the audience to assume an active role in its composition, extending to them a freedom comparable to her other collaborators.

In May 1997, the SITI Company experimented with producing its own work, with all the added responsibilities and financial risks which that entails; they mounted their "Miller season" in New York, showings of *The Medium*, *Small Lives/Big Dreams*, and *Going, Going, Gone* at the Miller

Theater on the campus of Columbia University. That fall, at the City Theatre in Pittsburgh, the SITI Company debuted their fourth original creation, *Culture of Desire*, a fractured meditation on American consumerism refracted through the Pop celebrity of Andy Warhol and undergirded by Dante's *Inferno*. While initial plans to collaborate with Chuck Mee on the piece did not work out, affinities between their aesthetic strategies around this time are apparent. Bogart's use of Albee, Chekhov, or Dante as a subtextual structure or frame as the basis for organizing an assortment of thematically related quotations parallels Mee's re-making of Greek tragedies by pinning borrowed passages on the bulletin board of their mythic actions. Both artists reject Newtonian notions of cause and effect in favor of a principle of explosive simultaneity, one that is tinged with millennial anxiety. Moving into and through the 1990s, both Mee's and Bogart's bodies of work featured images of cataclysm and catastrophe: an exploding corpse and an outbreak of revolution in *The Investigation of the Murder in El Salvador*; the First World War, a self-destructing Rube Goldberg machine, and the night before the first atomic bomb test in *The War to End War*; Orestes's mania and violent fight back in *Orestes*; the aftermath of war in the first half of *Trojan Women: A Love Story*; the murder-suicide that ends *True Love*; the idea of rape and the action of forty-nine brides slaughtering forty-nine brothers in *Big Love*; McLuhan's stroke in *The Medium*; the mysterious apocalypse in *Small Lives/Big Dreams*; the psychological savagery and implied Big Bang of *Going, Going, Gone*; and, in *Culture of Desire*, Valerie Solanas's assassination attempt on Andy Warhol. These plays are about other things as well, but the preponderance of entropy and ruin in them, juxtaposed with outbursts of manic energy, makes the happier themes, more upbeat tone, and vein of nostalgia of Mee and Bogart's eventual collaboration on *bobrauschenbergamerica* all the more conspicuous.

Over the course of the 1990s, the network of interest in the SITI Company widened to include such cities as Pittsburgh, Columbus, Chicago, Minneapolis, and San Francisco, which meant that once a piece premiered at a host institution, sometimes with the aid of a commission, the company could add it to their repertoire and tour it to performing arts centers and theater festivals around the country and abroad. (See appendix B for a production history.) When they traveled, company members often taught workshops or master classes, and as interest in their training methods grew, they began to travel more and more for that express purpose. Each summer, the company returned to Saratoga Springs to teach, to develop new work, and to re-work or perform established pieces. An annual rhythm evolved that enabled the company to grow while accommodating Bogart's teaching duties at Columbia and the need for others to work outside in order to make ends meet. In the process, the company developed a rhythm for generating new pieces that can be demarcated by three loose phases: (1) a lengthy and sometimes leisurely period of research and preparation; (2) sporadic periods of delay, interruption, and diversion that shift attention elsewhere; and (3) a short, intense period during which the piece is composed in rehearsal from the ground up for a premiere that is only a few weeks away.

During the initial preparatory phase, Bogart and an ad hoc team of researchers and dramaturgs collect large quantities of material pertaining to a given subject and then narrow it down to a bible of miscellaneous ideas, quotations, and extended passages that might go into the text of the piece. This "source-work," as it is sometimes called, provides fodder for exercises in Composition, preliminary sketches of possible scenes or performance sequences, created in workshop by members of the company or by students training with the company during the month-long Summer Intensive in Saratoga Springs. This brainstorming period often gives way to a hiatus in the work as the completion of other projects or a tour of finished work takes precedence. Whatever the impetus, this interim period, busy with other activities, is a crucial period of gestation, assimilation, and lack of direct attention. Individual collaborators have a chance to develop their own personal perspective or understanding of the subject at hand, free, for the moment, from the pressure to create something out of it or even to articulate their response to it.

Then, as the official rehearsal period approaches, more active work resumes. The design process gets underway. Additional research is done as needed. And table-work sessions are held to dissect the text line by line, or, lacking a text as of yet, to hash out what that text might contain. Finally, working full-time for a few weeks, the company goes into the rehearsal room and creates the piece on their feet, bit by bit, at a remarkably fast rate. Daytime rehearsals are used to generate material, if only to put *something* onstage for the being, and then, later, in conversation walking home or over a drink in the bar at night, the day's work is mulled over and new ideas emerge. As the piece, not quite finished, moves into technical rehearsals and opening night looms, the company shifts into overdrive, like adrenalin junkies in a high-stakes game of beat-the-clock. One day merges into the next, nerves fray, and sometimes, a marathon rehearsal – referred to by some as "SITI Company triage" – is needed to sort things out and make final decisions about what material should be 'rescued' and kept in the show and what should be left by the wayside. Depending on the company's satisfaction with the results, the finished piece is revised or tweaked before it moves on to be shown at a second or third venue.

In more recent years, with the company's success, this creative cycle has been complicated and enhanced by the fact that projects overlap and completed work remains in the repertoire. For example, here is a rough outline of the SITI Company's activities for the 2003 calendar year. In January and February, much of the company was in Cambridge, Massachusetts at the American Repertory Theatre rehearsing and performing a production of Marivaux's *La Dispute*, for which preliminary work was done during the 2002 Summer Intensive. In April, the company conducted a three-week workshop to continue development of a company-generated piece to be called *systems/layers*, which eventually premiered at Utah State University in September 2004. In May, the company spent two weeks at the White Oak Dance Plantation in Florida workshopping a piece about the Group Theatre to be called *Reunion*, which was the basis for compositions in the 2001 Summer Intensive. In June, the company retreated to their summer home in Saratoga Springs for the 2003 Summer Intensive, where work continued on *systems/layers* and the students made compositions based on *A Midsummer Night's Dream*, which Bogart went on to direct with the company at San Jose Repertory Theatre in early 2004. In August, a dozen company members joined Bogart at the Los Angeles Opera, where she directed the world premiere of Deborah Drattell's opera, *Nicholas and Alexander*, with Mstislav Rostropovich conducting and Plácido Domingo as Rasputin. In October, the company remounted *bobrauschenbergamerica* for the Brooklyn Academy of Music's Next Wave Festival. Also in the fall, *Score* and *War of the Worlds: Radio Play* were revived for limited tours to college campuses. And discussions were already under way for a number of future projects, including a production of the medieval play *Death and the Ploughman* and a new collaboration with Charles Mee around the work of artist Joseph Cornell.

In one calendar year, no fewer than ten SITI projects were in some active stage of development or performance, and that did not include other activities, such as fall and spring training sessions in New York, a summer workshop in Los Angeles, guest classes around the country, or teaching, performing, and design work conducted outside of the company (such as Ellen Lauren's continuing work with Tadashi Suzuki or Tom Nelis's stint as Pharaoh in the Disney *Aida* on Broadway). The company keeps busy, and even though not every SITI member is involved with every project, this means that in its life, from a spark of inspiration in Bogart's head to the last cue called by stage manager Elizabeth Moreau, each project overlaps with many others. In this regard, one piece interpenetrates another, influences it in the process of development, and informs it in retrospective analysis, fortifying the sense that the company has created a body of work, one that needs therefore to be seen as layered in several ways.

Even as the life spans of SITI creations are layered on top of each other, the creation of each new piece is characterized by a strategy of layering. First, the pattern of sustained preparation for a year or two and then quick creation in a matter of weeks amounts to a matter of building up a piece by layers, laying in one substratum after another so that the final product has both deep, sturdy roots and the feeling of a spontaneous event. Second, as mentioned, the piece itself will often combine three different continuities – a verbal, spoken text; a physical text of movement and gesture; and a design text of sound, light, music, and visuals – which maintain a measure of independence as they overlap, interweave, and sometimes crash into each other. This postmodern strategy harkens back to the experimental collaborations of John Cage and Merce Cunningham, some of which were joined by Robert Rauschenberg. Third, on any given day in rehearsal, the company will use a layering technique to rough out and build up a new scene. That is, an actor, or two, will introduce and establish a movement phrase, a physical action, perhaps a piece of text, some simple pattern. Another actor will join in, repeating the initial phrase and then elaborating on it, or sampling just a part of it and going off in a different direction. Others will jump in, extending what others have started, often with variation or counterpoint, until a spontaneous polyphonic composition is under way that yields ideas or performance material or the nugget around which a scene is constructed.

This strategy of accumulation – of building up layer by layer, and, quite often, building back 'down' to the initial phrase, perhaps in some fundamentally altered form – has roots in minimalism in postmodern music, most conspicuously Philip Glass, and in the structured improvisations of postmodern dance, such as the Accumulation pieces created in the early-1970s by Trisha Brown. One of the principal achievements of Bogart and the SITI Company has been their adaptation of these arithmetic structures of addition and subtraction to the manipulation of theatrical time and space. Among other effects, it has assured the primacy of performance as the organizing principle and bedrock of their work. This means that their original creations, from *The Medium* forward, need to be experienced, understood, and judged on the basis of performance, like a dance or a concerto, even though they may include extensive verbal texts that sometimes trigger conventional expectations about plot and character. And it means that their productions of plays based on those conventions – Shakespeare, Marivaux, Strindberg, Coward – gain a visceral immediacy that enlivens or subverts or refreshes what might seem old or familiar.

What this introduction to the SITI Company cannot begin to capture is the growing pains, the personal sacrifices, the ups and downs, the moments of doubt, the epiphanies and triumphs of the moment, the money problems, the emotional crises, the management crises, the breakthroughs, breakdowns, and breakups that marked the true evolution of the company. Nor is it easy to pinpoint a moment when its staying power was proven and its survival assured. There is little doubt, however, about what enabled them to stick together over the years: a fervent belief and abiding commitment to the ideal of company. They are quick to point out that in the cultural climate of the USA, where most professional theater is made by virtual strangers working together on a short-term basis, having a theater company amounts to a political act. The power of a group of individual artists working together over time with a shared vision and a common vocabulary makes things possible that can happen no other way. Over the years, Bogart and the members of the company found their own ways to create work, to give and take, to trust each other, to make sacrifices, to settle differences, to love each other's quirks and idiosyncrasies, and just to be together that enabled them to stay focused on the greater good, which is both the specific work at hand and, more generally, the health and continuance of the company. Many of them speak of the company as a kind of family, and they experience their bonds with each other as just as irrevocable as blood ties. In moments of crisis (and the group has weathered its fair share), the company bond has been a beacon in the storm and, at the same time, the source of much anguish. In better times, it is the basis for the rarest of joys: a communion in art and life.

5

SITI: the trainings
(Suzuki, Viewpoints, Composition)

WHEN ANNE BOGART AND TADASHI SUZUKI JOINED FORCES TO create the Saratoga International Theater Institute, two approaches to actor training came together that few would have thought compatible at the time. The Suzuki Method of Actor Training is pure, hard work. Its rigorous physical disciplines test a performer's will and stamina. By virtue of its improvisational nature, Anne Bogart's Viewpoints has an element of play, as does the collective approach to creating theater known as Composition. Prior to 1992, each of these practices existed independently of the other two, and they continue to be taught independently in the USA and around the world. But their combination as a system of actor training and the bedrock for an extensive body of work is unique to the SITI Company, which has demonstrated again and again, in the work of their students and in the work they put on stage, the powerful synergy of the two approaches. The two are not fused into one; they are taught side by side, establishing a kind of synaptic gap that asks to be bridged by the individual actor, who in the process must take increased responsibility for what he or she does, in mastering the work or in creating a performance. The SITI actors are adamant in their advocacy and disciplined in their practice of perpetual training, pointing out that, unlike dancers at the barre or musicians practicing scales, few actors engage in continuing training as a matter of professional routine. When the company teaches workshops in Suzuki and Viewpoints, they train along with their students. When they are in rehearsal or performance, they begin each session with "training," a half hour or more of Suzuki and Viewpoints work. The trainings in tandem aim to develop – and *maintain* – performers with a powerful and dynamic presence, even in stillness or when doing 'nothing' on stage, so that their work commands attention through its energy, focus, interest, and truthfulness. The goal is to be, in a word, undismissible.

Before outlining these three disciplines in detail, a few caveats are in order. First, the Suzuki and Viewpoints work are overwhelmingly physical in nature, and like any knowledge that lives in the body, their verbal articulation can only be an approximation of the corporal truth. I write here as an observer, not a practitioner, of these disciplines, and with an eye more towards how they generate and inform performances, particularly *bobrauschenbergamerica*, than towards how they influence and benefit individual performers. Second, the SITI training is a culture, and like any culture, it is defined by a slow but steady process of change. The company is in constant dialogue about what they teach and how, and a written account such as this runs the risk of making things sound more fixed and formulaic than they are. For example, for years, only certain SITI members taught Suzuki, while others taught only Viewpoints, but in 2001, fear of ghettoizing the training prompted the company to switch things around, so that everyone would come to teach both. As the teaching artists evolve and mature, so, too, does the training. Third, like any new methodology with growing popularity, the Viewpoints and Suzuki work have been met by misunderstanding, bastardization, pockets of controversy, internecine disagreement, and informed criticism.[1] A thorough study of these trainings is needed, one that might take full account of Mary Overlie's continuing theorization and practice of the original Six View Points and the dissemination of Suzuki training in theater programs around the USA and abroad.[2] Considerations such as these lay outside the scope of my project here.

The SITI Company teaches Suzuki and Viewpoints in a wide range of circumstances and situations: six-week sessions during fall and spring training in New York; single classes or weekend workshops when the company is on tour; an annual summer residency in Los Angeles; and so on. Some company members teach on an individual basis at schools such as Juilliard or New York University or Columbia. The most thorough introduction to the SITI training takes place each year in June at the company's summer home at Skidmore College in Saratoga Springs. Known as the Summer Intensive, this four-week workshop attracts participants from around the USA and all over the world. Part summer camp and part boot camp, the Intensive provides an immersion experience that maximizes the interplay between the three practices and the connections between training and creating new work. Five mornings a week, participants take a Viewpoints and a Suzuki class. Afternoons are filled with a once-a-week three-hour Composition class, additional Suzuki or

Viewpoints work, or "supplemental training" in voice, dance, developmental movement, and other special topics. Evenings are devoted to a once-a-week symposium, rehearsal and preparation of composition pieces, or occasional excursions. Each class session is led by one or two primary teachers, but there are often three or four more company members in the room on any given day, taking the class themselves, offering pointers, side-coaching, and keeping an eye out for those who are struggling with the work. Participants live in Skidmore dormitories and eat in the cafeteria along with the company members, thus providing informal opportunities for questions and feedback. Most participants would agree that the "Intensive" lives up to its name.

While other acting techniques focus on how to act (in the sense of creating a character, building a role, performing an action, or expressing an emotion), the SITI training centers on how to get ready to act. Emphasis is on achieving and maintaining a frame of mind, a physical and vocal condition, and a focus that prepares the actor to respond to an outside stimulus or event at any moment, to send and receive kinetic energy, and to execute a task or an action with clarity and precision. Because an actor can only respond to what he is aware of, the training places a premium on "paying attention," that is, being mindful, giving ongoing consideration to all that is outside the self and receiving a stream of sensory data as a result, some of which provide the basis for a response. These responses may not be flamboyant or even noticeable to a spectator; a shift of weight, a turn of the head, a release of breath may constitute a response, but the rate of response is acute, without necessarily becoming manic or rushed. In my observations of the SITI Company, in training, in rehearsal, and in performance, the back-and-forth exchange between actors is so frequent and continuous as to suggest a self-perpetuating feedback loop, one which roots an interaction in the present moment and propels it forward at the same time. This results in work that is both highly calibrated and seemingly spontaneous. The dual keys are "paying attention" and being "ready to act." These are not just practical skills; they are moral principles.

The Viewpoints

As she admits freely and often, Anne Bogart stole the Viewpoints from Mary Overlie, a postmodern dancer and choreographer from Montana who came to New York in 1971, where she was influenced by several of the Judson dancers, particularly Barbara Dilley.[3] For several years, they were both members of the Natural History of the American Dancer, a small group of women exploring the principles and techniques of improvisational movement. In 1975, Overlie began presenting her own solo works, duets, and, eventually, group pieces at downtown venues such as St. Mark's-in-the-Bouwerie and the Kitchen and at alternative spaces such as the window of an art gallery or a football field. Like the Judson dancers before her, Overlie's interest in improvisation, her use of quotidian as well as virtuosic movement, and the incorporation of text into choreography blurred the boundary between dance and theater. In the mid-to-late 1970s, she began sustained collaborations with experimental theater artists, notably Mabou Mines, and with Wendell Beavers, another Judson protégé, with whom she worked for many years at the Danspace Project, Movement Research, Inc. (which they co-founded), and the newly formed Experimental Theater Wing (ETW) of New York University.

Around this time, as part of her effort to expand and explore the frontiers of what dance as an art form might express, Overlie began to articulate the building blocks or basic elements out of which a dance is constructed:

> I'll start from the beginning. There are six viewpoints (not all that unusual). 1. Time; 2. Space; 3. Kinesthetics (what I call the subject of moving); 4. Emotion, which I feel is always there whether you want to acknowledge it or not; 5. Line. I'm most fascinated that the body is capable of making certain lines and line-shapes. Weight is not so much a factor, because weight is only experienced kinesthetically, whereas line is experienced visually. 6. Story. No matter what you are doing, dance happens through time, and you are adding image and experience on top of image and experience.[4]

Overlie considered each of these components, or viewpoints, to have equal value and importance in dance. Therefore, any one of them might provide the legitimate basis for structuring what she called her "abstract narratives," choreography that advanced the postmodern dance movement's "determination to bring dance away from the role of the performing bear, feats of mystery and great athletic show, into a more fully rounded and explored medium of artistic expression."[5]

Bogart got to know Overlie while both were at New York University. In 1980, with students in the ETW, they collaborated on *Artourist*, a piece about a group of Manhattan tourists, which combined pedestrian movement with choreography. During the 1980s, Bogart began to adapt the conceptual vocabulary of Overlie's Six Viewpoints to her own directing and teaching, altering some of the nomenclature at first and later adding new terms to the list in order to make it more applicable to theater. In 1988, when Bogart came to the American Repertory Theatre to direct Heinrich von Kleist's *Kätchen von Heilbronn* at the Institute for Advanced Theatre Training, she met Tina Landau, who became her friend, collaborator, and, for seven years, her partner. Over the years, both together and apart, Bogart and Landau continued to develop and refine the Viewpoints and related practices, resisting their rigid codification in favor of an open-ended, evolutionary approach. A set of Vocal Viewpoints was enumerated.[6] Though not yet as systematically taught as the "physical" Viewpoints, the mere fact of their enumeration reflected the widening influence of Bogart's methods and the pressure to articulate a comprehensive system. Eventually, Bogart and Landau wrote *The Viewpoints Book: A Practical Guide to Viewpoints and Composition.*[7]

In the 1990s, as the Viewpoints acquired more and more cachet as the leading edge of Bogart's theatrical innovations, tensions surfaced within the wider Viewpoints community over a lack of recognition for Overlie. A major Viewpoints conference at New York University in January 1998, featuring Overlie, Bogart, Beavers, members of the SITI Company, and others, went a long way towards mending fences and generating dialogue amongst various practitioners. At one panel discussion, the critic Elinor Fuchs offered some "anthropological notes," expressing sympathy for the impulse to enumerate tenets and principles – "we need these as fences to put around young trees" – but cautioning against a tendency "to give a greater impression of orthodoxy and fixedness to the entire system than it may have."[8] Since then, Overlie, Beavers, and others have continued to explore the original, more dance-oriented vision of the Viewpoints, while Bogart, Landau, and their protégés have brought them to bear on making theater.

The Viewpoints is a practical semiotics for the stage that provides performers with a dynamic orientation to theatrical time and space and promotes performances that are both specific and spontaneous. Bogart amended and expanded Overlie's original Six Viewpoints and came up with nine principal, physical Viewpoints. They are:

Shape: the form, contour, or position of the actor's body in space, either alone or with other bodies; the body as mass, 'statue,' or sculptural object;

Spatial Relationship: the distances between the actor's body and other actors or objects in a defined space, and by extension, the distribution and rhythm of empty, 'negative' space and occupied, 'positive' space on stage;

Floor Pattern: the path and design of the body's movement through space, on a line, a diagonal, a curve, or at random; also known as topography;

Architecture: the physical environment of the space through which the actor moves, be it the rehearsal studio or the stage set; its shape, dimensions, furnishings, textures, light levels, entrances and exits, and the actor's relation to them;

Repetition: the recurrence or duplication of any shape, gesture, movement, spatial relationship, spoken text, action, or other performance element, whether by two or more actors at the same time or in sequence or at distinctly separate moments in time;

Gesture: the movement of one or more parts of the actor's body, in a manner that is often understood as either behavioral/functional/mimetic or abstract/expressive/theatrical;

Tempo: the rate at which a gesture, movement, or action takes place on stage; how fast or slow, steady or varying, hurried or relaxed it is;

Duration: the period of time over which a gesture, movement, interaction, or event is extended; how long something lasts on stage;

Kinesthetic Response: the impulsive and spontaneous physical reaction of the actor to a gesture, movement, sound, event or other outside stimulus in the performance space.[9]

There is nothing mysterious or complicated about these terms. As Bogart herself is quick to point out, they are ways to describe something that already exists, a theoretical or descriptive vocabulary that divides theatrical performance into constituent aspects of time or space. Repetition, gesture, tempo, duration, kinesthetic response describe temporal qualities of performance, and shape, spatial relationship, floor pattern, and architecture pertain to spatial characteristics. Taken in aggregate, the nine viewpoints articulate a system of fluid and variable signs, which in staging a performance are arranged and combined for aesthetic or rhetorical purposes (whether or not an explicit Viewpoints vocabulary is used). More complicated sign systems, such as the one outlined in Keir Elam's *The Semiotics of Theatre and Drama* (London: Methuen, 1980), have proven to be of limited practical value for artists. What the Viewpoints lacks in complexity, it gains in usefulness. Most newcomers grasp the basics and put them into practice in short order, which makes the Viewpoints useful for establishing a working vocabulary and a rudimentary ensemble, which, in turn, facilitates the creation of stage material.

Viewpoints training often begins with a series of exercises designed to heighten the individual actor's sense of being part of a group, sometimes by working towards executing a simple movement task in complete unison with others. For example, a group will stand in a circle and be told to jump high in the air and land at the same time – without any single person initiating the jump or acting as leader. This takes practice, especially when the group is asked to jump even higher and then land without making a sound. On the same principle, the signature "12–6–4" exercise asks a group to begin by running in a circle, turned slightly towards the center so as to see or sense the whole group and maintain equal distances between runners. Then, over a period of minutes and in no particular order, the group has to reverse direction and run the other way a total of twelve times, jump in the air while running six times, and come to a complete stop (and start again) four times. The goal is to make each change spontaneous, simultaneous, and instantaneous, so that, with practice, the group operates as a single corporal entity with a single collective will.

Central to the Viewpoints training is an expanding and vigilant perceptual awareness of what is going on all around you. This is partly a matter of developing what is called "soft eyes," a way of seeing that combines looking ahead, peripheral vision, and sensing the presence of what is just out of sight, while remaining relaxed and ready to react to an ever changing field of view. In everyday life, soft eyes are what we use when driving a car, an action which requires a focus on the road ahead, a perpetual monitoring of the mirrors that show what is beside and behind you, and a readiness to swerve or brake to avoid sudden danger. In fast-moving team sports, such as basketball, soft eyes are what enables a good player to 'see the entire court,' even to the point of seeing where a team-mate will be before he gets there and passing the ball to that spot to meet him (without tipping off the opponent in the process). The Viewpoints asks for the same high level of perception. "Soft eyes" requires what Bogart refers to as "looking without desire," a matter of developing maximal attention with minimal intention, being ready to react to changing circumstances, anticipating what might happen without assuming that it will. In this way, the actor is better able to engage with what is already in process, rather than committing the twofold error of first entering a situation without taking notice of it and then blindly imposing his will on that situation.

"Soft eyes" and "looking without desire," along with what Bogart calls "listening with the whole body," are essential to the viewpoint of kinesthetic response, which is the heartbeat or engine of the Viewpoints in action. Something happens – a movement, a gesture, a sound – and then something else happens. The energy of the first is transferred and transformed in the second. This kinesthetic rhythm of stimulus and response, action and reaction, cause and effect provides the driving force and forward momentum for advanced Viewpoints work and an underlying principle for the Composition work as well. To isolate and practice kinesthetic response, introductory exercises often prescribe a limited set of physical actions. For example, a group of twelve people might stand in a circle and be told that at any given moment eight of them should be standing and four of them should be squatting. Four people squat down, and then, each time a person moves to squat or stand, somebody else must do the opposite instantly, so that the numbers up and down remain constant. At first, as more than one person rushes to react, split-second negotiations and frantic adjustments take place, but as the group becomes more in tune with itself, success is achieved with remarkable ease. The exercise gets more difficult when the members of the group are asked to stand in a line facing forward, either shoulder to shoulder or, harder still, one in front of the other. The 'horizontal' line-up requires peripheral vision and helps to develop "soft eyes." In the 'vertical' line-up, the people towards the rear have much more visual information about how many are up and down and thus learn that they must "take care" of the ones towards the front, who try to sense what is going on behind them and 'see' with eyes in the backs of their heads.

In practice, none of the Viewpoints exist independent of the others. That is, there is no gesture without tempo, no shape without duration, no floor pattern without architecture and so on, but in the early stages of training, the individual components are isolated as much as possible for the sake of introduction. So, to draw attention to floor pattern, actors are told to walk about the room only in straight lines, as if moving on a grid, turning at strict right angles to change direction. To draw attention to spatial relationships, a number of individuals are told to take a physically neutral position standing still somewhere in the room and then to observe the distances between bodies and to feel as viscerally as possible the gaps in the room; then, on cue, each person stands elsewhere in the room and the new spatial relationships are examined.

Introductory exercises such as these pave the way for extended movement improvisations, referred to as open Viewpoints, that bring most or all of the Viewpoints into play. With as few as five or a dozen or more participants, this exercise starts at five or ten minutes in length and can build to last for a half hour or longer. Performers take positions in the workspace, striking a variety of poses (shape) and noticing their proximity to others (spatial relationship). Then, without cue or instruction, somebody will begin to move. This is enough to trigger a reaction (kinesthetic response) from one or more of the others. Soon, everybody is engaged in some form of motion, moving in place (gesture) or across the room (floor pattern) and changing the motion in response to something happening either close by or across the room. Direct eye contact is minimal, but as one person crosses the room, he may 'collect' others, as they fall in beside or behind him for a few moments and then break off or drop out in response to something else. As kinesthetic responses multiply and overlap, clusters of bodies gather and then dissolve in different parts of the room. A changing rhythm of engagement and disengagement takes hold. Motion becomes perpetual. Energy moves in waves. The interactions generally are not behavioral or dramatic. Emphasis remains on the kinesthetic, although the natural progression of some encounters may suggest a character relationship or even a story. When this happens, it lasts for a while and then gives way to something else.

As participants become more adept, more variables are introduced. Participants may choose when to enter and exit the space, a decision which requires a heightened sensitivity to the ongoing event and an ability to 'enter in' or 'step out' in a way that does not disrupt the flow too much. Sometimes, music or sound effects will be played during all or part of a session, although for the novice this raises the danger of moving to the beat of the music (in effect, dancing) rather than responding in some less obvious kinesthetic fashion. On occasion, particularly when Viewpoints work is done in conjunction with a rehearsal process, a phrase or a sentence or a line of dialogue may be spoken as a kinesthetic response, and the Viewpoint of repetition will often lead to it echoing down through the improvisation as it continues. Here again, the speaking is not for the sake of communication in any narrative or dialogic sense. It is the word as sound, the breath as voice, speech as physical response, that are primary.

An open Viewpoints session is often fascinating to watch. Some rise to the level of an accomplished performance, all the more astonishing for being extemporary. When the mix and the mood of the group are right, the give and take of bodies in motion seems to take on an inevitable flow, as though some force of nature, a tumbling river or a chemical reaction, is at work. Yet, the players retain a sense of individuality and humanity. They are not wispy leaves in the wind; they exert themselves in reaction to what is around them. They take charge for a moment, before releasing control and reverting from willfulness to willingness. Combinations, patterns, and situations recur, some conspicuous enough to strike a tone or conjure an image or suggest a relationship that is more than kinesthetic. If there is music, it colors the action and often provides an emotional subtext.

Though no content or theme is stipulated for these improvisations, the observer's reflexive will to find meaning is often activated. The kaleidoscope of movement takes on a cumulative effect over time. Something like what Mary Overlie dubbed an "abstract narrative" seems to develop. When the free, unguided, movement achieves the aesthetic interest of form, something undeniable, if not quite definable, happens, and what feels like a complete, spontaneous theatrical event takes place.

My sense of understanding the Viewpoints in action took a quantum leap one summer morning in midtown Manhattan when I was rushing to a breakfast meeting. A bit behind schedule, I found myself scurrying down a crowded sidewalk, darting around slowpokes, dodging oncoming pedestrians and their umbrellas or briefcases, looking ahead to see where a gap might open up or when the traffic light at the cross street might change. And, in the midst of the hustle and bustle, it occurred to me that I was viewpointing with a thousand New Yorkers on their way to work. The simple task of walking down the street activated a keen awareness of spatial relationships (bunching up close at street corners), duration (waiting for the light to change), gesture (a man in a suit sips his coffee, a woman checks her make-up), shape (somebody stoops to tie a shoe, a homeless person sleeps on the sidewalk), tempo (speeding up in mid-block, slowing down at corners), floor pattern (weaving in and out, turning the corner), architecture (the curb, the corner of a building, the open delivery hatch in the sidewalk), repetition (many people on cell phones), and kinesthetic response (giving way to commuters pouring out of the subway, stepping back from a speeding taxi). This mad rush-hour dash amounted to a massive urban improvisation, informed by the same constant metamorphosis of time and space as a Viewpoints jam.

By articulating a shared vocabulary, the Viewpoints helps an actor to pay closer attention and to be more articulate in taking action. The greater the actor's awareness, the more frequent, precise, spontaneous, and varied are his reactions. Attention radiates outward, from the self to the immediate environment to an expanding horizon of possibilities. While this outward focus has its physical, perceptual limits, in principle it extends to infinity. In this sense, the ethos of the Viewpoints is open, inclusive, and all-encompassing.

Suzuki training

The most widespread early stereotype about the Suzuki training is that it amounts to moving around a room stomping your feet as loudly as possible over and over. While this emphasis on the feet as the actor's primary point of contact with 'the acting surface' is important and undeniable, it has led to misunderstanding. The chief corporal focus of the Suzuki technique is what is commonly known as the actor's center, the point in the lower abdomen – "two jiggers of scotch below the navel," as an irreverent friend of mine likes to say – that is both the center of gravity and the point of origin for the deepest breath. It is the source of energy and power and balance, the root of the voice, the crossroads of the upper and lower bodies, and a crucial nexus in the mind–body connection.[10] The Suzuki training develops the performer's capacity to initiate movement and speech (and, by extension, expressive stillness and eloquent silence) from this center through the repetition of codified exercises that test the limits of control, strength, and balance. The goal, to quote from the SITI website, is "to heighten the actor's emotional and physical power and commitment to each moment on the stage."[11]

Although the various postures, steps, walks, squats and other routines of the Suzuki training have roots in actual productions, they do not constitute a performance vocabulary per se. They are a method of actor training, one that poses physical and mental challenges that in their difficulty can become intensely personal for the individual actor. For novices and experts alike, the training presents what amounts to a series of diagnostic tests that help the actor, on any given day and over time, to assess the mind–body connection, the command and control of energy, and the integrity of his focus on his fellow actors, the stage environment, and his so-called "fiction." This last concern is important. Newcomers to Suzuki work are often coached to put their attention outside of themselves, on some point on the horizon or an imagined other, both as a way of building a kind of mental toughness and of reminding them that, even at the earliest stages, this is a practice for performance and therefore a form of interaction intended to be watched by others.

Central to a Suzuki class or training session is the atmosphere in the room and the student-teacher relationship (see figure 8). An air of discipline prevails, one marked by a sense of dignity and a seriousness of purpose. The room is clean, quiet, and uncluttered. Students wear standard workout clothes – shorts, sweatpants, leotards, and tights, tee shirts – generally in neutral colors of black, white, and grey. The traditional footwear is the *tabi* (heavy split-toed socks common in Japan), although white athletic socks are a frequent substitute. Each session is led by a single instructor (or one instructor at a time), who kneels on the floor at the front of the classroom or studio and projects an air of authority similar to a

Figure 8. The grammar of the feet: Tadashi Suzuki (center) and Leon Ingulsrud (right) instruct a student in the Suzuki workshop held during the inaugural season of the Saratoga International Theatre Institute (1992). (Photograph by Clemens Kalischer.)

martial arts teacher or a drill sergeant. Instructions are terse, questions are discouraged, and idle conversation or side comments are frowned upon, all in order to concentrate attention on the physical work itself and on learning by doing. Instructors bark out commands or counts for exercises in crisp, strong tones or, when appropriate, slap the floor with the *shenai* (a type of stick that makes a sharp, loud sound) as a "go" signal. Sessions start on time – latecomers are not admitted – with the instructor taking a place at the front of the room and the others expected to fall in automatically.

There are no group warm-ups or other preparations. Individuals are expected to be ready to work.

There are four fundamental exercises in the training, known as Basic #1, Basic #2, Basic #3, and Basic #4, each of which constitutes a physical template that the student aims to replicate with exactitude.[12] Beginners learn each of these in increments, building up step by step to complete a sequence of motions. Most begin with the student standing with feet in firm contact with floor, either together or shoulder's width apart, knees unlocked and legs energized, the center activated, shoulders relaxed, chin level, and eyes focused ahead on some real or imagined distant point. Basic #1 starts with heels pressed together and feet open to form a 90-degree angle. On the instructor's command, the right foot is lifted, moved to the right, and brought down with a vigorous stomp to the side, so that the body's weight is balanced over the right foot and the left leg is straight. On the next count, the trailing left foot is snapped back in to contact the right foot, so that the original position is restored. The next two moves involve lowering the center down into a low squat, with the back straight, pelvis open, and buttocks just above the heels, and then raising it back up again to the starting position. At first, this squat is done in a swift, sudden burst, but it can also be practiced in a variety of counts, with the instructor sometimes saying "Down in 3" or "Up in 10" before issuing the command to move. To complete Basic #1, this entire sequence is repeated in reverse with an initial stomp to the left. This and other exercises are often repeated multiple times before moving on to the next one.

Basic exercises #2, #3, and #4 are similar in nature and complexity, each with specific positions and variations for the feet, legs, arms, and head. Basic #2 includes a whip-like action of raising the leg and standing, stork-like, on one foot. Basic #4 begins in a half squat facing the back of the room and involves a corkscrew turn of the entire body that ends in a standing position facing forward. Difficult maneuvers like these can easily throw the novice off balance, a tendency that draws attention to a principle which informs much of the Suzuki work. Many of the movements ask for an activation of energy that is sudden and forceful enough to risk loss of physical control and then a re-assertion of control as a move is completed. "As fast as you can go is not fast enough," a teacher will say, challenging her students to push beyond their comfort zones. This pattern of unbalancing and rebalancing is paralleled by the irregular stop-and-start rhythm of the work, a practice which is sometimes described as "putting maximum acceleration next to maximum stillness." To make this as challenging as possible, the instructor avoids a regular count in leading an exercise, changing the tempo as she proceeds so that the student must respond in an instant to the sound of her voice and not to a predictable interval of time between steps. This need to be ready to spring into action promotes a more dynamic and energetic type of stillness, one which over time helps an accomplished performer to command attention even when doing 'nothing' on stage.

The training also includes a series of "Walks" and a practice called "Statues." Accompanied by up-tempo music, the Walks are performed by the group in single file, with each person crossing the room on a diagonal from one corner to the opposite. Emphasis is placed on driving energy down from the center through the legs and feet to the floor. While maintaining a forward focus, a relaxed upper body, and equal spacing with the person ahead and behind, the actor walks with a designated step, as if advancing his center across the room on a taut wire or cable. The Walks begin with a familiar forward stomping step and then progress to other types, including a high-toe walk, a pigeon-toed walk, a sideways stomp, and a duck walk. Here again, while the movement across the floor may appear steady and smooth to an observer, each step is approached independently with the same start-and-stop action that defines Basic #1, #2, #3, and #4. Motion is initiated and then halted, initiated and halted. The momentary break between steps is not a rest or a release. The flow of energy is continuous through the flicker of stillness.

The discipline of Statues is performed from two positions, sitting and standing (see figure 9). Sitting Statues start out with the trainee sitting on the floor with knees pulled up in a relaxed tuck position and then, at the instructor's command, moving into one of three different positions. In each one, the head is up, the back is straight, the center is opened out, weight is balanced on the tailbone and legs are held up off the floor. Standing Statues start in a crouched position and, on command, pivot into one of three different standing positions, each one balanced on the balls of the feet. Both forms are also executed "free style," which means that, when called for by the instructor, the actor strikes a more active and dynamic upper-body pose (of his own instantaneous choosing), with arms raised or extended in a gesture, torso twisted right or left, head turned, and so on. As in the four Basic exercises, once a move is completed and a Statue established, perfect stillness is sought, without wiggling or wobbling or writhing. Students are coached, colloquially speaking, to suck it up, to take the physical difficulty of the exercise inside the body and deal with it there, while maintaining an external demeanor of composure and even ease, with the lower body strong and rooted to the floor and the upper body relaxed, free, and expressive.

Figure 9. Perpetual training: *bobrauschenbergamerica* cast members begin a Lousville rehearsal with Suzuki work (2001). (Photographs by John Nation.)

Two more extended group exercises, known as "Stomping Shakuhachi" and "Slow Ten," should be mentioned here, in part because of their overt theatricality. Stomping Shakuhachi begins with the participants in the group moving slowly about the room in random fashion, all using the same basic stomp as a forward step. Set to a specific piece of music about three minutes long, the actors calibrate their movements so that they all arrive on the far side of the room as the music ends, lined up along the rear wall shoulder to shoulder, evenly spaced and facing forward. On the final beat of the music, they end as one with a final stomp and then collapse to the floor in a heap. Then, as a slow, ethereal melody plays on the Japanese bamboo flute known as the shakuhachi, the individual actors each come to a stand in their own gradual way and then proceed to walk forward across the room slowly and deliberately. For an observer, they seem as if they might be spirits rising from the dead and coming forth to make themselves known.

Slow Ten has a similarly powerful effect for an observer. It begins with two uniform rows of people facing each other on opposite sides of the room, right and left. Again, with music, these two rows move slowly across the room towards each other, and when they meet in the middle, each line passes through the other without pause or interaction and then proceeds onward to the other side. Once there, each person rotates 180-degrees, pivoting 'downstage,' facing back across the room, and, in the process, slowly adjusting the center to a higher or lower level and moving the arms, head, and torso into a freestyle statue. Without stopping, each row, now defined by a variety of poses, marches slowly back to the other side, once again passing in the middle before arriving where they started. The slow and steady approach of the two rows has the feel of a tremendous confrontation, as if two phalanxes of foot soldiers are meeting in battle. When the timing is right and two perfectly straight lines meet in the middle and become one, there is an instant of seeming unity before they separate and proceed to the far side. The second pass, anticipated all the more after the first and complicated by the various free-style positions, feels even more like a clash. Animated by the accompanying music, both Stomping Shakuhachi and Slow Ten can be haunting in their beauty, even though they are taught and practiced on a technical basis, without any explicit mimetic intention.

The ultimate focus of the various components of Suzuki is on the act of speaking, although the training does not include a series of specific voice exercises on the order of the four Basics. Instead, voice and speech are added to some of the physical exercises, often the Sitting and Standing Statues at the start. When the trainee is balanced on high toe in a Standing Statue or on the coccyx in a Sitting Statue, the teacher will issue the command "Speak," and as one, the group recites a short speech at a rapid but controlled rate, without particular inflection or emotion. Breaths are scored so that each one carries a sustained piece of text and so that the group can speak together with one voice. Memorized in advance, the texts are taken from past SITI productions. In recent years, the opening lines of Robert Pinsky's translation of Dante's *Inferno*, which figured in SITI's Andy Warhol piece, *Culture of Desire*, have become one of the standard texts used in their vocal training.

The Statue positions make it difficult to speak with full voice, and the act of speaking makes it difficult to maintain the Statue position. These reciprocal tensions are central to vocal training in Suzuki. The struggle in the body, fierce at first, to maintain physical balance and stillness and then to find within that access to breath and the vocal apparatus forces a connection between control of the center and control of the diaphragm. It produces a sound that, while often strident and flat at first, is powerful and resonant, and eventually supple. As company member Will Bond puts it, "as one finds the freedom of music internally while sustaining such rigorous and formal structures externally, speaking can be as varied, lyrical, surprising and textured as one would hope for in performance."[13] The built-in obstacles to speech provide a source of energy as the breath and voice push off from them in order to speak, just as the leg and foot send energy into the floor with a stomp and then take the rebounding energy of the resisting ground back and hold it at the center. The stern persona of the teacher and the martial bark of the commands are something else to push against, so to speak, as is the pressure to keep up with the group. This principle of dynamism, of operating in response to perpetual resistances, oppositions, and tensions (some real and physical, some imagined but, for that matter, no less real), informs every aspect of the Suzuki work and differentiates it from systems predicated on a state of maximal relaxation as the best place from which to work.

For well over a decade, the combination of the Viewpoints and Suzuki training have served the actors in the SITI Company as a dual platform for their collective playmaking. When I once asked the group to characterize the benefit of these collateral practices, Ellen Lauren answered in a single word: "Tenacity." Barney O'Hanlon elaborated:

> It has something to do with being in rehearsal and making choices. I think it is what makes us different from other people who have not worked with us. There is a fearlessness in making choices that is deeply influenced and fed by both trainings together. There is a presence, a listening, and an activation. You just keep going and going and going in rehearsal, with physical choices, intellectual choices, spiritual and emotional choices. If anybody sits back, it is dead in the water. I think that the two trainings together are the fuel for that kind of presence in rehearsal.[14]

In many ways, Suzuki and Viewpoints are yin and yang. While both practices work towards placing the actor's focus outside of the self, on paying attention and being ready to act, the Suzuki training starts off as a private discipline for the actor, one by which he can assess and improve his current levels of energy, strength, concentration, and centered-ness. The actor works on himself in preparation for acting with others, whereas, in Viewpoints, the actor works with others in preparation for creating a performance. The Viewpoints develops the ensemble and the actor's ability to join the group in a manner that is active and unselfish, willing and willful as the moment requires. Suzuki features a set of strict forms that demand discipline and hard work. Viewpoints is improvisational and therefore more playful and open in nature. The Viewpoints work is very much about flow, a changing, self-perpetuating rhythm of kinesthetic responses that makes one thing lead to the next in a manner that is smooth and organic. Suzuki is based on response, also, but on an 'atomic' level, its forms ask for a stop-and-start rhythm that alternates between motion and stillness. To borrow electrical terms, Viewpoints is direct current and Suzuki is alternating current. On a more theoretical level, Suzuki is spoken of as being vertical in orientation, whereas Viewpoints is more horizontal. That is, in Suzuki, the orientation is to the heavens above and the spirits of the earth below; even when moving forward, energy is directed downwards into the earth. In Viewpoints, the orientation is more inter-active, more collaborative, and in a general sense, more social. In this regard, Suzuki seems more rooted in the relationship of the individual to what is eternal and absolute, while Viewpoints centers more on the relationship of the individual to the group, on the material and social worlds, on the here and now of the moment. On this basis, I would suggest that, at its core, Suzuki implies the ethos of Tragedy and Viewpoints the ethos of Comedy.

Composition

The Suzuki work is pure, hard training. The Viewpoints work is a form of training that, by virtue of its improvisational nature, has an element of play; it can also be used during a rehearsal process to explore themes, discover impulses, and generate material towards a production. The third rail of the SITI training, Composition, is a method for creating theater. It represents the bridge from training into practice, and as such, it points to Anne Bogart's orientation to directing and her broader theater aesthetic.

Bogart's concept of Composition, as both a creative and a pedagogical tool, derives from her work with Aileen Passloff as an undergraduate at Bard College. Passloff is a choreographer, dancer, director, and actor who was an integral member of the influential off-Off Broadway dance and theater movements in Greenwich Village in the 1950s and 1960s. According to Sally Banes, "she became noted not only for her wit and theatricality, her collaborations with visual artists and avant-garde composers, but also for her independence."[15] In 1969, Passloff began teaching at Bard, where one of her courses was titled "Composition," which she defines in broad terms as "putting things together, putting one thing after another, listening to what the content is so you can find out what form it needs to take."[16] As Bogart recalls, students in Passloff's Composition class were asked to do such things as stage a dream in order to capture its feeling, rather than its story, or to "take a photograph and base a whole composition on it" or to "make a piece out of 2 percussive or vibrating moves, 1 sustained, 2 lyric, 1 gesture, 1 still."[17]

Along with Bogart's concurrent interest in Grotowski and the more general influence of the alternative performance movement in SoHo and the Village in the 1970s, Passloff's emphasis on performance as metaphorical and on finding a piece's rhythm and 'voice' in the process of creating it became a lasting influence on the young director's work. Before long, just as with Mary Overlie's Six Viewpoints, Bogart was using her own variations on Passloff's methods as a teaching and rehearsal tool in her productions at New York University's ETW. She often divided her student cast into smaller groups and asked them to come up with short, quickly prepared pieces that addressed some aspect of the play or the frame-world which she sought to create for it. For example, in an early stage of working on Büchner's *Danton's Death*, Bogart asked each group to create something that was set in a club and included an execution, the use of water, a master-of-ceremonies character who spoke only text from the play's stage directions, and "unusual audience/spectator relations."[18]

Bogart called these rehearsal creations, after Passloff, Compositions, and over the years, this practice became a fundamental aspect of her work as a director. Tina Landau calls Composition "an alternative method of writing. Rather than being alone in a room with a computer, Composition is writing with a group of people on their feet."[19] It is a form of sketching or making a rough draft, a way to generate raw material, test out creative impulses, and experiment with themes, characters, and situations, images, structures, pieces of text, and physical materials, any or all of which might contribute to the creation of a larger, more polished piece. As a shared activity, it has the added benefit of establishing an atmosphere of free play at the outset of a project, thereby proliferating, rather than eliminating, possibilities, and of inviting actors to take a creative role in making the piece, thereby generating a stronger, more active ensemble and a greater sense of individual responsibility. One of the virtues of Composition as a practical tool is its utter simplicity. As Bogart describes it:

> I make a list of everything that I imagine being in a show. I just make lists and lists, and I hand them to whoever I am working with and say, "Go make a show that is ten minutes long and has all this stuff in it." Then, I can watch it and say, "That works" or "That doesn't" or "I think I will use that." It is essentially a way of lateral thinking in planning a production.[20]

Bogart teaches Composition as part of the Master of Fine Arts directing program that she heads at Columbia, and she and members of the company also teach it during the annual Summer Intensive. In Saratoga, workshop participants are divided into three groups, each of which takes Composition one afternoon a week for four weeks. The focus is on the quick, impulsive preparation and presentation of short, original theater pieces on a designated theme or topic. On the first day, every student in the class creates and directs a 90-second, two-person play, composed on the spot and presented as a theatrical montage of five 15–20-second vignettes divided by blackouts. She encourages them to work physically and with precision and introduces the distinction between work that is descriptive (that is, behavioral, mimetic, objective, realistic, psychological) and work that is expressive (more abstract, lyrical, subjective, metaphorical). Subsequent sessions focus on presenting and analyzing longer Compositions that have been developed and rehearsed outside of class by working-groups of four or five people, or sometimes more. Often, a director is designated, but each group is expected to work as a team in conducting research, shaping the event, determining the text, tracking down props, staging the piece, and so on. Students are encouraged to work as much as possible on their feet, creating the piece as they go rather than hammering out a fixed script in advance and then staging it.

Individual Composition assignments consist of a general topic, a stipulated range of sources from which textual material might be drawn, a prescribed duration (seven minutes, fifteen minutes), and a long list of theatrical ingredients that are to be included in the piece in any way that the group sees fit. These ingredients tend to fall into two categories: actions that are repeated or sustained for a period of time and actions that are abrupt and surprising. Over the years, Bogart and Landau have developed a long list of standard ingredients that they assign with regularity. These include:

> fifteen consecutive seconds of stillness;
> fifteen consecutive seconds of simultaneous unison action;
> a sustained moment when you don't know if somebody is laughing or crying;
> a sustained moment when everyone is looking up;
> a sustained passionate kiss;
> an accident (planned and staged as such);
> a surprise entrance;
> an inappropriate interruption;
> one gesture repeated five times (or ten or fifteen);
> twenty seconds of stillness;
> twenty seconds of high-speed talking;
> the establishment of an expectation that is subsequently broken;
> the use of music in three different ways, one of which has the music coming from an unexpected source;
> revelation of an object (the discovery or exposure of some object that was not apparent up to that point);
> revelation of space (revealing some portion of the performance space that was not visible or recognized up to that point);
> revelation of character (a character's identity turns out to be other than first assumed or introduced).

Along with other givens, enough of these ingredients are called for in a single composition to generate an "exquisite pressure," one which promotes creativity by overwhelming collaborators with a lot to do in a short amount of time so that they do not have a chance to think too much. As Bogart describes it,

> Pressure is a central ingredient: pressure of collaboration, of time, of putting all this stuff together. Here is all this stuff that has to be in a composition. I cannot possibly control it, therefore I start to work on a more intuitive level, rather than on a logical level, which is what you are trying to get to because all creation is intuitive. It has nothing to do with intellect. It is more like information overload equals pattern recognition. It is like the Sistine Chapel. It is so complicated that your conscious mind breaks down and you start recognizing patterns.[21]

The rationale here alludes to Marshal McLuhan, the subject of SITI's *The Medium*, who asserted in *Counterblast* (and elsewhere) that "Faced with information overload, we have no alternative but to pattern-recognition."[22]

The pattern lurking in the list of oft-used ingredients pertains to certain fundamentals of playmaking and playgoing. On a simple, cognitive level, audiences remain interested in what is happening onstage in two basic ways, by taking notice over time of the differences that emerge out of sameness (a matter of gradual change) and by being caught off guard by sights, sounds, and events that are surprising and unexpected (sudden change). From moment to moment, incorporating change into the stage situation and their understanding of it is what an audience does. By calling for sustained or repeated actions or sudden, revelatory events, the Composition assignments compel directors to create pieces that, when performed, will stimulate the audience's attention and activate their spectatorial will.

The subject of Compositions often pertains to a current or upcoming SITI project. For example, in the summer of 2000, in anticipation of *bobrauschenbergamerica*'s opening at Humana the next March, students made Compositions based on the art and aesthetics of Rauschenberg and Mee's current draft of the script. In 2001, in anticipation of the piece to be called *Reunion*, students made Compositions about the Group Theatre, drawing on such sources as Harold Clurman's *The Fervent Years*, Wendy Smith's *Real Life Drama*, and the plays of Clifford Odets and other Group playwrights. One assignment that summer had to include, at some point, an acting lesson, a description of affective memory, text or dialogue taken only from actual words spoken by a Group member or from any play that the Group ever produced, and a group photograph (an ingredient inspired by Ralph Steiner's famous photograph of the Group all posing like Rodin's Thinker). In 2002, in advance of SITI's production of *La Dispute* at the American Repertory Theatre the following winter, Compositions focused on the plays of Marivaux. In this way, the Composition work serves not only the students but also the members of the SITI Company, who find themselves steeped in a subject matter (and dozens of creative responses to it) months and months before they face the task of building their own production. Students are warned that the company is looking for ideas, images, moments, texts, characters, and staging devices to 'steal' for their own future use. While some may balk at this, just as many take pleasure in being a part of the creative community of their instructors and having a chance to stimulate their imaginations. The Summer Intensive becomes not just a training ground but an artistic research-and-development laboratory, where preliminary experiments are carried out that stimulate thought about a SITI project in an embryonic stage.

Jo-ha-kyu

Both the Viewpoints and Composition employ a strategy of quick or instantaneous response in order to inhibit the tendency of aspiring artists to think too much, to impose premature judgments on work in progress, and to rationalize the creative process instead of trusting intuition, impulse, and accident. In Bogart's teaching and in her practice, this initial, indiscriminate embrace of whatever comes up is tempered by a sense of form and an aesthetic principle derived from Japanese culture: *jo-ha-kyu*. One of the most influential and insistent advocates of *jo-ha-kyu* was Zeami Motokiyo (1363–1443), the celebrated actor and playwright who transformed *noh* theater into a high art. In his nine major theoretical treatises, Zeami repeatedly emphasizes the importance of *jo-ha-kyu* in shaping an experience on a variety of levels: "It may be said that all things in the universe, good and bad, large and small, with life and without, all partake of the process of *jo*, *ha*, and *kyu*."[23] In simple terms, *jo* means beginning or preparation, *ha* means break or interruption, and *kyu* means fast or urgent. Together, they constitute a temporal progression that has affinities with more familiar tripartite patterns – such as slow-medium-fast or prelude-development-finale or beginning-middle-end or even exposition-rising action-climax – but is equivalent to none of them. As Kunio Komparu describes it, "The idea is that the most natural, human way of being and doing is to begin slowly and gradually build to a rapid climax, to stop, and begin again. The *jo-ha-kyu* of rhythm in noh, in other words, is the application of the theory that because human beings always exist in a state of unbalanced harmony, our aesthetic consciousness of rhythm also exists within a disharmonious construct."[24]

Jo-ha-kyu is an elastic concept that has been applied to a number of Japanese artistic structures, such as poetry, the tea ceremony, and ikebana (flower arranging). It also expands and contracts to fit a wide range of temporal contexts, from the training of an actor over a lifetime to the sequencing of several plays as a day's entertainment to the structure of a single play (or an act or a scene within that play) to the instantaneous action of making a single gesture or uttering a single word onstage. In "Finding Gems and Gaining the Flower," a treatise of 1428, Zeami writes, "The *jo* can be said to be represented by the stage of hearing the pitch and gathering in the breath. *Ha* is represented by pushing out the breath, and *kyu* by the production of the voice itself.[25] In *The Secret Art of the Performer*, Eugenio Barba describes the three phases of any action performed by an actor or dancer in similar terms:

The first phase is determined by the opposition between one force which is increasing and another force which is resisting the development of the first (*jo*, to restrain); the second phase (*ha*, to break, to interrupt) is the moment when the resisting force is overcome until one arrives at the third phase (*kyu*, speed), when the action culminates, releases all its power and suddenly stops as if meeting an obstacle, a new resistance.[26]

This understanding, with its emphasis on physical action and oppositional dynamics, has clear and direct links to principles at the heart of the Suzuki training and even to the execution of a single Suzuki movement. It also suggests the cyclical nature of *jo–ha–kyu* in certain contexts, with one *kyu* leading to another *jo* in a manner that is comparable to the Aristotelian concepts of action as a chain of causes and effects and of catharsis as the release of emotions stimulated by that action. Thomas Rimer calls *jo–ha–kyu* "a metaphor for the deepest psychological movement inherent in a successful theatrical experience." Without it, a *noh* play (or any aesthetic experience) cannot achieve what Zeami calls fulfillment, the proper and elegant completion of its form and the corresponding feeling of novelty and fascination (or awe) engendered as a result. To achieve this, Kunio Komparu argues, "the concept of *jo–ha–kyu* unifies the contradictions of the essentially opposing concepts of space and time, binding them with a breaking element. The result is the discovery of beauty in unbalanced harmony and a process for reaching fulfillment. We might say that it allows us to apprehend the spatial balance of heaven-earth-man within time, seeing position in space and speed in time as one."[27]

While the principle of *jo–ha–kyu* remains, at root, very Japanese, it resonates with the explicit focus of the Viewpoints on the dynamics of theatrical space and time and provides an underlying form for the work in Composition. While Bogart talks about the concept more in practical than theoretical terms, it penetrates the core of her work as a teacher, a director, and an artist. It is crucial to any understanding or evaluation of her theater, which revels in the contradictions of time and space and seeks the beauty of unbalanced harmony in its complex unity.

6

Two metadramas: Bogart's Cabin Pressure *and Mee's* Full Circle

TOWARDS THE END OF THE 1990S, WHEN *BOBRAUSCHENBERG-AMERICA* was little more than an idea, both Charles Mee and Anne Bogart completed projects of major importance. Mee's *Full Circle*, under its original title *Berlin Circle*, received its world premiere at Steppenwolf Theatre in October 1998 in a production directed by Tina Landau. Bogart and SITI's *Cabin Pressure* debuted months later at the Humana Festival in March 1999. Each play marks a moment of fruition and a moment of transition. Landau had already staged two Mee plays in abandoned Manhattan sites for En Garde Arts and made her Steppenwolf debut in 1997 with *Time to Burn*, Mee's remaking of Gorky's *Lower Depths*. By following that up with *Berlin Circle* a year-and-a-half later, she became the first director to carry Mee's work out of its 'off-Off' enclaves – downtown theater in New York, edgy young companies on the west coast, workshops at regional theaters or universities – and onto the main stage of an institutional theater with a national reputation. Aided by the tremendous success of *Big Love* a couple of years later, Mee found himself operating in a new, broader, more mainstream arena, a change of venue that coincided with a burst of productivity and his shift away from apocalyptic nightmares towards rambunctious romantic comedies.

After *The Medium, Small Lives/Big Dreams, Going, Going, Gone,* and *Culture of Desire, Cabin Pressure* was the fifth new piece that Bogart and SITI created on their own, that is, without a designated playwright. By that time, Bogart had already begun her collaboration with Irish critic and dramaturg Jocelyn Clarke, who "arranged" the texts for *Bob* and *Alice's Adventures* and would do the same for *Room, Score,* and *Reunion.* Following *Cabin Pressure,* the SITI Company began to pursue active collaborations with compatible contemporary playwrights, teaming up with Naomi Iizuka on *War of the Worlds* before turning to Mee to partner with them on *bobrauschenbergamerica* and subsequent projects. The collaborations with Clarke, Iizuka, and Mee, along with more frequent productions of established plays, signaled the inscription, so to speak, of the playwright into the company's process. The year 1999, the year of *Cabin Pressure*, was also the last one that Bogart directed outside of the SITI Company. She worked with Lola Pasholinski and Linda Chapman on their *Gertrude and Alice: A Likeness to Loving* and with Laurie Anderson on her *Songs and Stories from Moby Dick*.[1] Thereafter, Bogart limited herself to working with the company more or less exclusively, continuing to generate new projects from within or, when directing classic plays at regional theaters or new operas in New York and Los Angeles, including a major quotient of SITI actors and designers.

Full Circle and *Cabin Pressure* are also significant because each in its own way is a metadrama, and as such, they suggest Mee's and Bogart's respective thoughts about theater itself at the time they agreed to collaborate on *bobrauschenbergamerica*. *Cabin Pressure* scrambles time and other theatrical matters in order to examine the fundamental relationship of audience and actor. In this regard, it sits at the heart of Anne Bogart's body of work, reflecting her lifelong inquiry into the moment of performance and the creative role of the spectator. Intellectual in form, it is nevertheless one of the most emotional and personal works that Bogart has ever created, a valentine to those for whom theater has an irresistible magnetic pull. In Mee's metaplay, it is the role of the playwright that is in question, particularly the playwright who writes in the face of history and a social order in the midst of millennial change. While the overt model for *Full Circle* is Brecht, the play's exuberant public satire makes a case for viewing Mee as the American Aristophanes. The action of each play climaxes with a major confession, a *cri de coeur* that reflects the different personalities of Mee's and Bogart's artistry. Each play is a great work, a celebration of theatrical process, and an instance of playwright and director working at the peak of their creative powers. As such, a detailed look at them helps to pave the way for the second half of this book.

Cabin Pressure was created as part of a multi-phase project conducted at the Actors Theatre of Louisville (ATL) with the support of a National Theatre Artist Residency Program grant from the Theatre Communications Group and the Pew Charitable Trust. In the fall of 1997, Bogart and a team of dramaturgs recruited a demographically diverse "project audience" of roughly forty Louisvilleans, who agreed to sit in on a few rehearsals for her upcoming ATL production of *Private Lives*, see the show and participate in post-play discussions, answer an extensive written survey, and then be interviewed by Bogart about their peek behind the scenes and their experience of being an audience. The public talkback sessions and the private interviews were recorded, transcribed, and added to a ream of raw material that also included commissioned essays, excerpts from theoretical writings, monologues and dialogues from important plays in the history of western drama, and lists of theatrical conventions.[2] Bogart and the SITI Company would take this inch-thick sourcebook into a rehearsal room and use it, in their customary fashion, to create a theatrical essay around a question, an anchor, and a structure. The question, with variations, was clear: What is an audience? What is an actor? What is their responsibility to each other? In the moment of performance, what happens between them? The anchor, in this instance, was not a specific historical figure but the dual archetypes of Spectator and Performer. The structure would be based on various dramatic genres and theatrical conventions and on an audience talkback, the principal occasion in contemporary regional theater when the audience might be said to take the stage.

Bogart's production of *Private Lives* played for three weeks in January 1998, with SITI actors Karenjune Sanchez, Jefferson Mays, Stephen Webber, and Ellen Lauren as Sibyl and Elyot Chase and Victor and Amanda Prynne, respectively. That June, students in the SITI Summer Intensive at Skidmore created compositions based on the theater as a phenomenon and the audience's role in it. In July, members of the company gathered for two weeks in Louisville to review the assembled sourcework, Viewpoint around relevant ideas and images, and create Compositions that might be part of the larger whole. After a six-month hiatus, they resumed work in January 1999, initially in New York and then in Louisville, and premiered the play, after some nerve-wracking, last-minute changes, on March 18, 1999. The cast included Will Bond, Ellen Lauren, Kelly Maurer, Barney O'Hanlon, and Stephen Webber. *Cabin Pressure* ran for two weeks in ATL's Victor Jory Theater (just as *bobrauschen-bergamerica* would two years later), and then, over the next twenty-six months, it toured to Columbus, Chicago, Miami, Champaign-Urbana, Los Angeles, Edinburgh, and Jerusalem.

Cabin Pressure

As soon as the audience arrived in the Victor Jory's third-floor lobby, they heard dialogue coming from the theater, and when they took their seats, they discovered four characters – two couples, each smartly dressed, the women in stylish dresses and hats, the men in dapper suits – in the middle of a scene that seemed as if it came from a drawing room comedy. The play, some play, was already under way. Savvy theatergoers and ATL regulars recognized it as the final scene from Noël Coward's *Private Lives*. As the prim-and-proper foursome banter about the glories of travel, they share the ritual of morning coffee, with Sybil Chase, Victor Prynne, and Amanda Prynne placing their napkins, stirring their coffee, clinking their spoons, and raising their cups to drink at precisely the same time. The boorish Elyot Chase, out of sync with the others, finds that each time he clangs down his cup in its saucer the lights change noticeably, the first hint that the surface of theatrical events will not remain smooth. When a verbal spat between Sybil and Victor reaches its climax, the scene stops suddenly, the actors shift position, the lights change, and the scene begins all over again.

In this scene, when Victor asks the time, Elyot looks at his watch and identifies the actual time in the theater, reminding the audience that curtain time is still minutes away and that this is, in effect, an elaborate, live-action, pre-show loop that they may choose to ignore or watch while they wait for the 'real' show to begin. Those who care to watch will notice that the acting style is pushed a bit beyond the affected graces of a comedy of manners. It verges on parody. The actors' voices are miked and processed, and their movements mechanical, almost robotic. Their conversation is forced and fast and vapid as a result, the usual politesse acid-edged. It is Coward stretched tight between the opposite poles of Strindberg and Ionesco. And with each loop, one of the scene's first retorts – "Oh God! We're off again." – takes on an added resonance, an echo of Beckett's metaphysical merry-go-rounds that offers a metatheatrical wink to the audience. Some in the audience might be prompted to consider that this cycle of repetition defines the life of the actor, who comes out night after night and, for the benefit of that audience, performs the same actions again and again as if for the first time. Others just wait for the show to begin.

The Coward scene is the first of many quotations and allusions in *Cabin Pressure*, some to the work of the SITI Company itself, some to other dramatic genres and styles, past and present, some to the general routine of theatergoing. When it begins for the third time – or is it the fourth? – the houselights fade slowly, the audience takes its cue and quiets down, and the scene plays through, all the way to its original end this time, with Sybil and Victor coming to blows and Amanda and Elyot flirting madly. When the mayhem spills offstage, ending *Private Lives*, a large act curtain closes, sealing off an upstage proscenium arch, and then, a moment later, it opens again and the actors come out to take a curtain call, as canned applause plays on the speakers. After a scant few minutes' entertainment, the real audience faces the minor quandry of whether to clap as well. The actors exit and the houselights come up, just as they would at the end of a show, and nothing happens. The spectators sit and wait, looking (or not looking) at each other across the empty thrust stage, shifting in their seats, enjoying (or not enjoying) the ruse that suggests that the evening is over and they should go home. They wait – an audience alone and self-conscious – until there is some movement behind the curtain and the joke goes itself one better. A man comes out carrying two plain metal folding chairs. He wears a short-sleeved white shirt, a tie, and trousers with suspenders. He comes and goes, struggling to find the gap in the curtain, until he has set up five folding chairs in a line and sat down in the center one with a clipboard in his lap. The four Coward actors, now dressed in street clothes, come out from backstage and sit in the other chairs. They look at each other, at the audience, and at the man in the middle, who looks back and says, "Any questions?"

This simple query is the true beginning of *Cabin Pressure* and the punchline to an elaborate joke, too clever by half for some, yet dead serious in its ironic insistence that this play begins at the end, at that moment of ontological limbo in the theater when actors and audience release each from their mutual compact, shed the skins of aesthetic illusion, and revert to their everyday identities. This is the moment of the curtain call, followed by the houselights coming on and then the squeak of the chairs as people get up to leave, an ambiguous state that Bert States has described as "a seam in social nature" and "a decompression chamber halfway between the depths of art and the thin air of reality."[3] In the phenomenology of theater, the curtain call reverses and concludes what begins two hours earlier, when the 'cabin pressure' in the theater changes as a still comes over the rustling crowd, the houselights fade down, and the 'magic' curtain goes up. As her first order of business, Bogart conflates these two sublime liminal passages – beginning and end, engagement and disengagement, take off and landing, tension and release, walk in and sit down and stand up and walk out – in order to introduce her chief subject: the alchemy of actor and audience.

Cabin Pressure is earnest and explicit in its conviction that the audience has a crucial, creative role to play in the act of theater, mainly through the willing participation of the imagination. Its argument organizes itself around three fundamentals of performance:

- the sine qua non of shared presence, actor and audience, often figured in terms of being in "the room" together;
- the mutual agreement (or aesthetic contract) between audience and actor implicit in the idea of theatrical convention;
- the audience's experience of theatrical time, in terms of beginning, middle, and end, and the arousal, affirmation, and reversal of certain expectations.

All three of these subjects are raised by the initial sequence of *Cabin Pressure*, and as the piece advances, it instigates a self-consciousness about them that is, by turns, entertaining, mundane, provocative, tedious, and compelling.

The man with the clipboard, SITI actor Barney O'Hanlon, follows up his initial question with others designed to initiate a post-play discussion: "What did you think?," "What was your experience?," "What did you think it was about?," "What were your expectations?," "Did you have a good time?" The actors onstage begin to provide hesitant, monosyllabic answers – "I liked it," or "It was fun," or "It's just pretty" – and it soon becomes clear that they are not there now as actors in street clothes ready to talk about their Noël Coward play but as members of an audience called upon to offer feedback about their experience. With O'Hanlon as the innocuous dramaturg, coaxing reluctant responses from his guests, this initial question and answer session becomes a virtual parody of a typical audience "Talkback" in a regional resident theater. The four spectators, played by Ellen Lauren, Kelly Maurer, Stephen Webber, and Will Bond, come off as innocent boobs, marble-mouthed philistines who fidget in their seats and fumble for words to describe their responses (see fig. 10). As they hem and haw and wriggle in their chairs, they act as if they don't know what they are talking about or their answers are wrong, even though they are being asked to talk about their own perceptions and responses. There is an element of the actor's revenge in these cartoon characterizations – how often, after all, does a professional actor get to play the audience? – but this initial mockery is part of the piece's strategy, setting the stage, as it were, for a changing image of the audience, one which will ultimately confer on them a measure of fondness and respect and even a heroic dignity.

No sooner is the conceit of this first talkback scene established than it gives way to another, brief play-within-the-play, on the model of the *Private Lives* scene but referencing a different theatrical style altogether. The upstage curtain parts to reveal Ellen Lauren sitting on a high, narrow

Figure 10. Actors and audiences: *Cabin Pressure* at Humana (1999). (a) Barney O'Hanlon (center) as moderator and (from left to right) Ellen Lauren, Kelly Maurer, Stephen Webber, and Will Bond as everyday theatergoers in a talkback session. (b) The same five actors parody the theatrical conventions of the avant-garde. (Photographs by Richard Trigg.)

table, wearing a yellow paper crown, an ellipse of bright, white light splashed on the wall behind her. She leans to her left, in utter stillness, her body on a rigid diagonal, as she speaks through a head microphone that gives her voice the pretentious portent that was a convention – and then a cliché – of 1980s avant-garde performance. This is an allusion to the Theater of Images and, in particular, to the painterly images of Robert Wilson, an early preoccupation of Bogart's. Lauren's posture recalls the angular positions taken by Lucinda Childs in *Einstein on the Beach*, and her voice and text seem at moments to mimic the quirky inflections and sensibility of Laurie Anderson. Her text actually is taken from Peter Handke's *Offending the Audience*, a rarely performed *sprechstück* (speech play) from the 1960s. In its drive to instigate a complex self-consciousness in the audience, one that makes them both the object and the subject of the play, it can be seen as a paradigm for *Cabin Pressure* as a whole. The Handke excerpt intoned by Lauren features a litany of simple declarative sentences:

> You represent something. You are someone. You are something. You are no longer someone here. You are something. You are a society of sorts. You are an order because you come dressed, the position of your bodies, the direction of your glances. You also form an order with the seating arrangement. You are dressed up. With your dress you observe an order. You dress up. By dressing up, you demonstrate that you are doing something that you don't do everyday. You are putting on a masquerade so as to partake in a masquerade. You partake. You watch. You stare. By watching, you become rigid. You become something that watches. You are no longer someone here. You are something. You are no longer alone with yourselves. You are no longer left to your own devices. Now you are with it. You are the reason why. You are an audience. That is a relief. You can partake.[4]

By now, the audience recognizes that the object of representation, the "you" of this pile-up of sentences and the main subject of the play, is indeed them – or the idea of them. The play proceeds to dissect this subject as it weaves back and forth between the two established types of scene, talkback interviews with the audience and send-ups of various theatrical styles and genres. These mini-meta-plays include snippets of a Restoration pavane, with prancing actors in periwigs carrying fans and lace handkerchiefs; a nineteenth-century pantomimic melodrama, with a damsel in distress, a villain in black, and a handful of shredded white paper tossed in the air to indicate "Snow!"; an Agatha Christie-like English manor house murder mystery, set on a dark and stormy night, with a stuffy inspector who speaks standard lines like "No one may leave this room;" and a postmodern pageant à la the Wooster Group, with actors in dark glasses and postures of torpor lined up in a row speaking theoretical gibberish into table microphones (see figure 10, page 138 above). Bolstered by the musical selections of Darron West's sound design, each of these sketches exaggerates the conventions of the genre or style on display, for comic effect and for the sake of highlighting the nature of conventions as theatrical devices with a life cycle that begins as innovation, evolves into common practice, and then declines into cliché. Rather than conversational dialogue, the texts for some of these scenes consist of theoretical passages (about acting, audiences, theater in general) spoken as if they were dialogue, a Bogart technique familiar from *No Plays No Poetry*, *Going, Going, Gone*, and other pieces.[5]

As talkback scenes recur, the field of inquiry expands to include the actor. The gentle Interviewer also wants to know: "What is it that makes an actor interesting? . . . What is the actor doing? . . . If you could ask an actor anything, what would it be?" The answer to this last question is repeated word for word by the four Spectators in turn, sitting now in their folding metal chairs in four spotlights on the four corners of the stage: "Well, do– . . . do they min– . . . do they mind doing the– . . . you know, over and over again?" The cadence here, the self-interruption, and the inability to find a word to name what it is the actor does all reflect the vernacular source of the Spectators' lines, which were taken verbatim from the interviews Bogart conducted with members of the project audience attached to her production of *Private Lives*.

Each of the four spectators has what amounts to a monologue at some point. The anxious, excitable spectator played by Ellen Lauren works herself into a frenzy as she reveals her understanding of convention:

> You can do something that would look ridiculous, like somebody gets punched in the, stomach, and out comes a, a red cloth, for example. And you kind of go, 'Oh, okay.' I'm sposed to see blood. So I'll I'll buy that, into that with my imagination. So you actually get more involved because it's more artificial. You know what I mean? It is an extreme event.[6]

The persona played by Kelly Maurer is calmer, a bit world weary perhaps, but there is still a lilt in her voice when she observes:

> It's . . . It's difficult. It's more difficult. I'm learning that's not necessarily a bad thing . . . the effort. The effort to go. To get there. Like if you have to get through a snowstorm someday to get there, everybody feels more together because you all got through a snowstorm to get there.

I like that. I like that fact that it's a little bit difficult I mean. Some go cause they wanna be shocked, to be angered, challenged. All of the heavier emotions – I 'spose. Ya know, blah, blah surprise. But, for me it's it's just pretty.

In the context of *Cabin Pressure*, contrasted by the carefully composed dialogue of Coward, Shakespeare, Handke and others, this off-the-cuff vernacular speech takes on the lyricism of the inarticulate. As analysis, "it's it's just pretty" is dumb, but it takes on a homespun humanity when spoken as a direct quote from a local citizen, with inflections and verbal hems and haws intact. A personality makes itself felt, both an individual person and, more and more as the piece advances, the persona of the archetypal everyday theatergoer, who turns out to be just as preoccupied with the physical routine of theatergoing – wearing appropriate clothes, the fatigue of day's end, getting to the theater, parking, trying not to cough, hearing from up in the balcony, and so on – as they are with the aesthetic and intellectual challenges of the play itself. The audience is revealed as corporate and corporal all at once, a theatrical body whose imagination cannot be engaged if its stomach is growling or its butt is uncomfortable in the seat.

Just as *Cabin Pressure* plays with the experience of theatrical time, through repetition, acceleration, and fragmentation, it plays with the topography of theatrical space. This is most obvious in a sequence in the middle of the play that represents what goes on in the minutes before and after the curtain goes up for a performance. Reversing the standard arrangement, the Victor Jory's thrust stage represents backstage for a performance, as it turns out, of *Private Lives*. The actors appear in their now-familiar Coward costumes, getting ready to go on, as O'Hanlon, now a stage manager, calls places and makes sure all is in order. A portion of the play is seen upstage (visible from the backside through a sheer scrim-like curtain), but focus remains on the ethereal and liminal world of backstage. As before, this *Private Lives* sequence ends with a series of bows, the curtain closing, the houselights coming up, and the Interviewer coming out to set up the folding chairs for a post-play discussion. The actors come out, the Interviewer asks "Any questions?," and *Cabin Pressure*, after more than an hour, begins all over again, thus provoking a variation on an earlier question: does *the audience* mind "doing the, you know, over and over again?" Repetition, one of the Viewpoints, proclaims itself as the glory and essence of theater, the basis for comparison that allows an audience to figure out what is going on, the basis for conventions that compress time and space into a finite theatrical box, and the basis for its continued existence night after night, performance after performance.

This time though, the talkback segment yields and blends into another dramatic excerpt, one that kicks the play into a different register and prepares for its unpredictable final sequence. As the onstage Spectators go through their standard responses, Maurer says, "Why don't we dance?" The remark goes unnoticed at first, but when she repeats it, or words to that effect, Lauren chimes in, "Not a bad idea." And, in a moment, the Spectators have taken up roles in what many will recognize as an excerpt from Edward Albee's *Who's Afraid of Virginia Woolf?*, a psychologically savage sequence in the second act when Martha humiliates George in front of Nick and Honey until he erupts in anger and attacks her. As performed by Will Bond (George) and Ellen Lauren (Martha), this attack and its illusion of violence are palpable and convincingly real, even though everything that has come before has warned the audience to regard what they see on stage as a matter of convention and theatrical make-believe. At this climactic moment, significantly, the lights go out and a tight beam of light isolates the Interviewer downstage as he says, "I've become extremely interested in the relationship between the audience and the actors on the stage." The statement that follows sounds as if it must come from Bogart herself. If it contains ideas that have already been expressed – that the audience has a creative role to play, that the relationship between audience and actor is a circular one – their repetition here makes clear that *Cabin Pressure*, more than a theater essay, is a personal confession, the articulation of certain articles of faith, unashamed of their simplicity, profound and guileless in their honesty, as if the director stepped out from the protective shell of the production to say, "This is who I am. This is what I believe."

By the time this statement is finished, the four actors in the Albee scene have resumed their persona as Spectators and are sitting again in their metal chairs in four spots of light in the four corners of the stage. A single, plaintive piano note is heard, and the Interviewer, seated in the fifth chair, says softly, "Why do you go?" The mood is different now, more elegiacal. Each Spectator answers this question in turn, as if it were a matter of life or death. With simple, unforced sincerity, Lauren says, "I go because, for me, it's the sense that anything can happen. That anything can happen." The others provide their reasons: because life is unbearable, for the stillness, as an escape, for "the icing on the cake," because it's better than TV, "as a way of getting out of myself," for the mystery of what is behind the curtain. O'Hanlon joins them in this litany, releasing his persona as Interviewer to become, ultimately, another Spectator. As they speak, their attitude is reflective, almost melancholy, and their tones are soft, as if not to disturb the vacuum of empty space around them, even when, midway through this list, they start to move through that space. At first, all five pivot up and out of their chairs, fold them up, and cross to another spot in a curved motion. Some unfold their chairs and sit. Others remain standing. A rhythm of walking and sitting and standing and walking and speaking at odd irregular intervals takes hold, until Lauren speaks the play's final words, cribbed from Herbert Blau: "The theater remains the form most depended upon, fascinated with, drawn, quartered by, and fixated upon the body, its vulnerabilities, pain – and disappearance."

With this, the play might be over and the bodies might disappear, but before they do there is a coda, a movement sequence with these five actors and their innocuous clanging folding chairs, set to elliptical, pulsing, mounting music by a new music ensemble called Rachels. They line up in a diagonal across the stage, chairs in hand, and the line begins to rotate in a circle, like a propeller spinning faster and faster, until they fly off and end upstage seated in a line as they were at the very start. They are the audience again, and they go through a pantomime of audience reactions, stretching, wriggling in their seats, leaning forward with interest, leaning back in boredom, scratching, squirming, listening, watching. Sometimes these gestures are simultaneous, sometimes not. There is a gasp, a cough, a yawn, a sudden clap, a cry of "Yes!," a shush, a snore. There is weeping and laughter. And there is the joke of unwrapping hard candy and staring down the poor oblivious fool who crinkles and crinkles the wrapper. As the music builds into a more insistent sway, this orchestrated pantomime gives way to more abstract movement. As if yanked up out of their seats by some cosmic force, the actors lurch forward and then collapse back into their sitting positions. This movement repeats. Side by side in parallel lanes, they lunge forward at odd intervals, some falling to the floor, others reaching out in front of them, only to be pulled back upstage into the chairs, as if attached to an elastic cord that will stretch but not let go. Eventually, O'Hanlon breaks this routine, breaks free, dashes downstage and then walks back up slowly, takes up his chair, and clangs it down with a bang. The others follow suit, as the music pounds more like a march, slapping down their chairs all at once, and then dancing with them freely, twirling them around, twirling around them, folding and unfolding, standing on them, jumping down, falling out of them and falling back in, a chaotic ballet of five actors and five metal chairs. With the music loud and strong, they end up running in a circle and then finally dashing downstage, setting their chairs up in a row, their backs to the audience, making a new front row, becoming a part of them as everybody now stares at a blank white wall upstage. The music stops. There is a blackout. The play is over.

I can say without hesitation that this "audience ballet" (as it came to be known) is one of the most cathartic experiences I have had as a spectator. As a wordless six-minute coda to the ninety minutes of practical and theoretical theater talk that preceded it, it had an exquisite, wrenching beauty. On one level, it was just a variation on a Viewpoints exercise that limits movement to lanes, but it was executed with such passionate control that it exemplified the methods and vocabularies of the SITI Company: the physical discipline and gravity of Suzuki, the kinesthetic crackle of the Viewpoints, the total awareness of the performers, the spirit of collaboration, the precision of detail, and the freedom found within a tight structure. On one level, it might be seen as just a rip-off of some Judson-era improvisation with pedestrian movement, but in reinforcing the choreographic nature of Bogart's theater, it connected her with her teachers and her teacher's teachers and with popular and avant-garde traditions in American performing arts. As *Cabin Pressure*'s final portrait of the audience, it expressed a profound respect for what they bring to the play, including varying degrees of attention, various types of response, a preoccupation with physical comfort, and beyond that, a humanity edged in anguish and yearning, a willingness to be engaged, and maybe even an impulse somehow to rise up out of their seats and become a part of the fiction.

And as the conclusion to a ninety-minute theatrical essay, it restored the ineffable to the argument and insisted that the ultimate statement about the audience–actor relationship can only be made in the language of performance itself.

In a narrow, literal fashion, *Full Circle* offers a literal, textbook demonstration of Mee's conviction that culture is a perpetual process of remaking. It derives from a play that has been re-made many times. During the Yuan dynasty (1271–1368), the Chinese playwright Li Qianfu wrote *Huilan ji* (*The Chalk Circle*). As a *zaju* or "variety play," it was intended to entertain all levels of society with its combination of songs, often with new lyrics set to known court and folk tunes; movement sequences, in the form of dance, acrobatics, combat, clowning, and pantomime; dialogue, ranging from lyric poetry to colloquial prose to verbal buffoonery; and stock characters, defined by age, gender, and moral status. Its action centers on a down-and-out prostitute named Haitang, who becomes the concubine of a wealthy landowner and bears him a son, triggering the jealousy of his wife. When the landowner is murdered, Haitang is falsely accused of the crime and her maternity is contested. The case is referred to a provincial authority, Judge Bao, an archetypal character in Yuan drama, who uses the famous test of the chalk circle to restore the child to his rightful, biological mother. Justice prevails at the eleventh hour, rounding off the play's implicit social criticism with a happy ending.

Huilan ji journeyed to the west when it was translated by the scholar Stanislas Julien and published in French in 1832 as *L'histoire du Cercle de Craie*, but it had negligible impact until the German poet Klabund (pen name of Alfred Henschke) adapted it in 1925 as a vehicle for the popular Viennese actress Elizabeth Bergner.[7] Max Reinhardt directed *Der Kreidekreis* at the Deutsches Theater, and it became a tremendous boulevard success in Berlin, Vienna, and throughout Europe, thanks in large part to Klabund's substitution of fairy-tale sentimentality for the original's social commentary. This Weimar chinoiserie was precisely the sort of culinary theater despised by Bertolt Brecht, who was a dramaturg at the Deutsches Theatre shortly before Reinhardt's production and who went on to parody the play (among other things) in his *Elephant Calf* of 1926. As dramatic raw material, the Yuan fable proved to have abiding appeal for Brecht during his years of exile. In 1941, his story "The Augsburg Chalk Circle" was published in Moscow, and a couple of years later, while living in Santa Monica, he set to work adapting the chalk circle story as a Broadway vehicle for the Hollywood star Luise Rainer.[8] Brecht shifted the play's setting from China to the Caucausus and replaced Klabund's Orientalist romanticism with an epic folk legend set in ancient times and set off as a parable by a contemporary political frame. The concubine Haitang became the kitchen maid Grusha, and the contested child was not her own but the abandoned son of the ruling governor, who was assassinated in a palace coup in the beginning of the play. In the chalk circle scene at the end, Azdak, Brecht's Saturnalian twist on the original, incorruptible Judge Bao, awards custody to Grusha, endorsing her claim that her sacrifices for the child are the true sign of maternity.

The planned Broadway production of Brecht's *Der kaukasische Kreidekreis* (*The Caucasian Chalk Circle*) never came to fruition. Instead, the play had its unlikely world premiere in 1948 at Carleton College in Northfield, Minnesota in a translation by Eric and Maja Bentley. By that time, Brecht had left America and returned to Europe, where he formed the Berliner Ensemble, which eventually settled into its famous home at the Theater am Schiffbauerdamm in what was then East Berlin. Under Brecht's direction, the Berliner Ensemble gave the play its German premiere in 1954 and took it on tour to Paris in 1955 and London in 1956. These landmark tours, bracketing Brecht's death on August 14, 1956, accelerated his influence in post-war Europe and around the world. Eventually, that influence spread as far as China, where Brecht's theories and plays were used to invigorate the form of modern spoken plays known as *huaju*. In 1986, the director of a *huaju* performance of *The Caucasian Chalk Circle* presented by the Chinese Youth Artistic Troupe called upon a well-known Peking opera performer named Hu Zhifeng for help in adding classical Chinese techniques to Brecht's play. This led Hu Zhifeng to adapt, direct, and perform her own Peking opera version of the *Chalk Circle* tale, combining Li Qianfu's original *zaju* with Brecht's epic-theater master-piece. When *Huilan ji* (the original Yuan title) premiered in 1992 at the Dongpo Theatre in Hangzhou under the auspices of the Zhejiang Provincial Peking Opera Troupe, the nearly 700-year-old *Chalk Circle* had come full circle.[9]

This long, global history of adaptation and appropriation and the ever more intricate intertextuality of each successive *Chalk Circle* play could not help but appeal to Mee, who undertook his own version in the mid 1990s. Mee had studied and performed Brecht as an undergraduate at Harvard, even going so far as to track down Eric Bentley, the leading champion and scholar of Brecht in the USA, in New York to seek his advice. As a young playwright in New York and a staffer at *The Drama Review*, Mee saw the Living Theatre's productions of *In the Jungle of Cities* (1960) and *Man is Man* (1962) at their downtown theater on 14th Street.[10] A few years later, Brecht moved uptown, with productions of *The Caucasian Chalk Circle* (1966) and *Galileo* (1967) by the Repertory Theatre of Lincoln Center. But as Brecht was catching hold in the USA, Mee was drifting away from theater into political activism and writing history. When he returned to playwriting in the 1980s, he first found inspiration in the anarchy of dada, the collage work of Max Ernst and Kurt Schwitters, and the majesty of the Greeks, but Brecht – as a moralist who would not back off from the question of the public good; as a political vaudevillian who peppered his plays with popular songs, slapstick routines, and other variety acts; as a dialectical materialist who embraced contradiction and conflict as the engine of historical change; and as an unapologetic pilferer, some would say plagiarist, who borrowed from a wide range of sources – was always there lurking in the shadows as one model of what a playwright could be.

So, too, was the more contemporary figure of Heiner Müller, Brecht's theatrical heir and just as crucial to Mee and *Full Circle*. When Mee returned to playwriting in the 1980s, Müller, through his collaborations with Robert Wilson and the attention of PAJ publishers Bonnie Marranca and Gautam Dasgupta, was just gaining recognition in the USA as the embodiment of a postmodern playwright. Mee's *War to End War*, whatever its express debt to dada, has a Müllerian ring to it, in its attempt to blow history wide open, its myriad allusions and anachronisms, and its imprac-tical/impossible stage directions, which call for an inventive director who will construct a theatrical event around the play's borrowed texts. As Jonathan Kalb writes, "Müller's risky habit during much of his career was to adopt the styles and personas of other authors. He did not do this trivially, for the cheap thrill of mimicry, but rather out of a principled mistrust of originality and the historical construction of literary heroes."[11] Much the same could be said of Mee. Kalb organizes his book on Müller around a series of shadow-figures – Kleist, Mayakovsky, Shakespeare, Artaud, Genet, Wagner, Beckett – playwrights whose body of work Müller occupied like "a vampire or virus in order to explode it from within."[12] Mee crawled into the skin of his own shadow-figures to con-front his own national history with his own unique sensibility. Chief among Mee's shadow figures are Brecht and Müller. Both have a distinct and literal presence in *Full Circle*. If they are Mee's pater familias, *Full Circle* is part homage, part double patricide.

Full Circle

Crucial to Brecht's *The Caucasian Chalk Circle* was his addition of a prologue and frame to the traditional story. Set just after the end of the Second World War in a war-torn kolkhoz in Soviet Georgia, this prologue presents a dispute between two agricultural collectives over which of them should now own and farm a fertile valley.[13] The matter is resolved through peaceful deliberation in favor of the group that will make better use of the land, rather than in terms of property rights. To celebrate the settlement, a play is presented, under the direction of the singer and storyteller, Arkadi Cheidze; it takes the form of a fable set in "olden times" which tells of the heroic struggle of the kitchen maid Grusha to do the right thing and of the anarchic administration of justice by the rascally judge Azdak. This frame helped Brecht to demonstrate his vision of epic theater as a genre of drama that, through various means such as historicizing its subject matter and emphasizing the action as a theatrical presentation, sought to make the familiar appear strange (*verfremdung*) and, in so doing, to incite critical inquiry as a form of aesthetic pleasure for an audience. Within this frame, the twin tales of Grusha and Azdak constituted an extended play-within-a-play, and each episode within it was presented as a crux, a demonstration of an event more than an event in itself, focused on key decisions made by typical characters facing specific social, political, and economic circumstances. The frame story – in its resolution of the dispute over the valley at the start, the ongoing presence of the Singer as narrator, and his final, brief appearance summing up the moral of the story – is always there to forestall the narcotic illusionism of a play like Klabund's and to remind the audience that the chalk circle play is a play, that is, both a performance in celebration of a successful social praxis and a social praxis in and of itself.

The present-tense of Brecht's frame for *Caucasian Chalk Circle* coincides with the historical moment when the Allied victory that ended the Second World War gave way to the onset of the Cold War. This was just the period that shaped the USA of Mee's youth in the late 1940s and 1950s and later came to motivate many of his interests as a historian. Fast forward forty-five years to November 1989 and another liminal moment of history: the breaching of the Berlin Wall, the eventual collapse of the Soviet Union, and the end of the Cold War. This is the present-tense of *Full Circle*, which begins with its own play-within-a-play, which mimics Brecht in canny ways. Set in the late-1980s China of Deng Ziaoping, it features two American investment bankers, two Chinese investment bankers, a government expert in a Mao jacket, and a female translator, all of whom are played by Caucasian actors in exaggerated "Oriental" make-up. The Chinese characters speak a Chinese-y gibberish that, by Mee's instruction, should be as "offensive" and "politically incorrect" as possible. Here again a valley is at stake: the American businessmen are negotiating a deal in which they will sell back to the Chinese a genetically modified strain of the valley's native rice, on which the Yankees will hold a patent in perpetuity. Once a deal is struck between the men, all of them in pin-striped suits, the Chinese announce with a blithe but undeniable irony: "Thank God. We used to think that communism would solve all of our problems. Now we see that capitalism will solve all our problems."

Only at this point does the action reveal itself as a play-within-the-play. An irate member of the audience rises in anger to ask: "Is this some sort of political play?" This turns out to be Erick Honecker, Secretary General of the Communist Party and head of state in the German Democratic Republic. On this evening in 1989, he has come to what turns out to be the Berliner Ensemble expecting to see a quaint parable by Brecht. Outraged, Honecker demands to see the artistic director, who turns out to be none other than Heiner Müller. Historically, Müller did not become head of the Berliner Ensemble until 1995, less than a year before his death, but in 1989, he was the most produced playwright in both Germanys and a controversial national hero among artists and intellectuals. Mee's comic characterization makes clear that Müller is no more a sacred cow than Brecht is. Described as ill-shaven, red-faced, and vomit-soaked, Müller kowtows to Honecker and the State, kissing the hem of his long, leather coat and praising "a government that ensures the public order and nurtures the public good, sometimes even by giving grants to cultural institutions, god knows!, even though to be sure it is easier to give grants to ballet companies or to art museums rather than to theaters where words are used." He defends the Chinese agribusiness play as not political propaganda but "a human play, a play about how human beings feel, no doubt because of the way they were brought up, you know, their childhoods, their mothers and fathers." These clear and ironic allusions to the contemporary arts scene in the USA assert Mee's own metadramatic purpose in *Full Circle*. Even as the play seems to mock aspects of Brecht and Müller, it stumps for a contemporary American epic theater modeled on Brecht and Müller, one that fights back in the Culture Wars of the 1980s and 1990s, rejects the dominance of psychological realism, and calls into question the poverty of a genuine political theater in the USA.

This American dimension of *Full Circle* is fortified by Mee's injection of two flamboyant American characters into the chalk circle story: a ditzy socialite named Pamela Dalrymple, suggested by the real-life figure of Pamela Harriman, who has come to the House of Brecht as a cultural tourist; and the billionaire venture capitalist Warren Buffett, who shows up, cherry Coke in hand, looking for investments that will tap the new markets of the former Eastern bloc.[14] Pamela, in particular, proves central to Mee's revision of Brecht. In the first scene, when the revolution in the streets spills into the theater, Honecker and his young mistress Christa take flight, and in the hubbub, their love child – Karl Marx Honecker, "a name that bears some history," says Müller – is left in the custody of Pamela. Unable to cope with the messiness of child care, she immediately hires one of the student revolutionaries off the street as her au pair for $250 a week. This is the Grusha character, here named Dulle Griet, after the peasant figure in a famous Brueghel painting on which Brecht modeled

Grusha.[15] To protect the child, Pamela and Dulle Griet set off together on a difficult journey that turns Grusha's earnest flight into the Northern Mountains into a carefree shopping spree across the changing face of Germany. When they need milk for the baby and a night's lodging, Pamela checks them into a ritzy spa where she can get a massage and take the baths. Whereas Brecht's Grusha had to bargain with a peasant before paying half a week's wages for a cup of milk, Mee's Dulle Griet is taught by the hotel's kitchen staff how to say, "Put it on the tab." Mee even copies Grusha's famous Perils-of-Pauline escape across a rope bridge high above a mountain chasm, turning it into the occasion for a wry soliloquy about "that shadowy void just beyond the edge of the stage of human comedy" (see figure 11). The two clownish goons chasing the women get so nervous crossing the bridge that one drops his pants to take a leak on the audience below and the other tries to calm him down by getting him to sing the Village People's "YMCA."

Mee finds plenty of occasions to imitate Brecht's epic theater techniques as well, often with a hint of irreverence. He converts Brecht's use of projected scene titles into a vaudeville character called the Sign Man, who holds up placards introducing each new scene. Brecht's fondness for having his low-status characters exchange folk aphorisms as lines of dialogue is inverted when the wealthy Warren Buffett utters trite affirmations like "Never ask the barber if you need a haircut" and "My idea of a group decision is to look in the mirror." With the Berliner Ensemble, Brecht facilitated the march of historical time and the frequent changes of locale called for by his episodic plots by staging them on a revolve, most famously in his production of *Mother Courage and Her Children*. Mee writes *Full Circle* for a turntable stage as well, and after a sequence in which Pamela and Dulle Griet "travel à la Brecht" past a despoiled landscape littered with abandoned Soviet tanks, broken dolls and toys, old government file cabinets, and other rubble, Pamela cries, "Wait, wait! Stop!" and Dulle Griet says, "I think we're going in circles." Of course, they do go in circles in ending up back in Berlin and on trial for kidnapping little Karl Marx Honecker. The judge for this trial turns out to be Heiner Müller, summoned from jail by the young revolutionaries as "the man of conscience during the old regime" and therefore the best to administer the first round of justice in the new post-communist world.

The dispute over custody of the child, the symbol of the New Europe, shapes up as a three-way battle between Crista, Pamela, and Dulle Griet. As Mee's Müller sees it, "one of you brings money to the job. / One brings love. / One brings the bloodlines. / But I don't think any one of you / has it

Figure 11. Copying Brecht: two productions of *Full Circle.* (a) Amy Morton as Pamela followed by Marion Mayberry as Dulle Griet at Steppenwolf (1997). (Photograph by Michael Brosilow.) (b) Will LeBow as Heiner Müller at the American Repertory Theatre (2000). (Photograph by Richard Feldman.)

all." So, he resorts to the chalk circle test but with a twist. Reversing the wisdom of Solomon, Judge Bao, and Azdak, Müller declares that "we live in a new age now. / And the new rule is / the real mother is the one / who grabs the child and holds on for dear life / who holds on and keeps holding on / who never lets go / until she and she alone has the child in her grip." And in the rough-and-tumble tug-of-war that follows, Pamela, the epitome of the Ugly American, prevails. She immediately retains Dulle Griet as au pair so that she can run off with Warren Buffett to get married in Biarritz. Before stepping down from the bench, Judge Müller annuls Dulle Griet's marriage of convenience and proposes to her, paving the way for a double wedding out of Shakespearean romantic comedy. The play ends with the whole cast, "dressed in rags and holding out tin begging cups," singing the Beatles "All You Need is Love" in German – "Leib, Leib, Leib" – as "daisies rain down from the sky."

If Mee's intent was only to lampoon Brecht, *Full Circle* would be little more than an academic trifle, but the parody here is too grand, too intelligent, and too penetrating to be an end in itself. The madcap comedy, the slapstick hi-jinks, the wry satire all mask a bolder effort to invoke the comic sublime. Again and again, Mee prolongs a particular situation or passage well beyond a ridiculous extreme so that it passes through sentimentality or silliness and then through the sarcasm of exaggeration to regain a measure of sincerity. For example, early in their journey, Pamela and Dulle Griet contemplate what Brecht the moralist presents in *The Caucasian Chalk Circle* as the temptation to do good. "I'd like to do the right thing myself," says Mee's Dulle Griet. "Sometimes I feel such badness welling up in me . . . And still, I think: / there is some goodness too. / I have in me such an intensity of life." Her words are so simple and bland that she seems ludicrous, especially when she goes on to describe "how many beautiful songs there are in the world / choirs of all kinds / children in their schoolrooms / farmers in their fields." This would be sufficient to mimic the mawkish sentiment and folk wisdom that Brecht makes conspicuous in some of his characters, but the speech goes on at great length and with great lyricism as Dulle Griet describes her vision of "the Happy Life."

I think, one day, when my happiness is given to me
When my happiness is given me,
life will be
a nameless thing.
It will seethe and roar;

it will plunge and whirl;
it will leap and shriek in convulsions;
it will quiver in delicate fantasy;
writhe and twist;
glitter and flash and shine;
sing gently;
it will shout in exquisite excitement;
vibrate to the roots
like a great oak in a storm;
it will dance;
it will glide;
it will gallop;
it will fly;
it will soar high–high;
it will go down into depths unexplored;
rage and rave;
sound out like a terrific blare of trumpets;
chime faintly;
sob and grieve and weep;
revel and carouse;
it will go in pride;
lie prone like the dead;
it will float buoyantly on the air.
And when it comes my turn to meet face to face
with the miraculous vision of the Happy Life
I know I will be rendered dumb.
But my feeling will open up like the torrent of a summer rain
like a rain of summer flowers.

The passage comes from the autobiography of Mary MacLane (1881–1929), a free spirit from the mining town of Butte, Montana who wrote her life story at age nineteen and became a celebrity bohemian when it sold more than 100,000 copies. Mee found it in one of his favored places to look for texts to steal, an anthology of "outsider literature" written by psychiatric in-patients over the course of the twentieth century.[16] His inclusion of it in the middle of a scene throws things off balance. In its new context, the speech is too long to sustain irony and be just a joke, and nothing follows that undercuts or negates it – at least not until the play ends with just the rain of summer flowers that Dulle Griet dreams of. In the moment, all Pamela can say in response to her rhapsody is: "I must say, this is what I love so much about travel. / One meets such interesting people."

This yearning for the Happy Life surfaces in an explicit political form during the wedding bacchanal that celebrates Dulle Griet's marriage to a feeble-minded car mechanic named Gunter. Here is yet another Mee scene built around a ritual meal. As guests pass out in a drunken stupor left and right, Ursula, Dulle Griet's sister-in-law, raises her glass and says,

> On a serious note
> I say, let us pray that we find a third way
> neither communism nor capitalism
> but a third way
> some middle ground
> to get rich, like in the West
> and to share like in the East
> Because the choice that we are being given
> this should not be our only choice.

This prompts an argument about free will versus determinism and the possibility of social action, which climaxes when Dulle Griet plunks down her souvenir piece of the Berlin Wall on the banquet table and says, "Don't let anyone tell you / you can't change the way things are. / It happens all the time." In the moment, this might seem like so much drunken blather, but the heavy clunk of the prop on the table cuts through the fog and lends a ring of authority to what she says. There is a utopian urge here peeking out from behind the play's layered ironies, or, short of that, a neo-Brechtian provocation to consider the idea of utopia, the dialectics of historical process and political action, and the possibility of "a third way." The free-wheeling theatricality and carnivalesque spirit of the play conceal and reveal both at once its sincere concern with the state of the world, how it is to improve, and how the artist might participate in that process.

In 1961, the year the Berlin Wall was erected, Heiner Müller was an aspiring and promising thirty-two-year-old playwright when he triggered the wrath of East German authorities with – ironically enough in this context – his own play about agricultural disputes and land reform. *The Resettled Woman* was shut down the night before it opened, and Müller was kicked out of the Writers' Union, even after, on the advice of Brecht's widow, Helene Weigel, he composed a "self-deprecatory self-critique to try to save himself."[17] Mee, perhaps on this model, provides his Müller with a mind-boggling confessional monologue that constitutes the penultimate scene of *Full Circle*. It is a stunning meditation on the role of the artist in society that takes the form of a kind of psychological *hara-kiri*, an exercise in self-recrimination that turns the despicable playwright, and any who are as honest as he, into an ironic hero. The monologue's defiant length – it goes on for twenty minutes – recalls the extended text blocks found in many Müller plays. In a way, the whole play and all of its theatrical hijinks might be said to exist for the sake of this harrowing and unrelenting interrogation of the self, conducted, as Mee has it, under a single, naked light bulb (see figure 11, page 151 above).

The scene begins with Müller, "still sweating, covered with vomit," rotting in a jail cell and asking of no one in particular, "So? / What am I doing here? / What did I do wrong?"[18] He then launches into a series of diatribes that alternate between brutal self-excoriation and unapologetic self-justification. He defends his involvement with Stasi, the East German secret police, only to admit a moment later that he was in the wrong. He dismisses art as nothing more than "a way of supporting the status quo" and then valorizes it as an agent of social change and "the purest expression we have of human freedom." And then he says, "but really so what? / I mean if you really care / whether this fellow on the street has no food or clothes / the most useful thing to do is not to put on a play / but give him food." In a manner that mirrors the real-Müller's career-long posture of "belligerent subterfuge and protean elusiveness,"[19] in both his writing and his public persona, the Mee–Müller's train of thought careens from one contradiction to the next, unsaying what he has just said in a logorrheic effort to empty himself out, to evacuate himself, to rid himself of words, free himself of the past, and maybe even get to the end of history itself. With one breath he says, "You can't escape history," and with the next, he insists, "Now we are all Americans / We start without a history / Today is a new day."

In the end, Müller denounces himself as a criminal (whether he is guilty or not) and calls for his own punishment, listing at great length the forms of torture to which he wouldn't mind being subjected. He ends his screed on a note of aggressive ambiguity:

Whatever it is said
I may have contributed to
whether true or not
whatever it is I may have condoned
or consented to with my silence
or neglected to challenge as an artist or a human being
a citizen, a worker in the society,
OK
OK

let it be done to me
let justice take its course
I, for one, am ready.
You want to know
how should a man behave?
I say:
do as I do.
Do as I do.

Despite his will to be punished, he finds himself summoned by "the people in the streets" to administer justice in the present political vacuum because "Who's better to judge, they say, / than one who is himself guilty." In the next and final scene, the new judge uses his Darwinian version of the chalk circle test to resolve the child custody battle, moralizing that "people who let go / just get things taken away from them."

Even when his rhetoric is self-obfuscating or self-indulgent, even when he is disingenuous or vituperative, Müller is so unrelenting and ferocious in his honesty that his confessional tirade passes through the ridicule of satire to take on a measure of ironic heroism. It is difficult to imagine that Mee, as a playwright with his own history of political activism and as a historian with an interest in the role of the artist in society, could write such a speech and not project his own personal ambivalences, anxieties, regrets, misgivings, and self-doubt, as well as his profound convictions, into Müller here. The scene's title alone, "Ich Bin Ein Berliner," is enough to suggest Mee's identification with Müller (not to mention with the young American president who uttered those famous words near the Wall on June 26, 1963).[20] Brecht escaped from Hitler's Germany the day after the Reichstag fire in 1933 only to find himself facing the House Un-American Activities Committee in 1947. After the scandal of *The Resettled Woman*, Müller's plays were neither published nor performed in his homeland for a dozen years, yet following his death on December 30, 1995, a couple years before *Full Circle*, his memorial service was broadcast live on national television and a commemorative reading of his works lasted eight days. These were playwrights living and working in a society in which artists were important enough to be perceived as threats and in which theater had a chance, at least, to be as much public forum as private entertainment. In 1995, the subsidy provided by the city of Berlin to just one theater, the Berliner Ensemble, topped $15 million, while the entire theater budget of the National Endowment for the Arts that year totaled $8.3 million. No wonder then that Mee might wish to be able to say "I am a Berliner." *Full*

Circle is an Aristophanic fantasy set in a Cold War Cloud-Cuckooland where a playwright, of all people, is King for a Day.

Around the time of *Full Circle*'s creation, a major fact of life changed for Mee, one which adds resonance to the play's ruminations about state-supported theaters, the status of the playwright in society, the conundrum of patronage, and billionaire Americans like Warren Buffett. In June 1998, months before the play's Steppenwolf premiere, Mee contacted an old friend named Richard B. Fisher. Both polio survivors, the two had known each other since a few years out of college, and while Mee pursued a life of letters, Fisher joined the investment bank of Morgan Stanley in 1962 and worked his way all the way up the corporate ladder to become president and eventually chairman and chief executive officer, playing a pivotal role in the company's tremendous success in the process. Not long after overseeing the $10.9 billion merger in 1997 of Morgan Stanley Group, Inc. with Dean Witter, Discover & Company, Fisher retired from the company – a very wealthy man. At that same time, despite widening recognition, Mee was still working as an editor to support himself and his two pre-teen daughters. He found himself "at this strange moment in my life as a playwright, where I can't afford to succeed,"[21] so he swallowed hard and approached his old friend with an immodest proposal: that Fisher become his patron. They would partner in a joint venture "Playwriting Company," real or make believe; Mee would provide the labor (that is, plays) and Fisher would provide the capital (enough money to free Mee from the need to hold a regular job and still be able to support his loved ones). Fisher talked it over with his wife, Jeanne Donovan Fisher, and they soon proceeded to arrange a system of bi-annual disbursements that were enough for Mee "to live and send my kids to private school and summer camp and take care of the other folks who depend on me." There were no stipulations or conditions placed on this support in terms of what Mee wrote or how much or what he did with his income as a playwright or how long the arrangement was to last. He was free to write as he pleased. Since then, each new Mee play has had a simple note attached that says, "Charles Mee's work is made possible by the support of Richard B. Fisher and Jeanne Donovan Fisher." What the note does not say is how grateful he is.

> They've given me my life really, the life I've wanted since I got out of college at age 20, 40 years ago. Imagine what amounts of work would be released from others if there were more such patrons in the world, if the

NEA had ever been allowed to be a real patron of the arts – or maybe it never could have, probably this sort of support needs to come from extraordinary individuals. But it's an amazing thing – being able to give myself entirely to my work – it's indistinguishable from being rich and happy.[22]

And so, Mee's "miraculous vision of the Happy Life," as Dulle Griet and Mary MacLane call it, became an enviable reality, and he became king for more than a day of his own playwriting utopia financed by his own one-man NEA.[23] Rather than being "rendered dumb" by such good fortune, Mee began to write at a prodigious pace, the plays rushing out of him at the rate of three a year, "like the torrent of a summer rain / like a rain of summer flowers." Many of them were love stories, quirky, funky, less apocalyptic and lighter in tone that his first decade of plays. Some, like *True Love*, his remaking of the Hippolytus-and-Phaedra myth, end in catastrophe, but over time more and more of them hewed in their own idiosyncratic way to the happy end of romantic comedy, with lovers reconciled and a joyful celebration afoot. This was the general situation in Mee's life and art at the time he undertook *bobrauschenbergamerica*.

Part II

The making of bobrauschenbergamerica

7

Preliminaries: facing Rauschenberg, making lists, collecting stuff

IN 1955, LACKING THE MONEY FOR CANVAS (AS LEGEND HAS IT), Robert Rauschenberg took an old patchwork quilt left over from his days at Black Mountain College, stretched it across a frame, and then splattered the upper half of it (plus an attached bed pillow) with dribs and drabs of multicolored oil paints, as well as pencil marks, red nail polish, and toothpaste. He hung the piece upright, like a painting, and called it "Bed." That same year, Rauschenberg bought a stuffed long-horned Angora goat that he saw in the window of a used furniture store and made it the centerpiece of a work that took him several years to complete. Over time, he painted the goat's snout in many vivid colors, fixed an old automobile tire around its midsection, and mounted it on a wheeled platform – he called it a "pasture" – that was covered with a combination of paint, paper, printed reproductions, footprints, a shirt sleeve, a rubber shoe heel, a tennis ball, and pieces of lettered wood that suggest initials. He titled this piece "Monogram." *Bed* and *Monogram*, two of Rauschenberg's most famous creations and long since canonized as masterpieces, were shocking when first seen, without apparent precedent and seeming to defy comprehension. They are prime examples of what Rauschenberg called "combine paintings," paintings that incorporated three-dimensional objects into the picture plane or extending out from it, and "combines," more sculptural works that combined miscellaneous objects which were lathered with paint and imprinted with two-dimensional images (see figure 12).

With their striking incorporation of discarded materials scavenged from the back alleys and junk shops of New York, their defiant, messy, cryptic juxtaposition of personal and public iconography, and their conflation of horizontality with verticality, figure with ground, and two-dimensionality with three-dimensionality, the combines and combine paintings became the most famous of Rauschenberg's many innovations.

Figure 12. The artist at work and play: Robert Rauschenberg. (a) In his studio (1958), surrounded by his combines: (from left to right) *Interview*, *Untitled*, *Bed*, *Monogram* (second state), and *Odalisk*. (Photograph by Kay Harris.) (b) In *Pelican* at the First New York Theater Rally (1965). (Photograph by Peter Moore © Estate of Peter Moore/VAGA, New York.)

For his ceaseless experimentation with both materials and means and his prodigious output over a long and varied career, he has been described as the most significant visual artist of the second half of the twentieth century. That certainly was the implicit argument of a mind-boggling retrospective of Rauschenberg's art that took over Manhattan in the fall of 1997. Both the uptown Guggenheim Museum and the Guggenheim SoHo downtown were filled from stem to stern with more than 400 works drawn from every phase and period of the artist's career, and commercial galleries all over town presented independent, collateral exhibits. Curated by Walter Hopps, a long-term champion of Rauschenberg, and Susan Davidson, the retrospective placed a monumental capstone on a fifty-year career that continued on nevertheless well into the twenty-first century.[1] For many viewers, including critic Robert Hughes, the Guggenheim show was "too big, too profuse, too sprawling – too damned much all round – to take in with any sort of ease," but that did not prevent him from celebrating Rauschenberg as "the Great Permitter" and "the artist of American democracy, yearningly faithful to its clamor, its contradictions, its hope and its enormous demotic freedom, all of which find shape in his work."[2]

Charles Mee's appreciation of Rauschenberg dates back to the 1960s, when, as editor at *Horizon* magazine, it was his business to keep up with developments in contemporary art. In the 1980s, when he resumed playwriting, Mee embraced collage as a playwriting technique, taking inspiration from Rauschenberg, as well as earlier pioneers Max Ernst and Kurt Schwitters. In 1997, Mee took in the vast quantity of Rauschenbergs on view at the Guggenheim and began to imagine them as the basis for a new play. What would it be like, he wondered, to create a theater work in the manner of Rauschenberg, not so much about him in any explicit biographical sense, but drawing on his sculptural sense of collage, his use of found objects, his favorite images and motifs, his love of collaboration, his celebratory, often whimsical spirit, and his expansive vision of the USA? "The Guggenheim book is wonderful," he wrote at one point, referring to the exhibit's massive catalogue, "and if you just look at the pictures, some of them are the content and structure for a whole play – or maybe a bunch of them together are ten scenes for a play. Something."[3] At some point after seeing the exhibit, Mee approached Anne Bogart with the idea for a Rauschenberg project, just as she had approached him a few years earlier about working on *Culture of Desire*, the SITI Company's piece about Andy Warhol. Mee had passed on the Warhol project, and ever since, director and playwright had been looking for something to work on together. Though she knew little about Rauschenberg at the time, Bogart embraced Mee's proposal, largely on the basis of his enthusiasm for the subject.

Informal discussions took place on and off for a while before the project got going. On November 19, 1999, Mee met with the SITI Company as a group to discuss the Rauschenberg project for the first time. Efforts were already underway to find the resources and to schedule the time necessary to develop the piece. By this point, Mee had flipped through the Guggenheim catalogue and made two lists: "Stuff in Rauschenberg's works" and "Stuff it makes me think of" (as follows).

Stuff in Rauschenberg's works:
stuffed chickens
cardboard boxes
oil drums
chairs
JFK
ML King
an astronaut
coke bottle
goat
automobile tire
eagle's wings
clock
construction barricade
roller skates
electric light bulbs
one-way sign
car door
house window on wheels
laundry
soldiers in a jeep
a bathtub with crunched sheet metal above it
shoes
pillow
life jacket
wash tub
license plates

Stuff it makes me think of:
chicken jokes
a chicken farmer talking
his wife talking about something else at the same time

automobile race-track announcer
astronaut talking to Houston base
women talking at the laundromat
traffic cop talking
men and women talking to each other at the butcher shop
a shoe-repair guy talking about work
a window cleaner talking
an oil rigger talking
dialogue from Baywatch
pillow talk
prisoners talking about making license plates
a guy in a junk shop talking
a car-tow service operator talking
a guy in an automobile graveyard talking
the sound of a car door slamming
sound of oil drums being unloaded from truck
construction sounds
carpentry sounds
the sound of a conversation in Rauschenberg's studio while a print is being
    made

Mee used these lists again and again as a springboard for discussion about
Rauschenberg's work, asking others what it made them think of and then
revising and expanding his lists to incorporate their ideas and associations.
These two practices – making lists of associations and soliciting input from
others – became central to the process of developing *bobrauschenbergamerica*. Mee wanted to start with the actual "stuff" of Rauschenberg's art – its
materiality, its dominant motifs, its compositional strategies, and the
feelings that it generates – and see what might emerge from a lot of
people just reacting to that. Mee wanted to collect bits and pieces from
a variety of sources for possible inclusion in what was conceived from the
outset as a theatrical "combine" created in the manner of Rauschenberg.
Unlike previous SITI Company pieces about artists, Rauschenberg himself would not be a character in the play, nor would it chronicle his life in
any biographical sense, despite some eventual suggestion to the contrary.
Rauschenberg's life and art became a kind of subtextual inspiration for the
piece, and in that regard, an overview is in order.

   Milton Ernest Rauschenberg, as his parents named him, was born on
October 22, 1925 in Port Arthur, Texas, an oil refinery town on the Gulf of
Mexico.[4] His father, the son of a German doctor and his Cherokee wife,
worked for the local power company and loved duck hunting and bass

fishing. His mother was a religious woman who attended the fundamentalist Church of Christ and ran a modest household, making all of her son's clothes and keeping chickens in the backyard. A shy kid, Rauschenberg had a typical boyhood, riding his bicycle, building contraptions out of wooden crates and junk, looking after his many pets, going fishing with his dad, and the like. In high school, he was active in the drama club, designing sets and costumes and working backstage. He was religious in his youth (to the point that he considered entering the ministry), but his love of social dancing led him away from the Church of Christ, which regarded such activities as sinful. After high school, Rauschenberg attended the University of Texas at Austin, but he dropped out after a short while, due in part to his dyslexia (undiagnosed at that point) and his refusal to dissect a live frog in biology class. In the spring of 1944, at the height of the Second World War, he was drafted into the navy and, while stationed at Camp Pendleton, posted to hospital duty in San Diego, after making it clear that he had no desire to kill anybody. As a neuropsychiatric technician, he worked with combat veterans suffering from post-traumatic stress disorders, an experience that solidified his pacifist inclinations.

When he was young, drawing was one of Rauschenberg's hobbies. While in the navy, he made his first-ever visit to an art museum, and something about seeing actual paintings, including Gainsborough's *Blue Boy*, instead of reproductions in books or on the backs of playing cards, led him to take his artistic impulses more seriously. After the war, with help from the GI Bill, he attended the Kansas City Art Institute and then the Académie Julian in Paris. In Kansas City, he changed his name to Bob (thus Robert), and in Paris, he met Susan Weil, a fellow art student, who he married in 1950. By that time, Rauschenberg and Weil had already enrolled in Black Mountain College, the progressive art school in the mountains of western North Carolina. He studied – and clashed – with his teacher Josef Albers, the former Bauhaus instructor famous for his exacting discipline and his attention to the physical properties of the artist's raw materials. Black Mountain became Rauschenberg's artistic birthplace. Over the next few years, he shuttled back and forth between its pastoral remove and the metropolitan bustle of New York City. In May 1951, at age twenty-five, he had his first solo exhibition, at the respected Betty Parsons Gallery. Two months later, his son Christopher was born, but his marriage was in trouble. After traveling on a shoestring to Cuba, Italy, and Morocco with fellow artist Cy Twombly, he settled in New York, an ambitious young artist determined to carve his own path in an art world dominated by abstract expressionism and the New York School.

In the 1950s, Rauschenberg began to create works in series, as he would for the remainder of his career. White Paintings led to Black Paintings, which led in turn to Red Paintings and the first Combines. He showed his work at galleries of contemporary art, sold little, got mixed to negative reviews, and kept on working. He supported himself by designing window displays for fancy Fifth Avenue stores such as Bonwit Teller and Tiffany's. He began an intimate working and personal relationship with Jasper Johns that lasted for seven years. He spent the better part of two-and-a-half years creating a series of drawings based on Dante's *Inferno*. In these and other works, he experimented with solvent-transfer techniques, applying turpentine or lighter fluid to clippings from newspapers or magazines and then rubbing them face down against paper or canvas with a blunt implement so that image or text was transferred. This, aided by a nudge from his Pop Art contemporary, Andy Warhol, led to Rauschenberg's pioneering work in photomechanical silkscreen painting and then in lithography, printmaking techniques which he pushed beyond their assumed limits. With Tatyana Grosman and her studio Universal Limited Art Editions (ULAE), Rauschenberg revolutionized graphic arts by transferring images onto heavy lithographic stones, rather than drawing on the stones directly, an innovation which extended collage technique and photographic images into the realm of printmaking.

All this while, Rauschenberg was involved in various capacities with the avant-garde performance movement. In the summer of 1952, four of his White Paintings hung overhead at what has come to be regarded as the first Happening, instigated by John Cage in a Black Mountain dining hall, with Merce Cunningham improvising movement (followed around by a dog), David Tudor playing a prepared piano and a radio, Cage, M. C. Richards, and Charles Olson sitting atop stepladders and reading aloud, and Rauschenberg playing Edith Piaf records on an old Victrola at the wrong speed. In the 1950s and into the 1960s, Rauschenberg designed sets and costumes for both the Paul Taylor Dance Company and the Merce Cunningham Dance Company, accompanying the Cunningham group on its 1964 world tour as set, costume, and lighting designer and stage manager. This led to his involvement with the Judson Dance Theatre and his work as a choreographer of eleven dance pieces, starting with *Pelican* in 1963, in which he and Alex Hay roller-skated around with parachute-like constructions billowing behind them as a third performer, Carolyn Brown, danced on *pointe* between them, all to a sound collage created by Rauschenberg with music from Handel and Haydn and sound taken from the radio and television (see figure 12, page 162 above). To create "a kind of dim, oscillating illumination" for a section of *Spring Training* (1965), Rauschenberg attached flashlights to the shells of thirty turtles and set them loose on a dark stage, while he 'danced' around them on stilts.[5]

Rauschenberg also pursued experiments in combining art and technology, starting with his *Money Thrower*. This mechanical sculpture flipped silver dollars into the crowd that came to the Museum of Modern Art on March 17, 1960 to see Jean Tinguely's *Homage to New York*, a kinetic sculpture made out of junk that was designed to self-destruct after thirty minutes. This led to Rauschenberg's significant and lasting collaboration with Billy Klüver, an engineer at Bell Laboratories in New Jersey interested in humanizing technology and harnessing the creative potential of machines. Together, they were co-founders of Experiments in Art and Technology (EAT), an organization that arranged collaborations aimed at "the possibility of a work which is not the preoccupation of either the engineer, the artist, or industry, but the result of the exploration of the human interaction between these three areas."[6] One such attempt, Rauschenberg's *Soundings* (1968), consisted of a huge Plexiglas light box (8 feet tall and 36 feet long) ($2\frac{1}{2}$ by $9\frac{1}{2}$ meters) filled with dozens of silk-screened images of a simple wooden chair. The piece was wired with microphones that picked up voices and other sounds in the gallery, transformed them into electrical signals, and lit up different portions of the Plexiglas case in response to the presence of the viewer.

In December 1959, when seven of his Combines were included in a show at the Museum of Modern Art, Rauschenberg was still a relative unknown. In 1964, beating more than 500 artists from thirty-four countries, he became the first American artist to be awarded the prestigious International Grand Prize in Painting at the Venice Biennale, a controversial decision that launched him towards an 1960s art world celebrity surpassed only by Andy Warhol. His work was prominent in exhibits at the 1964 New York World's Fair and at Expo 67 in Montreal. He began to design posters as contributions to political causes he supported, starting with one for the Congress on Racial Equality (CORE) in 1965 and including posters for New York Senator Jacob Javits's 1968 re-election campaign and for the first Earth Day on April 22, 1970. In 1967, he received an honorary doctorate from Grinnell College in Iowa, where his meeting with Dr. Martin Luther King, released from jail to accept his own honorary degree that day, left a lasting impression on him. In 1969, he was one of a delegation of artists invited to Cape Canaveral by the NASA Art Program to witness the launch of Apollo 11, the space mission that made Neil

Armstrong the first human being to walk on the moon. Four months later, Rauschenberg was one of six American artists to have a drawing left on the face of the moon by the Apollo 12 mission. He created and endowed a not-for-profit organization called Change, Inc. that provided emergency funds for artists in need. He lobbied Congress on behalf of artists' rights. In 1976, as part of its celebration of the American Bicentennial, the Smithsonian Institution singled out Rauschenberg as a quintessential American artist with a solo retrospective. He became the first living American artist to appear on the cover of *Time* magazine. The accompanying article by Robert Hughes, titled "The Most Living Artist," credited Rauschenberg with almost single-handedly establishing:

> the basic cultural assumption that a work of art can exist for any length of time, in any material (from a stuffed goat to a live human body), anywhere (on a stage, in front of a television camera, underwater, on the surface of the moon or in a sealed envelope), for any purpose (turn-on, contemplation, amusement, invocation, threat), and any destination it chooses, from the museum to the trash can.[7]

In 1970, Rauschenberg withdrew from the high life of New York and shifted his base of operations to the Gulf Coast of Florida, where over the years he established an extensive studio compound on Captiva Island, off Sanibel Island near Fort Myers. He continued his relentless experimentation with materials and processes, creating series after series of new works with descriptive or evocative titles such as Cardboards, Cardbirds, Hoarfrosts, Jammers, Spreads, Scales, Publicons, Kabal American Zephyrs, Photems, Shiners, Gluts, Urban Bourbons, Borealis, Night Shades, Phantoms, Water-works, Anagrams, and Arcadian Retreat. In the 1980s, Rauschenberg's abiding interest in artistic collaboration and social change led to a long-term project called the Rauschenberg Overseas Culture Interchange or ROCI (pronounced "Rocky" after the twenty-year-old pet turtle that first appeared in *Spring Training*). Off and on for years, he traveled to political hot spots around the world in order to gather materials and photographic images and to learn traditional methods from local artisans, which he would then use to create new works of art. These became part of a traveling exhibit that toured to each subsequent host country. Based on Rauschenberg's conviction that "a one-to-one contact through art contains potent peaceful powers,"[8] ROCI sought to promote intercultural communication and understanding and to foster artistic freedom and expression in developing or politically repressive countries. Starting in 1984, the project had stints in Mexico, Chile, Venezuela, China, Tibet, Japan, Cuba, the USSR, Germany, Malaysia, and the USA, finishing up with an exhibition at the National Gallery of Art in 1991, which displayed all 125 works created through the project. Major corporate sponsorship for ROCI never materialized, so Rauschenberg "ended up spending eleven million dollars to finance it himself."[9]

ROCI is but one example of Rauschenberg's lifelong efforts to create art on a grand scale. As early as 1951, as a student at Black Mountain College, he conceived a project in which he would photograph the United States "inch by inch." At the end of the century, his ever-expansive vision was epitomized by a piece that aspired to be the longest work of art ever made. Known as " The 1/4 Mile or Two Furlong Piece," it is a sprawling, self-contained, single-work retrospective of Rauschenberg's life in art, an autobiography in images and objects that measured 190 feet (58 meters) long when first assembled at Edison Community College in Fort Myers, Florida. It had grown to 750 feet (228 meters) by the time it inaugurated the new Lila Acheson Wallace Wing of Twentieth Century Art at the Metropolitan Museum of Art, and it was longer still when it was shown at the Ace Gallery in conjunction with the 1997 Guggenheim retrospective. From beginning to end, Rauschenberg's carefree pursuit of limitlessness and his omnivorous engagement with the world around him combined with his roll-up-your-sleeves resourcefulness and his puckish imagination to make him the quintessential American artist of the second half of the twentieth century.

Collaboration was always a hallmark of Rauschenberg's art and career, from his pioneering days with John Cage and Merce Cunningham, his relationship with Jasper Johns, his partnerships with Billy Klüver, Tatyana Grosman, Steve Paxton and the other Judson dancers to his later work with Trisha Brown, the changing team of acolytes who gathered at Captiva, and the international ROCI participants. Making art was a social activity for him, one carried to extremes in *Synapsis Shuffle*, a huge multi-part work completed in the spring of 2000, right at the time that Mee was finishing the first draft of *bobrauschenbergamerica*. In imitation of a deck of cards, *Synapsis Shuffle* consists of fifty-two individual panels, each one $9\frac{1}{2}$ feet (3 meters) high and varying in width up to 5 feet ($1\frac{1}{2}$ meters), filled with mixed-media images from Rauschenberg's world travels. The "shuffle" of the title took place on May 15, 2000 at a Long Island City warehouse, where a dozen celebrity friends of the artist gathered, including Merce Cunningham, Martha Stewart, Chuck Close, David Byrne, Robert Hughes, Mike Wallace, Ileana Sonnabend, and Michael Ovitz. Each was to choose and arrange between three and seven panels as their own

Rauschenberg composition. To introduce an element of chance, they drew lots to determine how many panels each 'artist-for-a-day' would select and in what order, and then they put down their champagne and went to work, picking panels, bartering back and forth, and deciding on the order and position in which their collection would be displayed. The twelve pieces were installed as a composite work for public view at the Whitney Museum of American Art (June 29 – October 8) and then disassembled in anticipation of subsequent exhibits elsewhere, each one with a different shuffle to be made by different guest participants. Grace Glueck, whose coverage of Rauschenberg's work in the *New York Times* dates back to the mid 1960s, called it a "hollow exercise" and "the same old Rauschenberg deal, and it won't go away."[10]

Mee's strategy for his Rauschenberg play was the inverse of Rauschenberg's for *Synapsis Shuffle*. Instead of creating all the pieces and inviting a miscellaneous team of collaborators to put it together, he planned to collect miscellaneous pieces from a variety of collaborators, put it together himself, and then turn it over to the SITI Company to see how they would stage it. Starting with the twin lists "Stuff in Rauschenberg's work" and "Stuff it makes me think of," in late 1999 and early 2000, Mee began casting about for images, events, and chunks of text that might go into the script. For a while, he was assisted by a young dramaturg named Tali Gai, an undergraduate at Barnard College who volunteered her help after Mee gave a guest lecture in a course that she was taking on Greek tragedy. He set her to work tracking down everything from chicken jokes to play-by-play radio broadcasts of football games to transmissions between Apollo astronauts in space and mission control back home to Ben Franklin's argument about why the turkey should be America's national bird. When Mee learned that, through her mother, Gai was acquainted with the physicist Philip Morrison, he dispatched her to conduct an interview with him, instructing her to ask big, philosophical questions ("the stupider the better," he insisted). The scientist's responses to such queries as "What do you see when you look up at the sky?" or "How far into the future can we predict?" had a profound effect on the content of *bobrauschenbergamerica*.

Philip Morrison is a well-known physicist who studied with J. Robert Oppenheimer at Berkeley and then became one of the team of scientists involved in the Manhattan Project, the top-secret government effort to develop an atomic weapon that would win the Second War. As a group leader at Los Alamos National Laboratory, Morrison oversaw the final assembly of the first atomic bomb and rode with its plutonium core in the backseat of an Oldsmobile to Trinity Site, the test location in the

New Mexico desert 200 miles south of Los Alamos. On July 16, 1945 at 5.29 a.m., he was lying prone in a bank of sand ten miles from the original atomic "ground zero," watching through a piece of welder's glass as the device was detonated for the first time. A few weeks later, he was in the North Pacific helping to assemble Little Boy and Fat Man, the uranium and plutonium bombs dropped on Hiroshima and Nagasaki. Their devastating effect led Morrison, like many nuclear scientists of his day, to become an early proponent of nuclear disarmament and to steer his career in a different direction. In the 1950s, he co-authored an influential essay that proposed the use of microwaves for interstellar communications in search of extraterrestrial intelligence. Morrison went on to become an important science educator, popularizing public understanding of science through a regular column in *Scientific American* and many book, television, and film projects that he undertook with his wife, Phylis Morrison, including the widely seen and celebrated *Powers of Ten*. At the end of a long and illustrious career, he published two collections of his writings, *Nothing is Too Wonderful to be True* (1995) and *Reason Enough for Hope: America and the World of the 21st Century* (1998). Either title would serve as an apt subtitle for *bobrauschenbergamerica*.

On January 12, 2000 in Cambridge, Massachusetts, Gai interviewed the eighty-four-year-old Morrison, now a professor emeritus of MIT. The transcripts of that interview provided Mee with a gold mine of raw material and became the basis for one of the eight principal characters in *bobrauschen-bergamerica*, initially known as John, then as Herbert, and eventually as Allen. Mee edited and re-arranged Morrison's remarks, even splitting his words into a two-character dialogue at one point, but he was careful to quote him verbatim, preserving his jumbled syntax and verbal idiosyncrasies, his tendency to interrupt himself and revise his remarks as he talked, and his broad, seemingly goofy generalizations, such as "There is a great deal more space than time." Mee's strategy – similar to Bogart's use of audience quotations in *Cabin Pressure* – recalls a method practiced by actor and playwright Anna Deavere Smith, most famously in her solo performance pieces *Fires in the Mirror: Crown Heights, Brooklyn and Other Identities* (1992) and *Twilight: Los Angeles, 1992* (1993). Unlike Smith, whose virtuosic performances foreground the real-life models of her characters and the documentary nature of their speech, Mee's use of Morrison's words obscures their status as quotations and withholds the historical identity of their source.

This is important for understanding something about how Mee uses extended quotations from outside sources in *bobrauschenbergamerica* and other plays. He does not set off borrowed material in ways that make them conspicuous as such; nevertheless, the passages he borrows often feature a syntax that does not quite jive with the surrounding dialogue. To the extent that the listener can detect a slight dissonance on either a subliminal or conscious level, the words retain the aura of a textual artifact. Stripped of their original context, they take on new meanings and inflections, but as artifacts, they still carry a trace of their source, just as a ceramic shard unearthed at an archeological site implies (but does not identify) the ancient vase of which it was once a part. That missing or absent source gains a presence in a play as a type of historical or cultural subtext, as opposed to the psychological subtext more common in conventional realistic drama. Philip Morrison is not a character in *bobrauschenbergamerica*, but he is present in the words spoken by the character of Allen. As a man who spent a lifetime thinking and working in "powers of ten," harnessing the energy of the atom and contemplating the unfathomable reaches of the universe, the historical Morrison's words and sense of scientific wonder convey a cosmic perspective that became an important element of *bobrauschenbergamerica*.

Just as important for Mee the historian, Morrison's identity as a key participant in perhaps the single most important event of the twentieth century added an element of historicity to the play. In one of his longer speeches in the play, Allen, speaking Morrison's words, describes in cryptic terms a fascinating and beautiful place high in the mountains of New Mexico, hot in the summer, snowy in winter. He concludes:

> So it's the most beautiful place, Los Alamos . . . It was very grim, you knew the outcome couldn't work at all, that's what we all thought, but we weren't going to give it up.

This brief mention is as close as the play comes to pinpointing the real-life figure behind Allen. In the moment of performance, few spectators will have more than a vague impression of what he is talking about, but to the extent that Philip Morrison carries with him a significant chapter in American history, that history presses up from beneath the surface of everything that Allen says. In this way, Mee weaves nothing less than the making of the atom bomb into the fabric of *bobrauschenbergamerica*, giving the play a texture and a density that is not apparent to the naked eye. In a similar manner throughout his body of work, Mee's use of material borrowed from the culture at large carries that culture with it and allows its history to press up from beneath the surface in ways that lend a play dimension and amplitude.

On March 18 and 19, 2000, Chuck Mee led a weekend playwriting workshop that proved to be far more significant in the evolution of *bobrauschenbergamerica* than he anticipated at the time. Sponsored by the SITI Company, its purpose was to launch Mee into the writing of *bobrauschenbergamerica* by generating discussion, ideas, and raw material inspired by Rauschenberg's work. Participants were sent in advance a version of Mee's two lists and asked to brush up on Rauschenberg and bring in some writing in response.[11] Most of the eight participants had trained or worked with the SITI Company before; several were working for the company in staff or volunteer positions at the time. Few had playwriting experience to speak of, although all were active in theater or dance. They met in a basement rehearsal studio below the La Mama Gallery on 1st Street in the East Village on what proved to be an unseasonably cold late-winter Saturday; for most of the weekend, participants huddled around inadequate space heaters, bundled up in hats, scarves, and coats. By all accounts, the chill in the air was offset by the warm, collegial atmosphere.[12]

Mee started things off by sharing his impressions of Rauschenberg and his reasons for wanting to make a play inspired by his work. He made it clear that he hoped that the workshop would yield material that he would "steal" for the piece and that nobody's work would be used without permission. The eight participants – Rebecca Brown, Jane Comfort, Alec Duffy, Tali Gai, Jackie Goldhammer, Reba Herman, Carolyn Clark Smith, and Kathleen Turco-Lyon – shared their research: a copy of Anne Livet's *Contemporary Dance*, with a photo from *Pelican* of Rauschenberg in roller skates and parachute wings on the cover (see figure 12, p. 162 above); a long list of titles of Rauschenberg creations; a recording of the famous 1958 John Cage retrospective concert at Town Hall in New York. One of the more memorable contributions came from the choreographer Jane Comfort, who had studied with Merce Cunningham in the 1970s and, years later, met Rauschenberg a couple of times through a mutual friend. She strung a clothesline between two ladders and arranged a row of six or seven buckets of water on the floor beneath the clothesline; then, she dipped a different dancer's leotard into each bucket and hung them on the line, so that water dripped out of them into the buckets below – audibly. An allusion to a stage set Rauschenberg created for a Cunningham dance, Comfort's makeshift installation invoked a freedom of imagination well suited to the spirit of the workshop.[13] The colorful, limp leotards hanging in a line and the drip-drip-drip of water into the buckets were rich in connotation, suggesting the temporality of performance, the corporality of dance, the necessity of routine chores, and other associations. As an inspiring example of what could be seen as 'writing in three dimensions', the piece remained in place for the rest of the afternoon.

On that first day, Mee introduced another list, a simple outline of what he thought might be the first nineteen moments or segments of *bobrauschenbergamerica*:

music and viewpoints
parasols
a roller skater
chicken
first character enters/text
second character enters/they fall in love?
third character (a cross wind)
woman enters and sings
man enters and dances
someone serves drinks
there is a party
someone is assassinated
serious speech/not about assassination
welcome speech at an art gallery opening
tiny parachutes fall from the sky
people waltz
Rauschenberg's mom talks about her son
earlier lovers return/discuss break-up

Participants were asked to choose one item on this list and flesh it out on the spot with whatever it brought to mind: monologues, dialogues, stage action, further description, whatever. Each person read what they wrote and then they all brainstormed some more about what that brought to mind. The afternoon passed in much the same casual cycle of talking, writing, reading, and talking. Mee did not teach "how to write a play" in any systematic fashion, but he did share advice and experience. He introduced the notion of inducing character from found and borrowed texts. He warned against rushing to impose conscious or conventional structure on a piece, preferring instead to allow a shape to emerge from the inchoate enthusiasms, anxieties, and other emotional impulses that give rise to the work. Near the end of the first day, Mee gave the workshop participants a homework assignment to complete overnight. They were to make a list of what they thought the next nineteen bits or segments of the piece might be and then to select two or three of the total of thirty-eight and write them out by adding elements of text, visuals, sounds, plot, spectacle, and character. He encouraged them to make use of images, themes, characters, or situations that others in the group had already introduced. And he encouraged them to write whatever felt good to them, whatever they found fun or would please them as a piece of theater.

These two simple, practical ways to advance the task of writing – scavenge the world around you for items of interest and create what it pleases you to create – are basic principles of Mee's writing. They became a hallmark of the workshop, as ideas, images, and events that surfaced on Saturday were recycled and revised in the work that others wrote overnight and brought in to read on Sunday. This free exchange led to an openness and lack of judgment, engendering in turn a sense of possibility and, for some, creative joy. "I never felt like we were writing a play," said Rebecca Brown. "I felt like we were coming up with fodder for a play. It was about freeing imaginations and not about end product."[14] When the workshop ended late on Sunday afternoon, the participants went their separate ways and Mee went home with a folder full of "fodder" that proved useful when he sat down to compose a draft of the play. As it turned out, so many of the impulses that surfaced that weekend found their way into *bobrauschenbergamerica* that the script might be seen as Mee's amalgam of the workshop. For example, a discussion about Rauschenberg's use of discarded, devalued objects in his art led to more personal considerations of the role of material things in our lives, which led in turn to reminiscences about yard sales. Mee's script thereafter included a yard-sale scene as well as a monologue written by Rebecca Brown about her grandmother's precious collection of Italian cut glass, which he amended to say was sold at a yard sale after her death.

Two of the play's eight principal characters came out of the March workshop. Stimulated by Mee's idea for a segment in which "Rauschenberg's mom talks about her son," Jane Comfort went home on Saturday and flipped through her own family photo album, looking at snapshots from growing up in Oak Ridge, Tennessee and imagining a proud mother looking back on her son's boyhood misadventures. With her own mother's lilting rhythms and homespun syntax in her head, Comfort wrote a monologue for a doting mother looking back at photos of her beloved son.

> And that's Bob with Johnnie East in their canvas swimming pool
> when they were about four
> Johnnie popped that beach ball later that day
> and I told Bob I wasn't buying another one.

The descriptions had nothing to do with Rauschenberg's childhood in Port Arthur, Texas. A picture of "Bob's 1st birthday party on the back porch with the morning glories all in bloom" was actually Comfort's brother's first birthday party, and a picture of "Bob and his dog Jab" was Comfort herself and her dog Jab. Mee took Comfort's wistful memories and used them to make "Bob's Mom" the emotional core around which he constructed the text. Her series of recollections provided a semblance of continuity in what would prove to be a jumble of a play, and her evocations of growing up in middle America in the middle of the twentieth century were so vivid in detail and so saturated with maternal love that she became the heart and soul of *bobrauschenbergamerica*.

The creation of Bob's Mom reveals something fundamental about Mee's approach to character. For Mee, language precedes and creates character. Instead of conceiving a character and then imagining what that character would say, he gathers and combines various texts of interest and then imagines them being spoken by one figure onstage. One benefit of this strategy for Mee is that it populates his plays with surprising characters, because they speak in words and in ways that he himself could never write for them. And they become all the more surprising when a single character's words are drawn from different and even discordant sources. Mee complicated Bob's Mom by supplementing Jane Comfort's writing with additional speeches, including the monologue written by Rebecca Brown about her grandmother's glass collection. The hard edge of that speech cut back against the grain of Comfort's folksy charm. Later in the script's development, calls for "more Bob's Mom" prompted Mee to add material that he wrote himself, based on writing about Rauschenberg's childhood and family life.[15] Despite what audiences might think, this last Bob's Mom monologue contains the only genuine biographical information about Rauschenberg in the play.

Like many Mee characters, Bob's Mom needs to be understood as a collage of texts, the linguistic aggregate of disparate materials, found or original, that Mee fancied being spoken by one figure on stage. While discrepancies in syntax and speech patterns from one source to another are not so great as to be confusing or all that conspicuous, they do often generate a low-grade, subliminal dissonance that suggests the contradictory nature of human beings. Of course, the persona and voice of the actor, as well as the costume design, lend some automatic unity to the role, a fact which further emboldens Mee in his mixing of texts that do not always jive with each other. In his theater, a character is not imagined whole and then fleshed out with a psychology, a personal past, or a compelling objective that rationalizes who he is and what he does. Instead, character is induced from speech, from a combination of texts, and the more variegated their composite speech, the better. Characters do not determine what they say; what they say determines who they are.

The other character to emerge from the March workshop came from Kathleen Turco-Lyon, who brought in a letter from an old friend of hers, a big-rig truck driver who was working through a difficult period in his life. For all his troubles, he still saw himself as living a charmed existence, a combination of Sal Paradise in Kerouac's *On The Road* and Isaac Bashevis Singer's *Gimpel the Fool*, and his letter ended with a couple of paragraphs about the natural beauty of Colorado and setting out in his truck before dawn to haul rock. "Everywhere I go there is something to see," he wrote. "I don't know how I got so lucky. But here I am." Turco-Lyon used these paragraphs in her workshop composition about a truck driver who travels around naked in a bathtub as other odd events take place around him. The text struck a chord for Mee and became the seed of "Phil the Trucker," a character who tells chicken jokes and talks a lot about food in the play.[16] Like Bob's Mom and the Philip Morrison figure, he is endowed with an expansive vision and a genuine sense of wonder, qualities which came to define the play as a whole. Life is a marvel for the characters of *bobrauschenbergamerica*. They are all imbued with a mild, perpetual astonishment best described by Rauschenberg's real-life mom, Dora, when she came to New York in 1987 to see her son's autobiographical *The 1/4 Mile Piece* at the Metropolitan Museum. "Isn't it something," she said, "how he can see the beauty in almost anything?"[17] Mee made this the last line of the play.

In April 2000, after traveling to Louisville for performances of the Humana Festival production of *Big Love*, Mee set to work "full tilt" on *bobrauschenbergamerica*. His plan was to sift through the material from the March workshop and "put together notes, thoughts, an outline of a sequence of events, 30, 40, 50 moments, some of them movement, some music, some of them pieces of text, some I don't know what."[18] He would take that outline to Saratoga Springs in June, where students in the SITI Summer Intensive would make compositions based on it and Rauschenberg, thus providing more fodder from which he might pick and choose to add into the play. Over the summer, the plan went, he would fashion a rehearsal draft and, schedules permitting, work with the SITI Company would begin in the fall. A formal rehearsal period was scheduled to begin in February 2001 in anticipation of premiering the play at the 2001 Humana Festival. In this way, the script would build itself up through a series of approximations of its eventual, finished form, and the play would emerge through "a constant process of re-making," one which solicited not only feedback but actual performance material from a community of collaborators growing up around it, chief among them the members of the SITI Company.

In a matter of weeks, Mee generated in quick succession three early versions of *bobrauschenbergamerica*: a "working outline" with notes, a rough draft, and a first draft. The working outline amounted to a series of lists. It extended the initial list of nineteen possible segments that Mee presented to the workshop to an outline of forty-eight disjointed and open-ended "moments." Most of these items were brief and some were conjectural, as in:

> 1. John Cage music: viewpoints exercise with six folks . . . 8. a third character enters with a house window on wheels – and is jealous of the two, is a previous lover? . . . 12. a lone woman, wearing shower cap and towel, enters and sings a song – or is this man of gay couple? . . . 16. someone serves drinks – does someone need to say how they love parties or life itself is a party etc? . . . 23. woman opens purse, hundreds of ping pong balls fall out . . . 33. a boy dives over and over again into a pile of laundry while we hear an operatic aria . . . 42. now other miscellaneous things here that belonged neither in part one nor in party? . . . 48. at end of piece: a man's voice says "OK, that feels good to me."

This list was followed by a series of other lists with headings such as "characters," "recurring items," "texts to use," "text sources," "sounds to use," "tires," "chicken stuff," "songs and music," "things to use," "actions," "possible parties," and "possible settings." The texts to use list included such ideas as "automobile race track announcer," "women talking at the laundromat," and "Laurie dream," the last being a reference to Laurie Williams, whose vivid dreams had appeared verbatim as monologues in some of his recent plays. Possible settings included "Pina Bausch's Sicily, the Bowery, Rauschenberg's New York studio, Judson Church, Texas childhood, Omaha, Barrington," the last being the town in Illinois where Mee grew up. The working outline ends with a number of texts for possible inclusion in the play, including excerpts from the Philip Morrison interviews, an eyewitness account of the JFK assassination in Dallas, a few chicken jokes, the play-by-play commentary for a New York Jets football game, and several chunks of text written by participants in the March workshop.

What began as two simple lists became the March workshop's list of the first nineteen moments of the piece, and that, in turn, became the series of lists that comprised the working outline. This process of revising, expanding, and filling out lists reveals both Mee's basic playwriting technique and the aesthetic strategy behind it. At this early stage, writing *bobrauschenbergamerica* was a matter of selecting material from the various lists on the working outline and assigning it to one of its presumptive forty-eight moments. In the manner of a collage, he could move back and forth from one section to another, filling it out with this or that, trying out certain combinations or juxtapositions without getting locked in to a particular sequence. This approach is intuitive and trusts that some sense of a coherent whole will emerge from what I would call here the Integrity of the List. A list always makes sense to the person who made it. The items on a list – a to-do list, a grocery shopping list, a pro-con list – are permeated by the list-maker's subjective need to get organized or buy food for a dinner party or make a difficult decision. This subjectivity gives the list a meaning and a usefulness that is often obscure or inscrutable to another. In fashioning *bobrauschenbergamerica*, Mee made the strategic decision to trust that the Integrity of the List – both the more objective "stuff in Rauschenberg's works" and the more subjective "stuff it makes me think of" – would hold together the miscellany of dialogues, monologues, actions, dances, and songs that came to make up the play.

From the beginning, Mee recognized the risk in pursuing such an affective structure. "This is a tricky, slippery project," he wrote. "Free associating in this way maybe we'll just end up with such a disparate set of associations we'll have no center or shape."[19] Just in case, Mee had a fallback plan in mind:

> If it feels like the material begins to form itself into some shape, that's great. If it doesn't, then at some point I'll say, 'Oh, OK, let's pretend we're doing *Our Town*. Let's take all these pieces that we've collected and string them together as though it were *Our Town*, the American masterpiece.[20]

Ever since his *Orestes*, Mee had borrowed the structure or outline of a classic play to lend shape to his various impulses and appropriated texts. If the model of Rauschenberg's art did not provide that, maybe Thornton Wilder would. Further evidence that Mee conceived *bobrauschenbergamerica* with *Our Town* very much in mind is found in one of the last segments in the working outline: "Tiny parachutes fall in silence and people begin to do beautiful Viennese waltz or rain, and people put up tiny umbrellas (like *Our Town*)."

Mee's working outline was followed in short order by a rough draft and then a first draft of the play. These drafts took the forty-eight segments listed in the working outline, filled them out with material contained in the outline's other lists, and distributed it to a group of inchoate characters. In addition to Bob's Mom, the Philip Morrison figure (named John at this point), and the Trucker (named Jack at first, after Kerouac, and thereafter Phil), these characters included the Trucker's girlfriend, a Derelict, a pair of feuding lovers, and a gay couple. The rough and first drafts were essentially the same. Mee cut several segments that were in the rough draft, including a dialogue between the Trucker and his girlfriend fashioned out of a passage from Kerouac's *On the Road* and a discussion between the Trucker and the Derelict about "the importance of sports" as a source of pleasure for participants and spectators alike.[21] And he added several segments to the first draft, including an extended passage from Walt Whitman's *Leaves of Grass* that he was reminded about by Tali Gai's interview with Philip Morrison. The first draft, dated "Mayday," became the first version of the play to be circulated widely amongst the community of interest gathering around the project.

This Mayday draft had much of the substance of the play that would go into rehearsal eight months later in Louisville: flat, archetypal characters speaking all manner of borrowed texts, an absolute lack of plot, an interest in the vagaries of emotion, a winsome nostalgia for boyhood, a penchant for ironic undercutting and irreverent silliness, a compulsive embrace of variety, Rauschenbergian iconography, and lots and lots of chicken jokes. But by any conventional standard, its fifty-three separate segments amounted to a bewildering and random jumble of material. To read that draft and visualize how it might be staged in a coherent manner required a formidable imagination. There is no indication of setting or situation. The characters are known only by what they say. Jim is labeled "a derelict," but other than an oblique reference to him as "a dirtball," nothing he says or does reflects his impoverished condition. From one moment to the next, Carl is a dancer, Allen's lover, a chicken farmer, an actor who had a bad audition, an art gallery operator, and a victim of assassination, but why he is assassinated and by whom is unexplained, as is his subsequent reappearance alive and well. Things just don't add up the way they do in other plays. To go back to the historiographical terms of Mee's *Playing God*, there are no facts to know (or not know), no acts that have consequences (intended or not), no false precedents to lead characters astray, no contingency whatsoever. There is only the inevitability of surprise and plenty of spectacle. And what might give "such a disparate set of associations" a center or a shape was nowhere in evidence.

At the time, that was no cause for alarm. The Mayday draft was, by design, only a first approximation of a complete script. It was tentative, hypothetical, and very much open to change and elaboration as the process continued and others got more and more involved. This openness was epitomized by a segment Mee included in the script titled "The Beating," the entire text of which reads, "A beating occurs." That is the whole scene. Who is beaten? By whom? With what weapon? For what reason? These were among the many questions left to Anne Bogart and the SITI Company.

8

Summer 2000: messing around in Saratoga Springs

NEW YORK CITY SWELTERS IN THE SUMMER. STRETCHING BACK
at least as far as 1931, when the nascent Group Theatre rented what Cheryl
Crawford called a "vacation resort" in Brookfield Center, Connecticut,[1]
New York theater companies have fled summer in the city and retreated to
bucolic settings where they can live and work together without distraction,
clarify and advance their artistic missions, lay the groundwork for coming
seasons, and, in the process, beat the heat. For the SITI Company, that
Green World is the town of Saratoga Springs, New York. Since its incep-
tion in 1992, the company has spent part of every summer in residence
at Skidmore College, performing current work, developing future
work, and providing training in the company's three principal methods.
Over the years, the time in Saratoga has proven crucial to the company's
survival, growth, and identity. It has provided a period of concentrated
work under close-to-ideal circumstances, far from the daily grind of life in
New York. Just as important has been the opportunity to live together in a
relaxed summer-camp-like atmosphere, eating together in the campus
cafeteria, unwinding together after a long day's work, catching up with
each other's lives, and comparing notes and sharing ideas about the
company's evolving work.

All the same, it would be misleading to regard the company's time in
Saratoga Springs each year as a vacation. In the summer of 2000, for
example, the company pushed itself to the limit with the sheer volume of
work undertaken. The chief task was providing instruction for the sixty-
five students in the annual Summer Intensive, which was expanded that
year from three weeks to four. Classes were scheduled all day Monday
through Friday, with a symposium each Wednesday night to talk about the
company's history, aesthetic, or current projects. The initial plan for the
summer was for the company to use the other evenings to do preliminary

work on *bobrauschenbergamerica*, but preparations to take three SITI productions to the Edinburgh International Festival in August changed that. *War of the Worlds*, the company's piece about Orson Welles, needed extensive reworking after its shaky premiere at the Humana Festival a few months before. *Cabin Pressure* and *War of the Worlds (The Radio Play)* were also going to Scotland, and they needed to be brushed up, a task which included working Ellen Lauren and Tom Nelis into the cast of *The Radio Play* for the first time. Lauren was also knee deep in reading the works of Virginia Woolf in preparation for beginning work with Bogart in July on the one-woman show to be called *Room*. And Bogart, inspired by her interest in the Group Theatre, was already conceiving a metatheatrical piece about a theater company making a play about a theater company. All told, in addition to the training program, six different, original SITI creations were in some stage of conception, development, or production in June 2000. To make matters more arduous, the company's sudden, recent eviction from their work space in New York City had required them to move most of their equipment – computers, office furniture, file cabinets, props and set pieces for shows about to tour – with them to Saratoga Springs, until they could figure out what to do with it. The summer of 2000 was one of heavy lifting, literally and figuratively.

Even though active work by the company on *bobrauschenbergamerica* was put on the back burner, the Summer Intensive included two different activities designed in part to generate material that might have some bearing on the play. The composition work undertaken by the trainees would focus on creating short theater pieces inspired by Rauschenberg, and Mee would conduct a playwriting workshop that, on the model of the March workshop, might produce texts for him to "steal" and add into the mix. To launch these activities, to introduce the company to the larger group and the play to the company, and just for fun, Bogart decided to kick off the summer with a reading of Mee's Mayday draft of *bobrauschenbergamerica*. While Mee had met with the company on several occasions to talk about the project and to solicit their impressions of Rauschenberg, this marked the formal entry of the SITI Company into the process of developing *bobrauschenbergamerica*. It proved to be a memorable beginning.

On May 31, 2000, at the end of only the third day of training, the community gathered in a small chapel in the woods on the Skidmore campus. Company members had only received the script a day or two before, so it was to be a cold reading with no rehearsal, just sitting in chairs with scripts in hand contacting the text out loud for the first time. On a whim, sound designer Darron West decided it might be fun to mix in sound and music with the spoken text, so he set up his mountain of equipment (speakers, CD players, MD players, a mixing board, and an electronic sampler) and prepared a few quirky cues that he thought might be in the spirit of the play (such as barnyard animal noises and a bluegrass version of Marvin Gaye's "Let's Get it On"). That evening, West conducted the reading from the back of the room, signaling to the actors when to hold for a sound cue and when to continue, and the company responded by throwing themselves into what became an impromptu sit-down performance. The radical discontinuities of Mee's script took on an air of carefree unpredictability, one that was reinforced by the mid-reading arrival of company member Tom Nelis from London, where he had been touring in Laurie Anderson's *Songs and Stories from Moby Dick*. Delayed and jet-lagged, Nelis came straight from the airport to the Skidmore chapel and took over the reading of stage directions in the middle of a scene. The gathering generated an intoxicating thrill that seemed to capture the play's sense that anything could happen as well as the infectious, good-natured spirit of Mee himself. It inspired the workshop participants to make Rauschenberg compositions in the coming weeks that were just as wild and free. And it affirmed just how right (not to mention, how overdue) it felt for SITI to work with Mee, who Bogart, with the Group Theatre project in the back of her mind, was already identifying as "our Clifford Odets." For Ellen Lauren, among others, it was "like a tonic," an unexpected chance for the company, after some difficult months and a series of pieces with darker overtones, to reconnect and to fall in love again with each other and the way they sparked each other to do their best work:

> We went home that night blown away by being in the room together and being able to read something so quickly and so joyfully. The immediate response was "Oh, this is about fun. You mean it is all right to be happy?" Suddenly, Chuck was saying, "Hey, you're a human being. It is OK to play around with a yellow umbrella."[2]

On June 17 and 18, the third weekend of the 2000 Summer Intensive, Mee led an optional playwriting workshop. Despite the grueling training schedule and ongoing rehearsals for their final compositions, forty-five out of roughly sixty-five participants showed up for the first four-hour session on Saturday. Many of them had completed the assignment that Mee had given in advance: take Thornton Wilder's *Our Town* and write a five-minute distillation of the entire play, set in the year 2000 and refracted through the sensibility of Robert Rauschenberg. After a few introductory remarks, Mee asked for volunteers to read their miniature versions of *Our Town*. Exemplified by one piece titled "ourtown.com," these turned out to be mainly internet updates of Thornton Wilder, where Grovers Corners circa 2000 has a Starbucks on every corner and the Gibbs and the Webbs are replaced by non-traditional families of deadbeat dads, single moms, and mall-rat teenagers talking about the latest bomb scare at the high school. Many had Stage Manager-type narrators, stepladders as scenery, and grave-yard scenes in which the dead look back in wonder at the life they have left behind. Despite this awkward, derivative quality, the pieces displayed enough variety and sincerity to illustrate Mee's main point: everybody had the same assignment, read the same play, and looked at much the same Rauschenberg paintings, yet they wrote very different pieces in response, suggesting that a writer's individual voice can be drawn out by taking a classic play and writing a new one on top of it. He outlined three strategies or levels to this type of approach: first, outright parody; second, a simple allegorical update, in which present-day, one-to-one correspondences are substituted for elements of the original; and third, a metaphorical re-imagining of the sensibility of the whole, form and content alike, from a personal and contemporary perspective. While Mee would seem to favor the last of these three methods, he made no value judgments about them.

When asked what play he had appropriated as his point of departure for *bobrauschenbergamerica*, he admitted that he had been holding *Our Town* in reserve as a potential scaffolding but that he had not felt the need to use it so far. He told the group that with each new play he tests how free he can be in putting things together and therefore how much uncertainty, con-fusion, and even anxiety he risks imposing on an audience, whose natural reflex is to try to figure out what is going on. His goal is to generate a theatrical rhythm that encourages the audience to "float and float and float," but he recognizes the need for what he calls "tent stakes," elements or devices which anchor their experience, gather them back in to touch base, as it were, before propelling them out to float again. That was the reason that he put "lots of little love stories into *bobrauschenbergamerica*." Love stories provide an instant and efficient point of orientation for a bewildered spectator. A character can say as little as "Oh, yes, you love me / but you don't love me in *that way*," as Wilson does in *bobrauschenberga-merica*, and this is sufficient to invoke a complicated relationship with a long history, the details of which the audience does not even need to know to feel as if they have some understanding of the situation. For Mee, the art of playwriting is a matter of letting the imagination go and inviting an audience to follow along; the craft of playwriting is a matter of providing just enough structure and story that they do not feel so lost or disoriented that they give up along the way.

Over the course of the two afternoons, Mee offered more practical advice that demonstrated his intuitive approach to playwriting and suggested how the novice writer might get out of his own way. Here are a few examples:

> The structure of a piece is who you are. Structure is my statement about how it feels to be alive. When you sit down to write a play, think of it the way painters work: painters don't start in the upper left hand corner of the canvas and work their way over and down until they reach the lower right hand corner. They do this and they do that and they smoosh it around and stick something on it and then step back and then do something over here. This is the way to work on a play so that you are always in touch with the whole of the work, the whole of the structure, or maybe it is not even a structure yet, the whole of the experience. When you are in touch with the whole, you don't ever have to ask yourself what does it mean.

> Try to ask yourself constantly how you feel, and stay aware of your feelings rather than the assignment to write a play or the need to understand the character or have a motivation or structure the scene. Eventually you're going to assemble a pile of stuff and say to yourself, "Jesus, what is this? I feel hopeless. I don't know what this is all about or why anybody would want to look at this. But the stuff that feels to me as if it goes together is this, this, this, and this, and if I put those together, then I would think, 'Oh, this is about heartache,' or 'Oh, it is about revenge,' or 'Oh, I see, it is about a desensitized romantic relationship in a commodified late-capitalist society.' If I choose elements 6, 17, 18, and 22, that is an amazingly different way of making that remark!"

> If you bring this material out of yourself and you don't see a form or shape to it, then you are in the position that Shakespeare was in. He wandered around the world feeling happy or angry or in despair and he didn't know what to do with these feelings. So he stole John Lodge's novel *Rosalynde*, re-titled it *As You Like It*, stuck all his feelings on that plot, and he had a play. What I am saying to you is that if you get to that moment in your room where you have just this crap laying on the floor and something does not emerge from it, go and steal yourself a plot.

> One of the real uses of appropriation is to take stuff that is indigestible and difficult and not right for a play, inappropriate for putting on stage, wrong dramaturgically, and put that in the middle of the play and then

solve that problem. It forces you to do things that you otherwise would not force yourself to do. And it has another virtue: it is a piece of the real world or somebody else's way of looking at the world. It is not just you in your narcissistic little shell trying to imagine how somebody else feels. It *is* how somebody else feels; it *is* what they said. That forces your world view to open up and take them in.[3]

At the end of the Saturday session, Mee gave the group an optional assignment to complete overnight and bring in the next day. His original plan was to introduce the next step in developing a five-minute *Our Town* rip-off into a fuller piece, a process he sometimes refers to as "unfolding." That assignment, which Mee used when he taught playwriting courses at Brown University, is to choose five moments in the first, short draft and "open them up," either by extending an encounter between two characters or writing a new scene for them or inserting a piece of borrowed text or even sticking in a song or a dance, "whatever impulse allows what is there to have fuller expression." This process can be repeated for successive drafts by taking other moments in the new material and "unfolding" them in turn. Mee compares this procedure to scientific experiments with fruit flies that speed up the evolutionary process, so that "you go through 83 generations in a week and a half." In a similar manner, the playwright can evolve a script for as many generations as is necessary to get the material he needs or to find out what feels right. Mee recommended this strategy to the group as "an amazing way to work because, instead of starting at this point and working your way through from beginning to end, you work from association upon association upon association until you finally get to this fully flowered event with an astonishing array of material." Often, in the process, the connection to the source material grows so attenuated as to become unrecognizable.

But, in response to one of the pieces read on the first afternoon, Mee chose to assign a different exercise. He told the group to write a scene in a couple pages that captured a moment "between you and your lover, in your present or past life, either meeting or arguing or separating, but whatever the moment is, it needs to be truly humiliating or embarrassing or disgusting or offensive or twisted, but not made-up twisted or manufactured disgusting, something so fucking shameful from your life that you can hardly bear it – really the most intimate moment of your life." This task was based on Mee's conviction that "any time you are getting into material that you feel is too embarrassing or repulsive or shocking or you wouldn't want your mother to see it, you know you are on to something." There is a value and a pleasure, Mee explained, in humiliation because "it is a revelation of something deeper, something that we don't normally see, something essential about what it is to be a human being. And that is why we go to the theater. To feel that." Bogart echoes this idea in her handbook on directing when she identifies embarrassment as an artist's "key collaborator," "a teacher," and "an obstruction we encounter that helps us clarify our mission."

> If what you do or make does not embarrass you sufficiently, then it is probably not personal or intimate enough. Revelation is necessary to warrant attention. The feeling of embarrassment is a good omen because it signifies that you are meeting the moment fully, with an openness to the new feelings it will engender.[4]

The second day of the workshop proceeded along much the same lines as the first, with people reading material they brought in and Mee extrapolating from it to make general remarks. Throughout the two days, Mee continued to assert that anybody can write a play and to recommend "stealing" as a way of overcoming inertia. He reminded the group of the importance while writing of staying in touch first with their feelings and then with the world of others, bearing in mind that the cultural context for a play operates like an echo chamber, adding resonance and amplitude to whatever they might create. While any one of these principles might amount to little more than standard workshop advice, Mee's particular combination of them, conveyed with humor, passion, candor, and charm and backed by his considerable body of work, left a strong and positive impression on the group. For his part, Mee walked away with a stack of neo-*Our Town* scenes to sift through for ideas and inspiration. Earlier in the workshop, he had shared a quick anecdote about a time when he went to see a play with Martha Clarke, who turned to him at intermission and said, "Nothing to steal here. Shall we go?" Though he would be too discreet to make a point of it, that would seem to have been his response to the writing workshop that weekend.

The composition work that summer represented a more sustained exploration of the Rauschenberg materials and yielded more interesting results. The trainees were divided into Monday, Tuesday, and Wednesday afternoon classes, and from week to week, each class was divided into four groups, each of which created and rehearsed a composition on their own for in-class presentation. Keeping with Bogart's practice, each piece had to include a long list of ingredients, both standard items such as "revelation of

space" or "a broken expectation" and items specific to Rauschenberg and
Mee's Mayday draft for the play. The first assignment, titled "A Love
Story," had to be site specific, set and performed somewhere on campus
that "feels good," and based on a structure of accumulation, a gradual
building up of people, objects, and gestures. It was to include a party, a
square dance, and the moment of falling in love. The characters were to be
chosen from the following: a trucker, the trucker's girlfriend, an astronaut, a
Connecticut girl who went to prep school, Martin Luther King, an All-
American Boy, a derelict. Props were to be chosen from a list of objects
found in Rauschenberg's artwork or Mee's play. The second composition
assignment, loosely titled "The Astronaut's Journey," was also a site-specific
piece, based this time on a journey structure. It was to offer a tour through
the world of Robert Rauschenberg and take the audience to at least three
different places. Specific objects were to advance the journey, and at some
point there was to be a detour. A critical text about Rauschenberg, a pizza
delivery, a live country-and-western song, a piece of found text, a romantic
dance, five accidents, someone telling a joke, a specific use of color, an
element of chance, and a moment when the audience gets to make a choice
were all to be included. Emphasis in this piece was on place and particular
attention was to be paid to the matter of getting from one thing to the next.

As it turned out, an uncanny coincidence during one of these site-
specific performances provided a direct link to Rauschenberg and his
world. Each summer, in addition to the SITI Company, Skidmore College
hosts a major contemporary dance company, which teaches master classes
and presents a public performance. In 2000, the company in residence
happened to be the Trisha Brown Company, and one afternoon, attracted
by some curious activity going on near the dance building, Trisha Brown
herself wandered over to see what was going on and ended up walking
through a composition in progress. All of a sudden, here was the master
choreographer for whom Rauschenberg had designed sets and costumes
numerous times since 1983, the former Judson dancer with whom
Rauschenberg had performed as early as 1964 (in Steve Paxton's *Proxy* at
the Once Festival in Ann Arbor), popping up – oh, Angel of Serendipity! –
thirty-six years later in a student composition made in the spirit
of Rauschenberg (and in which he was a character). For Bogart at least, a
traditionalist at heart whose work has roots in the Judson era, it was a
thrilling moment.

At Mee's suggestion, the third and final composition in 2000 had no
list of ingredients. Each group was simply assigned to create their own
ten-to-twelve-minute version of *bobrauschenbergamerica*, one that had a

definite beginning, middle, and end (in other words, a *jo–ha–kyu*) and did not use any of Mee's text. That was the entire assignment. Rather than being site specific, these pieces were created for the black-box studio in Skidmore's theater building and performed there over two evenings as part of the public demonstrations that concluded the Summer Intensive. As the culmination of four weeks of hard training day and night, the final compositions, along with the Suzuki and Viewpoints jams, generate a palpable excitement for most workshop participants. While the SITI ethos makes clear that training is a lifelong proposition, there is still a sense of accomplishment in these final days – part preliminary mastery, part sheer survival – which is matched by a curiosity to see what the other groups have been working on. The final showings, in theater parlance, put 'a button' on the month's experience. They are the *kyu* that gives the Summer Intensive its sense of fulfillment.

On the evenings of June 22 and 23, 2000, twelve Rauschenberg compositions were performed, each of which had its own interest and its own flaws, its own minor technical snags, workshop in-jokes, and at least one glorious moment of aesthetic arrest. Each took the form of a theatrical collage, a chaotic jumble of images, movements, texts, and stage effects. Without access to the Skidmore lighting equipment or sound system, the teams had to be resourceful in meeting their technical needs. An all-important community boom box played odd or atmospheric bits of music that juxtaposed or commented on the action onstage. Clip lights, flash-lights, laser pointers, overhead projectors, and other makeshift devices helped to transform the space or provide focus with light. Slow motion movements were conspicuous, as was the use of the black-box theater's first-level walk-around as a performance area and the use of objects with wheels as props. A wheelchair, bicycles, tricycles, chalkboards on wheels, as well as car tires, hubcaps, shiny bicycle wheels, and even Hamm and Clov in *Endgame* arguing about the existence of bicycle wheels, all came into play. As might be expected, many of the pieces focused in part on the artistic process, including an artist figure who spoke lines pulled from Rauschenberg interviews or the use of picture frames as props (spinning one like a top, using an old tire as a circular frame). Several of the pieces included the action of painting in some form. A white sheet was hung from a clothesline, newspaper or white butcher paper or plastic sheeting was spread wide over the stage floor, a white tee shirt was worn, each as a canvas to receive paint as the performance went on. In one case, the paint was 'concealed' in a blown egg and then appeared, as if by magic, when the egg was smashed against a surface.

As theater, the pieces were rough and raw and messy, but mostly in a manner that suited the subject and spirit of Rauschenberg, his collage techniques, and his particular sense of wonder at being in the world. As a celebration of four weeks of hard work together, they generated excitement and a deep satisfaction. As part of the SITI Company's initial exploration (through the agency of their students), they fortified the importance of sheer silly fun in the piece. The compositions re-affirmed the message of the cold reading four weeks earlier: that *bobrauschenbergamerica* was exactly what the company needed at the present moment in their development. It offered them a script that really did feel like it was written for them, that shared their sensibility and left room for their considerable input. It challenged them to loosen up, release some control, work with a lighter touch and fewer rules. And, in the spirit of the "Great Permitter" himself, it gave them license to play, to have fun, to do whatever feels good. For a group of perfectionists, that was not as easy as it might seem.

Before decamping from Skidmore for the summer to focus on more pressing projects, Bogart conferred with Mee about possible revisions in the script in response to the work done during the June Intensive. They agreed to stick with the basic, loose structure of the script that Mee brought to Saratoga Springs, which had come so alive four weeks earlier in the reading in the chapel. *Our Town* would not be needed as an invisible scaffold on which to shape the play. The little love stories – between Susan and Wilson, Carl and Allen, and Phil the Trucker and Phil's Girl – and the event of a party would be enough, they hoped, to provide "tent stakes" to orient people in the audience if they started to get lost. Even though the script already had a Viewpoints improvisation, a song-and-dance number, a square dance, a waltz, and a "Last Dance," Bogart wanted the play to include a line dance. Other new material would be added to the middle of the play as rhythm and feel dictated. Mee was eager to look over his notes and the scripts that he had collected and to consult with company members via email about their responses to the Rauschenberg compositions and his Mayday draft. He did that in short order and, within a month, completed a revision of the play dated July 24 (hereafter referred to as the July draft or the pre-production draft).

While some changes in this draft are significant, the July draft affirmed what had become apparent in Saratoga: the script had come together sooner than Mee had expected. Despite its loose, disjointed form, the Mayday draft had a clear, infectious spirit, a palpable rhythm, and an odd integrity that Mee was hesitant to tamper with it. He described it this way:

The moment I add a Skidmore element, because it came from a sensibility other than my own, it seems almost instantly random, almost instantly to reduce the piece to inchoate rubble. I think maybe this happened because I did that original workshop at SITI headquarters in New York with folks who wanted to do playwriting; they brought in tons of stuff, and I chose from their mountain of "random" stuff and my own and – in that moment – put it into a form that is composed of nothing but my own sensibilities. But, having made that cohere then (as much as it does), it is weirdly hard to break it open again. I almost think that if I were doing *Agamemnon* or something with a strong plotline, I could add limitless amounts of other folks' associations, and the original plotline would be strong enough to hold it, but when you have composed a piece that is already – by design – on the knife edge of randomness, one or two bits can knock it right off the cliff.[5]

At this crossroads, Mee again made the conscious decision to trust that his affective "sensibility," reflected mainly in his selection and arrangement of materials at a particular moment in time, would provide a solid enough foundation on which the SITI Company could build a production. While material was not appropriated verbatim from the June compositions, they still had a major impact on the script and the performance. Something about them had made a strong impression that had to be taken into account. As Bogart put it:

> One thing that we learned by watching these compositions is the glory of mess, how human beings adore to watch other people get messy and roll in stuff. So I realized that the end of the play is going to be really messy. Everybody is going to get really messy, covered with food and paint. So I started talking about floor coverings.[6]

The July draft made sure that the "glory of mess" would be a palpable part of experiencing the play. Mee added three scenes to the middle of the play in short succession, each of which featured a rambunctious situation that grew messier and messier as it escalated to a chaotic climax. The first of these was "Becker's Movie," which replaced a short quotation from John Cage that Mee had rendered on the page as a concrete poem. In the new scene, now one of the longest in the play, Becker (the new name for Jim the Derelict) steps forward and says he has a great idea for a movie and proceeds to describe a complicated plot about a lone FBI agent trying to thwart "a conspiracy to blow up a train carrying nerve gas from the west coast to the east coast." He then coaxes the others to act out his screenplay on the spot, distributing scripts, assigning roles, and giving direction with a mania that matches the madness of the movie itself (see figure 17, p. 245 below). The motley group of conspirators – "a folksy meteorologist, an embittered homosexual, a Chinese cameraman, a Lesbian, a Mexican pistolero, a Negro castrated in his cradle by rat bites" – are posing as a film crew making a documentary about America (a nation, we might guess, which has no place for these racial, ethnic, and sexual freaks). What starts out as a wild Revenge-of-the-Other story quickly devolves into a rapacious orgy of cartoon sex and violence, like an old underground R. Crumb comic come to life.

The text for the scene comes from William S. Burroughs's *Exterminator!*, an experimental novel written with Brion Gysin and first published in 1960. In the Mayday draft, Mee had cut a scene cribbed from Kerouac's *On the Road*, so the insertion of the Burroughs's passage added a Beat writer back into the mix and strengthened its roots in the 1950s of Mee's youth. Also, taken metatheatrically, it supported the notion that *bobrauschenbergamerica* itself was a crazy documentary about America. As Mee later explained to the cast, he chose the Burroughs for several reasons. On a pop culture level, it represented every American's fantasy about making or starring in a Hollywood movie. On a thematic level, it served to introduce "the dark side" into the play, Mee's express incorporation of violence and madness into his portrait of America. On an aesthetic level, it helped to demonstrate that "the same country seen by different temperaments comes out so different."[7] Burroughs's temperament contrasted the explicit vision of America in the Walt Whitman passage at the end of the play and the implicit vision throughout not only of Rauschenberg but of Wilder's *Our Town*. The inclusion of multiple perspectives on the same thing (that is, the USA), an impulse that is both democratic and cubist, was important to Mee. He also took a secret pleasure in the political incorrectness of Burroughs's carefree and defiant use of racial epithets and pornographic sex scenes, liking some "double not-quite-put-away" thing about it. What he did not say was that acting out this preposterous, offensive, madcap movie would invite the SITI actors to indulge in a kind of messy, exaggerated, bad story-theater acting that is antithetical to their characteristic discipline and precision.

In the July draft, "Becker's Movie" is followed by one of Wilson's romantic tantrums about Susan's unsteady affections and then the next new scene, titled "Dessert," in which Susan explains to Becker "how it is for women" and how in her search for true love she is trying to trust her feelings and not censor things, even when the way she feels about somebody changes without notice or provocation. "Feelings are feelings / they come and go," she explains, and in the process of her impassioned self-defense, she outlines a theory of gender and emotion:

> Women feel what they feel when they feel it
> and then when they don't feel it any more they don't feel it.
> Unlike a man
> who won't know what he feels when he feels it
> and then later on
> he'll realize how he felt
> and so he'll talk himself into feeling it again
> when he doesn't feel it
> because he thinks he should be consistent about the positions he takes
> and stick to them
> so a man always thinks he feels things he doesn't feel
> and so he never really knows how he feels at all.

This 'men are from Mars, women are from Venus' debate, written by Mee himself, is amusing enough in its own right, but Mee adds to the fun by including a stage direction that asks Susan to eat cake or cupcakes non-stop over the course of the scene. She eats normally at first but then "more and more compulsively, until she is stuffing it into her mouth" as she speaks with greater and greater excitement. The unavoidable spray of crumbs and smear of icing that this food orgy would require guaranteed that the *bobrauschenbergamerica* would include a mess similar to ones in the June compositions.

The closest thing to a direct steal from the summer group was the very next scene, titled "Martinis." One of the final Summer Intensive compositions involved performers pouring out breakfast cereal and milk on a large plastic tarp and then rolling around in it with playful abandon. When Mee thought to add a similar sequence into the play, Laurie Williams suggested that he adjust the event to reflect the fact that some members of the company were "major, major martini drinkers."[8] In the July draft, the new scene reads:

> Phil's girl brings out an immense piece of plastic sheeting
> which she spreads out on the floor.
> She takes a bottle of gin
> and pours it out on the sheeting,
> then she takes a bottle of vermouth
> and waves it over the gin,
> then she takes a bottle of olives and pours it out onto the gin;
> she takes off her clothes and slowly begins to slide forward on the gin,
> licking it up with her tongue.
> After a few moments, Phil sees her,
> he takes off his clothes,

and he joins her
sliding forward on his stomach
and licking up the martini.

The scene, arguably the funniest in the play, is more than a private joke. In his effort to create, as he put it, in the gap between art and life, Rauschenberg made it his practice to include evidence of himself (old family photographs, keepsakes, newspaper clippings, whatever was lying around) in his work. Mee had already inscribed several pieces of himself in *bobrauschenbergamerica*: the opening paragraph from his memoir about his battle with polio, one of Laurie Williams's surreal dreams, a square-dance call that he used to perform as a teen for his high school exhibition team. The martini scene was a way of inscribing the SITI Company into the play. Eight months later, when the company rehearsed "Becker's Movie," "Dessert," and "Martinis" in order, the sequence had an explosive silliness that was crucial in launching the play into another dimension, as if to shake it up like a bottle of champagne and then open it.

In addition to the trio of glorious mess scenes, the July draft contained changes that reflected Mee's ongoing effort to find the right balance between the two thematic halves signaled by the play's title. From the beginning, Mee had decided against including Rauschenberg as a character, preferring to think of him more as the invisible dramaturg for the piece. He wanted the play to generate the same feeling that he got when he looked at Rauschenberg's work, "a feeling of his absolute permeating presence in all of it and his complete absence from it. It is sort of like pantheism. If Rauschenberg is God, he is in everything." This helps to explain why it did not matter that most of the biographical information in the play about "Bob" at this point was not true of Rauschenberg. The Mayday draft did include a segment called "Welcome Speech," in which Allen, speaking as a museum curator or gallery director or artist, welcomes people to an opening and describes "how we put the show together." The long, rambling monologue combined Mee's own heartfelt writing about the nature and purpose of art with quotations drawn from Rauschenberg interviews, such as "I don't want a picture to look like what it is, I want it to look like what it isn't" or "when I saw how beautiful the saris were in India for the first time I wasn't embarrassed by the look of beauty or of elegance."

In the July draft, Mee took "Welcome Speech" out and inserted in its place a new monologue titled "America" for a new character named Steve. The text came from an opinion piece in a Canadian newspaper, which had been forwarded in an email chain to Barney O'Hanlon, who had passed it on to Mee. The speech begins, "*This* Canadian thinks it is time to speak up for the Americans / as the most generous / and possibly the least appreciated people on all the earth." It proceeds to inveigh against the international sport of America bashing and to celebrate good old Yankee ingenuity:

> You talk about Japanese technocracy,
> and you get radios.
> You talk about German technocracy,
> and you get cars.
> You talk about American technocracy,
> and you find men on the moon
> not once, but several times
> and safely home again.

The tirade is so insistent and genuine in its pro-Americanism that for liberal-minded listeners (the play's likely audience) it must seem to flicker back and forth between utter sincerity and ironic bathos. It is a good example of Mee's penchant for taking "stuff that is indigestible and difficult and not right for a play" and sticking it into a script for the sake of the shock waves it will generate. Along with the addition of "Becker's Movie," it gave the July draft a much stronger focus on the idea of the United States of America as a nation (as differentiable from a culture). It would have been interesting to hear how it resonated on opening night and then later in performances of *bobrauschenbergamerica* after September 11, when national feeling underwent such a sudden transformation.

As it turned out, Steve the Canadian and his jingoistic monologue were cut before the play went into rehearsal. "Welcome Speech" was restored, as was the tag line that ended three of Bob's Mom's monologues – "Art. Art was not a part of our lives" – which had also been trimmed from the July draft. This cycle of change and change-back exemplifies Mee's effort to have the piece evolve and transform in response to the Summer Intensive and his discovery that the script was closer to being finished much sooner than anyone expected.

9

Fall 2000: getting ready in New York

O<small>N NOVEMBER 12, 2000, FIFTY-ONE WEEKS AFTER MEE HAD</small> first met with them to describe the Rauschenberg project, the SITI Company sat down to work on *bobrauschenbergamerica*. They met in a conference room at the New York Theatre Workshop on E. 4th Street in the East Village for the first of several informal "table work" sessions. They had not spent time on the play as a group since Saratoga Springs in June, and in the interim, the stresses and strains of taking three plays to the Edinburgh Festival, the high-profile engagement of *War of the Worlds* at Brooklyn Academy of Music, the creation and premiere of *Room* at the Wexner Center, transitions in management, and the search for a new office and teaching studio had pushed the company to the limit. If working on *bobrauschenbergamerica* was to be "a tonic," it could not have come at a more perfect time.

Table work

Table work – starting work on a play with a series of sit-down rehearsals during which production concepts are spelled out by the director and designers, the script is dissected line by line by the actors, background information is provided by the playwright and/or dramaturg, and open-ended impressions and ideas are shared by everyone involved – is a common theatrical practice. But for the SITI Company, table work is different. First, it is not also a get-acquainted period, as it often is for a group of actors brought together for a single production. For the members of the SITI Company, even a first rehearsal is a continuation of their work together. Strong working relationships are already well established, so right from the start the conversation tends to be free and open. Second, the table work is a continuation of the project at hand, which has already begun with preliminary research and composition work. Third, whenever schedules allow, the table work takes place weeks, if not months, before the formal rehearsal period begins, which leaves the actors what some in the company call "cooking time," a relaxed period before staging rehearsals begin in which to conduct individual research and mull over the play and live with its themes without the pressure to make immediate decisions. All three of these advantages are directly attributable to SITI's identity as a permanent ensemble.

Bogart began that first day by encouraging the group to engage in a process that she has promoted for years. "Lateral thinking" is the term dubbed in 1967 by Edward de Bono to describe an orientation towards creativity that involves free association, questioning assumptions, random juxtaposition, courting serendipity, responding to others with an attitude of "Yes, and. . ." instead of "No, but. . .," and other tactics for changing one's perception or perspective on the matter at hand. In technical terms, this is a matter of moving laterally across the asymmetric patterns generated by self-organizing information systems, such as the brain.[1] In more common terms, it is a matter of brainstorming. Over the course of several hours, the July draft was read segment by segment, with anybody in the room breaking in at any time to ask a question, make a point, share an association, or contribute an anecdote. Bogart asked Mee a lot of questions about how Mee imagined specific moments onstage. Others recalled some of the favorite tropes and motifs from the Summer Intensive compositions. Segment by segment, Mee identified the outside sources from which he stole material, confessing with mock apology, "I'm afraid I made that up," for ones that he wrote himself. Different moments or images in the play triggered free associations with, for example, carnival sideshows that feature chickens that play tic-tac-toe, the opening sequence of Frank Capra's *Meet John Doe*, and an episode of *The Dick Van Dyke Show* with a closet full of ping-pong balls. At times, the conversation wandered far afield, as when a question about the names mentioned by Bob's Mom caused Kelly Maurer to marvel at how rich and evocative names can be and then, spontaneously, Ellen Lauren got everybody to go around the table and say the name of their best friend growing up. This gesture changed the feeling in the room as a dozen adults each spoke a name in turn and all thought back for a moment to their separate childhoods at the same time.

For the SITI Company, table work focuses on identifying the questions that need to be borne in mind when they eventually get up on their feet to "build" the piece. A number of these questions, large and small, surfaced on that first day or at the second rehearsal, held on December 7, 2000 in a studio on the third floor of the New York Theatre Workshop. For Bogart, none is more basic than the question of the audience. Not until Bogart has "cast the audience" is she able to proceed with certainty. "As a director," she said, "I always have to know what the relationship to the audience is. Is the audience watching a graduation ceremony or are they peeping toms looking at something they shouldn't see? Who are they?"[2] Pressed for an answer to this question, Mee said he saw members of the audience as Bob's Mom's friends, regular folks who show up as she is flipping through her family photo album, just like they might show up for a Fourth of July parade or a local picnic at the town park. Ellen Lauren offered an opposite identity for the audience, suggesting that they were akin to alien anthropologists "shot from Neptune" who had landed in the theater with an hour and a half "to find out what this country is." The play offered them, without explanation, several dozen iconographic samples that add up to saying 'This is who we are. This is America.' In this light, J. Ed Araiza likened the play to the gold-plated copper disks (also known as the Golden Record) launched in 1977 aboard NASA's two Voyager spacecraft and headed for deep space with numerous sounds and images illustrating the range of life and culture on Earth.[3]

Another conceptual question that arose the first day pertained, in effect, to props. How was Rauschenberg's love of his working materials – paint, wood, paper, ink, metal, fabric, cardboard, wire, and all manner of everyday objects – to be incorporated? His art and the June compositions inspired by it demonstrated how important simple, found objects must be to the piece, but should they be presented *au naturel* or, on the model of Rauschenberg, manipulated or recontextualized in a way that made them also aesthetic objects? The script called for several characters to make their first entrances pushing or pulling sculptural collages suggestive of Rauschenberg. Should these be replicas of actual pieces or just allusions to the idea of combines? This gave rise to the short-lived idea that over the course of each performance the actors would bring on various materials, including perhaps junk harvested from the streets of Louisville on the way to the theater that night, and construct a combine-like assemblage bit by bit. This, in turn, raised another question: would the same sculpture be re-assembled every night or would the cast create something new and original each time? This was to ask, in effect, how improvisational this action would be, how spontaneous and unrehearsed, how much in the spirit of a Happening, taking place in the real time of any given night rather than in the recuperated present of a fully planned, scripted, and repeated performance.

This impulse had particular pertinence to Rauschenberg, who experimented with the incorporation of time into his paintings as early as 1961 in a work created live onstage at the American Embassy in Paris as part of a multi-media happening known as *Homage to David Tudor*. "During the action, Rauschenberg worked on *First Time Painting*, a combine which, since it faced away from the audience, was unseen. Because it had been fitted with a microphone that amplified the sounds of its construction, however, the picture was highly audible. When an alarm clock attached to the painting went off, a bellman from Rauschenberg's hotel appeared. Together they wrapped up the painting and carried it off the stage."[4] Bogart is always looking to incorporate a similar crackle of real time into her directing. At the first *bobrauschenbergamerica* table-work rehearsal, when excitement began to snowball about the prospect of an actual high school marching band coming through in the middle of the performance, she suggested that, rather than having a fixed cue for their entrance, they could come in – "in more of a Cage-Cunningham way" – so many minutes into the performance, no matter what was happening on stage at that point. She liked the tension and uncertainty that something like that injected into the performance, and to illustrate her point, she told an anecdote about Caryl Churchill's *Top Girls* at the Public Theater in New York. At the end of a long and successful run, before a matinee performance on Easter Sunday, the stage manager informed the cast that she had hidden a number of Easter eggs around the set and that whoever had the most when the show was over would win a prize. So, added to the theatrical fiction of the play, there was "a whole other drama going on that is not being addressed directly but that has to do with time."

Because the play itself was intended as a theatrical combine, the idea of building a junk sculpture-cum-combine during each performance was torpedoed, but the question of chance and improvisation did not go away. Mee's first scene, titled "Viewpoints," went like this:

Music.
Eight company members enter and do Viewpoints exercises.

As the playwright explained, this was part of a prologue sequence that announced the three vocabularies out of which the piece would be made: the physical, the verbal, and the emotional. The Viewpoints introduced the acting of the SITI Company. The next segment, a quote from Rauschenberg done as a voiceover and titled "What I Like," invoked the artist Rauschenberg and aspects of his creative process ("I start with anything, / a picture, / these colors . . . "), as well as Mee's own practice of making speeches out of appropriated texts. And "Country Music," in which a roller skater with a big red umbrella bursts onto the scene while a country-music song plays, represented themes of love, romance, betrayal, and heartache, all in a distinctly American musical style. As Mee told the group, "Country music, excuse me for saying this, has no intellectual agenda. It is all about heart, all about raw feeling."[5] With each idiom briefly invoked, a stuffed chicken with a title sign around its neck drops from the flies and the play proper begins – with crickets and slides and Bob's Mom talking about her son.

But starting the play with Viewpoints raised a practical question. Would the company create the opening Viewpoints sequence in rehearsal and repeat it as such each night? Or would they just go out and jam for a certain period of time, as they often do as part of the training that begins a rehearsal? The former would seem to be antithetical to the improvisational nature of Viewpoints work, and the latter would mean starting each show with a different impromptu beginning, one which might not set the right tone or lead into the rehearsed performance that followed. Whether he knew it or not, Mee had opened a can of worms concerning the re-lationship of the company's training methods to their carefully prepared performances. In the months ahead, the company was vigilant in their commitment to remain true to the play that Mee wrote for them and to perform it as written, but this initial Viewpoints scene raised issues that would not go away – all the way up until opening night.

Casting

Mee wrote the Mayday draft of *bobrauschenbergamerica* without knowing who or how many of the SITI actors would be in the play. Bogart's preliminary idea was to use as few as six, which would make the show more affordable to tour after its premiere at the Actors Theatre of Louis-ville (ATL). But the Skidmore reading generated such excitement about the play and such a palpable sense of how good it was for them as a company that Bogart was motivated to use as many actors as she could, even if it meant that the production was seen in Louisville and nowhere else. She negotiated with ATL for the show to be budgeted for eight com-pany members, plus unpaid extras drawn from ATL's apprentice company. Sometime before table work began, Bogart decided who those eight actors would be: Akiko Aizawa, J. Ed Araiza, Will Bond, Leon Ingulsrud, Ellen Lauren, Kelly Maurer, Tom Nelis, and Barney O'Hanlon. Of these, the inclusion of Ingulsrud is worthy of note, because it marked the first time in years that this long-term member of the company would function as a performer. A big, stocky Minnesotan with bright orange hair, Ingulsrud provided a physical presence that contrasted with the leaner, more sinewy profile of other cast members. Two SITI actors were not in the cast. Jefferson Mays had not performed with SITI since *Alice's Adventures* in 1998; his burgeoning career outside the company eventually led to him leaving the group.[6] Stephen Webber was coming off an exhausting eighteen months of creating and performing the role of Orson Welles in both *War of the Worlds* and *War of the Worlds: The Radio Play*. With mixed feelings on both counts, he and Bogart agreed that *bobrauschenbergamerica* might be the right project for him to sit out.

Casting is personal, all the more so for the members of an ensemble like the SITI Company, who work, train, teach, and, in some cases, live together on an ongoing basis. Although much of the company's decision-making is collective, casting has always been Bogart's exclusive province, and each year the actors renew their mandate that she cast each project as she sees best for that project. This requires trust, mutual respect, compassion, sensitivity, and, most of all, sustained commitment to the company ideal, even when the size of the company and economic realities make it impossible for every project to involve (and employ) every actor. As artistic director, Bogart must weigh such concerns as maintaining balance and promoting growth within the company alongside the desire to cast the best person for each role. For the initial reading at Skidmore in late May, she asked Mee to cast the roles, and then at the first read-through in November, not having settled on her own choices, she asked the five actors present (three others could not be there) to go around the table and pick roles for themselves. There was not the slightest hint of audition in this process. To the contrary, most people chose parts across gender and against type.[7] Over the course of the afternoon, as Bogart listened to the company read, she began to zero in on casting choices and drop comments indicating what some of them were. "This is Akiko," Bogart said as the company laughed over the new martini scene. A few scenes later, she interrupted Will Bond in the middle of reading one of Herbert's speeches about the night sky and said, "By the way, you're cast as Herbert. Herbert is you." At the end of the day, more by impulse than by plan and with no fanfare whatsoever, Bogart announced a preliminary cast: Bob's Mom – Kelly Maurer, Susan – Ellen Lauren, Phil's Girl – Akiko Aizawa, Phil the Trucker – Leon Ingulsrud, Wilson – Tom Nelis, Becker – J. Ed Araiza, Herbert – Will Bond, and Carl – Barney O'Hanlon. The chances are that these choices came as no surprise to the company. Nevertheless, the casual, offhand manner in which they were made known seemed to reinforce the pre-eminent value of the ensemble by downplaying the significance of individual roles and even Bogart's authority in assigning them. Ultimately, they would create and perform the play as a company.

Bogart's announcement left a few roles uncast and a few casting issues unresolved. Though none of the characters were defined in the script by race, Mee had made plain from early on how important it was that the cast of a play with "America" in its title reflect the racial and ethnic spectrum of the USA and, in particular, include at least one African American. There were no black actors in the SITI Company in 2001. One possible source of actors of color was the ATL apprentice company, a couple of dozen young actors spending a year in training in Louisville. In keeping with her penchant, whenever possible, for using a chorus of extras to surround and supplement the main action, Bogart wanted as many apprentices, black or white, as she could get. They might be used to play supernumerary roles in the script (a girl on roller skates, the boy who dives into the laundry, the man in the chicken suit) and perhaps even one of the three speaking roles that had yet to be cast (Allen, Steve the Canadian, and Bob the Pizza Boy). Not only did this fortify the possibility that *bobrauschenbergamerica* would be seen only in Louisville, but it raised questions about whether any of the eight principal actors would be double-cast and in what combinations of roles. In this regard, Bob the Pizza Boy represented a special case.

Bob the Pizza Boy

In 1991 at the Mark Taper Forum, when Robert Woodruff directed the initial workshop of what became Mee's *Orestes 2.0*, Mee remained at home in New York faxing pieces of text to Los Angeles that he thought might be interesting to stick on the scaffolding of Euripides. One of these was the transcript of a haunting television interview with a convicted murderer, which Mee assigned more or less verbatim to John and William, two of the damaged war victims confined to hospital beds. John begins:

> Uh, primarily, uh, uh, the, uh, the. . .primarily the question is does man have the power to forgive himself. And he does. That's essentially it. I mean if you forgive yourself, and you absolve yourself of all, uh, of all wrongdoing in an incident, then you're forgiven. Who cares what other people think, because uh.[8]

Punctuated by this terrible stutter, the speech proceeds to recount how he had some kind of vision or delusion of grandeur while reading the Aquarian gospels, which led him to take a knife and – "believing that I had the power to kill" – murder his sister, brother-in-law, and nephew after they turned him away when he was in trouble and needed a place to stay one night. This was years and years ago, and he has long since forgiven himself, but there is something in his calm demeanor and his rhetoric – "If I forgive myself, I'm forgiven. You know that's essentially the answer. I'm the captain of my ship. I run my own ship. Nobody can crawl in my ship unless they get permission." – that remains threatening and creepy. Like so many of Mee's favorite appropriations, it has some "double not-quite-put-away thing about it" that makes it difficult to digest or dismiss.

Mee has often made it a practice to use certain stolen texts in one play after another, partly for the difficulty that they injected into the play and partly to see how the same text resonated differently in different contexts. Sei Shonagon's *The Pillow Book*, Valerie Solanus's *Scum Manifesto*, and the collection called *In the Realms of the Unreal: "Insane" Writings* are just three examples of books that Mee has turned to again and again. For a performer and a director, insertions from outside sources often have a verbal/linguistic effect similar to that of a Suzuki exercise; that is, they throw things off balance with a burst of energy, triggering a more dynamic effort to maintain a certain equilibrium while proceeding with the task at hand. The tale of the triple homicide first used in *Orestes 2.0* became the most conspicuous of Mee's recycled texts. It shows up next in the middle of act one of *Summertime* (2000) when Bob, "a slimy young Italian guy," enters to deliver a pizza, and again in *Summer Evening in Des Moines*, written around the same time. On this occasion, Bob is explicitly identified as "a new character we've not seen before," not necessarily Italian, and when he finishes his seemingly endless confession, he asks in a matter of fact manner, "Who ordered a pizza?" When he is told that there must be some mistake, he responds:

> I think you are the one who is making a mistake
> if you think nobody
> is going to pay me for the fucking pizza.
> You know: pizza
> is not returnable.

Given his criminal history and menacing stutter, this threat, even when uttered in a calm, even-tempered voice, is enough to prompt quick payment from a character onstage and scattered laughter in the audience. The humor is macabre. For Mee, this character – someone from the community, a regular anonymous person, someone who might come to your door for legitimate reasons – came to represent what Mee refers to simply as "the dark side" of American culture:

He reflects that strain of unfathomable violence in America. You listen to him speak and you think, this is weird and funny, and then, this is horrifying, and then you begin to have sympathy. And you finally conclude that you don't understand where his violence is coming from. I think human beings remain unfathomable.[9]

For nearly the third play in a row, Mee threw this monkey wrench of a scene into *bobrauschenbergamerica*, which, like *Summertime* and *Summer Evening in Des Moines*, has a carefree mood, lots of silly romance, and a summer setting. Now titled "The Dark Side," it was assigned to Phil the Trucker in the Mayday draft and then switched to "Bob the Pizza Boy, a character we have not seen before" in the July draft. This did not necessarily mean *an actor* we have not seen before, and Bogart's initial inclination was to have Kelly Maurer, wearing a different costume and "a bad wig," double in the role. She felt that the scene would gain an added dimension and become "more hearable" if it came from the actor already familiar as Bob's Mom. Darron West was among the first to argue that the part should be played by an actor who had not been seen before at all, in order to maximize the impact of this strange character coming in, as he said, "completely out of the middle of nowhere." Bogart was concerned that this might come off simply as "an idea." What is more, if the Pizza Boy was not to be played by a company member, then at this point he would have to be an ATL apprentice. Counting on a young, less experienced actor to have "the chops" to pull off such a tricky cameo appearance in the play's longest scene would involve a calculated risk.

By the end of the second table-work session on December 7, many of the lingering casting issues were resolved. Sometime after the first meeting a month earlier, Tom Nelis decided for personal reasons that it was a bad time for him to be out of town for six weeks and pulled out of the cast. He was replaced by Danyon Davis, a black actor who had trained with the company off and on for many years, initially as a student at Juilliard and later in Los Angeles and New York. Davis was cast as Wilson and Steve the Canadian. Will Bond would play Allen, Carl's lover, as well as Herbert, the Philip Morrison figure. And, Leon Ingulsrud, not Maurer, would play Bob the Pizza Boy, along with his 'main role' of Phil the Trucker. Bogart made this change in response to Mee's concern that having Bob's Mom, as the heart and soul of the play and the avatar of motherhood itself, also appear as a "psycho murderer" would send the wrong message. At the December 7 table-work session, she admitted that she had been struggling with just who should play the role and switched it on the spot to Davis. Half an hour later, the situation changed again. As soon as the read-through ended, Will Bond proposed that Herbert and Allen, his two characters, might be "the same guy" and fused into one character. This suggestion had a domino effect. The idea of having Bob the Pizza Boy be a total stranger resurfaced and gathered steam. Mee took the opportunity to propose that the character of Steve the Canadian be cut and that the Welcome Speech be restored and assigned to Carl. Just like that, all eight SITI actors had only one designated role and double casting was eliminated from the production, a decision which strengthened the sense of ensemble and the archetypal profile of the individual characters.

This meant that Bogart would hope to find an actor in the ATL apprentice company who could play Bob the Pizza Boy. After looking at a number of audition tapes, she chose twenty-one-year-old Gian-Murray Gianino, a Manhattan native fresh out of Wesleyan University (see figure 13). He and Jennifer Taher, who played a non-speaking choral figure who came to be known as "Roller Girl," were the only two ATL apprentices in the production. In the end, Gianino acquitted himself impressively in his cameo appearance. He understood from early on that the key to this character was to present an outward demeanor of utter calm while describing his delusions of grandeur and bloody deeds. The stutter written into the text (and the implied effort to gain control of speech) were enough to suggest a latent, not altogether vanquished, demonic force within. And, all the more in his red, white, and blue Domino's Pizza uniform, Gianino's youth lent a boyish faux innocence to Bob the Pizza Boy, compared to the older SITI actors. After seeing *bobrauschenbergamerica* at the Brooklyn Academy of Music's Next Wave Festival in 2003, the *New York Times*'s John Rockwell was inspired to write a column about the peculiar, shocking experience of aesthetic arrest, especially in the performing arts: "Suddenly and unexpectedly we are lifted from our normal detached contemplation into another place, where time stops and our breath catches and we can hardly believe that those responsible for this pleasure can sustain it another second." Bob the Pizza Boy was Rockwell's primary recent example of such a jolt, and without giving Gianino all the credit, he celebrated how "he perfectly catches Bob's eerie singsong detachment."[10] Aided by Gianino's understated performance and the theatrical trick of introducing a new character (as if off the street) an hour into the show, "The Dark Side" segment played a pivotal role in shaping the audience's experience of *bobrauschenbergamerica*.

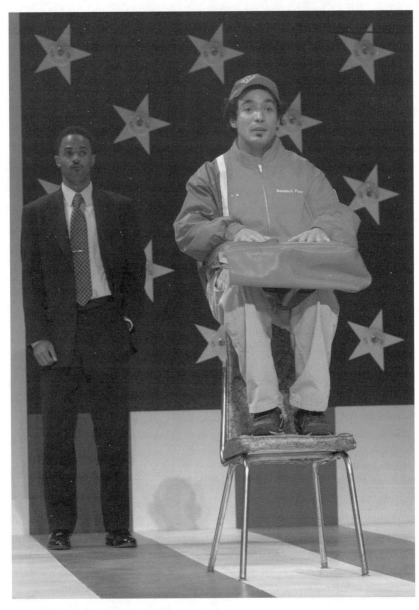

Figure 13. "The Dark Side": Bob the Pizza Boy (Gian-Murray Gianino) explains himself as a wary Wilson (Danyon Davis) looks on. (Photograph by Michael Brosilow.)

Design

On December 8, 2000, the SITI Company design team – Neil Patel (sets), James Schuette (costumes), Mimi Jordan Sherin (lights), and Darron West (sound) – received an EDDY Award from *Entertainment Design* magazine, an industry publication which covers "the art and technology of show business." Other honorees that evening included Anne Roth, the venerable costume designer for film and theater; the founding trio of Blue Man Group, heads by then of an expanding corporate empire; and Tait Towers, a designer of high-tech lighting towers and rock-and-roll concert stages. Bogart was tapped to present the award to her colleagues, and in doing so, she praised the beauty and intelligence of their designs, their capacity to hear "what the play wants," their willingness to let go of work and start again, and their ability to disagree with her and with each other. "There was a moment when I actually fell in love with each one of them," she said to open her remarks, concluding later, "Talent is actually very erotic."[11] (Eroticism is another "ally in the creative process" discussed in Bogart's *A Director Prepares* [London: Routledge, 2001].)

Earlier that day, Bogart had met with her design team for *bobrauschen-bergamerica*, which was a bit different from the established SITI foursome. Darron West had designed sound for every SITI production since *The Medium*, and *bobrauschenbergamerica* would be no exception. But an unforeseen scheduling conflict and a desire to remain in New York after the birth of his son prompted Neil Patel to drop out of the project, so arrangements were made for James Schuette to design the scenery as well as the costumes. In addition to their professional designer-director colla-boration, Mimi Jordan Sherin and Bogart had been personal partners for four years, but that relationship had ended about a year earlier. Company member Brian Scott, SITI's sometime technical director and a long-term apprentice to Sherin, was asked to design lights, as he had for *War of the Worlds: The Radio Play*.

The July draft for *bobrauschenbergamerica* contains no stipulation what-soever about the play's setting or scenery. The script is full of geographical references that suggest, as in "Becker's Movie," a broad American sweep "from the West Coast to the East Coast." Chicago, Cincinnati, Denver, the Malibu Highway, Port Arthur, New Mexico, Arkansas, Albany, the Grand Canyon, Seattle are all mentioned, but none of these is a setting per se. Some of the play's events or characters imply a type of locale: a derelict is an urban figure, a picnic suggests a backyard or a park, a marching band requires a main street or a football field. A yard sale, a square dance, a slide show, and so on all carry a sense of place, but none of these is general enough to encompass the play's full variety of events. To the extent that the numerous segments can be seen as individual works in an exhibit, the place of the play might be imagined as an art gallery or a museum, but to literalize this metaphor as a design concept would be a dull solution to the challenge of finding a scenic frame for the play. When asked what region of the USA he associated with the play, Mee said, "I think what I was thinking about all the time was Kerouac's *On the Road*, so I think the location slides through the Midwest to the West and a little bit down South."[12]

Bogart's impulses about scenery were influenced by the consideration early on that the show might tour. Inspired in part by the spirit of collaboration in the Rauschenberg Overseas Culture Interchange (ROCI) traveling project, Bogart imagined a series of two-week residencies in each city on the tour, during which the play would be rearranged to feature a different order of scenes, re-rehearsed to incorporate local people and objects, and redesigned to accentuate the architecture of whatever performance space they were in. This site-specific emphasis on the local, the found, and the theater-as-raw-space carried over into her thoughts about how to use ATL's Victor Jory Theatre. She wanted to base the set on what was already there, pull back the 'skin' of the theater and expose its structural materials, and then add complementary elements of brick or steel that would create an arena for the play rather than a specific environment. "I think it should be almost anonymous space," she said at the table-work session on December 7. In effect, she wanted a kind of theatrical blank canvas.

The next day, at the first major design meeting, James Schuette proposed a scenic approach that was anything but anonymous: he wanted to do the play on a giant American flag. A flat rear wall, 17 feet (5 meters) high and as wide as the Victor Jory thrust (22 feet) ($6\frac{1}{2}$ meters), would be constructed, and thirteen red-and-white vertical stripes would be painted down the wall and across the floor. As bold as it was simple, Schuette's idea for the flag set was a bit of a shock at first, but Bogart embraced it nearly at once, and she and the others set to brainstorming about some of its details and features. The blue field with white stars would fill the stage-left half of the wall, and each star would be big enough to hold a porcelain socket and a clear 60-watt light bulb at its center. Actors and objects could move on and off from all four corners of the stage, and a screen door built into the flag wall provided a fifth entrance, obscured at first sight by the dominant verticals of the red-and-white stripes painted across it. As a director, Bogart wanted levels to work with, so above the screen door two pop-open, window-sized openings were added, which came to be called "the Laugh-In doors" because they recalled the joke wall on *Rowan and Martin's Laugh-In*.[13] Another door, 6 feet ($1\frac{3}{4}$ meters) high, with its bottom edge 3 feet (*c.* 1 meter) off the stage floor, was designed into the star field. Like the screen door, it was unnoticeable until opened.

This basic design satisfied Schuette's desire to have color in the set and Bogart's need for an "arena" that would allow quick and easy entrances and exits for the play's fifty-plus segments. The light-bulb stars offered Brian Scott the opportunity for special lighting effects. And the flag made the unmistakable statement that all that took place in front and on top of it should be seen as Americana. But not all of the set's implications and repercussions were so immediately apparent. When put to use in rehearsal, the screen door, rigged with a nostalgic squeak, would take on tremendous significance. In performance, the light-bulb stars came to represent not just the fifty states of the union but the boundless heavens above (as often mentioned in the play by Allen), thus enhancing Mee's implicit connection between the vastness of the American continent and the infinitely greater vastness of the universe beyond. An art historian might find in the flag design a subtle allusion to Rauschenberg's relationship with Jasper Johns, who began his first *Flag* painting late in 1954, the same year he met Rauschenberg.[14] For the audience who saw the play in the intimate Victory Jory Theatre (particularly for those in the center section), the flag backdrop so filled their field of view as to be engulfing, a geometrical landscape that had a sense of open abstraction and grandeur at first and then, as the long straight lines and solid blocks of color became familiar, took on a rigidity and unrelenting sameness. Most of all, with an 'American,' in-your-face bravura, the flag set provided an undeniable visual unity for a play which on the page was a jumble of disparate and unrelated events, gathering them together in its stars and stripes in a manner that said, 'This is all the USA. This, too, is American.'

Schuette's costume designs had a similar unifying effect (see figures 14 and 15). They straddled the line between archetype and stereotype, giving the characters more definition (more character, so to speak) than the script itself did. And the range of clothing and hairstyles helped to suggest that the play took place across the second half of the twentieth century, rather than in a particular decade or period. Bob's Mom (Kelly Maurer) wore a simple cotton green dress from the 1940s, an apron, and "sensible shoes." Allen (Will Bond), in his short-sleeved white shirt, skinny tie, black pants, and hat, reminded me a bit of Dennis-the-Menace's father; the addition of a pocket

Figure 14. Costume renderings by designer James Schuette.

Figure 15. Costume renderings by designer James Schuette.

protector full of pens and thick black-framed glasses repaired with white adhesive tape gave him the look of a 1950s science geek. Carl (Barney O'Hanlon), barefoot, wore grey cotton sweat pants and a white-ribbed tank top in order to suggest the Judson dancers of the 1960s, in particular Steve Paxton, a frequent collaborator with Rauschenberg at that time.[15] Phil the Trucker (Leon Ingulsrud) looked like a trucker (or a biker) in his cowboy boots, blue jeans, black Harley Davidson tee shirt, and frayed jeans-vest covered with insignia patches, and Phil's Girl (Akiko Aizawa) recalled the swingin' chicks of the 1960s – part beach girl, part Bond girl – in her mod, hot pink and orange, full-cut bikini. Susan (Ellen Lauren) was more demure in a pale blue gingham sundress with a string of pearls at her neck, and Wilson (Danyon Davis) matched her in a contemporary, dark-blue business suit, with a conservative tie. Becker (J. Ed Araiza), also barefoot, with long, greasy, matted hair, worn pants, shirt untucked, and soiled, stained topcoat, was instantly recognizable as what in the 1950s was called "a bum" and in more politically correct times "a homeless person." All told, Schuette's carefully chosen everyday clothes portrayed a broad enough demographic – the blue-collar worker, the buttoned-down businessman, the casual hip artist, the nerdy scientist, the mangy street person, the girl next door, the sexy babe, the prim-and-proper homemaker-mom – to suggest a full spectrum of American types.

As would be expected, while the sound design and lighting design were roughed out in advance, many specific decisions were contingent on what Bogart and the actors came up with in rehearsal. Both Darron West and Brian Scott prepared for this by using a familiar SITI strategy: establishing certain "rules" for themselves, that is, setting parameters, guidelines, or limitations that offered a degree of structure within which they could operate with plenty of freedom. For Scott, the wall and floor of the flag set implied a cube-shaped space; he wanted to draw out that shape by outlining the stage floor with strip lights and placing fluorescent tubes in parallel overhead, by creating a uniform "ceiling" by using only one type of visible instrument above the stage floor, and by hanging other instruments in a symmetrical pattern. The moment he heard about the broad stripes on the set he knew that he wanted to light them individually or at least the red ones independent of the white, so that he might be able to create the effect of actors being "in" the flag as well as on it. West's "rules" often stem from what he calls "the pull," the large selection of CDs that he pulls in the months before a play goes into rehearsal from his vast library of sound and music. Once he "seals the vault," he will limit his sound design choices to what he has on hand – unless, of course, he feels the need to break the rules. In the summer of 2000, West's preliminary pull for *bobrauschenbergamerica* included everything from John Cage to Betty Page (the 1950s stripper), lots of bluegrass and country music, Earth, Wind & Fire's Greatest Hits, Milhaud and Moby, soundtracks from *Citizen Kane* and *Plan Nine from Outer Space*, and a wide variety of compilations. Taking cues from Rauschenberg, West wanted his sound design to be quirky, populist, all over the place, and "dirty," that is, with hiss or static or other evidence of it as *recorded* sound. As he anticipated it, the basic design question would be simple:

> What do I have to do musically in the play to say "America" without doing Scott Joplin or Aaron Copland or Leonard Bernstein? It is not that kind of America, it doesn't seem to me. It is the America I grew up with in Kentucky. Dirt roads and pickup trucks and normal folks. It is those great people that you run into in the grocery store that make your day for no apparent reason. It is those people that you run into in a park that give you directions. Everyday people.[16]

This populist impulse in the play made the decision to perform the play on a giant American flag appropriate, simple, perhaps even obvious, but in a way that was also daring and provocative, given the flag's status as a contested symbol and a flashpoint for political debate. What is the United States of America? What does the nation and its most ubiquitous symbol really mean to you? The size and omnipresence of the flag made these questions unavoidable. In this regard, it should be borne in mind that *bobrauschenbergamerica* was conceived at the end of the American century and written at the end of the happy-go-lucky Clinton era. The play premiered in Louisville six months *before* September 11, 2001. The national wound opened up on that horrible day was bandaged with millions of American flags, altering the symbolic meaning of the flag and the valence of its display for years to come. Late in the fall of 2000, when Schuette first proposed his design, the flag was something different, more an open symbol than a closed one. In fact, the design period overlapped with the ugly November limbo that followed the contested Bush–Gore election, when, at one press conference after another, the Vice President and the Governor of Texas took turns appearing in front of more and more American flags, as if their competing claims to the presidency might be settled by who had more flags behind him. When Mee heard about the proposed design in December, he wondered if an audience entering the theater and seeing a giant flag might get the wrong impression of the play to come, a concern that contributed to the decision to cover the stage with a large dropcloth and reveal the set as part of the play's opening sequence. This decision had practical repercussions that were not resolved until opening night.

One last ironic note on the flag design: it was wrong. In its vertical orientation, the star field was placed in the upper-right-hand corner (on the stage left portion of the set's wall), as if a horizontal flag had been rotated ninety-degrees clockwise. Less than a week after the first anniversary of the September 11 attacks on New York and Washington, *bobrauschenbergamerica* was revived for the first time since its Louisville premiere, and when the set was loaded in to the Stamford Center for the Arts, somebody on the IATSE stage crew pointed out that the proper way to display the flag is always with the star field in the upper-left-hand corner, whether it hangs vertically or horizontally. A year of ubiquitous patriotism seemed to have raised people's awareness of flag protocol. In retrospect, given the play's unconventional, scrambled form and its cautious, counter-cultural patriotism, the mistake – and it was a mistake – seems fitting.

In response to the first two table-work sessions, Mee made minor changes in the script and printed up a new draft dated January 1, 2001. This would be the script that the SITI Company took into rehearsal eight weeks later in Louisville (referred to hence as the rehearsal draft or the New Year draft). It had fifty-six numbered segments, most of them separate, independent units of action, each with its own title (indicated below in quotation marks). After the prologue of "Viewpoints," "What I Like," and "Country Music," the characters are introduced in a series of monologues and dialogues, one by one at first, and then as romantic couples: Susan and Wilson (complicated by her "Falling in Love" with Becker), Phil the Trucker and Phil's Girl, Carl and Allen. Suddenly, there is a "Tub Party," which concludes with "A Toast" from Becker, and then a picnic lunch is served, which is comprised of a series of "Table Talk" scenes that, in effect, zoom in on different private exchanges ("The Stars," "The Dispute," "A Couple Seeks Advice," "Lips," "Guy Talk") between the guests. This gives way to a highly unstructured sequence, which starts with "Becker's Movie" and includes "Line Dancing," "Martinis," "The Laundry Opera," a "Square Dance," "The Assassination," "Chicken Jokes," a "Welcome Speech," a "Yard Sale," "The Beating," "The Marching Band," and "The Dark Side," featuring the unforeseen Bob the Pizza Boy. With his departure, the play returns to its "Lovers" and their fragmented romances, ties those up with neat little happy endings and "The Waltz," pauses for a sample from "Whitman" and a final reminiscence about "Bob" from Bob's Mom, and then, in the spirit of the canonical ending of comedy, there is "The Last Dance," followed by "The Final Moment," in which a man's voice calls out, "OK! That feels good to me."

The New Year draft retained the same amorphous shape as the Mayday and July drafts. "The only thing that gives it coherence is a feeling," Mee told the company, knowing full well that they could not simply go out onstage and replicate that feeling. They would have to discover their own rationale for each and every fragment in the play and then decide when to stage the play in a way that made that rationale evident to the audience and when to withhold it, as Mee often does, as hidden subtext or the moment's secret cause. Without a sustained narrative that might lead from one thing to another, without conventional characters who act out of need or want, without even a specific time or place to lend a coherent setting to its many pieces, the play provided none of the familiar pegs on which a director and actors hang their interpretive hats. In his work, Rauschenberg combines materials in a manner that preserves and protects their differences. Each clipped image, found object, swatch of fabric, or swath of paint retains a degree of separation from the other elements. No matter how much they overlap, they remain somehow disconnected and independent. As critic Leo Steinberg said of *Washington's Golden Egg*, "Near and Next admit no felt neighboring, only disjunction by juxtaposition. The more closely pressed, the keener the dissociation. Items estranged by adjacency, like renters in urban apartments, or travelers, economy class."[7] This "triumph of the Immiscible" – a term borrowed from chemistry for two or more substances that will not blend together to form a single homogeneous substance – forestalls the closure of representation in Rauschenberg's work, makes the assignment of meaning to a piece highly speculative, and keeps things open: open-hearted in spirit, open in the sense of being in process or feeling unfinished, open to the interpretation, and even the participation, of the viewer. In keeping with its namesake, *bobrauschenbergamerica* sought to make that same openness part of its experience. Each scene, character, movement, speech, dance, and action needed to stand on its own as much as possible. Each piece of the collage asked to stand alone and stand apart.

bobrauschenbergamerica posed a particular challenge to the SITI Company in this regard. One of the hallmarks of their work is flow, the steady, organic movement of a performance from beat to beat, entrance to exit, beginning to end. In putting a piece together, the SITI people look for ways to maintain (with variety) the continuous and uninterrupted movement of theatrical time. Conspicuous scene breaks are rare, intermissions even rarer. Transitions are often blurred or bridged by sound and light cues or incidental movement or the business of secondary characters. Sometimes, the moment-to-moment progression is so deft that the stage picture will change altogether without a spectator being sure how it got so different. Just as an Open Viewpoints session will expand and contract space, speed up and slow down time, and shift focus from one actor to another or to the group as a whole, all without apparent agency, a SITI production plays out with the same paradoxical sense of spontaneous inevitability. For some viewers, this can make the work too controlled, tight, hermetic, or precious. For others, it is the key to the work's tremendous vitality.

Bogart and the Company faced the daunting, if exciting, task of making a million specific decisions about exactly what to do, without erasing or filling in the openness at the heart of the play. As an ensemble of highly trained, sophisticated actors, they were masters of flow, of making one thing lead to another, of taking a mountain of disjunctive, raw material and theatrical impulses and harmonizing them into a compact, powerful whole. On one level, the play wanted just the opposite. They had to find enough of a rationale to motivate – that is, to activate, to energize, to bring alive – each individual segment without letting that rationale carry over to other segments and evolve into some kind of overarching narrative. They had to create enough flow to hold the piece together and make it interesting, but not so much that the Rauschenbergian principle of dissociation was washed away in the process. They had to trust that a satisfying composite picture would emerge if they left room for the audience to assemble the pieces of the collage through their own act of perception. Alluding to *Monogram*, Rauschenberg's most famous combine, Leon Ingulsrud summarized their task this way, "At any moment, you are either playing the goat or you are playing the tire. You cannot express what results from those things happening together. You just have to be the goat or the tire. And then allow the thing to happen."

IO

Winter 2001: rehearsing in Louisville

Like other SITI projects, *BOBRAUSCHENBERGAMERICA* started off as a marathon and ended as a sprint. By the time rehearsals began in Louisville on February 27, 2001, sixteen months after Mee first met with the company, all concerned were chomping at the bit. In keeping with company practice, the SITI actors arrived in Louisville off book (or close to it) and ready to rehearse unencumbered by a script in hand. With the first performance scheduled for March 22, the company had just over three weeks (twenty Equity working days plus one preview performance) to put the show together. Given the amorphous nature of the script and the volume of material that needed to be invented virtually from scratch, this was not a luxurious amount of time, but the SITI Company was accustomed to working under pressure and working fast. In truth, they thrive on it.

Rehearsals were held on a typical Equity schedule, from Tuesday through Sunday, starting most days at noon and ending sometime around 8.00 p.m. On any given day, there were at least fifteen to twenty people in the room, starting with Bogart, Darron West, the eight principal actors, and the company's new stage manager, Elizabeth Moreau. The cast was rounded out by the two young actors from the Actor's Theatre of Louisville's apprentice company (Jennifer Taher and Gian-Murray Gianino); two other ATL apprentices worked as assistant stage managers. Chuck Mee was there for the first full week and the last few days of rehearsal (see figure 16). Tanya Palmer, the production dramaturg and a recent addition to ATL's literary staff, was in and out on a frequent basis, as was lighting designer Brian Scott. In addition, two scholars were in attendance, Julia Whitworth, a New York University doctoral student doing dissertation research, and myself. And these were just the regulars. From day to day, all manner of visitors would stop by for a few minutes or a few hours, from new ATL artistic director Marc Masterson to

Figure 16. Charles Mee and Anne Bogart (and mascot) on the first day of Louisville rehearsals. (Photograph David Perry/*Lexington Herald-Leader.*)

former ATL artistic director Jon Jory (back in town to debut another Jane Martin play at the Humana Festival) to Dot the receptionist and other ATL staffers to members of the board of directors to senior citizen or high school groups on a tour of the theater to friends and colleagues of the company. In this instance, at least, the SITI Company was operating in a fish bowl, an indication of the premium that Bogart places on making her work as open and transparent as possible. While many artists approach the creative process as a private act, best conducted with minimal distraction in the controlled environment of a studio, the SITI Company makes no effort to create in a vacuum, despite the frustrations and annoyances that constant or unannounced visitors can entail.

Although *bobrauschenbergamerica* was one of eight Humana productions in rehearsal at the same time, it was the only one scheduled that year in the Victor Jory Theatre, which meant that the company was able to create the piece in the space where it would be performed. This advantage was enhanced by the company's familiarity with the "VJ," the cozy 150-seat thrust theater tucked away on the third floor of the ATL complex. Having performed *Cabin Pressure*, *Going, Going, Gone* and *The Medium* there in recent years, they knew how to make good use of both the character and mechanics of the room. While *bobrauschenbergamerica* would go on to theaters that seated nearly a thousand, it was created in and for this intimate chamber theater, where no spectator is more than six or seven rows from the edge of the stage. This close proximity made the production's overt theatricality – characters rushing on from all four corners of the thrust, multiple dance sequences, the in-your-face backdrop of the flag set – all the more palpable and engulfing. The play would be as visceral as it was visual. It left no room for aesthetic distance.

The first couple of days of rehearsal were given over to getting-started formalities, additional table work, and a specially arranged lecture about Rauschenberg by Julian Robson, Curator of Contemporary Art at Louisville's Speed Art Museum. Even then, in keeping with strict company practice, rehearsal began with "training," a half hour or more of Suzuki work followed by an extended Viewpoints improvisation (see figure 9, page 122 above). For *bobrauschenbergamerica*, training was followed each day by work on the play's "specials," movement sequences that are technical enough to require instruction, regular practice, gradual development, or daily review. Although the wide, wild range of activities written into the script by Mee prompted a cast member to remark at one point that the play was composed entirely of specials, these were mainly the stipulated dance sequences: a square dance that morphs into a more ecstatic clog stomp, the line dance requested by Bogart, and a final waltz between Susan and Wilson. Barney O'Hanlon, SITI's resident choreographer and the actor playing Carl the Dancer, led the company through their daily paces in putting these dances together. This meant that on many days the company had done upwards of ninety minutes of vigorous physical work before dealing with the spoken text of the play or the acting of a specific scene. Each day, after training and specials, they picked up where they left off the day before, sometimes taking the time to review the work up to that point first. When contacting a scene for the first time, the effort was to discover and establish its rough parameters, either by talking it out or just jumping up on stage and trying something. As this was articulated, essentially through a process of trial and error, a basic shape for the segment at hand was sketched out and then filled in with detail through repetition and revision. If things were going well, precise blocking would be determined, minor adjustments would be made for the sake of timing, composition, or variety, and the sequence would be repeated in order to lock it in before moving on. In and of itself, this is a conventional way to rehearse any play, but the nature of *bobrauschenbergamerica* as an unconstructed collage and the SITI Company's commitment to collective creation made the process unique and, at moments, uncanny to observe.

First of all, all of the actors are there for all of every rehearsal, regardless of whose scenes are on the agenda. At any moment, the actors in the room are either working onstage or sitting in the house keeping an eye on the work onstage or preparing for an upcoming scene somewhere offstage. They are always working. They do not wait around for the director to tell them what to do. Each of them assumes a measure of responsibility not just for their individual performances but for the creation of the whole and even for the performances of their peers. They feel free to offer notes, comments, and suggestions to each other as they work, either in group discussion or tête-a-têtes off to the side or just simple hand signals from across the room. They look out for each other. In this regard, I could not help but notice the exquisite attention paid to ATL apprentice Jennifer Taher on just the third day of rehearsal, the first day the cast was up on its feet. Taher was cast in the role that came to be referred to as "Roller Girl," a girl-next-door choral figure who would skate through the action at selected moments and sometimes look on from a corner, as if watching over a backyard fence. As Mee's script had it, after the initial Viewpoints sequence, Roller Girl was the first character to appear onstage, which meant that on this first day of staging, Taher had the daunting duty of trying to figure out – in front of the cast of SITI veterans – how to enter on skates twirling a red umbrella, fall on her butt with comic aplomb, and then get up and skate off, closing the umbrella just in time to clear the exit doorway. The assembled company could not have been more supportive to the young actor, cheering her on, giving her all the time she needed, making suggestions, anticipating problems, providing funny off-stage crash sounds, and creating the moment with her.

This is the way the SITI Company works. They all create everything together, and most of the time, they manage to do so with a combination of civility, concern, and good humor that avoids stepping on toes. They joke around and have plenty of fun, but they also treat each other with a personal respect and professional courtesy that at moments might seem to belie their longstanding familiarity. They solicit feedback from each other in making the smallest of choices, oftentimes by asking the shorthand question "Is it A or is it B?" and then demonstrating two different ways to execute a move or shape a moment or sequence an action. Often there is a unanimous preference and the work proceeds apace, but a difference in opinion will often lead to a discussion, sometimes a lengthy, rambling discussion in which everyone has something to say. Some talk more than others, and when necessary, Bogart will exercise her directorial prerogative to resolve a situation or make a unilateral decision, but she is rarely in a hurry to do so. When the group is thinking something through, there is no rush to wrap things up. A long, pregnant pause in the conversation or Bogart asking "Anybody else?" at what seems like the end of a discussion can lead to one person broaching some new misgiving about the matter at hand or even a decision that has already been made. They don't move on until the air is clear. The work proceeds by general agreement, often more tacit than explicit. They create by consensus.

In this context, Anne Bogart's identity as the director in the room is remarkable in several ways, first and foremost for the quality of attention that she brings to the performers as they work. Bogart herself does not practice or teach Suzuki, yet she is there almost always at the top of the hour, front and center, sitting and watching as the actors go through each day's Suzuki training and Viewpoints work. While for another director this chunk of time might be an opportunity to grab a cup of coffee, confer with the stage manager, make a quick phone call, flip through the script, or finalize the day's agenda, Bogart pays direct and undivided attention to the actors as they stomp. She sits and watches, often perched on a wooden stool with a music stand in front of her that holds her script, and this simple act of paying attention stands as a paradigm – something like a gestus, in Brecht's sense – for Bogart's directorial role in rehearsal. She positions herself as an observer, more a respondent than an initiator:

> I am the first audience member. That is my job, and I am the only one.
> I really think that. Everybody else is trying to do things for me. It might
> sound like a big ego trip, but I think that is right. I am the first. And the
> actors know, too, no matter how many people are watching them and
> throwing out suggestions, their focus is me, ultimately. So, I try to be
> present and listen and react before I think about it. I listen to everybody,
> and I feel my way through their comments. I am completely dependent
> on that. I don't come in with a dramaturgical plan. I have some ideas, a
> couple things to start with, but I get that out of the way really fast. Half
> the time, the company will say, "Well, what about this?" and that is
> great because if the company did what I thought first, what would be
> the point? It would be a realization of some thought, as opposed to
> something else. So listening is the entire thing.[1]

By the time rehearsals begin and Bogart sits back to take it all in, her most active, willful work has already been done. In most instances, she has conceived the piece on the basis of a question, an anchor, and a structure, conducted extensive research and assembled voluminous raw materials, and gathered a talented group of artists. In these early stages, she leads from out in front of the project, but as others get more involved, she leads more from the middle of the pack, as another member of the ensemble. As rehearsals advance, she seems to lead from the rear, a change in position that allows her to hang back, tie up loose ends, and get a broader perspective on the action which she instigated months and months earlier. As necessary, she is the final arbiter of certain matters, but as much as possible, she conducts herself as "the first audience," paying close attention, listening, giving her collaborators a chance to do their work, seeing how things feel, and channeling energy back to the performers on stage as they all figure things out together.

In this and other ways, Bogart directs by indirection. While she is as concerned with how things look or sound as any director, she does not come to rehearsal with blocking in mind or an exact template of how a scene should be staged. She will often lead off a rehearsal by saying, "What I know is . . .," and complete the sentence by describing one or two things regarding the rhythm of the scene or a part of the stage to be explored or a general feeling or quality that seems right for the segment of text at hand. This intuition provides a few parameters or ground rules to provoke and to contain the actors' own inventions and explorations. Bogart will also use the locution "What I know is . . ." as a way of responding to that preliminary work without making many negative comments, trusting the actor to make whatever adjustments might be appropriate. Often, she will embrace raw work and first impulses with what seems like undiscerning enthusiasm, content for the company to weed things out as they go back over things. The company is there to create the piece as a company, and while she is present to move things along as needed, to offer her perspective, or to make her own contributions, the moment-to-moment progress of rehearsals does not always depend on her or flow through her. In fact, on occasions when she is called away from rehearsal, for an hour or even for a day, the company rehearses without her. At certain moments when she is there, an unknowing visitor who walked into rehearsal would have a hard time identifying her as the director in the room. On some of these occasions, the more likely guess would be Darron West.

Perhaps the most unusual aspect of the SITI Company's rehearsal process is the role played by Darron West. He is in the forefront of a new generation of sound designers who are taking sound beyond its traditional role as scene-change music and realistic offstage effects (barking dogs, squealing tires, etc.) and making it as pronounced and as integral as other design elements. Brian Scott describes what West does like this: "Darron hears the music that happens when people say words on stage and then he lifts that musical quality up by weaving things into it and around it, laying things underneath and on top of it. In a way, he is pushing it, holding it up, and punctuating it all at the same time."[2] West does not plan all his design in advance, review it with Bogart, and then introduce it during technical rehearsals when the lighting and costumes come into play. Unlike most sound designers and unlike the set, costume, and lighting designers for most SITI projects, West is in the room for every rehearsal, providing music for the training period and then collaborating hour by hour and day by day with Bogart and the actors in making the play. Not far from Bogart's director's stool, he sits in the house at a work table piled high with audio equipment, and while the actors work, he works right along with them, testing out impulses of his own, adding in sound on the fly in the middle of a scene, steering it in a particular direction by his choices, providing the actor with something to push off against. His relationships with his acting colleagues have developed to the point that he does not hesitate to introduce sound without warning while they are in the middle of working a scene. Most of the time, the actors welcome these surprises and find a way to feed off the energy they offer or ask him to try something different. Their dialogue is open and ongoing.

West feels just as free to offer comments and corrections to the performers as they work on a scene, calling for a change in posture or position for the sake of a better stage picture or even coaching the acting of a particular moment. To an outside observer accustomed to the singular authority of the director in rehearsal, such behavior is strange to behold at first, but it soon becomes another hallmark of the profound and intimate collaboration that defines the SITI Company's work. The sound that West creates is so closely and organically linked to what the actors are doing that he operates as another species of performer in the scene at hand, another presence with an entrance and an exit and something to say or do in between. Bogart often describes West as the best dramaturg she has ever worked with. He is, in a way, her alter ego in rehearsal. His masculine energy and 'guy's guy' persona provide a curious, countervailing effect to Bogart's female presence; in a loose Jungian sense, he is her animus, projected out into the room as another set of eyes and ears and a valued partner who is ready to pick up the slack or fill in a gap or throw out another idea as needed.

The SITI Company's modus operandi, with a Noël Coward play or a piece of their own invention, is to make as few assumptions as possible, to question everything, to consider every possibility, and then to build the theatrical world for each play from the ground up. This can result in lengthy and long-winded deliberations, passionate disagreements, a too-many-cooks feeling, creative false starts and dead ends, and sometimes a mistrust of the obvious that leads to making simple matters very compli-cated, but all of this is necessary to achieve the thorough investigation that makes their work so sturdy on their feet. Heading into rehearsals for *bobrauschenbergamerica*, Bogart's main concern was figuring out the dynamics of its quixotic form. "We have to learn how this play functions," Bogart said on the first day of staging, articulating the task that would beguile them for the next three weeks. They had devoted considerable time during table work to discussing the play's logic, knowing that for them the ultimate answers had to be found on their feet, by taking a stab at one scene at a time, improvising in order to generate possibilities, trying variations on those, and generally feeling their way through the play until it revealed its secrets. In company parlance, this is the ouija board approach, as in 'Let's ouija board this and see what happens.' The meta-phor, however casual, reinforces two things about the way they work: first, all hands are on the pointer as it floats about looking for answers; and two, those answers are to be found outside of themselves in the work itself. This is why two strategic questions – What is it? and What is it really? – are so important to Bogart's work on a text. Work on each new segment of the play began with one or both of these questions and the commensurate posture of willful naïveté needed to discover each thing in and of itself (for example, what is *a* waltz?) and in the context of the play (what is *the* waltz between Susan and Wilson at the end of the play?).

Starting on Day Three, the company began working their way in chronological order through the play's fifty-six segments. They made a first stab at the opening "Viewpoints" sequence, viewpointing on a muslin drop-cloth since it had been decided that the flag set and stage floor would be covered at the very top of the show. They came up with Roller Girl lazzi for Jennifer Taher to perform during the country-music song. And they roughed in the monologues and dialogues that introduced each character in turn, starting with Bob's Mom. The first segment that involved the full cast was "Tub Party," and their work in this instance exemplified their method of collective creation. The scene reads as follows: "All at once, there is a party. Music. Everyone has glasses in their hands – and everyone is trying to get into the tub at the same time, laughing and talking." That is all the script gave them to go on, but the company does not blanch in the face of such scant information. "How does the party start?" Bogart asked when they set to work, meaning 'what does the party come out of?' or 'what gives rise to it?' From his sound table, Darron West provided an immediate, cheeky answer by blasting the room with Three Dog Night's "Joy to the World," and the entire group jumped up from their seats and started to dance. But nothing is that simple for the SITI Company. A brainstorming discussion about the logistics of a party in a tub led, in typical SITI fashion, to the establishment of certain ground rules for the party: 1. You have to 'circulate' the full length of the tub, 2. You have to be careful not to spill your drink, and 3. Everybody you see is somebody you have not seen in a year. Then, it was "One, two, three, Go!" A free-for-all erupted, with seven actors stepping in and out of a cast-iron tub set up on a wheeled platform, making small talk in gibberish, pretzelling arms and legs as they squeezed around each other, and catching each other when somebody started to fall. This first attempt amounted to viewpointing in a very small space, and the hilarity of it prompted Ellen Lauren to compare it to the party game Twister. At one point, Bogart yelled out with glee, "Ladies and gentlemen, this is what we do for a living!"

The initial chaos led to a systematic effort to structure the party bit by bit so that it had its own *jo-ha-kyu*. Bogart called for the group to find seven tableau moments and then figure out how all seven actors could negotiate the shift from one to next so that each of them arrived in position at exactly the same moment. This led to marking off each shift with Suzuki-like precision and a specific count. At one point, concerns for safety prompted them to substitute a large cardboard refrigerator box on its side for the actual bathtub. At another moment, thinking ahead to exact performance conditions led lighting designer Brian Scott to rig the tub with a makeshift pipe and shower head to mark a place for the one that wasn't there yet, so that they did not set blocking that would have to be changed later. The decision was made at the start that Bob's Mom would not join the others in the tub; when the party flagged at one point, Kelly Maurer made the spontaneous decision to bring out a deli tray of leftover cheese cubes and cut vegetables that had been delivered earlier that day as a rehearsal treat for the company. When she placed it off one corner of the tub, the party picked up energy and definition as people tried to shimmy over and grab a snack.

As the company put things together bit by bit, Bogart chimed in with a combination of practical concerns ("Are you sure it's going to work with this tub?") and unbridled excitement ("I want a ticket to this play imme-diately"). When it became clear that what was shaping up was "a keeper," they figured out how the party would move into and climax with the next two segments, "Ping Pong," in which "Phil's Girl opens her purse, and

hundreds of ping pong balls fall out," and "A Toast," a homespun perora-
tion in which Becker celebrates the value of social rituals, from weddings
and funerals to just sitting down together for a meal. Then, they went over
the sequence again and again as if they were finetuning a dance, making
adjustments for the sake of efficiency, safety, or visual interest, trouble-
shooting problems, and eventually tying the action into specific cues
within the music provided by Darron West. Every shift of weight, twist
of a hip, and turn of a chin was linked to something. The whole process
took eight to ten hours over three rehearsals. It was a marvel to observe, all
the more for the irony of watching a wild, chaotic party in a bathtub be
created in such a workmanlike and methodical way. At one point, as a
dozen seasoned theater professionals stood around the tub with puzzled
faces, Leon Ingulsrud turned to Mee and remarked, "Hey, Chuck, how
tough is it when you are sitting at your desk to write 'tub party'?"
Moments like this exemplified the way in which Mee's script for
bobrauschenbergamerica – in its looseness, its frivolity, its conviviality, and
its messiness – rubbed up against the SITI Company's propensity to make
work that is tight, strict, exact, and controlled. Throughout the rehearsal
period, members of the company commented on what a boon it was for
them to be working on this play at this time and how invigorating it was
to be given permission to have fun and do whatever the hell they felt like.
The play called for a carefree quality, a lightness and an ease that was not
always easy for them to achieve. Freedom was the play's keynote, and they
worked hard to embrace it, sometimes falling back on ways of working
that made that freedom all the more elusive.

On Sunday, March 4, 2001, the last day of the first week, rehearsal began
with a discussion triggered by Kelly Maurer. Much of the rehearsal the day
before had been spent on creating the picnic that was the backdrop for the
"Table talk" conversations: Susan and Wilson have another lover's spat;
Carl and Allen seek advice about their plan to become chicken farmers;
and Susan and Phil gossip about the woman next door "having an affair
with an orchestra conductor in Cincinnati." One of these scenes, "Table
Talk: Bob's Mom's Grandmother," consisted of the monologue written for
the March workshop by Rebecca Brown about her grandmother's cut
Italian colored glass collection. Mee had assigned this speech to Bob's
Mom in order to complicate the more folksy material written by Jane
Comfort, and its placement in the middle of the picnic proved to be just as
complicated. Maurer wanted to know, as any actor would, "Who am
I talking to?" The question is simple on the surface, but it broached a

fundamental issue about how the play was to be staged. Where did Bob's Mom stand in relation to the other characters? Did she 'know' them? Where did she fit into the grand scheme of things? In effect, who was she? And who was she really?

Kelly Maurer had spent her first week of rehearsal exploring these questions on her own. In Mee's script, Bob's Mom is the only character who does not really speak to any other character. Her reminiscences about her son Bob stand alone, written as though she is flipping through an old family photo album while slides (that, as the script stipulates, don't match her descriptions) are projected behind her. On the page, her appearances are limited to four segments, but Maurer had been looking for appropriate moments to augment the main action onstage with Bob's Mom's presence. The inclusion of the screen door in the set's flag wall suggested a house, which came to seem more and more like her house as Maurer became the predominant actor to use that door to come on and go off. When it came time to figure out the transition out of Becker's "Toast," which ends with an unspecified voice calling out "Lunch is served!," Maurer spoke the line from offstage and proceeded to bring on a series of picnic dishes from the "house," stomping her foot to simulate the slam of the screen door that was not there yet. With this decision, Bob's Mom became the ostensible hostess of a backyard picnic and, by extension, the stage became her domain.

By end of first week, the presence of Bob's Mom was becoming pervasive, but to Maurer it also felt ambiguous. "I'm there, but I'm not there," she observed in specific reference to the staging of the "Tub Party," summing up her uncertain status vis-à-vis the other characters. This prompted discussion about the extent to which Bob's Mom was the font or secret cause of the entire play, as if perhaps the whole event sprang from her consciousness as a dream or a series of memories prompted by the photo album or an interview with an art historian or museum curator doing research on her son. Mee likened Bob's Mom to the Stage Manager in *Our Town*, who exists outside the action of the play yet participates in it at certain moments. "You're on the sidelines," added Bogart. "You're helping to make it happen, like Tadeusz Kantor," the Polish director known for placing himself on stage in his own memory plays, observing and sometimes correcting the actors in mid-performance. Maurer, too, saw her character as some kind of onstage facilitator of the action, and that raised questions about how the top of the play had been staged earlier in the week. If in some meaningful way, the play emanated from her, shouldn't she be the very first character to appear on stage, however briefly, after the initial Viewpoints segment? Shouldn't the Roller Girl business come after rather than before the audience meets Bob's Mom? Or, as others thought, was this initial back-and-forth roller skating better understood as part of "the opening credits rolling" or "a palate cleanser" between the Viewpoints prologue and the play proper? The script did not stipulate an exact structural function for Bob's Mom, nor did Bogart presume, as the director, to define one. This major conceptual concern was for the company to work out as a company. In a relaxed and civil manner, without a hint of contention, they hashed out these issues for more than half an hour, offering individual points of view while supporting the need for one of their number to get a firm handle on what she was doing. In this instance, Mee helped to round off the discussion by suggesting that the most Rauschenbergian approach would be if each and every character thought that the whole play sprang from his imagination. Bogart credited Maurer with helping her to see the need to organize space around the character of Bob's Mom in a particular way. In typical fashion, the discussion ended with a clearer sense of how to proceed without determining an exact course of action.

Over the next two weeks, as the group worked through the play, Maurer defined and refined the presence of Bob's Mom. If she was not the conceptual source of the action, she was nevertheless central to it as its penetrating spirit. Just as the metronomic slam of the screen door set the rhythm for the picnic scenes, her series of loving speeches about her son Bob set the rhythm for the play as a whole. She became a kind of maternal permitter of what went on there, looking on from the screen door at moments, dish towel in hand, making sure that things did not get out of hand, too busy with chores to join in the fun herself, but always happy to see that everybody was getting along and having a good time. She filled in gaps or added a dimension to a scene as needed. Each time the script called for the ch-ching! of the paper boy's bicycle bell, she came out to retrieve a folded newspaper tossed onstage by Darron West from up in the sound booth. For certain scenes, such as the "Yard Sale," she instigated the action and then retreated into the background. Though she made contact with others onstage with a wave or a smile or a wink or a look of concern, she never spoke to any of them directly. She was there and not there, appearing again and again to observe the action onstage, be it "Becker's Movie" or "The Laundry Opera" with Carl diving into a pile of clean white shirts or the several dance sequences that set her toes tapping or hands clapping. She, more significantly than Roller Girl, became an onstage audience, looking on but not quite joining in. And then, after her final tribute to her beloved Bob, after making clear that the dance pavilion on Lake Sabine "was definitely off limits" for her son when he was growing up, she loosened her apron strings, tossed it aside, and danced with wild and comic abandon to the Cuban rhythms of Ibrahim Ferrer, ending the play on a note of pure joy.

Maurer's warm, nurturing, friendly persona became essential to the experience of *bobrauschenbergamerica*. She made Bob's Mom the figurative ground on which the play took place and a figure on that ground in her own right. Her presence was always felt, even when she was silent or absent, and in that regard, her profile in the play might be said to mirror Bogart's presence in the rehearsal room.

On Saturday, March 10, midway through the twenty-day rehearsal period, Bogart shared her thoughts about why *bobrauschenbergamerica* was proving to be so exhausting to rehearse. "It's because every scene starts things all over again," she said. "Usually, when you work on a play, you get to the end of a scene and you go, 'Oh, I know where it goes,' and there is a kind of a flow. Every time we get to a new scene it is like starting with a completely blank page. It is like starting a new play every time we start a new scene." As in a Rauschenberg composition, nothing was contingent upon any-thing else, which meant that at face value the answer to Bogart's standard question "What does this come out of?" was, in effect, "It comes out of nothing. It is what it is." As a consequence, the company's reliable skill at carrying energy forward and finding what feels like a natural progression from one moment to the next ran the risk of connecting segments that wanted to remain separate and independent. Each day, they confronted the challenge of creating a transition that was not too smooth and not too logical. For example, in the script, "Yard Sale" was followed by "The Beating." As the company developed its version of a yard sale, it turned out that both Allen and Susan coveted a shiny vintage toaster that Bob's Mom had brought out to start things off. This object of desire kept eluding them as one person after another acquired it in turn, until Susan finally ended up with it, to Allen's chagrin. In brainstorming about the transition that followed, Bogart wondered if the baseball bat that Allen was to use in "The Beating" might be introduced as an object that first appeared in "Yard Sale." For some that raised concerns that Allen's act of violence might seem like he was venting frustration about not getting the toaster, thereby linking one scene to next with a narrative thread. In similar instances, the company found itself checking impulses to forge stronger connections than the play's Rauschenbergian aesthetic really wanted.

On Wednesday, March 14, 2001, Day Thirteen out of twenty, the SITI Company had a run-through of *bobrauschenbergamerica* for the first time. By SITI standards, this was early. A first run-through five days before technical rehearsals left them plenty of time to make adjustments, which, after Bogart's disappointment with what she saw, seemed to be called for. The initial concern was the running time of the show. From early on, Bogart and Mee had agreed that an optimal running time would be an intermissionless one hour and forty minutes, and the run that day was clocked at two hours and eleven minutes. Adding an intermission was never a serious consideration, so significant cuts would be needed to trim a half hour from the show. Bogart cancelled plans for that evening and called Mee in New York to get this process started. His characteristic response was to tell her just to get rid of everything that was not "lovely and wonderful" and keep what was left over. Of course, it was not that easy.

Over the course of the next week, a series of cuts and changes were made in the interest of zeroing in on the logic and the arc of the piece. Here again, the process was typical in many ways for any production in its final days, but the nature of the play and the company also made it unique. *bobrauschenbergamerica*'s status as a collage of fifty theatrical bits made it relatively simple to take material out. There was no plot or character development to be disrupted, so segments could be pulled or moved with little obvious repercussion. But, as with an actual collage, taking out an independent scrap of the composition left a kind of blank space that asked to be filled by adjusting the adjacent pieces. The subsequent ripple effect meant that to remove an entire scene was not as simple as it might seem at first. And internal cuts within a scene proved to be just as tricky because so many of the individual bits had their own integrity, be it temporal or thematic or structural. To speed things up or cut a few lines ran the risk of stripping away an essential aspect of the scene's fullness or rhythm.

"The Marching Band" scene is a good example. In the New Year draft of the script, this segment reads in full, "A 123-piece local high school marching band enters playing and marches through the center of the piece and out again." Protracted efforts to find a marching band (even a considerably smaller one) to be in the play were unsuccessful. So, a solo bagpiper in tartan and full regalia − a Louisville woman named Carol Cook − was substituted. As rehearsed, the scene had a definite beginning, middle, and end that depended on the following sequence: hearing the drone of the pipes far off backstage, recognizing the sound as it grew louder and closer, seeing the actors gather on stage in anticipation of the piper's arrival, taking in the slow march as she crossed the stage on a diagonal and exited into the lobby, and listening to the music as it faded into the distance. Sheer duration was crucial to the experience; speeding it up would kill it. And while, in the moment of performance, the unexplained arrival of a bagpiper played like a joke, it had subtle connections with motifs in the play, such as the feeling of an American summer holiday (a Memorial Day or Fourth of July parade), the inclusion of various types of music (from Cage to country), and the simple act of crossing the stage (echoing the girl on roller skates in the beginning and the man in the chicken suit in the middle). Plus, just as the segment seemed to slow down time to a marching crawl, the audible distance covered by the piper – from far offstage in one direction to nearby to right here onstage to near but gone to far offstage in the opposite direction – changed the sense of space for the moment and supported the subliminal feeling of expansion and opening out that was proving to be so important to the play. Finally, if the scene was eliminated altogether, it would put two instances of violence, "The Beating" and "The Dark Side," back to back and sacrifice the subtle way in which the unexpected bagpiper paved the way for the unexpected pizza boy. So, on balance, in this as in other instances, the ripple effect of a cut or a trim required careful consideration before the axe fell.

The first round of cuts, made by Mee in consultation with the dramaturg, Tanya Palmer, were mostly textual. "Lips," a fever dream of a monologue about Collagen implants and a botched audition, and "Fooling Around," one of Phil's long chicken jokes, were jettisoned with little regret all around. Internal cuts were made in Carl's "Welcome Speech," two of Bob's Mom's monologues, and "Whitman," although the *Leaves of Grass* material was later reinserted once the negative effect of its removal was felt. In the second run-through, on Friday, this knocked fifteen minutes off the show and helped to make clear that time was not the only problem. The first half hour still just did not feel right. For Bogart, "it was too Greek, too self-important and affected." It was stiff, stilted, strident, and 'stagey'; it lacked the necessary lightness and ease for all that was to come after, the simple pleasure of just being together onstage. And the rules of engagement for the audience were murky and misleading. As Darron West put it at the time, "Once we get to the picnic, we know what the play is, but there is still something with the beginning that is just not happening. It's like we are creating the opening for a play that we are not going to do."[3] This shared concern triggered a flurry of after-hours conversations between cast members and then a company-wide summit (this production's version of "SITI Company triage").

This meeting took place at the start of rehearsal on Saturday, March 17, five days before the first performance. Without any sense of panic, Bogart expressed her concern that the piece as a whole needed to recapture the lightness and improvised quality that had been so much a part of making the individual scenes. She quoted her phone conversation with Mee that morning in which he described the basic attitude of the characters as "We don't give a shit. We're just going to come out here and do this." Then, after giving notes on the run-through the night before, she opened the floor, asking each person in turn to make their own comments or propose a new order for the beginning of the play before responding to the suggestions of others. For the next couple hours, various possibilities were discussed. The "reveal" – removing the huge muslin tarp that masked the flag set – surfaced again and again as an issue. Should this chore be included as part of the Viewpoints scene, as it had been rehearsed, or separated from it? Should it be treated as more of a simple, workmanlike task and less of a "show-biz-y" curtain-up moment? What if it was cut altogether and the audience entered the theater with the flag already in view? Another idea that got renewed attention was shifting Bob's Mom's first monologue to right after "Viewpoints" and the reveal, so that it became more of a prologue and the play seemed to emanate more from her. Bogart and West announced their desire to cut the sequence of "Tub Party," "Ping Pong," and "A Toast" and have "Bathing Beauty" (the sex-talk scene in the tub between Phil the Trucker and Phil's Girl) lead straight into the picnic. Others felt that the monolithic formality of Becker's and Phil the Trucker's first monologues would be reduced if there were others on stage for them to talk to, a change which might also establish a more immediate sense of a whole community, rather than a series of individual characters. For a moment, recalling one of the final compositions from the previous summer, they considered blurring the start of the play with incidental preparations and other business, including the removal of the tarp, so that the audience did not know the play had begun until it was under way.

When the discussion was finished, the company spent the rest of Saturday and most of Sunday restaging the first quarter of the play: reconceiving the Viewpoints scene, testing out proposed changes and new orders, and trying to make transitions more "jagged." "Tub Party," "Ping Pong," and "A Toast" were indeed cut, as were a number of music cues and some of Roller Girl's business near the top of the show. Although exhausted, the group felt like they were well on their way to finding the right way to launch the play. Sunday night, the final regular rehearsal ended with a run-through of the revised piece. Though it ran only a few minutes shorter, the shape and rhythm felt much better, and thoughts of further cutting were postponed until Mee returned to Louisville and had a chance to see things in the technical rehearsals on Tuesday and Wednesday. Even as the company worked its way through tech and the introduction of Brian Scott's intricate and ever-evolving lighting design, even as some of the changes coming out of the weekend powwow were reversed when it turned out Mee was not so keen on them, even as other last-minute adjustments and notes were incorporated, the struggle to find the one true way to start the show remained a dominant concern. In the end, it all came down to the very beginning.

Bogart has often summed up her directing strategy in terms that she once heard used by the Japanese choreographer Yoshiko Chuma to create a dance piece. "One, two, three – Go! One, two, three – Go!," Chuma barked at her dancers in accented English, expecting them to jump up and just do something to get the ball rolling. Referencing Picasso, Bogart also expresses this idea in terms of making the first bold stroke on a blank canvas and then dealing with the provocation or disruption that is created by that beginning; the painting proceeds from the radical, violent gesture of that first stroke. This is precisely the process at which the SITI Company excels. After half a lifetime of training, more than a decade working as a company, a year of preparation and research for a given project, and, once in rehearsal, a preliminary discussion of the scene at hand, a time comes for "one, two, three – go!" and they step up on the stage, make a first stroke, and then deal with that initial expression. It is a matter of kinesthetic response, of looking without desire, of thinking with the body. Over time, Mee had seen these principles at work in a number of Viewpoints improvisations, some of which unfolded with such mystery, ease, and spontaneous beauty that he was prompted to make "Music. Eight company members enter and do viewpoints" the first brush stroke in his script for *bobrauschenbergamerica*. Committed, as ever, to doing what the playwright wrote, the company had labored long and hard to make that work. They had viewpointed on a drop-cloth so that the flag could be concealed. They had viewpointed to the same piece of music again and again, until Darron West pointed out that this effectively left him out of an exercise in which he was usually a key participant. They had viewpointed in a way that incorporated the conspicuously practical task of bending over to unfasten the dropcloth so that it could be removed and they could keep viewpointing.

At each stage, members of the company had misgivings. There was something unnatural about this effort to achieve the freedom of a genuine Viewpoints jam while giving it enough structure that it would begin each performance on more or less the same note. For some, the clincher came during dress rehearsals when for the first time the actors did the Viewpoints opening in the archetypal costumes designed by James Schuette. The iconic identities suggested by the clothes – Trucker, Bum, Dancer, Mom, and so on – made it impossible to see the actors onstage as only actors. Was that girl in a bathing suit Phil's Girl or Akiko Aizawa? Were those actors doing some kind of warm-up exercise or were these typical American characters doing some kind of abstract movement piece? In the end, despite the company's prolonged effort, Mee had asked them to do something – use their training as performance – that could not be done. The task amounted to starting with a different first stroke each night hoping to get the same painting every time. It did not make sense. So, on the afternoon before the first performance, by general agreement, the Viewpoints segment was cut from the play and, one last time, the first moments of the show were restaged. The first time they ran through the play in its ultimate final order was in front of an audience that night.

II

Spring 2001: the play in performance

O N MARCH 22, 2001, THREE AND A HALF YEARS AFTER MEE SAW
the Rauschenberg retrospective at the Guggenheim, *bobrauschenbergamerica*
received its world premiere as part of the 25th Annual Humana Festival of
New American Plays. In addition to Mee, Bogart, and SITI, Richard
Dresser, Eduardo Machado, Mac Wellman, and the pseudonymous Jane
Martin also received premieres that year, as did the up-and-coming
Melanie Marnich. On the model of old movie serials like *Buck Rogers* and
Flash Gordon, Arthur Kopit wrote a sequence of three ten-minute melo-
dramas about a young boy who receives a secret message from God. The
Actors Theatre of Louisville Acting Apprentice Company performed monologues and dialogues commissioned from various playwrights on the
general theme of "Heaven and hell (on earth)." A bank of pay telephones
in the upper lobby provided seven brief "phone plays," each one taking the
form of a telephone conversation which could be 'overheard' by picking up
the receiver and eavesdropping. All told, nearly thirty playwrights had work
on view.

Each year, the Humana Festival attracts critics, directors, agents, producers and other theater professionals from across the country and around
the world, especially during two "visitors weekends" in late March and
early April. With performances starting as early as 10.00 a.m. and getting
out as late as midnight, a lively festival atmosphere and a marathon
mentality are always a big part of the experience. During breaks and
intermissions, the lobbies, the bar downstairs and even the lines in the
bathrooms buzz with theater chatter, much of it concerning which shows
are 'missable' and which are not. The 2001 festival had an added sense of
occasion (and topic of gossip) because it marked a major transition in
artistic leadership. Jon Jory, who created the Humana Festival in 1976 and
developed it into the premiere new play showcase in the country, left the

theater in December 2000 after thirty-one years as producing director. Michael Bigelow Dixon, ATL's literary manager for sixteen years and a crucial partner in Humana's success, was in his last week before leaving for a new position at the Guthrie in Minneapolis. And Marc Masterson, after many years at the helm of the much smaller City Theater in Pittsburgh, was making a high-profile debut on the national stage as ATL's new artistic director. Change was in the air.

When the audience entered the intimate Victory Jory Theatre on the ATL's top floor to see *bobrauschenbergamerica*, they found the stage floor and the set covered with a muslin tarp, which in hindsight asked to be seen as a blank canvas. An old wooden stepladder sat upstage. The performance began when seven actors walked out on stage. One lifted the ladder and snapped it shut with a bang, and the others yanked the tarp loose from its moorings and removed it with a flourish, revealing the giant American flag painted on the floor and wall beneath. The broad stripes and bright stars made clear that the play at hand would feature American themes, as did the spirited fanfare from Aaron Copland's *The Red Pony* that filled the room. During this opening music, a stuffed chicken dropped from the flies with a sign that read: *bobrauschenbergamerica*. Roller Girl, dressed like a cheerleader in red, white, and blue, skated across the stage, blowing bubble-gum bubbles as she went and then falling on her backside and crawling off. The actors returned and crisscrossed the stage, pushing or pulling odd sculptural objects on wheels, recognizable to some as allusions to Rauschenberg's famous combines. And, a man's voice was heard coming from the speakers talking about how it is best to:

Start working when it's almost too late at night,
when your sense of efficiency is exhausted
and then just,
let it come on . . .

With this, the music swells, the lights fade, and the overture gives way to the start of the play. A screen door in the flag-wall opens and a prim, homespun matron in a simple green dress enters, a kitchen apron around her waist and a dish towel in her hands. Although she is never referred to as such, this must be the character listed in the program as Bob's Mom. In a soft, southern drawl, she describes a series of old family photographs featuring the apple-of-her-eye, her son Bob, and as she talks about him and his dog Jab, slides are projected on the flag. The images are difficult to make out against the red stripes and blue field, but they do not match what she is saying. Her monologue ends with a non sequitur which she will repeat a couple more times before the play is done – "Art. Art was not a part of our lives" – and then we hear the ch-ching of a bicycle bell, and a folded newspaper lands at her feet, tossed from offstage by some unseen paperboy. She smiles, gives a little wave, and goes back 'inside' through the screen door, where the strains of a television situation comedy can be heard. If it was loud enough, some in the audience would recognize it as *The Andy Griffith Show.*

Over the next ten minutes, the remaining seven characters make themselves known one by one. A mangy tramp in a dirty trench coat crawls out of a large cardboard box, eating french fries from a greasy paper bag and, odd as it might seem, he talks about the neighborhood where he grew up. A large man in a faded Harley Davidson tee shirt, with long carrot-orange hair tucked under a green mesh cap, sits up in a bathtub, turns on a light bulb fixed in the shower head, and talks about leaving home at 5.00 a.m. As he says this, he eyes a short, fetching woman in a bright two-piece bathing suit, with matching headband and heavy plastic bracelets, sipping on a McDonald's milkshake. Then, a pretty woman in a pretty blue dress bouncing a ping-pong ball comes on, and she falls instantly in love with the tramp, despite what she calls his "disgusting" appearance. She dashes across the stage and tackles him with a kiss, to the distress of a man in a business suit who claims at first that the pretty woman is his wife, then his fiancée, and then, at least, his girlfriend. "I thought we were going steady," he says pathetically. "What are you / some sort of biological creature?" After a brief lover's quarrel, the pretty woman storms off in a huff, just as a flat door in the middle of the flag's star field, hitherto unseen, opens. A half-naked man in a shower cap and a bath towel stands there, wearing black shoes and socks and thick black glasses. Holding a long-handled back scrubber as a microphone, he croons the Ink Spots 1950s doo-wop hit, "I Don't Want to Set the World on Fire." The others onstage provide backup vocals and then, midway through the musical number, a guy in a white undershirt and grey sweatpants runs on in bare feet, looks up at the singer with cartoonish adoration, and then expresses his love by dancing a soft-shoe to the music. Just as smitten, the singer comes down from his perch and joins the dancer in a campy pas de deux, which climaxes with a funny, running jump-and-throw before the two lovers scamper offstage holding hands.

For its sheer delight, this silly song-and-dance sequence draws applause from members of the audience, even as it prepares them to expect the unexpected. By this point, the eight main characters of the play have been introduced, however briefly, and half of them have fallen in love at first sight. All but two (Bob's Mom, Phil's Girl) have actual names, but those names are rarely, if ever, used. For the audience they are most easily identified by the costumes they wear, which lend them an archetypal character. Phil the Trucker represents the working man, and Phil's Girl embodies a 1960s version of a bathing beauty or a pin-up girl. Becker the Derelict is what used to be a bum but in more recent politically correct years is known as a street person. He is an outsider, one of the downtrodden and dispossessed. He gets caught in an unexpected romantic triangle with Susan, who he later accuses of being fickle ("a sort of a tease / or worse"), and Wilson, the possessive, uptight boyfriend, who justifies his jealousy at one point by explaining, "I am from Chicago, Susan." The man singing in the shower is Allen, whose interest in astrophysics will later reveal him as a man of science and a bit of a nerd. His partner is Carl, a postmodern dancer, and therefore a man of art. Last but not least, Bob's Mom is the quintessence of motherhood. Even as an archetype, she cannot be separated from the idea of her beloved son "Bob," a seeming reference to Robert Rauschenberg that is never truly confirmed or denied. She seems to occupy a different world from the others. She sees them and interacts with them at moments, but she never talks to them, not even when she serves them a picnic lunch in her own backyard. Although she dwells in memory, her salt-of-the-earth spirit comes to ground the play.

As a gallery of familiar types, they are diverse enough to suggest the American "melting pot" that is so central to the nation's self-image. From a bum to a businessman, a socio-economic range is indicated. None are referred to by race or ethnicity, although Wilson is played by an African American actor and Phil's Girl by a Japanese woman. These and other casting choices reinforce stereotype by contradicting it. Sometimes, the costume and the performer do not quite jive, which makes the type more 'visible' (as Bogart might say) and foregrounds the actor as, first and foremost, a performer. These are not characters in the traditional sense of the term. Except perhaps for Bob's Mom, they do not have a past that comes back to haunt them or a compulsive temperament that makes them behave in a certain way. When they meet onstage, they seem to know each other without really having a specific relationship, except, of course, for the lovers, Phil and Phil's Girl, Susan and Wilson, and Carl and Allen. Whatever coherence they have as characters stems from their emblematic costumes and the personae of the performers who 'play' them. They are figures who come and go, who perform whatever text or task concerns them at the moment and then, in effect, disintegrate until they come back on again.

After Carl and Allen's doo-wop song-and-dance routine, the play continues with a brief bathtub conversation between Phil the Trucker and Phil's Girl about having sex in public places and the types of feelings that creep up on them "every fifteen minutes." Then, from offstage, Bob's Mom calls out, "Lunch is served," and the stage erupts with another flurry of action as the actors come rushing on to set up for a picnic. Suddenly, it is summer. The lights pop up bright and full, and the sound system plays a silly novelty song from the 1940s – Cab Calloway's "A Chicken Ain't Nothin' But a Bird" – as people scurry about, weaving in and out of each other as they bring on a picnic table and an assortment of mismatched kitchen chairs, spread a table cloth, shift the objects-on-wheels to different positions, and work up an appetite. In the midst of it all, Bob's Mom brings out dishes of picnic food which she sets out with a bashful smile. Each of her exits and entrances is punctuated by the familiar bang of the screen door slamming shut, evoking summertime memories and marking the American rhythm of the play. On one of these slams, the chicken song cuts out in mid-phrase, the hustle and bustle ebbs, and the characters are suddenly sitting in silence with plates on their laps, eating fried chicken, potato salad, and corn-on-the-cob, while birds twitter in the background. The mood is abruptly serene and bucolic and contemplative. The action slows to a halt. Nothing happens.

After a long moment, Allen, now wearing a short-sleeved white shirt with a skinny necktie, napkin tucked under his chin, gazes up overhead and talks about the marvels of "the night sky," even though it seems like the middle of the day. "There is a great deal more space than time, you know," he says with a sense of wonder that is undercut by gesturing skyward with a drumstick in his hand. This is the first of several speeches that reveal his fascination with cosmology, an interest that will broaden the play's horizons far beyond the American continent. The picnic continues with a couple of lover's spats. First, Wilson storms on and accuses Susan of never really loving him "in that way," and then, Carl and Allen dash onstage, seeking advice about their plan to start a chicken farm. They talk with breathless excitement, until Carl reveals that Allen is afraid that if they go into the chicken business he will end up looking like a chicken. "Look at Frank Perdue," says Allen defensively, getting a laugh, but Carl ridicules his logic and Allen slams down his glass of lemonade and leaves in a huff. The others chase after him, leaving Bob's Mom alone to deliver a monologue about her secret passion for the color red and her grandmother's collection of "cut Italian colored glass decanters and glasses."

I valued those objects deeply. I wanted to play with them, to make new shapes of them, to make new surfaces for them. I wanted to smash them and see what they looked like as heaps, to see how light played on their shattered surfaces. My grandmother always wore a large rectangular ruby pendant on a gold chain. I dreamed of having that one day. Of having that color. When my grandmother died I asked what became of the ruby. It turned out she had gone into the home years before and everything was sold at a yard sale. The objects she collected – beautiful objects – all discarded. Thrown out. No one wanted them. Cast off. I would have preferred to smash them against brick walls to see what they might have become.

Though it passes in a minute, this speech is notable for a number of reasons. First, it contrasts the prevailing silliness, suggesting that there is more going on in this play than fun and games. Second, it is the only time that Bob's Mom focuses on herself or her own feelings. As she speaks with a sense of resignation that masks a suppressed fury, we catch a glimpse of an all-American mom with her own private needs and secret desires. Third, this passage draws attention to the play's Rauschenbergian interest in the aesthetic of things, in "beautiful objects" stripped as much as possible of the material culture and ownership history that surrounds them and presented as things in themselves. Fourth, the image of smashing fragile objects and making something new out of the broken pieces is Mee's favorite image for how he writes plays. Though the audience might not know it, *bobrauschenbergamerica* itself is constructed out of bits and pieces of text thrown together in a seeming heap, their rough and shattered surfaces set against each other in surprising ways. There is no logical progression from moment to moment here, no story or overarching event. The numerous segments of the play, most of which last only two or three minutes, stand on their own in loose affiliation with what comes before and after.

This speech is one of several in the play that provide clues about the play's dramaturgy and cues to the audience about how to engage with it. The voiceover in the play's prologue has already said:

Look,
everything overlaps doesn't it?
Is connected some kind of way.
Once you put it all together, it's just obvious.
I mean, tie a string to something, and
see where it takes you.
The biggest thing is

don't worry about it.
You're always going to be moving somewhere so
don't worry about it.

Moments later, in his initial monologue, Becker articulated much the same idea when he recalled his boyhood adventures exploring the forests and fields at the edge of the neighborhood where he grew up.

You could just go and go
you didn't know where you were headed
but you were a free person
you'd see where it was you'd been
after you came out of the woods at the end.

More obvious in print here than in the passing moment of performance, these passages orient the audience to the disorienting nature of the play, which asks for what art historian Brian O'Doherty, writing about Rauschenberg, once dubbed "the vernacular glance."

The vernacular glance is what carries us through the city every day, a mode of almost unconscious, or at least divided, attention. Since we are usually moving, it tags the unexpected and quickly makes it the familiar, filing surplus information into safe categories . . . Easily surfeited, cynical about big occasions, the vernacular glance develops a taste for anything, often notices or creates the momentarily humorous, but doesn't follow it up. Nor does it pause to remark on unusual juxtapositions, because the unusual is what it is geared to recognize, without thinking about it. It dispenses with hierarchies of importance, since they are constantly changing according to where you are and what you need.[1]

O'Doherty credits Rauschenberg with challenging "the etiquette of vision" and "the museum-goer's chew-the-cud regard" by creating work in the 1960s that demands to be seen with "the city dweller's rapid scan," a mode of perception that in the hustle and bustle of urban life grabs on to a view or a scene and lets go just as quickly. He traces this aesthetic to Rauschenberg's early days as a designer of window displays for fancy Fifth Avenue stores like Tiffany's. This work "was in fact a public theater to test his ideas. Window dressing could not be more consistent with his aims of provoking perception, of jogging attention and measuring its decay."[2] The miscellaneous fragments and quick hits of *bobrauschenbergamerica* work on just this principle, jolting the spectator with the unexpected or the illogical and then counting down the half-life of its interest, thus instigating a vernacular glance that "can tolerate everything but meaning (the attempt to understand instead of recognize) and sensory deprivation (voids and absences). It is superficial in the best sense."[3]

The picnic continues with an idle conversation over a game of checkers between Phil the Trucker and Susan. In the middle of discussing an extra-marital affair between an orchestra conductor in Cincinnati and a stewardess in Denver, Susan says, "I have to pee," and gets up and goes offstage. Everything onstage stops for a conspicuously long moment as actors and audience alike wait – and wait and wait – for Susan to return. The sound of a flushing toilet provides the punch line to this metatheatrical joke. Here again, the production abuses the audience's trust in a playful, teasing manner, even as it makes them self-conscious about how time passes differently in a theater and in real life. "Times have changed," says Susan when she returns, a statement that cuts several different ways. In a moment, Becker pops out of his cardboard hut like a jack-in-the-box and yells, "OK. I have an idea for a movie." He passes out old, rusty license plates like they were scripts and enlists the others to act out his preposterous story about a conspiracy to blow up a train headed across the country. His maniacal energy is contagious. Soon the others (all but Bob's Mom, who peeks in on the action from above) are engaged in a wild improvisation of Becker's crazy plot (see figure 17). Just as the frenzy of sex and violence reaches its zenith, Becker stops the action and says, "That's as far as I've gotten so far. How do you like it?" A long pause seizes the stage as the players stand still, look at each other dumbfounded and then back at Becker, not sure how to respond. Everything stops. Time, again, is held in suspension. And then, in the play's most surprising leap so far, the sound system blares Earth, Wind, & Fire's "September," and instantly everybody on stage lurches into a line dance. With pure delight, seven actors, in two lines, move to the music in unison, matching turns and steps, head bobs and hand jive. Becker's movie is gone, and they are dancing – with the joy of the young at heart.

This radical shift epitomizes many transitions in the play, which, in their abruptness and lack of logic, generate a dizzying energy and forward thrust for the play and a sense of frolic for the spectator who is willing to "tie a string to something, and see where it takes you." The line dance, pure fun, goes on for a minute, and then, mid-song, the music cuts out as abruptly as it started and the actors fall out of their ranks and walk off, leaving Susan and Wilson alone onstage for another of their impetuous confrontations. "We are in a relationship that is sick," The Boyfriend argues, explaining that when he is there for her, she rejects him, and when he withdraws from her and withholds his feelings, she comes forward to

Figure 17. (a) "Becker's Movie": Wilson (Danyon Davis), Phil's Girl (Akiko Aizawa), Susan (Ellen Lauren), Allen (Will Bond), and Phil (Leon Ingulsrud) take direction from Becker (J. Ed Araiza, kneeling). (b) "Square Dance": as Bob's Mom (Kelly Maurer) looks on, the cast executes a right and left grand. (Photographs by Richard Termine.)

him in love. This push-me-pull-you rhythm will drive them insane, he insists, and so he storms off once more, but with greater finality this time. Bob's Mom brings out a sheet cake for dessert, signaling that the picnic has almost run its course, and when she goes back in, Susan, thinking she is alone, sneaks a fingerful of icing. Just then, Becker pops out of his box once again, and he, too, confronts her about the sincerity of her feelings, accusing her of being "some kind of seducer and dumper kind of person who is just a loose cannon cutting a swath through men." She defends herself by describing "How it is for women," and as she does, she sidles over to the picnic table, takes a small piece of cake, and nibbles on it. As she explains the difference between men and women, she gets more and more animated and her eating gets more and more compulsive, until she is stuffing cake into her mouth with two hands, spraying crumbs and spreading icing everywhere before storming off in an emotional huff. Becker follows after, clearing the stage for one of the play's funniest bits.

Phil's Girl, still in her mod two-piece, walks on with a bounce in her step and a sense of purpose, while the sound system begins to play an old tune by Herb Alpert and the Tijuana Brass. She takes a folded plastic tarp from out of the bathtub and proceeds in a methodical and unhurried fashion to cover the stage with it. She goes off and returns with a large bottle of Bombay Sapphire gin, which she displays to the audience before emptying its contents on the plastic sheet. She goes off and returns with a small bottle of vermouth, which she waves over the puddle of gin at her feet, and then, just as the Herb Alpert tune ends, she opens her purse and pours out a cascade of olives. So far, she has prepared this giant martini with the cool indifference of a runway model, but when the music changes to the Captain and Tennille's "Love Will Keep Us Together," her attitude changes. She slips off her plastic bracelets, tosses her purse aside, kicks off her wedge sandals, and dives headfirst into the pool of gin at her feet, mixing the martini with her body as she slides across the wet plastic on her belly. She splashes like a baby in a bathtub, and then, Phil the Trucker comes running on, dressed for the beach. He peels off his Hawaiian shirt, kicks off his sandals, and he dives in, too, a sight all the more amusing for his big-guy size. While the Captain and Tenille sing, these two frolic on the 94-proof slip-'n-slide, spitting olives at each other, splashing, sliding together holding hands. He spins her around by her ankles like a top, and when she grabs his ankles and does the same to him, his greater weight, pivoting on his stomach, causes the plastic tarp to pull towards the center in a pinwheel motion, bringing the routine to a hilarious conclusion (see figure 18). Others dash on to help with the clean up, and a moment

Figure 18. (a) "Martinis": Phil's Girl (Akiko Aizawa) amd Phil (Leon Ingulsurd) stir a giant martini. (b) "The Laundry Opera": Carl (Barney O'Hanlon) dances like a super hero. Bob's Mom (Kelly Maurer), perpetual witness, looks on. (Photographs by Michael Brosilow.)

later, still toweling off as they go, Phil the Trucker and Phil's Girl walk slowly offstage, talking to each other, oddly enough, in Japanese. In the nation of bobrauschenbergamerica, Phil the Trucker speaks Japanese.

The stage is empty now. The high spirits of Becker's movie, the line dance, Susan's cake eating, and the giant martini have vanquished any sense of a picnic. The lights go dark and ethereal music plays, signaling that the play is shifting into another gear. From the up-right corner of the stage, in a thin strip of light just in front of the flag wall, a man in a bright yellow chicken suit, with red tights and rubber chicken feet, enters and walks slowly in a straight line towards the up-left corner. As he does, a voiceover states the obvious, "A man in a chicken suit crosses the stage." A half-minute later, just as he is about to disappear from view, the voice asks, "Why does he cross the stage?" This might be just another one of the play's wry metatheatrical jokes – and it is that! – if not for the sound design layered on top of it. In addition to the pulsing deep-space music, we hear what sounds like radio static punctuated by a steady series of beeps and then the fuzzy, static-y voice of a NASA astronaut on a space walk talking to the command center back on earth. Some of his chance remarks – "I feel ridiculous," "Man in space, where would we be without him?" – ring with a special irony when heard while watching the giant chicken moving along the giant flag, who now seems to suggest some silly astronaut walking on the moon. Another layer of sound – "Never My Love," the soft 1960s love song by the Association – gradually becomes audible and bleeds into the mix of sound, adding a sweet, gentle twist to the moment, which seems now in some odd way to celebrate, without chauvinism or sentiment, the American urge to explore, to head out into the unknown.

This feeling is extended as the chicken man exits and others enter the near darkness, all moving in a slow, deliberate motion that suggests that they, too, might be floating in space. Allen pulls an old car door on wheels. Susan can be seen in the car window and, when the door is gradually spun around, it turns out that Phil's Girl is there, too. The two women kiss, release each other, and drift off. Wilson comes on, sets down a golf ball, and takes a slo-mo swing with a three-iron, conjuring images of Apollo 14 astronaut Alan Shepard playing golf on the moon. Roller Girl appears and eats doggie treats from a box of Milkbones. Phil the Trucker pushes Carl across the stage on a boy's bicycle in a slow, steady motion, even as Carl dismounts the bike and Phil continues on and exits. Each of these overlapping, living tableaux is independent of the others. Each one includes its own tiny light source – a hand-held flashlight, a bike light, a tiny head lamp – suggesting perhaps that these human bodies in motion are distant stars moving across the night sky (and alluding perhaps to Rauschenberg's use of turtles with flashlights strapped to the shells in his 1965 dance piece, *Spring Training*). During all this, Allen shares another one of his cosmic profundities, explaining that because light takes time to travel from an object to the eye, however short or long the distance, when we look at the Milky Way or even just look in the mirror, we are looking at the past: "All any human being can ever observe is the past. / You never see the present. / And everything you look at is younger than it is right now."

The spirit of this space montage carries forward, but its rhythm changes abruptly when a huge pile of white laundry drops from above and knocks Carl to the ground. The lights come up full, the music changes to a Puccini aria, and in a manner that recalls Phil's Girl and the giant martini, Carl frolics in the laundry, diving into the pile, tossing white shirts into the air, bounding about with a white sheet like a super-hero's cape (see figure 18, page 247 above). All the while, Bob's Mom looks on with a smile. Carl could almost be her son Bob at this point, or she could be seeing Bob in him, but the connection is never made explicit. When he runs off, she steps forward and resumes her family slide show with the same subdued but hardy sense of maternal pride as before. When she is finished describing a series of snap-shots – Bob in his Lone Ranger costume; Bob on the roof fixing his short-wave radio antenna; Bob at "Ethel Howell's Ballroom Dance Class end of the year formal" – the bicycle bell rings again. A newspaper is tossed on. She picks it up, waves, and goes inside. The screen door slams. This routine is familiar now. Then, Allen returns with a stepladder, which he uses to change a light bulb high in the star-field as he ruminates again on the mysteries of the universe. "This connection between time and space is everything," he says from atop the ladder, with a sense of wonder that echoes Phil the Trucker's earlier observation that "Everywhere I go there's something to see." This simple amazement – and the sense of the beautiful, the delight in mystery, and the yen for discovery that underpin it – pervades *bobrauschenbergamerica* like a vapor, inspiring an openness and a curiosity that make its many improbable twists and turns much easier to follow.

As the play moves forward, those twists and turns become even more dizzying and, if possible, more random. Carl cries out, "OK. Square up," and suddenly, eight of the actors, including Roller Girl (sans skates), dash to the center of the stage and launch into a boisterous square dance (see figure 17, page 245 above). Again, Bob's Mom looks on. After a minute, this morphs into an even more energetic clog dance, with whooping and cheering, heavy foot stomps, and ankle slaps. Once again, things have come to a point where a dance erupts all of a sudden and ends just as suddenly. Three gunshot blasts ring out and Carl falls dead in Allen's arms. Becker's movie made a comedy of rape and murder, but this seems more serious. After a moment's panic, the others stand around in shock and

sadness and then slowly filter off without a word, leaving Allen on the
floor holding his lover's limp body and Phil the Trucker standing there
center stage not knowing what to do. The long, somber silence – there are
so many different moments of stillness in this play – is broken when Phil
takes off his green mesh cap and says, in a tone that suggests a eulogy at
first, "A chicken went into a library and went up to the circulation desk
and . . . " And as Allen lays Carl on the floor and walks off in mourning,
Phil finishes what turns out to be a shaggy dog story of a chicken joke and
then follows it with more chicken jokes that get more and more corny as
he proceeds. Even though the audience is accustomed at this point to odd,
abrupt transitions, this one is the most provocative yet as it veers from the
seriousness of Carl's supposed murder to the silliness of Phil's chicken
jokes. It challenges the audience's willingness to let go of what they have
just seen and move on to the next segment. It demands the vernacular
glance.

As if to prove the point, Phil gives a little bow and exits like a schoolboy
at a talent show, and then, proving again that no reality lasts for long in
this play, the 'dead' Carl pops up off the floor and says, suddenly undead,
"OK. How we put the show together." He launches into a monologue in
which he thanks the audience for coming and speaks to them directly
enough that "the show" he refers to seems to be the one they are in the
middle of watching. In the final analysis, of course, it is, but his literal
words indicate that he is, for the moment, a curator of an art museum
opening a new exhibit.

> We don't often get to do a show like this
> where we can just put on whatever we like
> figure OK what the hell
> lets just do whatever we feel like
> and hope you'll enjoy it.
> I often feel those of us who are in the museum world
> are particularly blessed.
> Because we get to explore our feelings
> whatever they may be
> that's a sort of freedom.
> You know, that's how it is to deal with art
> because art is made in the freedom of the imagination
> with no rules
> it's the only human activity like that
> where it can do no one any harm
> so it is possible to be completely free

and see what it may be that people think and feel
when they are completely free
in a way, what it is to be human when a human being is free
and so art lets us practice freedom
and helps us know what it is to be free
and so what it is to be human.

If *bobrauschenbergamerica* were a church service, this would be the hom-
ily. The speech articulates and connects the play's major underlying themes:
the value of trusting and following one's feelings, even in their insistent
mutability; art as the free expression of the imagination and therefore an
arena to practice freedom; and Americans as a people whose love of freedom
makes them patient, open to adventure, and driven to pioneer new frontiers.
The speech is appealing enough that it does not seem to matter that it has
the familiar, suspicious ring of a playwright speaking his big ideas through a
character. And as if it would be too raw or naked if left unadulterated, it is
undercut by a series of disruptions. The first one – the sound of something
being dropped backstage – is inconspicuous enough to be ignored by a
forgiving spectator, dismissed as a this-night-only accident. But as the
disruptions become louder and more frequent – power tools buzzing, the
clanging of a heavy shop door – this next metatheatrical joke makes itself
known: things go wrong backstage at the most inopportune moments. Just
as Carl's supposed assassination did not allow the audience to pretend for
long that something fictive had really happened (i.e. that Carl had been
killed), now, the audience was not allowed to pretend for long that something real did not happen (i.e. the proverbial "noises off"). Having elicited
again and again the audience's willingness to trust what is going on and just
see where it leads, the play makes sport of that good will, like the high
school buddy who points towards your shirt and says, "What's this?," and
then, as you look down, raises his finger and pokes you in the face. That the
play can pull this stunt again and again and remain in the audience's good
graces is a sign of its charm.

When Carl finishes his welcome speech and leaves, Bob's Mom comes
out carrying a shiny vintage toaster, which she places with loving care in
the center of the now-bare stage, arranging its electric cord just so. This
begins an impromptu yard sale, another helter-skelter movement sequence
in which the characters come and go without dialogue, moving in rhythm
with a perky bluegrass instrumental by Bela Fleck. Each brings some
old, unwanted object to sell or trade – a box of record albums, an old
portable television, an ironing board, a table lamp with a hideous tasseled

lampshade – and as they do, Phil the Trucker comes on with an aluminum lunchbox, goes up the stepladder in front of the star-field, eats lunch, and talks about food. "Eat / in any municipal, state or national park is my advice," he says, before reciting a litany of his favorite foods, with garlic topping the list.

The yard sale is followed by one of the play's most exquisite and bizarre bits. Allen comes out with a baseball bat and a shiny, brand-new aluminum trash can with a rolled-up square of green Astroturf inside it. Like Phil's Girl in the martini scene, he goes through an elaborate and methodical preparation, taking his time as he hangs his hat on one of the star-field light bulbs, rolls out the artificial turf, centers the garbage can on it, and lays out the bat alongside it. When he takes out a pair of earplugs and affixes them in his ears, the audience knows, if they did not already suspect, what he is up to. Still, suspense builds as he claps his hands to test the earplugs, drawing attention to the silence (again) onstage. Satisfied, he turns the trash can onto its side, picks up the bat, and starts to walk away only to turn suddenly, raise the bat high over his head, and bring it down on the can with all his might. The crash is loud and jarring, even though expected. He reaches back and hits it again. In workmanlike fashion, with no outward sign of fury or rage, he proceeds to beat the can again and again until it is nearly flat. When he is done, he reverses his preparation procedure – earplugs out, hat retrieved, bat under arm – and drags the turf with the mangled can offstage. Though it draws applause, Allen does not seem to perform this act directly for the audience. Nor does he behave as if he is getting something out of his system. In presenting the simple physical task itself, without context or explanation, as an act of pure violence, plain and simple, it becomes more comic, more abstract, and more disturbing all at the same time.

By now, the audience has long since come to expect the unexpected, so they might not be surprised to hear the drone of a bagpipe offstage and then watch as a female piper in tartan kilt and full regalia enters down-right. The actors come out with the same odd assortment of old chairs as earlier, take a seat, and become an audience themselves. Bob's Mom looks on from the pop-out window above, waving a tiny American flag as if at a Fourth of July parade. They all watch and listen as the piper crosses the stage on a diagonal and vanishes in the distance, not noticing at first the arrival from the lobby of another unforeseen visitor: a pizza delivery boy in cap and shirt holding a bright red pizza warmer. The sight of him generates an instant laugh – here we go again! – but when Bob the Pizza Boy (as the program identifies him) speaks, the mood in the room begins to change. Standing in the aisle, not really onstage yet, he says, "And yet, I think, nonetheless, forgiveness is possible." "You do," says Susan, and with that, the young man proceeds to speak in a calm, almost flat, voice that is plagued by a terrible stutter. He alludes to some crime or personal wrongdoing, and when asked what that was, he says as a matter of fact:

Triple murder.
Sister, husband. Sister, husband,
and a nephew, my nephew.
And uh, you know, uh, manic depressive.

He moves onto the stage and in a rambling and oddly tranquil fashion tells of the gruesome incident which "has already become part of my past." The others give way to him, some nervous, some curious. As he sits atop the back of a kitchen chair, his pizza warmer resting on his lap, his hands resting gently on it, his stillness and his lack of outward emotion make his presence all the more eerie and menacing (see figure 13, page 208 above). "If I forgive myself, I'm forgiven," he says, wrapping up his tale, and then, after a pause, he asks, "Who ordered a pizza?" When nobody claims it, he demands payment – "You know: pizza is not returnable" – and then, after receiving a generous tip, makes a good-natured exit, leaving the others a bit stunned, caught up in another suspended moment, an unordered cheese pizza in hand. Before any of them can figure out what to do, Bob's Mom comes out and reacts with delight at the sight of the pizza. She grabs the box and goes back in, bringing the episode to a benign conclusion.

Coming ninety minutes into the play, the pizza scene is conspicuous for its duration and its content. Lasting ten minutes, it is more than twice the length of any other scene. Its tale of murder harkens back to the exaggerated cartoon mayhem of Becker's movie, the sudden assassination of Carl, and Allen's beating the aluminum trash can, as if to make clear that the nation of bobrauschenbergamerica includes a culture of violence, crime, and destruction as well as square dances, picnics, and silly lovers' quarrels. The community of archetypes onstage listen, without judgment, to what he has to say. They neither embrace nor reject him. They pay attention to him, another datum in the play's cornucopic inventory of Americana. He is of them. His name, after all, is Bob.

With his exit, the mood onstage changes, thanks in part to a wistful, lazy piano tune that suggests coming to the end of the day. Bob's Mom appears at the screen door and opens it, inviting the others in for pizza. If the play began in the morning, with Phil talking about setting out in his truck at 5.00 a.m., and moved into an afternoon picnic in the backyard, now the cool of evening has set in and it is time to go inside for a light dinner or a snack. This is significant because it is the first time the group has joined Bob's Mom indoors. It suggests a winding-up, as do the few segments that remain. Carl and Allen sit close together downstage, staring out in the same direction, and share a brief, romantic dialogue which asserts that taking "delight" in another person is the key to true love. Allen goes in to join the others, and Carl improvises a freeform dance as he talks to Phil's Girl about falling in love. In turn, she speaks of her infidelities and jealousies and fear of being "tied down to one guy." They, too, go into the house, as Susan comes out and Wilson appears in the pop-out window above. They repeat verbatim the same "delight" dialogue that Carl and Allen just shared a moment earlier, except that they speak from opposite sides of the stage. Then, Wilson comes down from the window, and he and Susan dance a spirited Strauss waltz, effecting a genuine, perhaps lasting, reconciliation in their tempestuous romance. As they whirl about the stage, Allen appears in the door in the star-field and talks about the stars one last time. He says that it is easier to predict the positions of the planets hundreds of years in the future than it is to predict what is going to happen two years from now in Haiti – "because the human system, that's a very complicated system." The Strauss swells again, and Phil the Trucker and Phil's Girl shower the waltzing couple below with a cascade of ping pong balls (a remnant from the cut Tub Party).

Lights fade to a softer level as Becker comes out, barefoot still, one hand in the pocket of his dirty trench coat. He says,

> O take my hand Walt Whitman!
> Such gliding wonders! such signs and sounds!
> Such join'd unended links, each hook'd to the next,
> Each answering all, each sharing the earth with all.

Becker proceeds to recite a lengthy passage which some will recognize as coming from Walt Whitman's *Leaves of Grass*, an encomium that pays tribute to the connectedness of all peoples and cultures of the planet, past and present. As his catalogue spreads across borders and historical eras, music begins to play – Aaron Copland again – and one by one the others come out of the house, pick up a chair left over from the bagpiper scene, and move off. They do this quietly and slowly, functionally, but in a way that connects them to the parade of people that Walt Whitman talks about. It is a solemn procession, not sad, but reverent, the reverse of the parade of objects-on-wheels that started the show.

I see the male and female everywhere,
I see the serene brotherhood of philosophs,
I see the constructiveness of my race,
I see the results of perseverance and industry of my race,
I see ranks, colors, barbarisms, civilizations, I go among them, I mix
    indiscriminately
And I salute all the inhabitants of the earth.

Becker's rhapsody does not conclude so much as it trails off as he wanders offstage just as Bob's Mom comes out for one last nostalgic slide-show memory of her beloved son. She mentions his bicycle and a go-cart he built. She mentions the family's strict Christian lifestyle and a dance pavilion on Lake Sabine that was "definitely off limits. Everything you did, / if it could be possibly interpreted as an indulgence, / was evil. That's how it was then." There is a touch of melancholy, but no remorse, in her voice as she talks of her handsome, humble, sweet boy.

You knew he was going to go someplace,
you just didn't know where.
Isn't it something
how he can see the beauty in almost everything!
We were ordinary working people.
Art was not in our world.

She turns to go as an up-tempo dance tune with a strong Latin beat begins to play. She stops – or the music stops her – and with a physical flair and freedom we have not seen from her before, she tosses aside first her dish towel and then her apron. She puts one hand behind her head and cocks her hip, and she begins to dance to the music (see figure 19). She lets loose, and as she dances, the others dance on to the stage one by one, starting with Becker, who partners with her for awhile, and then expanding to include the entire cast, including Roller Girl, Bob the Pizza Boy, and even the lady bagpiper. A few minutes earlier, the others had all joined Bob's Mom inside 'the house' for the first time; now Bob's Mom has come out and joined in the spirit of the dance which has overcome the others on numerous occasions. After a minute, they dance off in couples, Roller Girl and Pizza Boy, Phil and Phil's Girl, Carl and Allen, Susan and Wilson, leaving Bob's Mom and Becker together again for a moment, and then he leaves her to dance alone again and to end the play with a grand solo flourish as the music blares a big-band brassy flourish that draws the audience's exuberant applause. The play is over.

Figure 19. "The Last Dance": Bob's Mom (Kelly Maurer) cuts loose in the final moments of *bobrauschenbergamerica*. (Photograph by Richard Termine.)

On the surface, *bobrauschenbergamerica* is a postmodern variety show, a latter-day Ted Mack's Amateur Hour or Ed Sullivan Show or Laugh-In, with Bob's Mom as a kind of homespun host and master of ceremonies. Some of the acts in this show are gratuitously weird or pseudo-avant-garde or just plain corny. Others smack of an ironic self-consciousness that inspires mistrust. But the audience learns that if they don't like the act on stage at the moment, another one is not far behind. And on balance, the sense of wonder or simple fun that energizes them gives the play an appeal that is difficult to resist. The radical shifts in tone or mood or event seem to be designed to test the limits of the audience's willingness to go with the flow, take satisfaction in whatever is happening at the moment, and then let go and move on, like thrill seekers at an amusement park or strollers at a state fair. Like so much American popular culture, *bobrauschenbergamerica* places a premium on sensation, one which might turn the play into a one-trick pony if it did not serve a subtler theatrical purpose.

To the extent that the play seduces or cajoles the audience into tying a string to something to see where it leads, it asks them to withhold aesthetic or moral judgment for the interim and just to take things for what they are. It confers an integrity, even a dignity, on the individual segments, however cryptic or silly or bizarre they may be, and then draws them together in a kind of theatrical democracy of solo acts and group numbers. In a similar fashion, the play presents individual archetypes that come together as a momentary community for such activities as a picnic, a backyard theatricale, a square dance, a yard sale, and so on. When Bob's Mom tosses aside her apron and dish towel in the end to join in the dance, the circle of community is complete. A dance is the canonical end of classical comedy, a celebration that signals the restoration of community and a return to balance and harmony after a spell of madness and runaway egoism. Unlike some comedies, there are no scapegoats or outcasts in *bobrauschenbergamerica*. Everyone is included, even Becker the Derelict and, in the last dance, the murderer who is Bob the Pizza Boy. In this way, *bobrauschenbergamerica* evokes a utopian vision of American democracy as open and inclusive and free, a vision that here is epitomized by the freedom of the artist. This connection is made explicit in Carl's welcome-to-the-gallery speech when he argues that art, as the free expression of the imagination, offers a model of freedom and that Americans, as a free people, are more tolerant of that expression. When we look at an artist's work, Carl says, we see "how this fellow sees the world / and there's a certain pleasure in seeing things from his point of view." This capacity for empathy, the aesthetic ability to see through another's eyes, to identify with another's feelings, or at least to pay attention to another for a few moments (and then move on) becomes, in the play's terms, the key to democracy.

The play structures the audience's experience in a manner that offers the palpable feeling of that democracy. The sheer variety of disparate events, ideas, images, and characters put on stage defies ready assimilation or integration. Be they "interesting" or "stupid" or "cool," each thing asks to be taken for what it is, independent of the rest. By jumping from one thing to the next with as little outward logic as possible, the play exercises with abandon the freedom of the imagination and invites the spectator who is willing to go along for the ride to experience that same freedom right there in the theater. In the process, it associates it with other experiences of freedom, with the limitless possibilities of boyhood and a youthful spirit of adventure; with being "on the road," traveling to far-flung destinations, and moving out to explore unknown territories; and even with being a citizen of the same United States of America represented by the likes of Walt Whitman, William S. Burroughs, Philip Morrison, Thornton Wilder, and Robert Rauschenberg. The play practices both an overt and a subtle patriotism, one that commingles love of country with love of art, love of another, and love of life itself to produce a rambunctious celebration of the joys (and a few of the miseries) of being human.

The SITI Company performed *bobrauschenbergamerica* thirteen times during the 2001 Humana Festival, with five of those performances coming within a span of fifty hours over the first Visitors Weekend. Many performances were sold out, and the house was always full enough for the audience to relax and give over to the play's infectious comedy, which elicited standing ovations on many nights. Critical reception was positive, often enthusiastic, with a handful of critics lauding *bobrauschenbergamerica* as the festival's "dazzling centerpiece" (*St. Louis Dispatch*) or "high point" (*New York Times*) or "best in show" (*Lexington Herald-Leader*).[4] The temptation to pick a winner at Humana each year reflects the festival's status as what some have called "the Kentucky Derby of American theater." Critics come from the four corners of the USA – Boston, Seattle, San Diego, and Miami all sent reviewers in 2001 – as well as overseas (Ireland, Germany, Italy, Hungary); they return home to write omnibus reviews that guess which plays have "legs" and what is on the mind (this year) of the American Playwright. As analysis, this stuff tends to be superficial – *bobrauschenbergamerica* was variously summed up as "a peppy physical romp," "a feast for the eye, the brain, the heart, and the funnybone," "a relentlessly cheery, Norman Rockwell-esque, 1950s-style cornucopia of Americana," and "a sensuous ebullient meditation on the relation between art and life"[5] – but the sheer geographical spread of the coverage, enviable by any measure, argues for seeing the Humana Festival as a true national theater, at least for two weekends each spring.

This adds a populist significance, albeit a middle-class populism, to the fact that nearly every Humana review that gave *bobrauschenbergamerica* more than one sentence mentioned the martini scene. In Bruce Weber's *New York Times* review, it took the lead paragraph; others touched on it in passing, but the widespread and lasting impression left by this four-minute scene testifies to *bobrauschenbergamerica*'s success in capturing the pure spirit of play. Though it might operate in the piece as "a stand-alone snapshot, both an appreciation and send-up of suburban hedonism,"[6] its power to delight depended on its situation in the midst of a complex collage, the comic pairing of tiny Akiko Aizawa and burly Leon Ingulsrud (wife and husband in real life), the *jo-ha-kyu* of their performance, and the sprightly, nostalgic musical choices of Darron West (Herb Alpert, Captain and Tennille). That the play's most memorable and emblematic scene derived from "the glory of mess" that characterized several of the Summer Intensive compositions and from the social life of the SITI Company is an indication of how deeply rooted the whole play was in the creative community that surrounded it. It might have been easy to write "Martinis," but it requires an extended collective effort to create the layers of context that made the scene spring to life.

That seeming ease was mocked in one negative review that argued that a Rauschenberg tribute was unnecessary because "we have abundant examples of his actual work in many publicly accessible collections across the country." Tony Brown went on to dismiss the play's formula as follows:

> Take a bunch of writers, put their words together in a stream of consciousness, punctuate them with some popular songs. Add eight actors, a roller skater and a bagpipe player, and dress them up in bikinis, pajamas, homeless rags, whatever is handy. Have them do a series of unrelated routines on a set that is a giant American flag.[7]

This cynical analysis of the piece's strategy has a surface accuracy – remember the importance of surfaces – which for other viewers, including reviewer Kevin Nance, resulted in a more positive experience:

> It's all very nutty, and you have to master your impatience for things to make sense; the piece is a test of your willingness to suspend, not your disbelief, but your ideas about what theater is and can be. If you pass,

you're rewarded with performances of surpassing sweetness, all of which illustrate Rauschenberg's aesthetic of the ordinary, his delight in the random. In this tribute to the artist as the finder of beauty in everything, we find beauty in everything, and that's enough.[8]

Is it enough? The answer, of course, is a matter of individual response, but these two comments, taken in tandem, make plain the essence of *bobrauschenbergamerica*.

bobrauschenbergamerica *forever*

A HANDFUL OF 2001 HUMANA CRITICS, INCLUDING CHICAGO'S Richard Christiansen and Chris Jones, came away from Louisville expecting (and encouraging) *bobrauschenbergamerica* to tour. But when the play closed on April 1, 2001, there were no plans in place for it to be seen again. When Mee and Bogart each returned to the 2002 Humana Festival with new pieces, prospects were still up in the air.[1] Possible runs of the show at the New York Theatre Workshop and Manhattan Theatre Club did not transpire; neither did discussions about a commercial run of the show backed by True Love Productions, the production company created by Jeanne Donovan Fisher to present *True Love* in 2001. A full year after its premiere, it appeared as if *bobrauschenbergamerica* was to be a one-shot deal.

Nevertheless, the SITI Company had found its playwright of choice, and within weeks of the play closing Mee was made an official member of the group.[2] He immediately set to work in laying the groundwork for their next collaboration, conceived as something like the European equivalent of *bobrauschenbergamerica*. It took as its inspiration the city of Paris and was intended to be developed in the same way as the Rauschenberg piece, starting with a writing workshop led by Mee to generate raw material, then compositions by participants in the SITI Summer Intensive, and finally a rehearsal period during which the company would create the piece in the flesh. Mee conducted the workshop and went on to write a draft for a collage play titled *Fêtes de la Nuit*, which celebrates (at moments, with tongue in cheek) Paris as the locus of all things French: white asparagus and escargots, Eric Rohmer and Edith Piaf, boredom and arrogance, Foucault and Derrida, *ennui*, *la nausée* and, most of all, *l'amour*. The play drew some of its sweet romance straight from Mee's personal life. In July 2001, he met and fell in love with Michi Barall, an actress cast in a workshop of his *Wintertime* at the Sundance Theatre Laboratory in Utah.

Two years later, they were married. At the Chinese wedding banquet held to celebrate their union, the mistress of ceremonies was Anne Bogart.

For various reasons, the SITI Company and Mee elected not to develop *Fêtes de la Nuit* together; the play languished for several years before receiving its world premiere in January 2005 at the Berkeley Repertory Theatre, in a production directed by Les Waters. By that time, Waters had already made a major contribution to Mee's movement into the theatrical mainstream with his successful and boisterous productions of *Big Love* and *Wintertime*. Each of these plays went on to numerous professional and amateur productions around the country. *Big Love* became Mee's big hit, garnering dozens of productions at institutional theaters, small professional companies, and colleges and universities around the country and in India and Australia (see appendix C). By 2005 – as a sign of Mee's penetration of the culture at large – it had already been produced at high schools in Palo Alto, California; Portland, Oregon; Plano and Leander, Texas; and Bellevue, Washington. Along with *Summertime, First Love, Limonade Tous les Jours*, and *A Perfect Wedding*, these successes marked a concerted shift for Mee into more whimsical and more plotted celebrations of the mysteries of love. Taking inspiration now from Shakespearean comedy rather than Greek tragedy, these love plays draw on the structures of romantic comedy and bedroom farce in a manner that was, by Mee's earlier standards, conspicuously conventional. As discussed in chapter 3, this shift was foreshadowed by *True Love* and *Big Love*, which were still tethered to Greek models and retained the trace of tragic form. *Summertime* and *Wintertime*, which Mee himself described as "frothy romantic comedy,"[3] completed the transition, partly by reducing the ancients to a topic of idle conversation for some of the characters. "I've seen Greek plays, you know," says Maria in *Wintertime*, "There's not a single one that's a love story," to which the character of Bob replies, "Every single one of them is a love story."

Summertime and *Wintertime* marked another departure for Mee. Both plays take place in the same elegant summer house, a magical retreat that is (as in other Mee plays) inside and outside all at once, with grass growing on the desk in summer, snow piling up on the piano in winter, and a surrounding forest of white birch that is the equivalent of Shakespeare's Arden. And both plays center on the same dysfunctional family, a pack of impetuous lovers whose affections are so skittish and insecure that they find reasons to feel jealous or betrayed where none exists. In each play, lovers of various stripes chance upon each other at awkward moments, misunderstandings flourish, tempers flare, doors are slammed, and futures look bleak, before all is set right and sealed with a kiss or a celebratory dance. The wedding often promised by such a canonical resolution provided the dramatic occasion for *A Perfect Wedding*, which received its world premiere as the inaugural production at the Center Theatre Group's new Kirk Douglas Theatre in Culver City, California in October 2004, directed by Gordon Davidson (forty-five years after he and Mee first met). It forms something of a trilogy with *Summertime* and *Wintertime*, bringing together many of the same characters (and just as many new ones) for a crazy wedding-turned-funeral-turned-wedding in the woods, catered by four radical fairies who bring to mind the "Fab Five" make-over mavens from the hit television show *Queer Eye for the Straight Guy*.

Written when Mee was in his sixties, these love plays refresh the tradition of romantic comedy in their focus on love in later life, featuring as many middle-aged and older lovers as young ones. This includes a memorable pair of feisty old lesbians named Hilda and Bertha in *Wintertime* and Edith and Harold in *First Love*, two irascible Old Lefties in their seventies, first played by Mabou Mines veterans Ruth Malaczech and Frederick Neumann. *Limonade Tous les Jours* features a nebbishy American man in his fifties, who comes to Paris to forget a failed marriage and ends up having a casual, spontaneous "fling" with a sexy French chanteuse "young enough to be my daughter." As this mismatched pair say goodbye again and again, agreeing what a lousy couple they would make, they fall deeply in love, their attraction magnified by their effort to deny it. Here and elsewhere, the prevailing theme is what Anne Carson, after Sappho, calls Eros the Bittersweet, the paradoxical quality of desire, which can only want what it does not have. "Perfect desire is perfect impasse," writes Carson. "What does the desirer want from desire? Candidly, he wants to keep on desiring."[4] Mee's rush of romantic comedies before and after *bobrauschenbergamerica* suggested a playwright who wanted to keep on desiring, writing love letters to love and celebrating the second chance in life that it offers to anybody who did not get it right the first time. The citizen playwright of the American Century plays had become, for the moment at least, an acrobat of the heart, more Marivaux than Aristophanes, more Coward than Brecht, more preoccupied with private passions than the decline of civilization, seeking love without the ruins, Eros without Thanatos.

In their own way, during this same period, Bogart and the SITI Company went through their own exploration of the vagaries of love, with a series of classic comedies produced by regional theaters in mid-winter: Noël Coward's *Hay Fever* at the Actors Theatre of Louisville (January 2002),

Marivaux's *La Dispute* at the American Repertory Theatre (January 2003), and Shakespeare's *A Midsummer Night's Dream* at San Jose Repertory Theatre (January 2004) (see figure 20). These productions extended SITI's long-term affiliation with ATL to other institutional theaters, a trend which continued when Bogart directed an unknown, never-produced Sophie Treadwell play, *Intimations for Saxophone*, at the Arena Stage in Washington, DC in January 2005. These regional partnerships enabled the company to do larger cast shows (keeping more company members employed more of the year), while continuing to develop their own self-generated work.

In this regard, the fall of 2004 marked a significant event in the history of the company. When it premiered at Utah State University on September 16, 2004, *systems/layers* became the first original SITI creation not spearheaded by Bogart.[5] After a protracted period of collective development, the piece was directed and choreographed by Barney O'Hanlon and created in concert with a contemporary music ensemble from Louisville called Rachels, whose music had been included in several prior SITI productions. *systems/layers* combined music and movement to create a meditation on the nature of life in the big city, with its mind-boggling layers of overlapping, 'invisible,' technological systems – communications, energy and power, water and sewage, the subway below, the skyscraper above – all in the service of millions of people living cheek by jowl as strangers, criss-crossing each other's paths and each other's lives with odd, syncopated anonymity. The piece's fascination with the patterns of daily urban life was played out on a series of grids, recalling the structuralism of the Viewpoints, its philosophy of theatrical time and space, its patterns of accumulation, and its reliance on what Brian O'Doherty, in reference to Rauschenberg, called "the vernacular glance." The kinesthetic rhythm of coming and going, speeding up and slowing down, engaging with others and then releasing to move on to something else remained a SITI signature.

In 2002, while in London, Anne Bogart attended a production at the tiny Gate Theatre of Michael West's new translation of *Death and the Ploughman*, a text written in 1401 by Johannes von Saaz, a notary and grammar school headmaster from Prague. The original takes the form of a medieval *disputatio*, an intricately structured rhetorical debate between two interlocutors, in this case the figure of Death and an angry and grief-stricken Bohemian ploughman who demands justification for the premature loss of his young wife. Haunted by the lyricism of West's translation, Bogart conceived her own elaborate staging of the piece, which she went on to create

Figure 20. SITI's *La Dispute* at the American Repertory Theatre (2003). (a) Akiko Aizawa and Barney O'Hanlon are partners in the elaborate dance prologue. (b) Carise (Lizzy Cooper Davis, left) helps the innocent Églé (Ellen Lauren) to find her lover Mesrin (Will Bond). (Photographs by Richard Feldman.)

with Stephen Webber (Death), Will Bond (the Ploughman), and Ellen Lauren (as a fluid figure who suggested at various moments the Ploughman's wife, Death's handmaiden, the Eternal Feminine, and finally God). Many aspects of the piece – its density, its abstract and precise choreography, the radical disjunction between its textual, gestural, and visual/aural scores, and the physical and vocal rigor of its performance, to name a few – harkened back to early SITI works like *The Medium* or *Small Lives, Big Dreams* and to the more recent solo trilogy of *Bob*, *Room*, and *Score*. This latest of Bogart's theater essays premiered at the Wexner Center in Columbus, Ohio in April 2004 and went on to become one of the more widely traveled pieces in the SITI repertoire.

By the time that *Death and the Ploughman* played at Australia's Melbourne International Festival in October 2005, the SITI Company was more than thirteen years old and on as firm a ground as they had ever known. For an American ensemble doing work of international scope, their stature and longevity was rivaled only by Mabou Mines and the Wooster Group. (The Group Theatre in the 1930s and the Open Theater in the 1960s and 1970s each lasted around ten years.) Some members of the company – Ellen Lauren and Kelly Maurer, for example, or Anne Bogart and Barney O'Hanlon – had been working together for more than twenty years. Still, in August 2004, when I asked Anne Bogart what she wanted most for the company at that moment, she replied, "Unity. I would wish for unity. It is always a question. You always think, 'Can this possibly survive? Is it possible?' Because the nature of a company is that it is always in crisis."[6]

That is not to suggest that at mid-decade Mee, Bogart, or the SITI Company were showing any signs of slowing down. To the contrary, their partnership was very much alive. On the model of *bobrauschenbergamerica*, Mee created a text for a piece called *Hotel Cassiopeia*, inspired by Joseph Cornell, the American sculptor and filmmaker famous for his box constructions, curious reliquaries filled with everyday objects such as marbles, metal rings, cut-outs of parakeets, and pieces of maps. At the SITI Summer Intensive in 2004, compositions were based on Cornell and the early drafts of this play, which turned out to be one in a broadening series of Mee plays about visual artists. For the SITI Company, Mee also wrote *soot and spit (the musical)*, about the outsider artist James Castle, and *Under Construction*, inspired by the work of illustrator Norman Rockwell and installation artist Jason Rhoades. And following the revival of *Vienna: Lusthaus* in 2002, Mee's renewed collaboration with Martha Clarke led to a series of developmental workshops at the Lincoln Center Theater that resulted in *Belle Époque*, a piece that sought to do for *fin-de-siècle* Paris what their first success did for *fin-de-siècle* Vienna. Set in a Montmartre nightclub, it was based on the figure and the famous paintings and posters of Henri de Toulouse Lautrec, reluctant aristocrat, chronicler of French bohemia, absinthe drinker, womanizer, and, because of brittle bones that had stunted his growth in his teens, a physical outsider. Unlike *bobrauschenbergamerica*, Mee's other plays about artists included a character that represented the historical figure of the artist himself, a choice that nudged the plays towards psychobiography.

As 2006 dawned, both Mee and Bogart had other independent projects in various stages of development as well. Bogart was still looking for the right place to complete *Reunion*, her long-awaited piece about the Group Theatre. Also, the compositions at the 2005 Summer Intensive were based on Tennessee Williams's *A Streetcar Named Desire*, part of the preparation for an eventual SITI production of the American classic that Bogart first deconstructed as *Sehnsucht* in 1982. And Durrenmatt's *The Visit* was scheduled for San José Repertory Theatre in 2007. In 2003, Chen Shi-Zheng directed Mee's *Snow in June* at the American Repertory Theatre, a commissioned adaptation of the Yuan drama *The Injustice Done to Tou O* transposed to the contemporary, multi-ethnic New York City borough of Queens. Despite Mee's general endorsement of any director's free interpretation of his texts, Chen cut and rearranged the playwright's adaptation enough that Mee was prompted to reclaim his original after the American Repertory Theatre production, circulating it to prospective producers under the new title *Utopia Parkway*. Other new Mee plays awaiting their premieres included *Mail Order Bride*, a cocktail of Molière excerpts, and *Cardenio*, written with the Shakespearean scholar Stephen Greenblatt and based on the supposed 'lost' Shakespeare play by the same name.

In March 1968, the art critic Leo Steinberg gave a lecture at the Museum of Modern Art that introduced an idea that became a cornerstone of Rauschenberg criticism. He began by taking issue with some of the distinctions between twentieth-century painting and the Old Masters made by Clement Greenberg in his influential essay "Modernist Painting." Then, he proposed that Rauschenberg was central among a number of contemporary artists whose work was having the radical effect of shifting the conceptual orientation of artist to image and of image to viewer from the vertical to the horizontal. Painting from the Renaissance all the way through Cubism and even recent Abstract Expressionism, Steinberg argued, implied "acts of vision" predicated on a "normal erect posture";

they were to be viewed standing up, and that head-to-toe orientation coincided with a visual hierarchy in the picture plane itself. The picture had a top and bottom, an up and down, an above and below. Rauschenberg changed all that, or at least his early work "proposed the flatbed or work-surface picture plane as the foundation of an artistic language that would deal with a different order of experience." Steinberg elaborated on this theory in his essay titled "Other Criteria,"

> The flatbed picture plane makes its symbolic allusion to hard surfaces such as tabletops, studio floors, charts, bulletin boards – any receptor surface on which objects are scattered, on which data is entered, on which information may be received, printed, impressed – whether coherently or in confusion . . . To repeat: it is not the actual physical placement of the image that counts. There is no law against hanging a rug on a wall, or reproducing a narrative picture as a mosaic floor. What I have in mind is the psychic address of the image, its special mode of imaginative confrontation, and I tend to regard the tilt of the picture plane from vertical to horizontal as expressive of the most radical shift in the subject matter of art, the shift from nature to culture.[7]

Steinberg found implicit horizontality everywhere in Rauschenberg's early work: in the maze-like imagery of *The Lily White*; in his prankish creation of a canvas that contained patches of growing grass; in the action of erasing a de Kooning drawing and by extension his experiments with image transfer and printmaking techniques, all of which involve pressing down on a flat surface. The tire track of *Automobile Tire Print*; the 'pasture' of *Monogram*; the quilt of *Bed*; and other combines with objects hanging off them and resting on the floor; all "kept referring back to the horizon-tals on which we walk and sit, work and sleep." Collage, by its very nature, is a form often practiced by arranging and rearranging materials laid out on a flat surface before being set upright on a vertical axis. For Steinberg, Rauschenberg's one-man paradigm shift – with roots in Mondrian and Duchamp – had sweeping implications. It did not directly represent a world, yet it "let the world in again," including familiar, everyday objects, the artisan's mechanical process of making, and the artist's personal human interests. It maintained "a symbolic continuum of litter, workbench, and data-ingesting mind," as a result making art a more accurate reflection of consciousness. And, in the heady, booming 1950s, it extended the inroads of art into non-art, further eroding traditional distinctions between high and low culture, fine art and popular entertainment, connoisseur and philistine.

Steinberg's theory of the flatbed picture plane offers a pertinent way to think further about *bobrauschenbergamerica*. On a simple level, Mee's procedure in writing the play was, in effect, to lay out a blank canvas and then arrange the various pieces of gathered text on it like scraps of paper in a collage. Bogart's directing was similar in principle. As much as possible, she scattered actors and objects around the playing space in non-hierarchical relationships, letting things accumulate to the point of making a mess and then clearing things away to restore a pristine, empty plane. Covering the stage with a canvas tarp at the outset and with a plastic sheet for the martinis scene in the middle accentuated the general idea of a flat surface and the specific use of the American flag as the platform on which the play was performed. The most potent symbol of the nation became the shared ground on which the play's variety of actions took place rather than a figure on that ground (except when, conspicuously, Bob's Mom waved a tiny American flag as the bagpiper paraded by). The community of characters danced, picnicked, stargazed, killed, and told chicken jokes on the flag. In this subtly transgressive manner, the play converted the flag from its prevailing vertical orientation (think flagpole) to the horizontality of the flatbed picture plane. In the process, a different idea of America was insinuated, one that is more expansive and more inclusive all at once, more small-d democratic, as Mee described Rauschenberg's work, the America of Walt Whitman and Huckleberry Finn and Woody Guthrie.

If the traditional picture plane operates on the longitudinal axis of head-to-toe, up-and-down, north-and-south, the flatbed picture plane invokes the latitudinal path from here to there, from near to far and, by extension into geopolitical and social realms, from east to west and from me to you. It suggests a moving outward from some point of origin or departure (be it the self or home base in baseball or a Cape Canaveral launching pad or a nation's thirteen original colonies along the Atlantic seaboard) towards unknown others and distant realms (a lover, the woods at the end of your block, the vast frontier west of the Mississippi, outer space) and then perhaps coming back to where you started, that is, returning home. *bobrauschenbergamerica* operates on just this dynamic. It invokes images of restlessness, of heading out into the territories and exploring the unknown, and it balances them with moments of gathering as a community to share a meal or a joke or a dance. The play is all lines and circles, and if there is a vein of nostalgia in it – a harkening back to lost boyhood, to the first decades of Cold War America and the Beat era and seeing the USA in your Chevrolet, to the birth of the American avant-garde in Cage and Cunningham and Rauschenberg – it is the measure of one or two generation's dreams of what art and life in America might be. For Mee and Bogart alike, this sense of history is important to carry forward into the new century.

As it turned out, *bobrauschenbergamerica* carried itself a few years into the new century, being revived for presentation in 2002, 2003, 2004, and 2005. George E. Moredock III, artistic director of the Stamford Center for the Arts (SCA), was among those delighted by the play at the Humana Festival, and eighteen months later, he brought it to suburban Connecticut. It was a bold choice for a presenting organization whose patrons were more accustomed to seeing shows on their way to or from Broadway, often with big-name actors attached. The piece was part of a subscription series that included the musical revue *Cookin' at the Cookery: The Music and Times of Alberta Hunter*, Elaine May's off-Broadway-bound comedy about porn actors called *Adult Entertainment* (with Danny Aiello), and Stephen Belber's *Tape*, already a "major motion picture" starring Ethan Hawke, Uma Thurman, and Robert Sean Leonard.[8] While stereotyping audiences is always suspect, the crazy-quilt collage of *bobrauschenbergamerica* proved to be too 'avant-garde' for many SCA subscribers. Attendance was disappointing, and many who came left scratching their heads. "Was there a message there?" asked one gentleman during an audience talkback, giving voice to those who feel the need to "get it," that is, to tie off their theater experience with a tidy moral or meaning. Walk-outs, though few in number, were not unusual, and during the opening-night performance, in the middle of Bob the Pizza Boy's gruesome tale of murder, a disgruntled spectator made quite a spectacle of her early departure, shouting "Outrageous! Outrageous!" as she stormed up the aisle before throwing down her program in disgust and banging out the door.

The play's run in Stamford was further conditioned by the fact that it opened within a week of the first anniversary of the terrible events of September 11, 2001. Over that year, the outpouring of national feeling, the ubiquitous display of the American flag, and the new concept of "homeland security" raised questions about whether audiences would respond differently to the piece in a USA with a different sense of itself. Bogart had no plans for post-9/11 changes in the production because there was "just no way to tell until there is an audience in the room whether it resonates a different way." Nevertheless, going into rehearsals for the Stamford run, she admitted some doubt whether "we would have chosen an American flag as a set design if we rehearsed this after September 11. The fact that it is on an American flag is more dangerous now than it was before."[9]

Bogart did have changes to make in the face of taking a piece that had been created for a cozy 150-seat thrust theater and reconfiguring it for a large picture-frame stage with a 750-seat house (including two balconies). Enlarging the scale of the set to fill a bigger stage and then re-blocking the entire show was never an option, so this was a matter of making lots of smaller adjustments, most of them geared towards maintaining the intimacy of the original production while projecting the action out over the footlights to the back of the house. The flag set, which seemed so panoramic and monumental in the tiny Victor Jory, became a floating island on the 42-feet (13 meters) wide proscenium of the SCA's Truglia Theater. Bogart felt no compunction to keep all the action on the flag surface, so she took what opportunity she could to pull moments out of the frame of the red-and-white stripes and into the surrounding moat of negative space. The tire swing used in the play, with its long rope and large metal hook, hung over this fringe area downstage left, suggesting more than ever a Rauschenberg combine painting with some odd pendant hanging down outside its established frame.[10] One of Bogart's concerns in restaging the piece was to resist the hierarchical organization of space induced by a pictorial stage. "The things on the stage have to have equal value," she said at the time. "Therefore the visual composition has to be not quite as satisfying in a traditional sense. It has to be a little bit more lumpy."[11] In effect, she had to work a little harder to keep the play on Steinberg's horizontal flatbed plane.

Once the company got onto the Truglia stage for technical rehearsals, more practical concerns took precedent. Bogart kept opening up the action and cheating it downstage in an effort to contact the audience and regain the immediacy that it had in Louisville. In the end, the coziness and community spirit of the Humana production could not be fully recaptured in a large proscenium house. Nevertheless, the play still made itself felt during its ten-day run at the SCA in September 2002, and then again, a month later, when it made a brief tour to Chicago and downstate to the University of Illinois.

The play's revival a year later as part of the Next Wave Festival at the Brooklyn Academy of Music (BAM) was something of a fluke. The original plan was to take the SITI Company's production of *La Dispute*, produced by the American Repertory Theatre early in 2003, to Brooklyn that fall. To Bogart's initial disappointment, Joseph V. Melillo, BAM's executive producer, determined that the Marivaux, with a large set and a cast of twenty, was too expensive for a one-week run and invited her to bring *bobrauschenbergamerica* instead. The programming choice amounted to a virtual reunion: the same week that the Rauschenberg piece played at BAM's Harvey Lichtenstein Theatre on Fulton Street, Merce Cunningham's *Split Sides* was having its world premiere at the BAM's opera house a block away. A half-century after their early collaborations, the two avant-garde pioneers were still, in a sense, working side by side. For Mee, Bogart, and SITI, the run at BAM marked a return engagement, since SITI's *War of the Worlds* played the Next Wave Festival in 2000 and Mee's *Big Love* did the same in 2001. It was a welcome chance to perform for a hometown audience in a high-status venue better known for programming European cultural giants from Pina Bausch to Ingmar Bergman to Peter Brook.

Even though BAM's Harvey seated more than SCA's Truglia, its more fan-shaped, more steeply raked house, its stage being on the same level as the first few rows of seats, and its curious faux-archaic decoration all made it a friendlier environment for the play. Most of the flag set extended below the proscenium line onto the forestage, with the downstage edge being only a few feet from the front row, recapturing a sense of contact with the audience absent in Stamford. This left a vast, cavernous area upstage of the playing area, which Bogart and lighting designer Brian Scott chose to draw attention to at moments, invoking the play's trope of expansive, wide open spaces. Relatively minor changes were made at BAM – the yard sale was tweaked; the slide projections, never all that visible, were changed – but, all in all, it was the same production that the company had created two-and-a-half years earlier in Louisville. The big question was how it would go over with a very different audience, the hip, avant-garde savvy, tough-to-please Brooklyn crowd, the antithesis of the Stamford suburbanites. Was *bobrauschenbergamerica*, as Bogart put it, truly "BAM-able?"

At each of the five performances, enough of the crowd was won over by the play's ebullience and the skill of the players to give a rousing ovation. The New York critics were more divided. In the *New York Times*, Neil Genzlinger gave credit to the "brashly, unapologetically entertaining" production and its Rauschenbergian ethos of seeing the beauty in almost anything, admitting that it altered his perception of the Dollar Dreams store and the Popeye's Chicken restaurant near the theater after he left the show. Other writers characterized the piece as:

> a curveball ode to front-porch Americana, short on substance but with a healthy sense of fun that, by the show's end, begins to feel hearteningly like optimism   (Gordon Cox)

> an entry in the 9/11 playwriting sweepstakes . . . when it misses, the effect is reminiscent of 60s avant-garde theater, something Ronald Tavel might have turned out on a bad day   (David Finkle)

not collage on stage, but a variety show, Anne Bogart and Charles Mee's
Laugh In – in short, the perky postmodernism that the world has been
waiting for   (Martin Harries)[12]

What is curious about these and other New York reviews is their misgivings or disregard for the play's accent on fun and entertainment. Perhaps
assumptions about what a piece in the Cage-Cunningham-Rauschenberg
spirit might be or the downtown roots of Mee, Bogart and SITI engendered
expectations of depth, substance, nuance, complexity and other such aesthetic qualities. When the piece turned out to be a romp, a lark, a frolic, a
whimsy, a picnic, a ride on a merry-go-round, and so on, that is, as it
revealed that it did indeed revel in a certain type of superficiality and in
the literal and obvious surfaces of things – different types of old kitchen
chairs, the obvious reason why the chicken crossed the road, the shininess of
a toaster, the sheer noise of destroying a garbage can with a baseball bat, the
simple pleasure of social dancing, of making a mess (and cleaning it up and
making another one) – then these expectations asked to be adjusted.

Daniel Mufson may have been right when he wrote in the *Village Voice*
that "*bobrauschenbergamerica* gets carried away by its own effervescence,"[13]
but that very concern raises critical issues about what a work of art means,
how it makes meaning, and the aesthetic contract between the play and its
audiences. One type of audience, in Stamford or elsewhere, that is, the
spectators who mistrust their own responses and get disoriented by elaborate stage metaphors, the audience that Bogart portrayed and paid
tribute to in *Cabin Pressure*, might see the play and dislike it because they
did not "get it." Another audience, some theater aficionados, some critics
too smart for their own good, some of the BAM-in-black crowd, might
see the play and dislike it because they found nothing to "get." The
Stamfordians and the Brooklyn-ites might seem like opposite constitu-
encies – one does not want too much art with its entertainment and the
other does not want too much entertainment with its art – but in both
cases, much the same hermeneutic impulse is frustrated. Both groups want
something to hold on to. The mind's grasping effort to conquer with
knowing, to crack the code, penetrate the veil, reveal the secret, and get
the prize buried in the Cracker Jacks runs up against *bobrauschenbergamerica's* casual attitude towards meaning, its glorification of surfaces and
sensations, its theatricalization of the flatbed picture plane, and its "OK,
that feels good to me!" aesthetic. The individual experience of the play
depends on how each viewer navigates this gap.

Even with a cast of ten and a mountain of one-of-a-kind props, *bobrauschenbergamerica* went on to become one of the more widely traveled pieces in the SITI repertoire. In June 2004, *bobrauschenbergamerica* was taken out of mothballs in order to make its European premiere at Biennale Bonn, a multidisciplinary arts festival which that year focused on the contemporary New York scene and featured among its theater offerings the Wooster Group's *To You, The Birdie! (Phèdre)*, the Classical Theatre of Harlem's production of *Macbeth*, and Rinde Eckert and Foundry Theatre's *And God Created Great Whales*. Less than a year later, the SITI Company took the play to MC93 in Bobigny, outside of Paris, where it was part of the theater's Festival Le Standard Idéal, along with Frank Castorf's *My Snow Queen*, René Pollesch's *Telefavela*, both from Berlin, Árpád Schilling's *BLACKland* from Budapest, and other works. A month later came a run at the Walker Arts Center in Minneapolis. Despite the prohibitive costs of touring, the play found a wide audience, and this must be because its celebration of Rauschenbergian values, of collaboration, of sensation and feeling what you feel when you are feeling it (to paraphrase Susan in the play), of the democratic spirit of the United States of America and of the imagination, of being in the moment and the preciousness of life itself was more than a matter of entertainment.

The piece pulsed with the conviction that being a spectator or an American or in love or a speck of dust in a tiny solar system in a corner of the universe is defined by freedom, or at least by the potential for freedom, by the condition of possibility. Writ large, this is the theater of Charles Mee and the theater of Anne Bogart. Both practice possibility. In production after production, Bogart's prime objective is to make something happen, to conjure an event, to elicit a quality of attention and then to trigger a moment of aesthetic arrest that jumps the gap between actor and audience and even seems to transcend time and space. In script after script, Mee fashions open-ended blueprints for theatrical free-for-alls, each one predicated on the knowledge and the belief that life can change in the blink of an eye, that anything is possible.

Their art offers a kind of freedom. Tie a string to something and see where it takes you. The biggest thing is don't worry about it. You're always going to be moving somewhere, so don't worry about it. You'll see where it was you were after you come out of the theater at the end.

Appendix A

bobrauschenbergamerica: *personnel and performance history*

Personnel

Written by Charles L. Mee
Directed by Anne Bogart
Created by the SITI Company

Bob's Mom   Kelly Maurer
Susan   Ellen Lauren
Phil's Girl   Akiko Aizawa
Phil the Trucker   Leon Ingulsrud
Becker   J. Ed Araiza
Allen   Will Bond
Carl   Barney O'Hanlon
Wilson   Danyon Davis
Bob the Pizza Boy   Gian-Murray Gianino
Girl   Jennifer Taher

Scenic/Costume Designer   James Schuette
Lighting Designer   Brian Scott
Sound Designer   Darron L. West
Properties Designer   Amahl Lovato
Stage Manager   Elizabeth Moreau
Dramaturg   Tanya Palmer

Performance history

2001 March 22–April 1: Louisville, Kentucky
Actors Theatre of Louisville/Humana Festival of New American Plays
Victor Jory Theatre (seating capacity: 159)
Performances: 13
Attendance: 2,058

2002 September 20–29: Stamford, Connecticut
Stamford Center for the Arts
Truglia Theatre in the Rich Forum (seating capacity: 757)
Performances: 9
Attendance: 3,236

2002 October 5: Urbana, Illinois
University of Illinois at Urbana-Champaign
Krannert Center for the Performing Arts
Tryon Festival Theatre (seating capacity: 921)
Performances: 1
Attendance: 625 (approx.)

2002 October 17–20: Chicago, Illinois
Performing Arts Chicago
Athenaeum Theatre (seating capacity: 985)
Performances: 4
Attendance: 760

2003 October 14–18: Brooklyn, New York
Brooklyn Academy of Music/Next Wave Festival
BAM Harvey Theatre (seating capacity: 845)
Performances: 5
Attendance: 3,915

2004 June 12–14: Bonn, Germany
Biennale Bonn: New York 2004
Kammerspiele/Theater Bonn (seating capacity: 473)
Performances: 3
Attendance: 644

2005 April 13–17: Bobigny, France
MC93 Bobigny/Festival Le Standard Idéal
Grande Salle Oleg Yefremov (seating capacity: 400)
Performances: 5
Attendance: 1,172

2005 May 3–7: Minneapolis, Minnesota
Walker Art Center
William and Nadine McGuire Theater (seating capacity: 378)
Performances: 6
Attendance: 1,140

In addition to the SITI Company production, *bobrauschenbergamerica* has been produced by several college and university theater organizations, including ones at Dartmouth College (May 2003), Southern Illinois University Edwardsville (February 2004), University of Puget Sound (April 2005), Brown University (April 2005) and Whittier College (May 2006). Also, in August 2004, a group in Hollywood, California called The S. O. B. Theatre Company presented a "loose adaptation" of *bobrauschenbergamerica* with the title *29 Things to Do on a Rainy Day (Or, This is not a Play about Art in America)*, directed by Erin McBride Africa.

Appendix B

SITI Company: production history

Chronologies make time seem more orderly than it ever is. Rather than independent events, the plays listed here are better regarded as strands in a braid, some longer than others, depending on how long each play remained in the SITI repertoire. Productions are listed here in chronological order by premiere, but many projects had a development timetable that went back a year or more before that and that continued after the first showing. The month listed is that of the first performance in a run; from venue to venue, runs ranged from one or two performances to more than two dozen.

All productions are directed by Anne Bogart, unless otherwise indicated. Productions marked with an asterisk are SITI originals, either "conceived and directed by Anne Bogart and created and performed by the SITI Company" or created by the group in direct collaboration with a playwright. Some resident theater productions of established plays included non-SITI actors in the cast. For a list of Anne Bogart's productions (1976–95) that includes her work independent of the SITI Company, see "Directorial Credits" in *Anne Bogart: Viewpoints*, ed. Michael Bigelow Dixon and Joel A. Smith (Lyme, NH: Smith and Kraus, 1995).

Orestes

By Charles L. Mee, Jr. Based on Euripides. Premiere: Toga Festival, Toga-mura, Japan (Aug. 1992) and Saratoga Springs, NY (Sept. 1992). Inaugural production of Saratoga International Theater Institute. Presented in tandem with Suzuki Company of Toga's *Dionysus*, directed by Tadashi Suzuki.

The Medium*

Based on Marshal McLuhan. Premiere: Toga Festival, Toga-mura (Aug. 1993) and Saratoga Springs (Sept. 1993)
ALSO: New York Theater Workshop, New York, NY (June 1994); Modern Masters Festival, Actors Theatre of Louisville, Louisville, KY (Jan. 1995); Theater Artaud, San Francisco, CA (April 1995); Irish Life Theater Festival, Dublin, Ireland (Oct. 1995); Walker Arts Center, Minneapolis, MN (Jan. 1996); City Theater, Pittsburgh,

PA (Oct. 1996); Wexner Center for the Arts, The Ohio State University, Columbus, OH (Nov. 1996); and the Miller Theater, New York, NY (May 1997).

Small Lives/Big Dreams*

Based on Chekhov. Premiere: Toga Festival, Toga-mura (Aug. 1994) and Saratoga Springs (Sept. 1994).

ALSO: Hamilton College, Clinton, NY (Sept. 1994); Modern Masters Festival, Actors Theatre of Louisville (Jan. 1995); PS 122, New York (Feb. 1995); The 1996 Olympic Arts Festival, Atlanta, GA (July 1996); and the Miller Theater, New York (May 1997).

Going, Going, Gone*

Based on quantum physics. Premiere: Humana Festival of New American Plays, Actors Theatre of Louisville (Mar. 1996).

ALSO: Toga Festival, Toga-mura (Aug. 1996); Magic Theater, San Francisco, CA (May 1997); and the Miller Theater, New York (May 1997).

Miss Julie

By August Strindberg. Actors Theatre of Louisville (Jan. 1997).

Culture of Desire*

Based on Andy Warhol. Premiere: City Theatre, Pittsburgh, PA (Sept. 1997).

ALSO: Portland Stage Company, Portland, ME (Mar. 1998); the International Theater Festival, Bogotá, Colombia (Apr. 1998); and New York Theatre Workshop (Sept. 1998).

Private Lives

By Noël Coward. Actors Theatre of Louisville (Jan. 1998).

Seven Deadly Sins

Music by Kurt Weill. Libretto by Bertolt Brecht. New York City Opera, New York, NY (Sept. 1998). Conducted by Derrick Inouye. With Emily Golden as Anna 1 and Ellen Lauren as Anna 2.

Bob*

Based on Robert Wilson; arranged by Jocelyn Clarke. Premiere: Wexner Center, Columbus, OH (Feb. 1998).

ALSO: New York Theatre Workshop (Apr. 1998); Hebbel Theater, Berlin, Germany (Sept. 1998); International Theater Festival, Tbilisi, Georgia (Sept. 1998); Irish Life Theatre Festival, Dublin (Oct. 1998); Walker Arts Center, Minneapolis (Jan. 1999); On the Boards, Seattle, WA (Jan. 1999); PICA, Portland, OR (Jan. 1999); Exit Festival, Paris, France (Mar. 1999); Theater Archa, Prague, Czech Republic (Apr. 1999 – first seen here as work-in-progress, Nov. 1997); Performing Arts Chicago, Chicago, IL (Apr. 1999); Holland Festival, Amsterdam, The Netherlands (June 1999); Contemporary Art Center, Warsaw, Poland (Nov. 2000); and Magic Theater, San Francisco (Mar. 2002).

Alice's Adventures Underground*

Based on Lewis Carroll; arranged by Jocelyn Clarke. Premiere: Wexner Center, Columbus (Nov. 1998).

ALSO: City Theater, Pittsburgh, PA (Dec. 1998); City Stage, Springfield, MA (Jan. 1999).

Cabin Pressure*

Based on Audience Project. Premiere: Humana Festival of New American Plays, Actors Theatre of Louisville (Mar. 1999).

ALSO: Wexner Center, Columbus (Sept. 1999); Performing Arts Chicago, (Dec. 1999); Miami Light Project, Miami, FL (Jan. 2000); Krannert Center for the Performing Arts, University of Illinois, Champaign-Urbana, IL (Apr. 2000); UCLA, Los Angeles, CA (Apr. 2000); Skidmore College, Saratoga Springs (June 2000); Edinburgh International Festival, Edinburgh, Scotland (Aug. 2000); and the Israel Festival, Jerusalem, Israel (May 2001).

War of the Worlds

Radio play by Howard Koch. Based on H. G. Wells novel. Directed by Anne Bogart and Darron L. West. Premiere: West Bank Café, New York (Oct. 1999).

ALSO: Joe's Pub, Joseph Papp Public Theater, New York, NY (Jan. 2000); Kennedy Center for the Performing Arts, Washington, DC (Feb. 2000); Edinburgh International Festival (Aug. 2000); Utah State University, Logan, UT (Jan. 2001); Edison Theatre, Washington University, St. Louis, MO (Apr. 2001); College of New Jersey, Ewing, NJ (Oct. 2001); University of California, Santa Barbara, Santa Barbara, CA (Oct. 2001); Stanford University, Palo Alto, CA (Nov. 2001); George Mason University, Fairfax, VA (Oct. 2003); Connecticut College, New London, CT (Nov. 2003).

War of the Worlds*

By Naomi Iizuka. Based on Orson Welles. Premiere: Humana Festival of New American Plays, Actors Theatre of Louisville (Mar. 2000).

ALSO: Edinburgh International Festival (Aug. 2000); Next Wave Festival, Brooklyn Academy of Music, New York, NY (Oct. 2000); University of California, Santa Barbara, (Oct. 2001); and Edison Theater, St. Louis (Apr. 2001).

Room*

Based on Virginia Woolf; arranged by Jocelyn Clarke. Premiere: Wexner Center, Columbus (Nov. 2000).

ALSO: City Theatre, Pittsburgh (Jan. 2001); Skidmore College, Saratoga Springs (Jun. 2001); On the Boards, Seattle (Oct. 2001), UCLA, Los Angeles, CA (Jan. 2002); Magic Theatre, San Francisco (Mar. 2002); University of Maryland, College Park, MD (Apr. 2002); Miami University, Oxford, OH (Apr. 2002); Performing Arts Chicago (Apr. 2002); Classic Stage Company, New York, NY (May 2002); and Emory University, Atlanta (Mar. 2003).

bobrauschenbergamerica*

By Charles L. Mee. Based on Robert Rauschenberg. Premiere: Humana Festival of New American Plays, Actors Theatre of Louisville (Mar. 2001).

ALSO: Stamford Center for the Arts, Stamford, CT (Sept. 2002); Krannert Center/University of Illinois at Urbana-Champaign (Oct. 2002); Performing Arts Chicago (Oct. 2002); Next Wave Festival, Brooklyn Academy of Music (Oct. 2003); Biennale Bonn: New York 2004, Theater Bonn, Bonn, Germany (June 2004); MC93 Bobigny, Bobigny, France (Apr. 2005); and Walker Arts Center, Minneapolis (May 2005).

Lilith

Music by Deborah Drattell. Libretto by David Steven Cohen. Premiere: New York City Opera (Nov. 2001). Conducted by George Manahan. With Lauren Flanigan as Eve, Beth Clayton as Lilith, and SITI actors in non-singing roles.

Hay Fever

By Noël Coward. Actors Theatre of Louisville (Jan 2002).

Score*

Based on Leonard Bernstein; arranged by Jocelyn Clarke. Premiere: Wexner Center, Columbus (Mar. 2002).

ALSO: Humana Festival of New American Plays, Actors Theatre of Louisville (Mar. 2002); Wesleyan University, Middletown, CT (Sept. 2003); University of California-Davis, Davis CA (Feb. 2004); Act II Playhouse, Ambler, PA (Nov. 2004); The Egg, Albany, NY (Jan. 2005); Purdue University, West Lafayette, IN (Jan. 2005); Pike Performing Arts Center, Indianapolis, IN (Jan. 2005); University of Maryland

(Feb. 2005); University of Notre Dame, South Bend, IN (Feb. 2005); and New York Theatre Workshop (Apr. 2005).

La Dispute

By Marivaux. American Repertory Theatre, Cambridge, MA (Feb. 2003).

Nicholas and Alexandra

Music by Deborah Drattell. Libretto by Nicholas von Hoffman. Premiere: Los Angeles, Opera, Los Angeles CA (Sept. 2003). Conducted by Mstislav Rostropovich. With Plácido Domingo as Rasputin and SITI actors in non-singing roles.

A Midsummer Night's Dream

By William Shakespeare. San Jose Repertory Theatre, San Jose, CA (Jan. 2004).
ALSO: Alabama Shakespeare Festival, Montgomery, AL (Apr. 2006).

Death and the Ploughman

By Johannes von Saaz. Translated by Michael West. Premiere: Wexner Center, Columbus (Apr. 2004).
ALSO: Dartmouth College, Hanover, NH (Sept. 2004); Classic Stage Company, New York (Nov. 2004); George Mason University, Fairfax, VA (Mar. 2005); SUNY-Purchase College, Purchase, NY (Mar. 2005); Skidmore College, Saratoga Springs (June 2005); On the Boards, Seattle, WA (June 2005); National Ensemble Theater Festival, Blue Lake, CA (June 2005); Melbourne International Arts Festival, Australia (Oct. 2005); Edison Theatre, St. Louis (Nov. 2005); University of California-Davis, Davis, CA (Feb. 2006), Flynn Center for the Performing Arts, Burlington VT (Feb. 2006), Williams College, Williamstown, MA (Feb. 2006), Wesleyan University, Middletown, CT (Feb. 2006), and Singapore Arts Festival, Singapore (June 2006).

systems/layers*

Directed and choreographed by Barney O'Hanlon. Music by Rachels. Premiere: Utah State University, Logan, UT (Sept. 2004)
ALSO: Krannert Center/University of Illinois at Urbana-Champaign (Mar. 2005).

Intimations for Saxophone

By Sophie Treadwell. Arena Stage, Washington, DC (Jan. 2005).

Hotel Cassiopeia*

By Charles L. Mee. Based on Joseph Cornell. Premiere: Humana Festival of New American Plays, Actors Theatre of Louisville (Mar. 2006).

At the time this chronology was completed, the SITI Company had the following projects in the works but not yet scheduled: a version of Durrenmatt's *The Visit*, a version of Tennessee Williams's *A Streetcar Named Desire*, *Reunion* (with Jocelyn Clarke), and two more plays by Charles Mee inspired by artists, *Under Construction* and *soot and spit (the musical)*.

Appendix C

Charles L. Mee: plays and productions

There is often a considerable time lag between when a play is written and when it comes to fruition in production. Some plays take longer than others to find sympathetic producers. Some theaters commission a play and then choose not to develop it. Some plays are written for specific directors and become dependent on their schedules. All of these have been true of the plays of Charles Mee.

In an effort to capture the trajectory of Mee's writing as well as the history of his productions, his plays are listed here in the order in which they were conceived and written (rather than the order of their first professional production). Such an order cannot be absolute, but to support it, readings, workshops, or early amateur productions of certain plays are listed, especially when the period between script and professional premiere is more than a year. (This is not to suggest that only these plays had readings or workshops; others did, as well.)

While the listing of productions is extensive, it is not complete. First, no effort has been made to chronicle Mee's early plays – Constantinople Smith, Anyone! Anyone!; Player's Repertoire; The Gate; and God Bless Us, Every One – most of which had showings at various off-Off Broadway venues in the early to mid 1960s. Second, while Mee has grown increasingly popular on college and university campuses since 2000, a school production is listed only if it came early in a play's production history or the play is seldom performed or the director is a noteworthy Mee director. Third, Mee's invitation on his website to take the scripts posted there, chop them up, re-arrange and supplement them, and then present them as a new work has spawned a number of productions inspired by one or more plays; generally, these are not listed.

The month indicated is that of the first performance in a run (including preview performances). A reading or a workshop might have had only one or two showings, perhaps for an invited audience only; a run at a resident regional theater might have lasted a month or more. A theater's location is included only in its first listing. All plays, even those with French titles, were performed in English, unless indicated otherwise.

The Investigation of the Murder in El Salvador

1984. Workshop: Mark Taper Forum/Center Theater Group, Los Angeles, CA. Dir.: Peter Brosius.

May 1989. Premiere: New York Theatre Workshop, New York, NY. Dir.: David Schweizer. Music: Peter Gordon.

Nov. 1991. Institute for Studies in the Arts, Arizona State University, Tempe, AZ. Dir.: Bill Akins.

Apr. 1993. Skidmore College, Saratoga Springs, NY. Dir.: Gautam Dasgupta and Phil Soltanoff.

Apr. 1999. NOSE Productions, Santa Monica, CA (inaugural production). Dir.: Juan Carlos Tonda.

May 2001. defunct theatre at Raindog Theatre, Portland, OR. Dir.: James Moore.

Vienna: Lusthaus

Apr. 1986. Premiere: Music-Theatre Group/Lenox Art Center at St. Clement's Episcopal Church, New York, NY. Dir./Chor.: Martha Clarke. Music: Richard Peaslee. Moved to the Public Theater (now Joseph Papp Public Theater) and then toured to Washington DC, Venice, Vienna, Paris, and elsewhere.

Apr 2002. New York Theatre Workshop. Dir./Chor.: Martha Clarke. Presented as *Vienna: Lusthaus (Revisited)*. Toured to Princeton, Washington DC, Chicago, Minneapolis, and Ann Arbor.

The War To End War

June 1989. Reading: New York Theatre Workshop (during run of *Investigation . . .*)

Sept. 1993. Premiere: Sledgehammer Theatre and California Repertory Theatre, San Diego, CA. Dir.: Matt Wilder.

Apr. 2004. University of California-Irvine, Irvine, CA. Dir.: Annie Loui.

The Constitutional Convention: A Sequel

June 1989. Reading: New York Theatre Workshop (during run of *Investigation . . .*)

Jan. 1991. Company One Theater at the Wadsworth Atheneum, Hartford, CT. Dir.: Juanita Rockwell.

July 1996. Premiere: Clubbed Thumb, Inc. and Theater ATM at the House of Candles, New York, NY. Dir.: Pam MacKinnon. Remounted at HERE Arts Center, New York, NY (Oct. 1996).

Nov. 2000. University of Iowa, Iowa City, IA. Dir.: Liza Williams.

Oct. 2002. Suffolk University, Boston, MA. Dir.: Thomas Derrah.

The Imperialists at the Club Cave Canem

May 1988. Premiere: Home for Contemporary Theatre and Art, New York, NY. Dir.: Erin B. Mee. Music: Guy Yarden. Moved to the Public Theater (July 1988).

Apr. 2001. Market Theater, Cambridge, MA (inaugural production). Dir.: Erin B. Mee. Music: Neptune and Jessica Rylan Can't. Presented on a bill with Robert Auletta's *Amazons*.

Sept. 2001. The Evidence Room, Los Angeles, CA. Dir.: Bart DeLorenzo.

Another Person is a Foreign Country

Sept. 1991. Premiere: En Garde Arts, New York, NY. Dir.: Anne Bogart. Site specific performance in the courtyard of the Towers Nursing Home.

Orestes 2.0

Mar. 1991. Workshop: Mark Taper Forum/Center Theater Group. Dir: Robert Woodruff.

Jan. 1992. Workshop: Institute for Advanced Theatre Training, American Repertory Theatre, Cambridge, MA. Dir.: Tina Landau.

Mar. 1992. University of California-San Diego, La Jolla, CA. Dir.: Robert Woodruff.

Aug. 1992. Premiere: Saratoga International Theatre Institute, Toga-mura, Japan and Saratoga Springs, NY (inaugural production). Dir.: Anne Bogart.

June 1993. En Garde Arts. Dir.: Tina Landau. Site specific performance at the old Penn Yards pier on the Hudson River at 59th Street.

July 1993. Act 1 Company, Williamstown Theatre Festival, Williamstown, MA. Dir.: Phil Soltanoff.

Mar. 1994. Actors' Gang Theatre, Los Angeles, CA (inaugural production in new theater). Dir.: David Schweizer. Presented on a bill with Mee's *Agamemnon 2.0* (Dir.: Brian Kulick) and Ellen McLaughlin's *Electra* (Dir.: Oskar Eustis) as *The Oresteia*.

May 1995. Annex Theater, Seattle, WA. Dir.: James Keene.

Jan. 1995. The Fifth Floor, San Francisco, CA (inaugural production). Dir.: Kenn Watt.

May 1996. Roadworks Productions at Famous Door Theatre, Chicago, IL. Dir.: Abby Epstein. Presented as *Orestes 2.0: An Alternative Rock Odyssey*, a rock opera with music by Andre Pluess and Ben Sussman, performed by the Halfbreeds.

Oct. 1998. Masonic Temple, Seattle, WA. Dir.: Joseph Seabeck.

May 2001. eb&c (Ellen Beckerman and Company) at HERE Arts Center. Dir.: Ellen Beckerman. Remounted by LightBox at Phil Bosakowski Theatre, New York, NY (Jan. 2004).

Apr. 2002. Beyond the Proscenium Productions at California Stage, Sacramento, CA. Dir.: Ann Tracy. Under the title *Orestes 2.5*.

June 2002. Gift Theatre Company at Chopin Theatre, Chicago, IL. Dir.: Michael P. Thornton.

Jan. 2003. Open Fist Theater Company, Hollywood, CA. Dir.: Matthew Wilder. Combined with *The Trojan Women: A Love Story* and presented as *Songs of Joy and Destitution.*

July 2005. Rogue Theater at the Athenaeum Theatre, Chicago, IL. Dir.: Nate White. Presented in repertory with Euripides's *Iphigenia at Aulis* and Hugo von Hofmannsthal's *Elektra* as "Rogue's *Oresteia*."

The Bacchae 2.1

Aug. 1993. Premiere: Undergraund! Inc. at Wild Child Place, San Diego, CA. Dir.: Ivan Talijancic. Site specific performance at five sites around a downtown warehouse.

Sept. 1993. Workshop: Mark Taper Forum/Center Theater Group. Dir.: Brian Kulick.
July 1994. Act 1 Company, Williamstown Theatre Festival. Dir.: Phil Soltanoff. Site specific performance.
Mar. 2001. Rude Mechanicals Theater Company at The Flea Theater, New York, NY. Dir.: Kenn Watt. Presented in repertory with *A Mouthful of Birds*, Caryl Churchill and David Lan's adaptation of *The Bacchae*.

Agamemnon 2.0

Mar. 1994. Premiere: Actors' Gang Theatre (inaugural production in new theater). Dir.: Brian Kulick. Presented on a bill with Mee's *Orestes 2.0* (Dir.: David Schweizer) and Ellen McLaughlin's *Electra* (Dir.: Oskar Eustis) as *The Oresteia*.
May 2000. Access Theatre, New York, NY. Dir.: Tali Gai.

The Trojan Women: A Love Story

June 1995. Workshop: Institute for Advanced Theatre Training, American Repertory Theatre. Dir.: Robert Woodruff.
July 1995. Act 1 Company, Williamstown Theatre Festival. Dir.: Phil Soltanoff. Site specific performance.
Aug. 1995. Undergraund! Inc. at University of California, San Diego. Dir.: Ivan Talijancic.
Apr. 1996. Workshop: University of Washington, Seattle, WA. Dir.: Tina Landau.
June 1996. Premiere: En Garde Arts. Dir.: Tina Landau. Site specific performance at the East River Park Amphitheatre.
June 2001. Crowded Fire Theater Company at the Next Stage, San Francisco, CA. Dir.: Rebecca Novick.
Dec. 2001. California Institute for the Arts, Valencia, CA. Dir.: Matthew Wilder.
Oct. 2002. Theater Schmeater, Seattle, WA. Dir.: Sheila Daniels.
May 2003. Double Helix Theatre Company at Phil Bosakowski Theatre. Dir.: Ellen Beckerman.
Apr. 2004. Speaking Ring Theater Company, Chicago, IL. Dir.: Kevin Gladish.
May 2004. The Quixote Project at the Attic above the Blue Lagoon, Santa Cruz, CA. Dir.: Erik Pearson.

My House Was Collapsing Toward One Side

Mar. 1996. Premiere: Dance Theater Workshop, New York, NY. Solo dance-theater piece with text choreographed and performed by Dawn Akemi Saito. Music: Myra Melford.

Chiang Kai Chek

Apr. 1996. Premiere: Institute for Studies in the Arts, Arizona State University. Dir.: Bill Akins.
Jan. 2005. Yale Cabaret, Yale University, New Haven, CT. Dir.: Tea Alagic, Nelson Eusebio III and Jessi Hill.

Time to Burn

Feb. 1997. Premiere: Steppenwolf Theatre Company, Chicago, IL. Dir.: Tina Landau.

June 2004. Resonance Ensemble at Manhattan Ensemble Theatre, New York, NY. Dir.: Leland Patton. Presented in repertory with Gorky's *The Lower Depths* (on which it is based).

Full Circle (Berlin Circle)

Oct. 1998. Premiere (under the original title *Berlin Circle*): Steppenwolf Theatre Company. Dir.: Tina Landau.

Jan. 2000. American Repertory Theater. Dir.: Robert Woodruff.

May 2000. International theater festival, Novi Sad, Serbia. Dir: Vida Ognjenovic. Also seen at City Theatre, Budva, Serbia. In Serbian.

May 2000. The Evidence Room (inaugural production in new theater). Dir.: David Schweizer.

Dec. 2003. Karma Drama Theatre, Istanbul, Turkey.

Nov 2005. Infernal Bridegroom Productions at Axiom Theater, Houston, TX. Dir.: Anthony Barilla.

True Love

Aug. 1998. Reading: New York Theatre Workshop at Dartmouth College, Hanover, NH. Dir.: Matt Wilder.

June 2001. Premiere: Toneelgroep Amsterdam and the Holland Festival, Amsterdam, The Netherlands. Dir.: Ivo von Hove. In Dutch.

Nov. 2001. American premiere: True Love Productions (inaugural production) at the Zipper Theatre, New York, NY. Dir.: Daniel Fish.

Oct. 2002. Deutsches Theater, Berlin, Germany. Dir.: Martin Kloepfer. In German.

Big Love

Feb. 1999. Workshop: University of California-San Diego. Dir.: Les Waters.

Mar. 2000. Premiere: Humana Festival of New American Plays, Actors Theatre of Louisville, Louisville, KY. Dir.: Les Waters. Remounted and presented at Long Wharf Theatre, New Haven, CT (Mar. 2001); Berkeley Repertory Theatre, Berkeley, CA (May 2001); Goodman Theatre, Chicago, IL (Oct. 2001); and Next Wave Festival, Brooklyn Academy of Music, Brooklyn, NY (Nov. 2001).

Apr. 2001. University of Calicut, School of Drama, Thrissur, Kerala, India. Dir.: Betty Bernhard. In Malayalam.

Apr. 2001. ACT Theatre (formerly A Contemporary Theatre), Seattle, WA. Dir.: Brian Kulick.

Aug. 2001. Rude Mechanicals at the Off Center Theater, Austin, TX. Dir.: Darron L. West.

June 2002. Woolly Mammoth Theatre Company at AFI Film Theater, Kennedy Center for the Performing Arts, Washington, DC. Dir.: Howard Shalwitz.

Oct. 2002. Pacific Resident Theatre, Venice, CA. Dir.: Mel Shapiro.

Nov. 2002. Salt Lake Acting Company, Salt Lake City, UT. Dir.: Meg Gibson.

Feb. 2003. Dallas Theater Center, Dallas, TX. Dir.: Richard Hamburger.

Feb. 2003. Blue Room Theatre, Chico, CA. Dir.: Margot Melcon.

Mar. 2003. Wilma Theater, Philadelphia, PA. Dir.: Jiri Zizka.

Sept. 2003. Out of Hand Theater, outdoors at Atlanta Contemporary Arts Center, Atlanta, GA. Dir.: Ariel de Man.

July 2003. Actors Theatre at Luther Burbank Center, Santa Rosa, CA. Dir.: Paul Draper.

Oct. 2003. Theatre Vertigo at the Electric Company, Portland, OR. Dir.: Sarah Jane Hardy.

Feb. 2004. Redwood Curtain at Eureka Mall, Eureka, CA. Dir.: Michael Fields.

Feb. 2004. Early Stages at Theater for the New City, New York, NY. Dir.: Jeff Griffin.

May 2005. Experimental Theatre Chicago at Chopin Theatre, Chicago, IL. Dir.: Jaclyn Biskup.

May 2005. Red Herring Theatre Ensemble at Vern Riffe Center for Government and the Arts, Columbus, OH. Dir.: Mo Ryan and Jeanine Thompson.

July 2005. Chance Theater, Anaheim Hills, CA. Dir.: Jocelyn A. Brown.

Summertime

June 1999. Workshop: The Fifth Floor and Magic Theatre, San Francisco, CA. Dir.: Kenn Watt.

Apr 2000. Reading: Joseph Papp Public Theatre. Dir.: Brian Kulick.

June 2000. Premiere: Magic Theatre. Dir.: Kenn Watt.

Apr. 2002. Lookingglass Theatre Company, Chicago, IL. Dir.: Joy Gregory.

June 2004. Theater @ Boston Court, Pasadena, CA. Dir.: Michael Michetti.

First Love

Dec. 1999/Apr. 2000. Reading: New York Theater Workshop. Dir.: Erin B. Mee.

Aug. 2001. Premiere: New York Theater Workshop. Dir.: Erin B. Mee.

Jun. 2002. Magic Theatre. Dir: Erin B. Mee.

Jun. 2002. Maui Academy of Performing Arts, Wailuku, HI. Dir.: Tim Wolfe. Also presented at Amari Rincome Hotel in Changmai, Thailand (Jan. 2003).

May 2003. Odyssey Theatre Ensemble, Los Angeles, CA. Dir.: Allan Miller.

Nov. 2003. European premiere: Schauspiel Köln, Bühnen der Stadt Köln, Cologne, Germany. Dir.: Uwe Hergenröder. In German.

Nov 2004. StageWorks, Hudson, NY. Dir.: Laura Margolis.

Summer Evening in Des Moines

2000. Commission completed (under the working title *The Great Escape*): Joseph Papp Public Theater.

Feb. 2002. Boston College, Chestnut Hill, MA. Dir.: Scott T. Cummings.

Mar. 2003. Live Arts, Charlottesville, VA. Dir.: Chris Courtenay.

Requiem for the Dead

June 2003. Workshop: Magic Theatre. Dir.: Erin B. Mee.

June 2004. The Red Eye Collaboration, Minneapolis, MN. Dir.: Barbe Marshall. Adapted from original script and presented as *Requiem*.

bobrauschenbergamerica

June 2000. Workshop: compositions at SITI Summer Intensive based on draft of the play.
Mar. 2001. Premiere: SITI Company at Humana Festival of New American Plays, Actors Theatre of Louisville. Dir.: Anne Bogart. Later toured to Stamford, CT, Urbana-Champaign, IL, Chicago, IL, Bonn, Germany, Paris, France, Minneapolis, MN.

Wintertime

July 2001. Workshop: Sundance Theatre Laboratory, Sundance Institute, Sundance, UT. Dir.: Les Waters.
Aug. 2002. Premiere: La Jolla Playhouse, La Jolla, CA. Dir.: Les Waters. Co-production with Long Wharf Theatre (Oct. 2002).
Aug. 2002. ACT Theatre. Dir.: Brian Kulick.
Oct. 2003. McCarter Theatre, Princeton, NJ. Dir.: David Schweizer. Co-production with Second Stage Theater, New York, NY (Feb. 2004).
Jan 2003. Guthrie Theatre, Minneapolis, MN. Dir.: John Miller-Stephany.
Nov. 2004. San Jose Repertory Theatre, San Jose, CA. Dir.: Timothy Near.
Mar. 2004. Wilma Theatre. Dir.: Jiri Zizka.
Dec. 2004. Live Arts. Dir.: Betsy Rudelich Tucker.
Jan. 2004. Round House Theatre, Bethesda, MD. Dir.: Lou Jacob.
Jan. 2005. Blue Room Theatre. Dir.: Paul Stout.
Nov. 2005. Reverie Theatre Company at Live Bait Theater, Chicago, IL. Dir.: Chris Pomeroy.
Jan. 2006. Baton Rouge Little Theater, Baton Rouge, LA. Dir.: Keith Dixon.

Limonade Tous les Jours

Mar. 2002. Premiere: Humana Festival of New American Plays, Actors Theatre of Louisville. Dir.: Marc Masterson.
Jan. 2003. Zachary Scott Theatre Center, Austin, TX. Dir.: Dave Steakley.
May 2004. Bay Street Theatre, Sag Harbor, NY. Dir.: Zoe Caldwell.
Feb. 2005. Asheville Community Theatre, Asheville, NC. Dir.: Jess Wells.
Feb. 2006. MOXIE Theatre, San Diego, CA. Dir.: Esther Emery.

Fêtes de la Nuit

Feb. 2002. Workshop: Utah State University, Logan, UT. With members of the SITI Company.
Jan. 2005. Premiere: Berkeley Repertory Theatre. Dir.: Les Waters.

Salomé

Apr. 2003. Premiere: Needcompany at Théâtre de la Ville, Paris, France and Kaaitheater, Brussels, Belgium. Dir.: Jan Lauwers. Monologue included in *No Comment*, three monologues and a solo dance, conceived, directed, and designed by Lauwers. Toured extensively in Europe. In French, at some venues in Flemish.

Utopia Parkway (Snow in June)

Nov. 2002/May 2003. Workshops: American Repertory Theater. Dir.: Chen Shi-Zheng.
Nov. 2003. American Repertory Theatre. Dir.: Chen Shi-Zheng. Music: Paul Dresher. Presented in altered version as *Snow in June*, the script's original title.

Belle Époque (with Martha Clarke)

Nov. 2002/Feb. 2003/Mar. 2004. Workshops: Lincoln Center Theater. Dir./Chor.: Martha Clarke.
Oct. 2004. Premiere: Lincoln Center Theater, New York, NY. Dir./Chor.: Martha Clarke.

A Perfect Wedding

Oct. 2004. Premiere: Center Theatre Group at Kirk Douglas Theatre, Culver City, CA (inaugural production in new theater). Dir.: Gordon Davidson and Yehuda Hyman.
Dec. 2005. European premiere: Toneelgroep Amsterdam, Amsterdam, The Netherlands. Dir.: Ivo von Hove. In Dutch.

Hotel Cassiopeia

Jun. 2004. Workshop: compositions at SITI Summer Intensive based on draft of the play.
Mar. 2006. Premiere: SITI Company at Humana Festival of New American Plays, Actors Theatre of Louisville. Dir.: Anne Bogart.

The Mail Order Bride

Sep. 2004. Reading: LAByrinth Theater Company at Joseph Papp Public Theater. Dir.: Rebecca Marzalek-Kelly.

Cardenio

Unproduced as of January 2006

soot and spit (the musical)

Unproduced as of January 2006

Under Construction

Unproduced as of January 2006

Appendix D

Postscript: an email from Betty Bernhard

Just days before work on this book drew to a close, I received an email from Betty Bernhard, a professor of theater at Pomona College with a research interest in folk, classical, and political theater in India. Erin Mee, the playwright's daughter, had identified her to me as the director of a production of *Big Love* at the School of Drama in Thrissur, Kerala, India. Bernhard's reply to my inquiry about the production offered such an unadorned testament to what I like to call "the will to theater" that I asked her for permission to include it here (unedited) at the back of the book as a reminder of the lengths to which a group of people will go to put on a play – even for a single night.

From: Betty Bernhard, <bbernhard@pomona.edu>
Date: Sat Jul 23, 2005 6:56:30 PM US/Eastern
To: Scott T. Cummings, <scott.cummings@bc.edu>
Subject: BIG LOVE

Dear Scott,
   I can't believe anyone knew about this production! Erin and I met on Fulbrights a long time ago in Trivandrum, India. First, I do not know of any other productions of Mee's work in India. The advanced drama students at the University of Calicut, School of Drama, in Thrissur translated the play from English to Malayalam in 4 days. We had severe time limitations of 10 days from start to production due to funding problems. The Fulbright office in Chennai came through for us in their first ever grant for a production by one of their "fellows." I believe the date was April 6, 2000. I will have to check on the year. [It was, in fact, 2001.]
   We set it in a kind of European mode (blazers, suits, wedding dresses etc.), that is, we did not "Indianize" the production. We only used a tub, a table for the cake, a bicycle, rows of candles and some wine glasses for the set. The costumes were mostly from their stock and the wedding dresses were made by local tailors. The theatre has built in performance spaces of concrete, high ceilings, and openings for air circulation (no AC) and fans. We used the end of the performance space that had a sort of Italianate arch, painted it pink and white, and found the tiered stairs to be most useful. The cast was an all-male one due to the cultural factors of families not wanting their daughters to perform in drama. We had one young woman we pulled in from designing

to play Oed, but she fractured a wrist in one of the wilder scenes, and so it was all male. This worked well by the way. They played it straight.

The music was a combination of all of our CD collections, including The Eagles. The lighting was difficult as we had to put some of the light trees outside the building to shine through the openings in the walls. Since it was in the extreme high heat and humidity of pre-monsoon weather, the 220 volts combined with people in bare feet on metal ladders was a worry. We did have one little explosion. The cables to a primitive rheostat light board were ganged across the puddles like giant nagas (snakes). During breaks someone shimmied up the trees outside for tender coconuts to drink. I added a song for the brides of "Going to the Chapel" that they learned by rote in English and did in a kind of 1950 Hollywood meets Bollywood dance routine.

One big challenge was getting a cake built since these tiered cakes are rarely made in that climate (they collapse and the frosting melts). And, getting it from town out to the theatre in a rickshaw presented a challenge. Getting the bathtub – not a standard household item there – to us in a three-wheeled rickshaw was also quite a sight.

We did one performance only to a packed crowd of 300 people with another 200 standing outside in the light rain and soon to be full blown monsoon beginning to descend. We could only pray that the usual blackouts did not occur during our 1hr 20 play. The gods descended for us however and then unimaginable rains came full force one hour after we finished. There was a lot of discussion about the play as one can imagine since the issue of unwilling brides and women making their own marriage choices is still a serious issue there. The recent spate of honor killings and suicides of young women who seek to not have an arranged marriage made the play even more relevant. I think the kalari training the young men receive in martial arts made it much easier for them to do the thrashing and throwing of themselves on concrete than it would have been for a western actor.

I am doing this play at Pomona College in April. So comparisons will be interesting. I only hope it is as much fun as it was doing it in India.

Let me know if this will do for you.

Best, BETTY

Notes

Introduction: of hiccups and fireflies

1. Leo Steinberg, *Encounters with Rauschenberg* (University of Chicago Press, 2000), 18.
2. For an anecdotal response to *Erased de Kooning Drawing*, see Steinberg, *Encounters with Rauschenberg*, 15–22. Steinberg calls the piece a prophetic gesture that "opened the portals of art to all wannabe artists with no talent for drawing. This open-door situation would have arrived anyway, what with digitized animation, video, installation, etc. But Rauschenberg anticipated and legitimized the process from within art" (22). He calls the piece "famous as the Library of Alexandria is famous, and for the same reason" (22).
3. Mary Lynn Kotz, *Rauschenberg, Art and Life* (New York: Harry N. Abrams, 1990), 108.
4. Anne Bogart, interview with the author, Waltham, MA, August 7, 2004.
5. Charles Mee, interview with the author, Saratoga Springs, New York, June 19, 2000.
6. In order of their premieres, those nine plays are *Full Circle* (1998), *Big Love* (1999), *Summertime* (2000), *bobrauschenbergamerica* (2001), *True Love* (2001), *First Love* (2001), *Summer Evening in Des Moines* (2002), *Limonade Tous les Jours* (2002), and *Wintertime* (2002). For a detailed production history, see Appendix C.

1. Mee: from accidental historian to citizen playwright

1. Charles Mee, interview with the author, New York, January 30, 2001.
2. Charles L. Mee, *History Plays* (Baltimore: Johns Hopkins University Press, 1998), vii.
3. Charles L. Mee, Jr., *A Visit to Haldeman and Other States of Mind* (New York: M. Evans and Company, 1977), 108.
4. Charles L. Mee, *A Nearly Normal Life* (Boston: Little, Brown & Company, 1999), 21.
5. *Ibid.*, 119.
6. Mee, *A Visit to Haldeman*, 170.
7. Mee, *A Nearly Normal Life*, 178.

8. The plays were directed by Stephen Aaron, Mee's classmate at Harvard, who went on to become a clinical psychologist, an acting teacher, and author of *Stage Fright: Its Role in Acting*. Writing in the *Village Voice*, Michael Smith called *Anyone! Anyone!* "an evocation of frustrated love in the midst of a collapsing world," a prophetic description of Mee plays to come thirty years later. Michael Smith, "Theatre: 3 by Mee," *Village Voice*, November 22, 1962, 9.

9. While generally praised for their engaging style, Mee's histories were criticized by some for their reliance on secondary sources. Of Mee's 1988 biography of Rembrandt, Simon Schama warned that "the innocent reader might not realize just how much of a casual scissors-and-paste job is being served up in the guise of a new book" ("Art for Money's Sake," *New York Times*, May 15, 1988, 7–34).

10. Personal correspondence, April 4, 2003.

11. Press coverage was extensive. In the *New York Times* alone, the following pieces appeared: Frank Rich, "'Vienna,' From Martha Clarke," *New York Times*, April 21, 1986, C-13; Leslie Bennetts, "Dream Imagery of 'Vienna: Lusthaus,'" *New York Times*, April 23, 1986, C-15; Mel Gussow, "Martha Clarke Speaks the Language of Illusion," *New York Times*, June 22, 1986, 2–3; William H. Honan, "Theater of Images Discovers the Word," *New York Times*, August 10, 1986, 2–4. Rich mentioned the piece favorably in several other articles that year.

12. A member of André Gregory's the Manhattan Project in the early 1970s, Tolan gained immediate and widespread attention as a playwright with her first play, *A Weekend Near Madison* (Actors Theatre of Louisville, 1983). Other plays include *Kate's Diary* (Public Theater, 1989), *Approximating Mother* (Women's Project and Productions, 1991), *A Girl's Life* (Trinity Repertory Company, 1998), *The Wax* (Playwrights Horizons, 2001), and *Memory House* (Actors Theatre of Louisville, 2005; Playwrights Horizons, 2005).

13. There are numerous accounts of the "Culture Wars." For one example, see John Houchin, *Censorship of the American Theatre in the Twentieth Century* (Cambridge University Press, 2003), 230–45.

14. Charles L. Mee, Jr., "When in Trouble, Start More," *New York Times*, July 8, 1990, Arts and Leisure-5.

15. Quoted in Leslie Bennetts, *New York Times*, April 23, 1986, C-15.

16. Mee charts a different movement through the plays, based on where the characters fit in hierarchies of power and political engagement. *The War to End War* centers on world leaders. *The Investigation of the Murder in El Salvador* and *The Constitutional Convention: A Sequel* feature members of the ruling class and custodians of empire. And *The Imperialists at the Club Cave Canem* presents mocking portraits of everyday, middle-class East Villagers. "So you've gone from the leadership class to ordinary people in the course of these four pieces." Charles L. Mee, Jr., interview with Alisa Solomon, "The Theater of History," *Performing Arts Journal* [31] 11, 1 (1988), 75.

17. Charles L. Mee, Jr., *The End of Order: Versailles 1919* (New York: E. P. Dutton, 1980), xviii.

18. Quoted in Welton Jones, "In 'War to End War,' concepts float free, ideas fly about and explode on stage," *San Diego Union-Tribune*, September 5, 1993, E-1.

19. On October 13, 2002, I saw an inspired undergraduate production of the play at Suffolk University, staged by Thomas Derrah of the American Repertory Theatre,

which demonstrated how successfully an inventive director can flesh out the Mee scenario, even with the limited resources of a college theater program.

20. In 1988 Mee said the piece was "meant to have music by John Zorn," who he had seen in performance at BAM. "It's this wild, hair-raising, cacophonous mess that finally leaves you feeling completely exhilarated and joyful. It's chaotic, but in this wonderful way, and that's really the promise of liberation." Mee, Jr., "The Theater of History," 69.

21. *Ibid.*

22. Eileen Blumenthal, "Blitzed-Out Lovers Tell a Tale for Our Time," *New York Times,* July 3, 1988, 2–3.

23. Erin B. Mee, "Shattered and Fucked Up and Full of Wreckage: The Words and Works of Charles L. Mee," *The Drama Review* [T175] 46, 3 (fall 2002), 85. Forty years earlier, Mee-the-father wrote about the Living Theatre for this same fabled theater journal, when it was known as *Tulane Drama Review.* On both occasions, the journal's editor was Richard Schechner.

24. Critics Alisa Solomon and Mel Gussow both experienced the original production this way. "As a historian who believes history is made from the bottom up, Mee is also accusing his East Village types of being unwitting participants in the crumbling American empire," wrote Solomon in her review ("The Mee Generation," *Village Voice,* May 17, 1998, 106). Gussow saw the piece as "a put-on" that expressed "Mr. Mee's own evident dismay about the incipient self-indulgence of the avant-garde" ("'Club' Lets The Air Out Of Post-Mod Pretensions," *New York Times,* May 6, 1988, C-3).

25. Charles L. Mee, Jr., *Playing God: Seven Fateful Moments When Great Men Met to Change the World* (New York: Simon & Schuster, 1993), 13.

26. *Ibid.,* 14.

27. *Ibid.,* 99.

28. Mee, *A Nearly Normal Life,* 40.

2. Bogart: engendering space, or building a nest

1. Anne Bogart, *A Director Prepares* (London: Routledge, 2001), 11.

2. Anne Bogart, interview with the author, New York, NY, April 21, 2003.

3. Anne Bogart, caption for production photograph from *At the Bottom,* SHOW PEOPLE at Exit Art, New York, NY, May 11–August 17, 2002.

4. Eelka Lampe, "From the Battle to the Gift: The Directing of Anne Bogart," *The Drama Review* [T133] 36, 1 (spring 1992), 35.

5. Bogart interview, April 21, 2003.

6. *Ibid.* Information for the biographical sketch that follows comes from this and other interviews by the author and from M. B., "Anne Bogart," *Current Biography Yearbook* 60, 2 (February 1999), 77–82; Bogart, *A Director Prepares,* 7–19; Anne Bogart, untitled self-profile, *American Theatre* 18, 6 (July/August 2001), 34–35; Lampe, "From the Battle to the Gift," 14–47; and other sources.

7. William Gale, "Anne Bogart Trinity Rep's new leader finds freedom in order, emotion in control, vitality in a brush with cancer," *Providence Journal,* April 23, 1989, M-6.

8. Anne Bogart, interview with the author, New York, NY, October 14, 2003.

9. Jessica Abbe, "Anne Bogart's Journeys," *The Drama Review* [T86] 24, 2 (June 1980), 85–100. Other articles in this issue profiled work by Ellen Stewart, Roberta Sklar, Joan Holden, Laurie Anderson, and Yvonne Rainer, among others.

10. Bogart, *A Director Prepares*, 14.

11. *Ibid.*, 25.

12. This account of *No Plays No Poetry* is based on anecdotal descriptions as well as Erika Munk, "Cross Left," *Village Voice*, March 29, 1988; Mel Gussow, "'No Plays No Poetry,' But Brecht's Theories," *New York Times*, March 31, 1988, C-20; and Stephen Holden, "Brechtian Collaboration in Experimental Theater," *New York Times*, March 18, 1988, C-32.

13. Holden, *New York Times*, March 18, 1988, C-32.

14. William Gale, "Anne Bogart," *Providence Journal Sunday Journal Magazine*, April 23, 1989, M-8.

15. As it turned out, Barbara Orson, the actor who played Lady Macbeth in that production, was on the search committee that made Bogart its unanimous choice. William Gale, "Theater for the '90s: New Trinity Director Ready to Break Molds," *Providence Journal*, December 14, 1988, G-1.

16. The occasion was all the more momentous for the fact that, after twenty years at Trinity Repertory Company, Hall was among the first of the regional theater's pioneer artistic directors to leave an institution after leading it through decades of growth. In 1989, Zelda Fichandler (at Arena Stage since 1950), Gordon Davidson (at Mark Taper Forum since 1967), Jon Jory (at the Actors Theatre of Louisville since 1969) were all still on the job.

17. William Gale, "Anne Bogart Resigns as Trinity Director," *Providence Journal*, May 24, 1990, A-1.

18. William Gale, "The Transition Team: Adrian Hall Passes Trinity's Torch to Anne Bogart," *Providence Journal*, April 18, 1989, E-1.

19. Kevin Kelly, "Brecht's Rich, Raw *Baal* sets Trinity Rep Afire," *Boston Globe*, March 27, 1990, Living-63. In a prescient review in the *Boston Phoenix*, Carolyn Clay wrote of Woodruff's *Baal*, "It's hard to predict what will happen at Trinity Rep if there's much more theater like this – raunchy, demanding, exhilarating, and definitely hazardous to the health of matinee ladies. New artistic director Anne Bogart's regime may go down in flames, but it will also go down in glory." (Carolyn Clay, "Great *Baal*'s Afire," *Boston Phoenix*, March 30, 1990, 3–13.)

20. Bogart, *A Director Prepares*, 16.

21. Bogart credits Machado for getting her in the door at ATL, saying "Actually, I'm fairly sure that Jon was initially apprehensive about hiring me. He either expected me to be bad-tempered, demanding or expensive, but I certainly felt kid gloves around the arrangement. Looking back, though, I must thank Eduardo from the bottom of my heart because this initial invitation led to a decade of adventure at ATL, both in the Humana Festival and during the regular mainstage seasons. And it led to a remarkable relationship with Jon and the theatre culture he nurtured." "An Artistic Home," in Michael Bigelow Dixon and Andrew Carter Crocker (eds.), *Humana Festival of New American Plays: 25 Years at Actors Theatre of Louisville* (in-house publication, 2000), 50–53.

22. Robert Hewison, "Evoking the Ghosts of Theatre Past," *The Sunday Times*, March 11, 1990.

23. Glenn Collins, "Street Theater Audience Must Make a Choice," *New York Times*, July 19, 1990, C-17.

24. Elinor Fuchs, *The Death of Character: Perspectives on Theater After Modernism* (Bloomington IN: Indiana University Press, 1996), 105.

25. James Schlatter, "En Garde Arts: New York's New Public Theatre," *Performing Arts Journal*, 21, 2 (May 1999), 5–6.

26. Charles Mee, interview with the author, Brooklyn, NY, April 22, 2003. The account here of the genesis of *Another Person is a Foreign Country* is based on this interview and an interview with Anne Hamburger in New York, NY on May 19, 2003.

27. Bogart interview, April 21, 2003.

28. Arnold Aronson, *The History and Theory of Environmental Scenography* (Ann Arbor, MI: UMI Research Press, 1977), 3. As an early example of the use of found space, Aronson points to Max Reinhardt's famous staging of *Everyman* in front of a cathedral in Salzburg, Austria.

29. The facts about *Out of Sync* are drawn from Jessica Abbe, "Anne Bogart's Journeys," *The Drama Review* [T86] 24, 2 (June 1980), 85–100. Abbe's account includes an example of how site-specific theater can blur the boundary between theater and life. "During a performance of *Out of Sync*, one actor was helping another to a waiting car after a fight scene on Second Avenue when an ambulance stopped. The concerned attendants got out to investigate. Bogart tried to stop them, explaining they were actors in a play, to which one replied, 'And all the world's a stage, right, lady?' At that point, the as yet unnoticed audience came to the rescue; thirty people burst into applause. As Bogart describes it, 'The street shrank'" (88).

30. Bogart interview, April 21, 2003.

31. One sign of this development, the Non-Traditional Casting Project, was founded in 1986 as a not-for-profit advocacy organization that promoted the full participation of artists of color and artists with disabilities in the theater, film, and television industries.

32. Jan Stuart, "Muted Waters For Seas of Outcasts," *Newsday*, September 12, 1991, 61.

33. Mee interview, April 22, 2003.

34. All quotes are from a manuscript copy of the script provided to the author. The play is not published or posted on Mee's website.

35. Michael Feingold, "Divided We Dance," *The Village Voice*, September 17, 1991, 89.

36. Stuart, *Newsday*, September 12, 1991, 61.

37. Erika Milvy, "'Another Person' is harping on bizarre," *New York Post*, September 9, 1991.

38. Vincent Canby, "They're Dancing as Fast as They Can," *New York Times*, March 20, 1994, 2–1.

39. Helen Epstein, *Joe Papp: An American Life* (New York: Little, Brown & Company, 1994), 98.

3. Mee: putting on the Greeks

1. Charles Mee, interview with the author, Brooklyn, NY, April 22, 2003.

2. Around the time that Mee returned to playwriting, Müller's work became known in American avant-garde circles, initially through his association with Robert

Wilson and the attention of PAJ Publications. *Hamletmachine* (1977) was first seen in New York at Theater for the New City in 1984 and then, more famously, in a version directed by Robert Wilson with students at New York University in 1986. Elinor Fuchs was among the first to take note of a "family resemblance" between Müller and Mee when she wrote, "The sense of a total environment of cultural failure inversely links both Müller's plays and Mee's *Orestes* to the nostalgia of the pastoral tradition, here sickened into dispastoral." Elinor Fuchs, "Play as Landscape: Another Version of Pastoral," *Theater*, 25, 1 (spring/summer 1994), 50.

3. The play was first presented simply as *Orestes*. As Mee revised the piece, he labeled subsequent drafts 2.0, 2.1, 2.2, and so on. The version that was posted on Mee's website was *Orestes 2.0*, and more by accident than design, that is the title that stuck.

4. Twice more in the coming years, Landau and Woodruff directed their own separate productions of the same Mee play. Landau staged *The Trojan Women: A Love Story* for En Garde Arts in 1996 and *Full Circle* (under its original title *Berlin Circle*) for Steppenwolf in 1998; Woodruff mounted his version of these two plays at the American Repertory Theatre Institute in 1995 and the American Repertory Theatre itself in 2000.

5. For an extended, if inconclusive, comparison of Euripides and Mee, see Robert J. Andreach, "Charles L. Mee's Orestes: A Euripidean Tragedy as Contemporary Transvaluation," *Classical and Modern Literature*, 16, 3 (spring 1996), 191–202.

6. The imagery of a cadaver here recalls the final lines of *Vienna: Lusthaus* ("What colors does a body pass through after death?") as well as the mysterious corpse in *The Investigation of the Murder in El Salvador*. The motif resurfaces more than a decade later in Mee's *A Perfect Wedding* (2004), in which the second act begins with the delivery of a coffin and corpse by two workmen, who, in a manner reminiscent of the gravediggers in *Hamlet*, proceed to ruminate on how bodies decompose under different circumstances.

7. See Elaine Scarry, *The Body in Pain: The Making and Unmaking of the World* (New York: Oxford University Press, 1985), 123.

8. Michael Feingold, "War and Pieces," *Village Voice*, July 9, 1996, 67.

9. This passage, included in the version of the play posted on Mee's website, is not included in the version published in the PAJ publication *History Plays*, which omits other passages as well. It is important to bear in mind that Mee's cut-and-paste writing strategy results in scripts that are more fluid and variable than traditional plays. The postmodern instability of the text is a comfortable part of their nature.

10. For a discussion of Landau's prior workshop of the play with students at the University of Washington, see Sarah Bryant-Berteil, "*The Trojan Women a Love Story*: A Postmodern Semiotics of Tragedy," *Theatre Review International*, 25, 1 (spring 2000), 40–52.

11. As the inaugural production in a new theater carved out of an old zipper factory on West 37th Street, *True Love* was directed by Daniel Fish and designed by Christine Jones in a manner that made good use of the industrial character of the space. Jeanne Donovan Fisher and Laurie Williams went on to form True Love Productions, a commercial producing company that, among other projects, presented *The Retreat from Moscow* (2003) and *The Mambo Kings* (2005) on Broadway and supported the touring of *bobrauschenbergamerica*.

12. In addition to borrowings from Euripides, Seneca, and Racine, the version of the script on Mee's website acknowledges the incorporation of texts from "Leo Buscaglia, Kathryn Harrison, the letters of Simone de Beauvoir, Andy Warhol, Valerie Solanas, Wilhelm Reich, the transcript of the trial of the Menendez brothers, Gerald G. Jampolsky, M. D., Jean Stein's biography of Edie Sedgwick, and texts posted on the Internet, among others."

13. The book, brought to the bedridden Mee by his high school English teacher, Miss Maude Strouss, was seminal in his intellectual development. He later wrote, "I loved the dialogue form, the opposing arguments, the turmoil of conflicting ideas and feelings; [Plato] spoke to my own warring mind and heart." Charles L. Mee, *A Nearly Normal Life* (Boston: Little, Brown & Company, 1999), 32.

14. The archaic prominence of Aeschylus's chorus – its status as group protagonist, its large size (perhaps fifty in number), and the preponderance of choral material – led to this valuation, but the publication of a papyrus fragment in 1952 triggered scholarly debate and made the more likely date circa 468 BCE, thus shifting the status of oldest extant play to *The Persians* (472 BCE). For one classicist's review of the controversy, see Hugh Lloyd-Jones, "The *Suppliants* of Aeschylus" in Erich Segal (ed.), *Greek Tragedy: Modern Essays in Criticism* (New York: Harper & Row, 1983), 42–56.

15. Aeschylus, *The Suppliants*, trans. Peter Burian (Princeton University Press, 1991), xxi.

16. Purcarete made memorable use of the fifty suitcases carried on in the beginning by his female chorus. As one critic wrote, the production "offers 101 ingenious uses for an empty suitcase. The Danaïdes, permanent, restless refugees in both life and death, lug their cases about, one minute using them as coffins or cutlery draws and the next using them as large, lego-style building bricks." Lyn Gardner, "First Night: Filling the Gaps in 'The Foreign Thing,'" *The Guardian*, October 9, 1996, Home-2.

17. The English Server, which evolved into today's EServer (www.eserver.org), was started in 1990 by eight graduate students in English at Carnegie Mellon University as an online publishing community. Before switching to the world wide web in 1998, it used a now-obsolete Gopher server to organize and display files on the internet. Mee's *Agamemnon 2.0*, *Bacchae 2.0*, and *Orestes 2.0* can still be found at http://drama.eserver.org/plays/contemporary.

18. This wording comes from a version of Mee's website archived on December 5, 1998 on the Internet Archive Wayback Machine (www.archive.org), a digital library of internet sites.

19. Todd London, "Stealing Beauty: Playwright Charles L. Mee Rips Off the Culture To Make It Anew," *Village Voice*, June 25, 1996, 84.

20. Charles Mee, interview with Rick Karr, *All Things Considered*, NPR, August 17, 2000.

4. SITI: from Toga to "New Toga" and beyond

1. Basic information on Suzuki is drawn from a number of sources, including Paul Allain, *The Art of Stillness: The Theatre Practice of Tadashi Suzuki* (New York: Palgrave Macmillan, 2003); Ian Carruthers and Yasunari Takahashi, *The Theatre*

of Suzuki Tadashi (New York: Cambridge University Press, 2004); Yukihiro Goto, "The Theatrical Fusion of Suzuki Tadashi," *Asian Theatre Journal*, 6, 2 (fall 1989), 103–23; Marie Myerscough, "East Meets West in the Art of Tadashi Suzuki," *American Theatre*, 2, 10 (January 1986), 4–10.

2. Suzuki reiterated this idea as recently as 2001, as he was preparing for his first US tour in years: "The terrible events of Sept. 11 confirm my belief that the world is a hospital, where no one is immune from the risk of becoming atrocious and mad. It is the urgent duty of theater art to make a deep analysis of the spiritual illness in which humankind is trapped, generally and eternally, but with particularly scathing desperateness now." Quoted in John Freedman, "An Art for the Ailing; That Is, for Everyone," *New York Times*, October 28, 2001, Arts and Leisure-6.

3. J. Thomas Rimer (trans.), *The Way of Acting: The Theatre Writings of Tadashi Suzuki* (New York: Theatre Communications Group, 1986), 9.

4. Leon Ingulsrud, interview with the author, Saratoga Springs, NY, May 30, 2001.

5. James R. Brandon, "Training at the Waseda Little Theatre: the Suzuki Method," *The Drama Review* [T80] 22, 4 (December 1978), 29–42.

6. Among the very first Americans to travel to Japan to train with Suzuki was Milwaukee Repertory actor and playwright Larry Shue, who drew on his experience of being a foreigner for the first time to write a comedy about an introverted Englishman visiting a fishing lodge in rural Georgia. Shue was killed in a plane crash in 1985, but that play, *The Foreigner*, went on to tremendous success and widespread production.

7. For analyses of Suzuki's *Clytemnestra*, see Marianne MacDonald, "Suzuki's 'Clytemnestra': Social Crisis and a Son's Nightmare" in Sally MacEwen (ed.), *Views of Clytemnestra, Ancient and Modern* (Lewiston, NY: The Edwin Mellen Press, 1990), 65–83, and John J. Flynn, "A Dramaturgy of Madness: Suzuki and the Oresteia" in "Madness in Drama," *Themes in Drama*, 15 (1993), 159–70.

8. Hewitt went on to become a successful Broadway actor, taking over the role of Scar in *The Lion King*, playing Frank 'N' Furter in the 2000 revival of *The Rocky Horror Show*, and starring in the title role of *Dracula, The Musical* in 2004.

9. According to Leon Ingulsrud, this spreading interest in the USA was a major factor in the codification of the training. Prior to that, the forms were known by simple descriptions or the pieces of music that accompanied them. Official names, such as Basic #1, came later. Ingulsrud, who grew up in Japan and first came to know Suzuki as his American translator, tells an amusing anecdote about a public demonstration of the training for which he was interpreting. When Suzuki gave a certain command in Japanese to his actors, Ingulsrud heard his sister, also fluent and sitting in the audience, laugh out loud at hearing the actors be told to get into "the crapping position." Ingulsrud interview, May 30, 2001.

10. Arthur Holmberg, "Hamlet's Body," *American Theatre*, 8, 12 (March 1992), 17.

11. Hill's *Hamlet* began as an in-house project at StageWest, was further developed for presentation at Suzuki's Toga Festival in the summer of 1991, and then was included in StageWest's mainstage season. Only at that point did Hightower, a StageWest intern, join the cast as Ophelia and Lauren switch from playing Guildenstern into the role of Gertrude.

12. "Towards a New International Theater Center," manifesto by Bogart and Suzuki included in the playbill for *Orestes* and *Dionysus* in Saratoga Springs in 1992.

13. Tracing Suzuki's production history is difficult and confusing because of his career-long practice of revisiting a few canonical plays and revising earlier productions, sometimes by restaging a Japanese production with an international cast and a bilingual text, sometimes by reconceiving a production and changing the title. For example, Suzuki first directed *The Bacchae* in 1978 in Tokyo with the great *noh* actor Hisao Kanze as Dionysus and Shiraishi Kayoko as Agave. He mounted a bilingual Japanese-American version in 1981 at UWM with Tom Hewitt as Pentheus and Shiraishi as Agave and Dionysus. In 1990, after Shiraishi left the company, he created *Dionysus* as the inaugural production of the Acting Company of Mito, with Dionysus represented by a chorus of priests and, eventually, Lauren in the role of Agave. This production was revised for SITI's inaugural season in 1992 and included, after further modification but with Lauren still as Agave, in the five-city American tour of three Suzuki productions in 2001.

14. Eelka Lampe, a long-time Bogart observer, found tremendous promise but also uncertainty and even a "tension between common goals and clashing cultures" in SITI's first summer of operation. See Eelka Lampe, "Collaboration and Cultural Clashing: Anne Bogart and Tadashi Suzuki's Saratoga International Theatre Institute," *The Drama Review* [T137] 37, 1 (spring 1993), 147–56.

15. Bogart quoted in Daniel Mufson, "Cool Medium: Anne Bogart and the Choreography of Fear," *Theater*, 25, 3 (1995), 60.

16. Mike Steele, "Go Reconfigure: Anne Bogart Still Breaking Down Barriers," *Minneapolis Star Tribune*, January 4, 1996, Variety 1-E.

17. The original cast of *The Medium*, when first seen at the Toga Festival in August 1993, was Will Bond, Mark Corkins, Kelly Maurer, Tom Nelis, and Puk Scharbau, a Danish actress pursuing Suzuki training. Starting with the 1994 run at the New York Theatre Workshop (NYTW), Scharbau was replaced by Ellen Lauren and Corkins by J. Ed Araiza. Nelis played the McLuhan role in Japan and Saratoga Springs, at NYTW (winning an Obie), and in SITI's Miller season in 1997. When *The Medium* toured in 1995 and 1996, Will Bond took over the McLuhan role and Stephen Webber joined the cast.

18. Ben Brantley, "McLuhan's Old Message, As the Medium Mutates," *New York Times,* May 17, 1994, C-20; Aileen Jacobson, "Echoes of McLuhan Bombard 'Medium,'" *New York Newsday,* May 20, 1994, B-16; Erika Milvy, "Nightmarish Message Inspires Hope," *The Press Democrat*, April 30, 1995, 18.

19. Fintan O'Toole, "Performing a Balancing Act," *The Irish Times*, October 11, 1995, ARTS-14.

20. 1996 Olympic Arts Festival program, 9.

21. When first presented in 1994 at Toga and Saratoga Springs, the cast was J. Ed Araiza (*Ivanov*), Will Bond (*Three Sisters*), Kelly Maurer (*The Cherry Orchard*), Jefferson Mays (*The Seagull*), and Karenjune Sanchez (*Uncle Vanya*). At the ATL Modern Masters Festival and at PS 122 in New York in 1995, Barney O'Hanlon replaced Jefferson Mays, who returned to his role when the show was performed at the 1996 Olympic Arts Festival in Atlanta.

22. While the piece was not intended as a pièce à clef, Chekhov fans could decipher the correspondence between actor and play. A man with a bandaged head carrying a birdcage recalled the suicidal Treplev and *The Seagull*. The spirit of *Uncle Vanya* could be found in a woman who put a gun in her mouth, pulled the trigger without

result, and said, pathetically, "Missed." A woman in a Victorian dress with a tattered parasol and hollow eyes spoke Ranevskaya's lines from *The Cherry Orchard*: "Oh, my childhood, my innocent childhood! Happiness awoke with me every morning! It was just like this, nothing has changed. All, all white."

23. Ben Brantley, "Chekhov in Small Doses by 5 Actors, Set to Music," *New York Times*, February 7, 1995, C-14; Alisa Solomon, "Bogart's Elegy," *Village Voice*, February 21, 1995, 82.

5. SITI: the trainings (Suzuki, Viewpoints, Composition)

1. One high-profile incident featured a testy exchange between Anne Bogart and her colleague at Columbia, master acting teacher Kristin Linklater, in the pages of *American Theatre*. The dust-up was triggered by Linklater's brief remarks on the risks and benefits of studying foreign theater traditions for an omnibus article titled "Far Horizons" in the January 2000 issue. She warned about the diluting effect of "transcultural grafting" on actor training, mentioning Suzuki among other tempting eastern performance traditions. She argued that actors "and their teachers sell themselves short when they bow down to foreign gods" (*American Theatre*, 17, 1, 38). In a letter signed by "Anne Bogart and the SITI Company" in the April 2000 issue, Linklater's remarks, characterized as "xenophobic, exclusionary, and border-line racist," were said to have "dangerously demonized the possibility of cross-cultural exchange" (*American Theatre*, 17, 4, 3). To resolve matters, the magazine followed up by organizing and publishing what turned out to be a rather civilized exchange between Bogart and Linklater. David Diamond, "Balancing Acts: Anne Bogart and Kristin Linklater Debate the Current Trends in American Actor-Training," *American Theatre*, 18, 1 (January 2001), 30–34, 104–06.

2. For an interview with two well-known American teachers of the Suzuki Method who are not affiliated with the SITI Company, see Terry Donovan Smith, "Method(ical) Hybridity: Stanislavsky Meets Suzuki: An Interview with Steve Pearson and Robyn Hunt," in David Krasner (ed.), *Method Acting Reconsidered: Theory, Practice, Future* (New York: St. Martin's Press, 2000). For another version of hybridity, see Catherine Madden, "The Language of Teaching Coordination: Suzuki Training Meets the Alexander Technique," *Theater Topics*, 12, 1 (March 2002), 49–61.

3. Between July 6, 1962 and April 29, 1964, a group of young choreographers who referred to themselves as the Judson Dance Theater, including Trisha Brown, Deborah Hay, Steve Paxton, and Yvonne Rainer, presented a series of concerts at the Judson Memorial Church in Greenwich Village. As such, they became the nucleus of a more widespread avant-garde dance community in the 1960s and an associated heterodox aesthetic, loosely suggested by the catch-all term Judson dancers. Rauschenberg choreographed and performed in several pieces with the Judson Dance Theater, including *Pelican* (1963), *Shot Put* (1964), and *Spring Training* (1965). See Sally Banes, *Democracy's Body: Judson Dance Theater 1962–1964* (Durham: Duke University Press, 1993).

4. Sally R. Sommer, "Mary Overlie: I Was a Wild Indian Who Happened to Dance," *The Drama Review* [T88] 24, 4 (December 1980), 57.

5. "Mary Overlie: A Letter," *Dance Scope*, 14, 4 (1980), 32.

6. The Vocal Viewpoints are pitch, dynamic (volume), acceleration/deceleration, timbre, silence, as well as the aural equivalents of tempo, duration, repetition, kinesthetic response, shape, gesture, and architecture.

7. Anne Bogart and Tina Landau, *The Viewpoints Book: A Practical Guide to Viewpoints and Composition* (New York: Theatre Communications Group, 2005). While my account here is based on firsthand observation and other sources, the publishers were kind enough to allow me to consult the book in manuscript.

8. Elinor Fuchs, quoted in "Viewpoints: A Muscle of Presence," *The Journal for Stage Directors & Choreographers*, 12, 1 (spring/summer 1998), 41. In the same section of *The Journal* on the New York University conference, Mary Overlie said, "I am sympathetic to the idea that for Ann [sic] Bogart and Tina Landau, the Six View Points began to change as they worked with them. It was a natural and inevitable path, since Anne, who collaborated with me on several productions, did not fully understand the complete work from the start." Mary Overlie, "Six View Points Theory," *The Journal for Stage Directors & Choreographers*, 12, 1 (spring/summer 1998), 38.

9. Tina Landau, "Source-Work, the Viewpoints and Composition: What are They?" in Michael Bigelow Dixon and Joel A. Smith (eds.), *Anne Bogart: Viewpoints* (Lyme, NH: Smith and Kraus, 1995), 13–30. The title of the Smith and Kraus book was unfortunate and confusing. It is a not a guide to Viewpoints practice but a collection of essays on Bogart's work that came out of the "Modern Masters" symposium at the Actors Theatre of Louisville in January 1995.

10. There are connections that might be made to eastern understandings of physiology and to the flow of vital energy, known as *ki* in Japanese, *chi* in Chinese, and *prana* in Sanskrit, through the body. The SITI training rarely, if ever, makes explicit mention of these terms, so in the interest of an accurate account, I eschew the connections here.

11. SITI Company, "Suzuki Method," http://www.siti.org.

12. My account of the Suzuki work is based primarily on my direct observation of training sessions conducted by SITI Company members. It has also benefited from conversations with company members and from consulting Paul Allain, *The Art of Stillness: The Theater Practice of Tadashi Suzuki* (New York: Palgrave Macmillan, 2003). The first account of the training in English is James R. Brandon, "Training at the Waseda Little Theatre: The Suzuki Method," *The Drama Review* [T80] 22, 4 (December 1978), 29–42. For more recent reports, see Paul Allain, "Suzuki Training," *The Drama Review* [T157] 42, 1 (spring 1998), 66–89; Stephanie Coen, "The Body is the Source: Four Actors Explore the Rigors of Working with Master Teachers Anne Bogart and Tadashi Suzuki," *American Theatre*, 12, 1 (January 1995), 30, 34ff.; Randy Gener, "Where Mystique Meets Technique," *American Theatre*, 19, 1 (January 2002), 42, 44ff.

13. Will Bond, correspondence with the author, January 4, 2005.

14. SITI Company, interview with the author, Cambridge, MA, January 24, 2003. In addition to O'Hanlon and Lauren, Akiko Aizawa, Will Bond, Kelly Maurer, and Stephen Webber were present. The interview took place at the end of a long day's rehearsal for *La Dispute* at the American Repertory Theatre, and when I broached the subject of how the two trainings inform each other, a collective sigh was followed by silence. This is not the company's favorite question, because it has

been asked so often and because a short answer runs the risk of being pat and reductive. On this occasion, O'Hanlon's response was met by nods of agreement and a friendly chorus of "Good answer!," "Good answer!"

15. Banes, *Democracy's Body*, xvii.

16. Aileen Passloff, interview by the author, June 16, 2003. At the time of this telephone interview, Passloff continued to teach at Bard College, where she is Wallace Benjamin Flint and L. May Hawver Flint Professor of Dance. In the world of modern dance, to which Passloff and others were reacting in the 1950s and 1960s, the term "Composition" is associated with Louis Horst (1884–1964), who advocated musical forms as a structure for modern dance and collaborated with Martha Graham for many years. In the era of Merce Cunningham and the dancers who gathered at the Judson Memorial Church, the idea of composition became less mannerist and more experimental, less Classical and more Romantic, less a matter of finding an established musical form to flesh out with choreography than finding some rubric or conceit or strategy for "putting things together" to make a dance.

17. Anne Bogart, interview with the author, New York, NY, April 21, 2003; and Eelke Lampe, "From the Battle to the Gift: The Directing of Anne Bogart," *The Drama Review* [T133] 36, 1 (spring 1992), 19.

18. *Ibid.*, 34.

19. Landau, "Source-Work, the Viewpoints, and Composition," 27. Landau goes on to describe a hypothetical Composition assignment that "Anne or I might give to actors in the first week of rehearsal for a Chekhov play or a piece about Chekhov."

20. Bogart interview, April 21, 2003.

21. *Ibid.*

22. Marshal McLuhan, *Counterblast* (New York: Harcourt, Brace & World, 1969), 132.

23. J. Thomas Rimer and Yamazaki Masakazu (trans.), *On the Art of the No Drama: The Major Treatises of Zeami* (Princeton University Press, 1984), 137.

24. Kunio Komparu, *The Noh Theater: Principles and Perspectives* (New York: John Weatherhill, 1983), 29.

25. Rimer and Masakazu (trans.), *On the Art of the No Drama*, 139. In "An Account of Zeami's Reflections on Art," Hata No Motoyoshi, Zeami's son, reiterates this idea. "In everything, a thorough knowledge of the principle of *jo, ha,* and *kyu* is paramount. Even in terms of the individual syllables themselves, even one syllable can be said to provide an exhibition of this relationship. For example, when a person, in answering, pronounces the syllable *o* ["yes"] too suddenly, the working of these principles cannot be observed. Generally speaking, the moment of silence before the person speaks should constitute the *jo*, the word *o* itself constitutes the *ha*, and the moment after the actor's voice stops constitutes the *kyu*." Rimer and Masakazu (trans.), *On the Art of the No Drama*, 205.

26. Eugenio Barba and Nicola Savarese, *The Secret Art of the Performer: A Dictionary of Theatre Anthropology* (London: Routledge, 1991), 214.

27. Komparu, *The Noh Theater*, 25.

6. Two metadramas: Bogart's *Cabin Pressure* and Mee's *Full Circle*

1. For a brief, informative overview of this Gertrude Stein/Alice B. Toklas play, see C. Carr, "Inventing the Century," *Village Voice*, June 1, 1999, 69. Carr mentions that

Bogart "asked the two actresses to look at photos of the couple and choose their favorite poses, which were then used in blocking the play," a technique that also figured in Bogart's creation of *Room* with Ellen Lauren. For Laurie Anderson's high-tech, multi-media meditation on Melville and modern life, Bogart was credited with "staging," although one source reported that she was "not currently attached to the project" at the time it premiered in Philadelphia in May 1999. Sean McGrath, "Laurie Anderson's *Moby Dick* to World Premiere at Philly Prince, May 12–22," *Playbill*, May 11, 1999, http://www.playbill.com/news/article/45384.html.

2. In the interest of full disclosure, I should mention that I was the author of one of the commissioned essays. Otherwise I was not involved in this project – until I saw it in performance (several times) in March 1999. For Anne Bogart's description of the project and portions of the script, see Anne Bogart, "Notes on Cabin Pressure" in Michael Bigelow Dixon and Amy Wegener (eds.), *Humana Festival '99: The Complete Plays* (Lyme, NH: Smith and Kraus, 1999), 1–13. For a more detailed account of its development, see Joan Herrington, "Breathing Common Air: The SITI Company Creates *Cabin Pressure*," *The Drama Review* [T174] 46, 2 (summer 2002), 122–44.

3. Bert O. States, *Great Reckonings in Little Rooms: On the Phenomenology of Theater* (Berkeley: University of California Press, 1985), 198.

4. Peter Handke and Michael Roloff (trans.), "Offending the Audience" in *Kaspar and Other Plays* (New York: Farrar, Straus and Giroux, 1969), 17.

5. The list of theater thinkers whose writings were anonymously sampled in the play included Herbert Blau, Joseph Chaikin, Jacques Copeau, Robert Edmond Jones, Harley Granville-Barker, Jerzy Grotowski, Martin Esslin, Michael Kirby, Julius Novick, and Peggy Phelan.

6. This and other quotes come from the unpublished rehearsal script of *Cabin Pressure*.

7. For an English-language version of Klabund's liberal adaptation, see James Laver, *The Circle of Chalk* (London: William Heinemann, 1929). For an English-language rendering of Julien's 1832 translation into French of the original play, see Frances Hume (trans.), *The Story of the Circle of Chalk* (Emmaus, PA: Rodale Press, 1954). The preface to this edition by Gwyn Williams draws attention to the liberties taken by Klabund in his adaptation.

8. Like Elisabeth Bergner, Luise Rainer was a popular Viennese actress who worked with Max Reinhardt before leaving Germany in the face of Hitler's rise. Rainer won back-to-back Best Actress Oscars for *The Great Ziegfeld* (1936) and *The Good Earth* (1937) and was married to American playwright Clifford Odets for four years (1937–1940). Sometime after Brecht's arrival in the USA in 1941, he and Rainer met, and by February 1944, Brecht had a contract with backer Jules J. Leventhal to write *The Caucasian Chalk Circle*. For detailed accounts of the play's genesis, see Bertolt Brecht, "Introduction" in Ralph Manheim and John Willett (eds.), *Collected Plays*, vol. VII (New York: Vintage Books, 1975), xvii–xix and James K. Lyon, *Bertolt Brecht in America* (Princeton University Press, 1980), 113–31.

9. For a thorough account of the chalk circle plays, including the fable's return to China, see Wenwei Du, "The Chalk Circle Comes Full Circle: From Yuan Drama through the Western Stage to Peking Opera," *Asian Theatre Journal*, 12, 2 (fall 1995), 307–25. For an overview of Brecht's influence in China, starting in 1959, see

Rong Guangrun, "Brecht's Influence in China: A Chinese Perspective," *Modern Drama*, 42, 2 (summer 1999), 247–52.

10. At the time, Mee wrote of *In the Jungle of Cities*: "It is in many ways a fine play, but I find it diffuse, full of fireworks and distracting theatrical debris. My feelings about the play may have added to my distaste for the production." Charles L. Mee, Jr., "The Becks' Living Theatre," *Tulane Drama Review*, 7, 2 (winter 1962), 200.

11. Jonathan Kalb, "A Postmodern Hamlet by a Driven Provocateur," *New York Times*, October 15, 2000, Arts and Leisure-6.

12. Jonathan Kalb, *The Theater of Heiner Müller* (New York: Limelight Editions, 2001), 15.

13. My friend and mentor, the Brecht scholar Peter W. Ferran, points out to me that, from the perspective of when Brecht wrote *The Caucasian Chalk Circle*, the prologue and frame – and by extension, therefore, Arkadi Cheidze's entire present-tense action of showing and telling legendary events in ancient Grusinia – take place in 'the future,' since Brecht finished the play by September 1944, a full nine months before the Allied victory that ended the war.

14. Pamela Harriman (1920–97) was a socialite, celebrity, and, late in life, US ambassador to France, well-known for her marriages and affairs with extremely wealthy and powerful men from all over the world. Warren Buffett (1930–) is an American investor and businessman, who in 2005 was ranked the second richest man in the world. In a 1991 letter to shareholders in his company, Berkshire Hathaway, he claimed to drink five cans of cherry Coke a day.

15. In "Notes to *The Caucasian Chalk Circle*," Brecht wrote: "All art embellishes (which is not the same as glossing over). If for no other reason, it must do so because it has to link reality with enjoyment. But this kind of embellishment, formulation, stylization, must not involve phoniness or loss of substance. Any actress who plays Grusha needs to study the beauty of Brueghel's *Dulle Griet*." Mannheim and Willett (eds.), *Collected Plays*, 295. Brecht's first three typescripts of the play included a picture of Dulle Griet glued on the title page.

16. John G. H. Oakes and Donald Kennison (eds.), *In the Realms of the Unreal: "Insane" Writings* (New York: Four Walls Eight Windows, 1991). The Montana Historical Society reissued *The Story of Mary MacLane* on its one-hundredth anniversary in 2002. For more information on her, see http://www.marymaclane.com/mary/explorerindex.html.

17. Kalb, *The Theater of Heiner Müller*, 8.

18. In Robert Woodruff's staging for the American Repertory Theatre, the scene began when an act curtain lifted just two feet off the stage floor to reveal Müller laying flat on the floor in bright light. This narrow horizontal band eventually widened as the curtain slowly raised during the scene, revealing a cell-like room. This gradual reveal was part of an ongoing compression and expansion of space that was central to Woodruff's thrilling mise-en-scène.

19. Kalb, *The Theater of Heiner Müller*, 9.

20. Mee once wrote of his youthful identification with John F. Kennedy: "I identified with John Kennedy. I identified with his Catholicism (knowing he must not really believe that stuff any more than I did); I identified with his Irish name; I identified with his years at Harvard; I identified with his injured back; I identified, too, with his taking of speed, for I, too, in those days of moving along, was just beginning to

ingest quantities of bennies and dexies and other tabs and capsules and what-not; I identified with his vitality; I identified with his rumored sexual appetites; and, most of all, I identified with his worldliness, with his assumption that what mattered in life was wheeling and shaking in the public arena. Me and Jack Kennedy, we were world beaters: with our bad backs and Harvard degrees, our quickness to ferret out the political angle, to spot other good political operators, our desire to hoard compensations, our drive, our stamina, our capacity to outlast all others, to overcome by surviving, by hanging on, by having the last play, and our wit, our self-deprecating wit, the sharpness of our sense of humor, and our stylish friends, our gift for the rousing speech, the soaring phrase, the dream to lift the spirits of others and of ourselves, we had that, Kennedy and I." Charles L. Mee, Jr., *A Visit to Haldeman and Other States of Mind* (New York: M. Evans, 1977), 183.

21. Charles Mee, personal correspondence with the author, n.d. (August 2000). The other quotes from Mee in this last section of this chapter come from this same correspondence.

22. *Ibid.*

23. In 2000, Richard B. Fisher donated $25 million to Bard College for a performing arts center designed by Frank Gehry. In October 2004, he gave $10 million to the Brooklyn Academy of Music. On December 16, 2004, he died of complications from prostate cancer. Joseph B. Treaster, "Richard Fisher, 68, Chairman of Morgan Stanley in 1990s," *New York Times,* December 17, 2004, C-9. For background on Mee and Fisher's agreement, see Jennifer Schlueter, "Patronage and Playwriting" in Robert Schanke (ed.), *Angels in American Theatre* (Carbondale, IL: Southern Illinois University Press, 2006).

7. Preliminaries: facing Rauschenberg, making lists, collecting stuff

1. A May 2005 *New Yorker* profile of the seventy-nine-year-old Rauschenberg revealed that he had completed twenty-seven large collage paintings in a new series called "Scenarios," despite a broken hip in 2001, a stroke that paralyzed his right side in 2002, and extensive damage from Hurricane Charley in 2004 to his Florida studio compound on Captiva Island. Calvin Tomkins, "Everything in Sight: Robert Rauschenberg's New Life," *New Yorker,* May 23, 2005, 68–77.

2. Robert Hughes, "The Great Permitter: A Vast Retrospective Celebrates the Whitmanesque Profusion of Robert Rauschenberg," *Time,* October 27, 1997, 108ff. For other responses to the Guggenheim show, see Roni Feinstein, "Rauschenberg: Solutions for a Small Planet," *Art in America,* 86, 2 (February 1998), 66; Lisa Wainright, "Rauschenberg's American Voodoo," *New Art Examiner,* 25, 8 (May 1998), 28–33; Catherine Craft, "Much Too Much," *Art Journal,* 57, 2 (Summer 1998), 108–11; and James Fenton, "The Voracious Eye," *New York Review of Books,* 44, 17 (November 6, 1997), 8. Rauschenberg has always had his naysayers, and some of them came out for the retrospective. "Self indulgence is what Rauschenberg has persuaded the world to accept in place of imagination, and the stupefying size of his success this fall leaves little doubt that there are very few people who can any longer tell the difference," wrote Jed Perl ("Transformations," *The New Republic,* 217, 22 [December 1, 1997], 46). After dismissing Rauschenberg's work as "flimsy" and "the pictorial equivalent of channel surfing," Mario Naves concluded his peevish review:

"The notion that anything can be art may once have been the cynical joke of an avant-gardist crank. It is now, however, the reigning orthodoxy. Once everything is art then nothing is art, and we are left in a world without distinctions. This is the world Robert Rauschenberg has disastrously ushered in." "A World without Distinctions: Rauschenberg at the Guggenheim," *The New Criterion*, 16, 3 (November 1997), 49.

3. Mee, personal correspondence to Tali Gai, November 10, 1999. The "Guggenheim book" is the massive retrospective catalogue: *Robert Rauschenberg: A Retrospective*, edited by Walter Hopps and Susan Davidson (New York: Guggenheim Museum Publications, in association with Harry N. Abrams, 1997).

4. Basic information about Rauschenberg's life and career was gathered from a number of sources, including Mary Lynn Kotz, *Rauschenberg: Art and Life* (New York: Harry N. Abrams, 1990); Barbara Rose, *An Interview with Robert Rauschenberg* (New York: Vintage, 1987); Calvin Tomkins, *Off the Wall: Robert Rauschenberg and the Art World of Our Time* (New York: Viking Penguin, 1980); Joan Young with Susan Davidson, "Chronology," in Hopps and Davidson (eds.), *Robert Rauschenberg: A Retrospective*.

5. Nancy Spector, "Rauschenberg and Performance, 1963–67: A 'Poetry of Infinite Possibilities'" in Hopps and Davidson (eds.), *Robert Rauschenberg: A Retrospective*, 237. One of those turtles, named Rocky, became a legendary Rauschenberg pet and was still living in his New York headquarters on Lafayette Street forty years later. Tomkins, "Everything in Sight," 77.

6. Young and Davidson (eds.), "Chronology" in *Robert Rauschenberg: A Retrospective*, 567.

7. Robert Hughes, "The Most Living Artist," *Time*, November 29, 1976, 54.

8. Robert Rauschenberg, Tobago, October 22, 1984, statement included on page 154 of the catalogue published in conjunction with the ROCI exhibit at the National Gallery of Art, Washington, DC (May 12 – September 2, 1991).

9. Tomkins, "Everything in Sight," 76.

10. Grace Glueck, "A Card Trick as a Celebrity Shuffle," *New York Times*, July 7, 2000, E-32.

11. Copies of these lists, along with other materials pertaining to the March writing workshop, as well as copies of early drafts of *bobrauschenbergamerica* (to be differentiated as working outline, rough draft, and first draft) were all provided to the author by Mee.

12. This account is based on interviews and correspondence with Mee and six workshop participants: Rebecca Brown, Jane Comfort, Alec Duffy, Tali Gai, Jackie Goldhammer, and Kathleen Turco-Lyon.

13. Efforts to identify exactly what Cunningham dance this was have been unsuccessful, but there is some likelihood that it was included in one of his early Events, "full evening performances made up of excerpts from various pieces, which the dance company began to present in 1964" David Vaughan, *Merce Cunningham: Fifty Years* (New York: Aperture, 1997), 76. The year 1964 was the year of Merce Cunningham Dance Company's first (tremendously successful) thirty-city world tour, which Rauschenberg traveled with as set, costume, and lighting designer and stage manager. Not long after, Rauschenberg and Cunningham had a falling out that lasted for the next thirteen years. The use of water as 'musical sound' can be traced

back at least to John Cage's *Water Music*, first performed by David Tudor at Black
Mountain College in 1952.

14. Rebecca Brown, interview with the author, New York, NY, January 6, 2001.
15. The immediate source for this monologue would seem to be Kotz, *Rauschenberg:
    Art and Life*, 43–55. Several passages here demonstrate how Mee converted Kotz's
    straightforward prose into the folksy idiom established for Bob's Mom by Jane
    Comfort. For example, on page 52, Kotz writes, "The fundamentalist Church of
    Christ frowned on drinking, movies, any kind of gambling, even card-playing for
    fun, kissing – before marriage – and dancing. Pleasure Pier on Lake Sabine, with its
    dance pavilion, was definitely off limits." In Mee's first-person, free-verse dialogue
    form, this became:

> We belonged to the Church of Christ
> so of course there was
> no drinking, no movies, no gambling
> not even card-playing for fun,
> no kissing before marriage,
> no dancing.
> You can be sure the Pleasure Pier on Lake Sabine,
> which had a dance pavilion,
> was definitely off limits.

16. Before using this text, Mee asked Turco-Lyon to get permission from her friend,
    whose name was Fred Becker. Mee later changed the name of the derelict character
    (not the trucker character who was 'assigned' this text) from Jim to Becker. Phil the
    Trucker's other speeches in the play came from other sources. The idea of the
    bathtub as vessel and vehicle, introduced by Turco-Lyon and carried into the script
    by Mee, recalls Rauschenberg's *Sor Aqua (Venetian)* (1973), a sculpture that com-
    bines an old, cast-iron, claw-foot bathtub (with a glass jug floating in it) with a
    'cloud' overhead of torn, rusted sheet metal and an old wooden beam.
17. Kotz, *Rauschenberg: Art and Life*, 263.
18. Mee, interview with the author, Louisville, KY, April 2, 2000.
19. Mee, personal correspondence to Tali Gai, December 1, 1999.
20. Mee interview, April 2, 2000.
21. The *On the Road* material came from the first paragraphs of chapter 10, when Sal
    and Dean arrive in "old brown Chicago" and head out for a night on the town. Jack
    Kerouac, *On the Road* (New York: Penguin Books, 1991), 239–40. The sports talk
    included such armchair philosophy as:

> say you have a situation
> third and two
> and you have to decide to play it safe
> go for the two yards through the middle
> or take the risk go for the surprise and uncork the long pass
> this will separate the two kinds of people there are in the world

8. Summer 2000: messing around in Saratoga Springs

1. Wendy Smith, *Real Life Drama: The Group Theatre and America, 1931–1940* (New
   York: Grove Weidenfeld, 1990), 32.

2. Ellen Lauren, interview with the author, Saratoga Springs, NY, June 23, 2000.
3. These extended quotations, as well as shorter quotes in this section, are drawn from the author's direct observation of the weekend playwriting workshop, June 17–18, 2000, and from an interview with Mee in Saratoga Springs, June 18, 2000.
4. Anne Bogart, *A Director Prepares* (London: Routledge, 2001), 116.
5. Charles Mee, personal correspondence with the author, July 31, 2000. When Mee taught playwriting at Brown, *Agamemnon* was a play that he had his students 'smash apart' and then re-assemble in their own way. Mee's version of the play, *Agamemnon 2.0*, was first performed in 1994 at the Actors' Gang Theatre in Los Angeles.
6. Anne Bogart, interview with the author, Saratoga Springs, NY, June 24, 2000.
7. Charles Mee, in rehearsal, New York, NY, November 12, 2000.
8. Charles Mee, quoted in Celia Wren, "Combines in Red," *American Theatre*, 18, 7 (September 2001), 58.

9. Fall 2000: getting ready in New York

1. With over sixty publications, a promotional website (http://www.edwdebono.com), and worldwide training seminars in the practical application of his ideas, de Bono turned himself into a one-man industry.
2. Unless specified otherwise, all quotations and information in this section come from the author's observation of these table-work rehearsals on November 12, 2000 and December 7, 2000.
3. When *bobrauschenbergamerica* opened on March 22, 2001, Voyager 1 was just past twelve trillion kilometers from earth and still sending back signals. For more on the Golden Record, see http://voyager.jpl.nasa.gov/spacecraft/goldenrec.html. For a detailed account of its creation, see Carl Sagan, *Murmurs of Earth: the Voyager Interstellar Record* (New York: Random House, 1978). This book was reissued in 1992 by Warner New Media with a CD-ROM that duplicates the Golden Record.
4. Mary Lynn Kotz, *Rauschenberg: Art and Life* (New York: Harry N. Abrams, 1990), 118.
5. Mee, in rehearsal, New York, NY, November 12, 2000.
6. In the summer of 2000, at the Sundance Theatre Festival, Mays was already at work on Doug Wright's *I Am My Own Wife*, the one-person play about German transvestite Charlotte von Mahlsdorf that in 2003 went from Playwrights Horizon to Broadway and won Mays the 2004 Tony award for Best Actor. Ten years earlier, Mays had won an Obie for his portrayal of Orestes in Tina Landau's production of Mee's *Orestes* for En Garde Arts.
7. At this rehearsal, Will Bond read Bob's Mom and Herbert. Ellen Lauren read Susan and Allen. Kelly Maurer read Wilson, Phil the Trucker, and Bob the Pizza Boy. Barney O'Hanlon read Phil's Girl, Carl, and Steve the Canadian. J. Ed Araiza read Becker. Akiko Aizawa, Leon Ingulsrud, and Tom Nelis were absent.
8. Mee's recollection of the exact circumstances around this source is hazy. Independent efforts to track it down have been unsuccessful.
9. Charles L. Mee, interview with Celia Wren, "Combines in Red," *American Theatre*, 18, 7 (September 2001), 58.
10. John Rockwell, "Living for the Moments: When Contemplation Turns to Ecstasy," *New York Times*, October 24, 2003, E-4.

11. Anne Bogart, EDDY Award Ceremony, New York, NY, December 8, 2000.

12. Mee, in rehearsal, New York, NY, December 7, 2000.

13. In performance, *bobrauschenbergamerica* ended up having some of the same helter-skelter rhythm and comic exuberance of *Rowan and Martin's Laugh-In*, a popular comedy-variety program on NBC from 1968 to 1973. From week to week, its running gags included Jo Anne Worley's loud-mouthed objections to making fun of chickens with chicken jokes.

14. For six years in the mid to late 1950s, when Rauschenberg created his first combines and Johns began his *Flag, Target, Numbers*, and *Alphabet* series, the two painters were close friends and companions who commented on each other's work in progress freely. Rauschenberg introduced the shy Johns to the art world crowd, including John Cage and Merce Cunningham, and it was Johns who suggested that Rauschenberg complete *Monogram* by placing the goat with a tire around its middle in a "pasture," a square, wheeled platform covered with collage and paint. They had separate loft studios in the same building on Pearl Street, and they supported themselves for a while by teaming up in a commercial window-display business under the composite name "Matson Jones." For one account of their friendship, see Calvin Tomkins, *Off the Wall: Robert Rauschenberg and the Art World of Our Time* (New York: Viking Penguin, 1980), 109–20. Of *Flag*, created shortly after Johns destroyed all previous work in his possession, Tomkins writes,

> Johns' flag was something very strange. It was not a "real" flag, to be sure, but neither was it an artist's image or representation of a flag. Its proportions were exact, its stars and stripes in the right order. The technique of its making seemed to qualify it as a work of art, but the "realness" of the image simultaneously made one uncertain. Johns' flag was a paradox. In common with almost everything he has done since then, it asked a question about art, or about the difference between art and reality, or about the faculty of human perception that differentiates between the two – a question that remained unanswered.

Rauschenberg's work, of course, might be said to ask the same unanswered question. Some literal-minded reviewers of *bobrauschenbergamerica* commented that the flag set would have been more apropos of a Jasper Johns-inspired work than a Rauschenberg play, given Johns's many variations on the flag image. Still, one astute critic pointed out that an American flag (an actual one, not painted on) figured prominently in Rauschenberg's *Pegasus' First Visit to America in the Shade of the Flatiron Building* (1982). Carolyn Clay, "Kentucky-Tried: The 25th Humana Festival of New American Plays," *Boston Phoenix*, April 12, 2001, ARTS-8. In 1955, in a mischievous gesture of defiance, Rauschenberg included a Jasper Johns *Flag* painting (as well as a painting by his former wife, Susan Weil) within a combine painting called *Short Circuit* that was included in the invitational "Fourth Annual Painting and Sculpture Show" at the Stable Gallery. To Rauschenberg's chagrin, XJohns and Weil were not invited to participate. Leo Steinberg, *Encounters with Rauschenberg* (University of Chicago Press, 2000), 12.

15. XThe caption to Schuette's costume rendering for Carl mentions Paxton by name. His presence is evoked again in the "Yard Sale" segment of *bobrauschenbergamerica* when Phil the Trucker, speaking a passage clipped from John Cage, says "On the way out of Albany / we stopped at Joe's Eat All You Want restaurant ($1.50). / Just for dessert Steve Paxton had five pieces of pie." For an overview of Paxton's work,

see Sally Banes, *Terpsichore in Sneakers: Post-Modern Dance* (Hanover, NH: Wesleyan University Press, 1987), 56–74. For Paxton's description of Rauschenberg's dance theater work, see Steve Paxton, "Rauschenberg for Cunningham and Three of His Own" in Walter Hopps and Susan Davidson (eds.), *Robert Rauschenberg: A Retrospective* (New York: Guggenheim Museum Publications, in association with Harry N. Abrams, 1997), 260–67.

16. Darron West, interview with the author, Saratoga Springs, NY, June 23, 2000. In this interview, nine months before the play opened, West said he "knew for a fact that you will not hear any Aaron Copland in this play," but as it turned out, he had a change of heart and used the fanfare from Copland's *The Red Pony* to open the show.

17. Steinberg, *Encounters with Rauschenberg*, 67.

10. Winter 2001: rehearsing in Louisville

1. Anne Bogart, interview with the author, Louisville, KY, March 1, 2001.
2. Brian Scott, telephone interview with the author, February 25, 2001.
3. Darron West, telephone interview with the author, March 17, 2001.

11. Spring 2001: the play in performance

1. Brian O'Doherty, *American Masters: The Voice and the Myth* (New York: Random House, 1973), 201.
2. *Ibid.*, 198.
3. *Ibid.*, 201.
4. Judith Newmark, "The Play's the Thing . . . Providing the Audience is Willing," *St. Louis Post-Dispatch*, April 8, 2001, F-3; Bruce Weber, "A Festival of Images, via Rauschenberg and Others," *New York Times*, April 7, 2001, A-15; Rich Copley, "'Bob' saves the day for Humana Festival," *Lexington Herald-Leader*, April 1, 2001, K-7.
5. Michael Phillips, "America, the Bountiful," *Los Angeles Times*, April 3, 2001, F-8; Charles Whaley, review of *bobrauschenbergamerica*, March 2001, www.totaltheater.com; Leslie (Hoban) Blake, "Louisville Sluggers: The Humana Festival of New American Plays Reaches the Quarter-Century Mark," *Theater Mania.com*, April 10, 2001, http://www.theatermania.com/content/news.cfm/story/1332; and Jennifer de Poyen, "New Plays Mirror Transitional Theme," *San Diego Union-Tribune*, April 8, 2001, F-8.
6. Weber, *New York Times*, April 7, 2001, A-15.
7. Tony Brown, "Festival Plays Range from Politics to Comedy," Newhouse News Service, *Birmingham News*, April 8, 2001, 2-F.
8. Kevin Nance, "In a Disappointing Year, Play Festival offers Consolations," *Nashville Tennessean*, April 5, 2001, D-3.

12. *bobrauschenbergamerica* forever

1. At Humana in 2002, Marc Masterson directed the world premiere of Mee's *Limonade Tous les Jours* and Bogart directed *Score*, the third piece in SITI's trilogy of one-person shows about twentieth-century artists, featuring Tom Nelis as the

figure of Leonard Bernstein. This was the third Humana Festival in a row that included Mee and Bogart; neither were back again until 2006.

2. At this same time, Susan Hightower, a long-term SITI associate and a member of the cast of the original SITI production (Mee's *Orestes*) ten years earlier, was also made a full company member.

3. Charles Mee, interview with Michael Bigelow Dixon, Guthrie Theatre study guide for *Wintertime*, October 10, 2002.

4. Anne Carson, *Eros the Bittersweet* (Normal, IL: Dalkey Archive Press, 1998), 136.

5. Other company members had staged pieces in the past. In 1999, in tandem with SITI's original piece about Orson Welles, Darron West and Anne Bogart co-directed a theatrical version of the infamous October 30, 1938 radio broadcast of H. G. Well's *War of the Worlds*, written by Howard Koch for Orson Welles's "Mercury Theatre on the Air." In 2004, Leon Ingulsrud directed a production of *Macbeth* for Swine Palace Productions, the professional arm of the theater program at Louisiana State University, with a SITI design team and five company members or associates (including Susan Hightower as Macbeth), two LSU faculty members, and two dozen graduate and undergraduate actors in the cast. But, as SITI's first creation built from scratch without Bogart as a principal collaborator, *systems/layers* was different.

6. Anne Bogart, interview with the author, Waltham, MA, August 7, 2004.

7. Leo Steinberg, "Other Criteria" in *Other Criteria: Confrontations with Twentieth Century Art* (New York: Oxford University Press, 1972), 55–92. The quotations included here can be found on pages 87, 84, and 89, respectively. On the occasion of the Rauschenberg retrospective at the Guggenheim, Steinberg revisited his ideas in a lecture that he gave at the museum on October 21, 1997, dismissing them as "old hat" and coming "like most criticism, with built-in obsolescence." See Leo Steinberg, *Encounters with Rauschenberg* (University of Chicago Press, 2000).

8. In the Small World Department, *Tape*, in its 2000 world premiere at the Humana Festival and its 2003 production at Stamford Center for the Arts, was directed by Brian Jucha, Anne Bogart's former student and co-founder with her of Via Theater.

9. Anne Bogart, interview with the author, New York, NY, September 9, 2002.

10. For examples of Rauschenberg works with such pendants, see *Canyon* (1959) and its pillow on a string; *Trophy IV (For John Cage)* (1961) and its flashlight on a rusty chain; *Gold Standard* (1964) and its ceramic dog on a 'leash' tied to a folding Japanese screen; *San Pantalone (Venetian)* (1973) and its coconut on a rope; *The Interloper Tries His Disguises (Kabal American Zephyr)* (1982) and its fraying tire tread trailing an old iron wheel.

11. Bogart interview, September 9, 2002.

12. Neil Genzlinger, "A Collage of Sly Tricks in Honor of a Collagist," *New York Times*, October 16, 2003, E-5; Gordon Cox, "Rauschenberg Plays with Found Objects," *New York Newsday*, October 17, 2003, B-23; David Finkle, "*bobrauschenbergamerica*," *TheaterMania.com*, October 16, 2003, http://www.theatermania.com/content/ news.cfm? int_news_id=3989; and Martin Harries, "Having Your Cage," *HotReview.org* (*Hunter On-Line Theater Review*), http://www.hotreview.org/articles/havingyourcage.htm.

13. Daniel Mufson, "Love American Style: Bogart and Mee's Homage to Rauschenberg's Homeland Spirit," *Village Voice*, October 22, 2003, 82.

Index

DATE DUE

GAYLORD

PRINTED IN U.S.A.